State Responsibility for 'Modern Slavery' in Human Rights Law

State Responsibility for 'Modern Slavery' in Human Rights Law

A Right Not to Be Trafficked

MARIJA JOVANOVIĆ

Great Clarendon Street, Oxford, OX2 6DP,
United Kingdom

Oxford University Press is a department of the University of Oxford.
It furthers the University's objective of excellence in research, scholarship,
and education by publishing worldwide. Oxford is a registered trade mark of
Oxford University Press in the UK and in certain other countries

© Marija Jovanović 2023

The moral rights of the author have been asserted

First Edition published in 2023

All rights reserved. No part of this publication may be reproduced, stored in
a retrieval system, or transmitted, in any form or by any means, without the
prior permission in writing of Oxford University Press, or as expressly permitted
by law, by licence or under terms agreed with the appropriate reprographics
rights organization. Enquiries concerning reproduction outside the scope of the
above should be sent to the Rights Department, Oxford University Press, at the
address above

You must not circulate this work in any other form
and you must impose this same condition on any acquirer

Public sector information reproduced under Open Government Licence v3.0
(http://www.nationalarchives.gov.uk/doc/open-government-licence/open-government-licence.htm)

Published in the United States of America by Oxford University Press
198 Madison Avenue, New York, NY 10016, United States of America

British Library Cataloguing in Publication Data

Data available

Library of Congress Control Number: 2022947803

ISBN 978-0-19-286708-7

DOI: 10.1093/oso/9780192867087.001.0001

Printed and bound in the UK by
TJ Books Limited

Links to third party websites are provided by Oxford in good faith and
for information only. Oxford disclaims any responsibility for the materials
contained in any third party website referenced in this work.

Acknowledgements

A few people are owed special credit for the completion of this book. My dearest friend Andrea Grgić-Naron helped me conceive this project during our time together at Oxford in 2010/11, and has been a constant source of encouragement and inspiration along the way. Yet, no one deserves more gratitude than my supervisor and dear friend Liora Lazarus, who has been a steady and stern steward, as well as a role model, on a long and sometimes perilous journey. I am also greatly indebted to Ryszard Piotrowicz and Miles Jackson, my generous and thoughtful DPhil examiners, whose reassuring support made me dare to believe that my doctoral thesis could become a book. Further along the way, Damian Chalmers' piercing and insightful feedback helped me transform the doctoral thesis into a publishable piece of work. In the final stages of this work, I benefited immensely from the magnanimous and inspiring advice of Virginia Mantouvalou. I am equally grateful to Geoff Gilbert for his profound and sharp comments on the final draft. The ultimate reassurance came from Judge Davor Derencinovic, whose review of the completed manuscript made me believe that the effort invested in this project has been worthwhile. Most special thanks are owed to my dear friend Petra Weingerl, who obligingly read and commented on innumerable drafts of this manuscript and offered a compassionate ear in the moments of despair and self-doubt. I must also thank the two anonymous reviewers for their exceptional, albeit challenging, advice on improving the manuscript, as well as the encouraging and patient editors from the Oxford University Press—Merel Alstein, Robert Cavooris, and Rebecca Lewis—who have helped me bring this project to a successful completion.

The work on this book took place across several academic institutions (and countless coffee shops in a range of countries and continents). Oxford University, and the Faculty of Law and Wolfson College in particular, offered a fertile ground for the project idea to develop and mature. Chance had it that the completion of the doctorate and significant work on revising the thesis for this book took place at the National University of Singapore. NUS Law Faculty allowed me to use their premises for an online *viva voce* examination, which was at the time an unusual and challenging endeavour—rather strikingly in the context of today's Covid-19-transformed world. Professor Andrew Simester was instrumental in ensuring that the centuries-old regulations were followed in full and provided quiet support throughout the process. The finishing touches on the manuscript were put in place at the UCL Faculty of Laws during my Visiting Fellowship in Spring 2022, and ultimately at the Essex Law School as my current academic home. I am grateful for the institutional support and intellectual power provided by these diverse and animating scholarly communities. I am also immensely grateful to Petya Nestorova who hosted me during a research visit at the Council of Europe's Group of Experts on Action against Trafficking in Human Beings where this book started to take shape.

Finally, the engine of this project has been my parents, Nadica and Gvozden Jovanović, who believed that my doctoral studies at Oxford University would be the best investment of their lives—I cannot thank them enough for unwavering support, confidence, and love. For my dear husband and son, Erik and Markus, the work on this book stretches back as far as they have both known me, and its completion truly represents the end of an era for our family. Last but not least, I have been blessed with so many friends who have lightened up my journey and been an endless source of support, comfort, and fun, most of all my beloved Vilija and Petra.

Without you all, this book would have never come to light and I will always be grateful for that.

West Malling, England
June 2022

Contents

Table of Cases   ix
Table of Legislation   xiii
List of Abbreviations   xvii

1. Introduction   1
   1.1 The Case for a Right Not to Be Trafficked   1
   1.2 One Definition, Two Legal Contexts: Individual Criminal Responsibility versus State Responsibility under Human Rights Law   5
   1.3 The Scope of the Book: Human Trafficking and the European Legal Space   9
   1.4 Book Structure   10

PART I HUMAN TRAFFICKING AND HUMAN RIGHTS LAW

2. On the Legal Nature of Human Trafficking   15
   2.1 Human Trafficking as a Complex and Contested Phenomenon   15
   2.2 A Brief History of Human Trafficking in International Law: From Law Enforcement to Human Rights and Not the Other Way Around   19
   2.3 Competing Narratives on the Relationship between Human Trafficking and Human Rights Law   26
   2.4 Human Trafficking as a Hybrid Legal Concept   30
   2.5 The Value of the Human Rights Approach to Human Trafficking   36
   2.6 Final Remarks on the Relationship between Human Trafficking and Human Rights Law   38

3. A Right Not to Be Trafficked?   40
   3.1 From Palermo to Strasbourg: The *Rantsev* Case and the Inclusion of Human Trafficking in the Human Rights Framework   41
   3.2 Saving *Rantsev*: A Case for the Right Not to Be Trafficked   44
   3.3 The Notion of 'Modern Slavery' in Human Rights Law   62

4. The Notion of Exploitation: Theoretical Foundations of the Human Rights Prohibition of 'Modern Slavery'   64
   4.1 The Insufficient Engagement with the Notion of Exploitation and International Law   66
   4.2 Exploitation in Moral Philosophy   72
   4.3 The Emerging Contours of the Concept of Exploitation in Human Rights Law   81

PART II STATE RESPONSIBILITY FOR 'MODERN SLAVERY' IN HUMAN RIGHTS LAW

5. Positive Obligations as a Means of Establishing State Responsibility for 'Modern Slavery' in Human Rights Law   95
    5.1 Non-state Actors and Human Rights Law: A Doctrine of Positive Obligations   98
    5.2 The Rationale, Legal Basis, and Scope of Positive Obligations   100
    5.3 Positive Obligations and 'Absolute' Rights   102
    5.4 Positive Obligations versus Remedies when Rights Are Infringed by Non-state Actors   107
    5.5 The Range and Classification of Positive Obligations: General and Specific Duties   116

6. Human Rights Obligations of States to Address 'Modern Slavery'   123
    6.1 General Obligation to Establish an Effective Legal Framework   124
    6.2 Specific Obligations: A Procedural Duty to Investigate 'Modern Slavery'   127
    6.3 Specific Obligations: A Duty to Protect Victims of 'Modern Slavery'   143
    6.4 Remedies for 'Modern Slavery': Individual Justice, Structural Change, and the Tale of the Two Courts   157
    6.5 'Modern Slavery', 'Absolute Rights', and State Responsibility for Acts of Private Violence: New Horizons for the Human Rights Jurisprudence   162

7. The Role of Specialised Anti-trafficking Instruments in Shaping Human Rights Obligations of States to Address 'Modern Slavery'   164
    7.1 The Palermo Protocol and States' Obligations to Tackle Human Trafficking   166
    7.2 The Victim-centred Approach in Post-Palermo Instruments and the 'Key Distinction' between Victim Protection and Victims' Human Rights   169
    7.3 From Victim Protection Measures to Victims' Human Rights: The Criminal Justice Context   172
    7.4 From Victim Protection Measures to Victims' Human Rights: Beyond the Criminal Justice Context   181
    7.5 The Future of 'Modern Slavery' Jurisprudence   192

8. Conclusion: Human Rights Law, Slavery, and State in the Twenty-First Century   194

Bibliography   199
Index   213

Table of Cases

EUROPEAN UNION

A, B and C v Latvia (2018) 67 EHRR 31 173–74
A v United Kingdom (1999) 27 EHRR 611 .... 83, 98–99, 102, 105
Airey v Ireland (1979–80) 2 EHRR 305 100–1
Alajos Kiss v Hungary (2013) 56 EHRR 38 83
Ali v United Kingdom (2011) 53 EHRR 12 191
Ali and Ayse Duran v Turkey [2008] ECHR 289 138
Aksoy v Turkey (1997) 23 EHRR 553 .... 108, 109, 112, 157
Artico v Italy (1981) EHRR 1 100–1
Assenov and Others v Bulgaria (1999) 28 EHRR 652 .... 112–13, 157
Axen v the FRG (1983) Series A No 72 177–78
Aydin v Turkey (1998) EHRR 251 .... 108, 109, 157
Bati and Others v Turkey [2008] ECHR 246 114
Beganovic v Croatia [2009] ECHR 992 .... 108–9, 112, 115, 138–39, 141
Belgian Linguistic (No 2) (1968) 1 EHRR 252 99
Bevacqua and S v Bulgaria [2008] ECHR 498 105
Breukhoven v The Czech Republic [2011] ECHR 1177 .... 141–42, 176–77
Bricmont v Belgium (1989) Series A No 158 177–78
Budayeva and Others v Russia [2008] ECHR 216 .... 98–99, 117
Calvelli and Ciglio v Italy [2002] ECHR 3 .... 47, 144
Case 'relating to certain aspects of the laws on the use of languages in education in Belgium' v Belgium (Belgian Linguistic Case) (1968) 1EHRR 252 191
Centro Europa 7 SRL and Di Stefano v Italy [GC] [2012] ECHR 974 117
Chowdury and Others v Greece App no 21884/15 (ECtHR, 30 March 2017) ... 82, 194–95
Chowdury and Others v Greece [2017] ECHR 300 .... 2–3, 7–8, 36–37, 42–43, 46–47, 124–26, 127–28, 129, 144, 149, 150, 151–52, 162–63, 164, 181, 188–89, 195
Christine Goodwin v United Kingdom (2002) 35 EHRR 18 .... 100–1, 147
CN v United Kingdom (2013) 56 EHRR 24 .... 2–3, 6, 42–43, 45, 47, 124–25, 129, 135–36, 139, 140–41
CN and V v France App no 67724/09 (ECtHR, 11 October 2012) 2–3, 42–43, 49, 53–55, 86–87, 88, 124–26, 127–28, 129, 157–58
D v United Kingdom (1997) 24 EHRR 423 98–99
Denis Vasilyev v Russia [2009] ECHR 2078 .... 109, 112, 115, 135–36
Denizci and Others v Cyprus [2001] ECHR 351 .... 47, 144
DJ v Croatia [2012] ECHR 1642 105
DH v Czech Republic (GC) [2008] ECHR 646 191
Doorson v Netherlands (1996) 22 EHRR 330 177–78
Dudgeon v United Kingdom (1982) 4 EHRR 149 100–1
E and Others v United Kingdom (2003) 36 EHRR 31 .... 47, 94, 102, 105, 109, 121–22, 143, 144, 145
EK (Article 4 ECHR: Anti-Trafficking Convention) Tanzania v Secretary of State for the Home Department [2013] UKUT 313 (IAC) 186

x TABLE OF CASES

Fadeyeva v Russia (2007) 45 EHRR 10 105
Giuliani and Gaggio v Italy [GC] [2009] ECHR 23458/02 94
Graziani-Weiss v Austria App no 31950/06 (ECtHR, 18 October 2011) 54–55
Gul v Switzerland (1996) 22 EHRR 93 102
Horvath and Kiss v Hungary (2013) 57 EHRR 31 191–92
Hugh Jordan v United Kingdom (2001) 37 EHRR 52 .... 112–13, 135–36, 157
İlhan v Turkey [GC] (2002) 34 EHRR 36` 112, 113–14, 157
J and Others v Austria, App no 58216/12 (ECtHR, 17 January 2017) 35–36
J and Others v Austria [2017] ECHR 37 .... 2–3, 40, 42–43, 45, 46, 58, 72, 106–7,
                                              111, 120–21, 125–27, 129, 136, 137, 140,
                                              142–43, 151–53, 156, 181, 189
Kilic v Turkey (2001) 33 EHRR 58 .... 47, 144
Klass and Others v Germany (1980) 2 EHRR 214 127
Kok v Netherlands [2000] ECHR 706 177–78
Kontrová v Slovakia [2007] ECHR 419 .... 47, 124–25, 127–28, 142, 143, 144
Kostovski v Netherlands (1989) Series A No 166 177–78
L v Lithuania (2008) 46 EHRR 22 107–8
LE v Greece [2016] ECHR 107 .... 2–3, 42–43, 135–36
Loizidou v Turkey (1997) 23 EHRR 513 164
Ludi v Switzerland (1992) Series A No 238 177–78
M and Others v Italy and Bulgaria [2012] ECHR 1967 .... 2–3, 42–43, 47, 130, 147–48
Marckx v Belgium (1979) 2 EHRR 330 .... 99, 100–1, 102
MC v Bulgaria (2005) 40 EHRR 20 .... 102, 105–6, 109, 117–18, 124–25, 138
McCann and Others v United Kingdom [1995] ECHR 18984/91 112–13,
                                                                     119–20, 127, 157
Medova v Russia [2009] ECHR 70 105
Menson and Others v United Kingdom (Admissibility) (2003) 37 EHRR CD220 109,
                                                                     124–25, 135–36
MSS v Belgium and Greece [GC] (2011) 53 EHRR 2 .... 83, 105
Öcalan v Turkey (2005) 41 EHRR 45 164
Öneryıldız v Turkey (2004) 39 EHRR 12 .... 47, 138, 141–42, 143, 144–46
Öneryıldız v Turkey [GC] (2005) 41 EHRR 20 .... 98–99, 117
Opuz v Turkey (2010) 50 EHRR 28 .... 47, 83, 102, 105, 108–9, 117–18, 124–25,
                                              127–28, 131–32, 142, 144–46, 149, 190
Oršuš and Others v Croatia [GC] (2011) 52 EHRR 7 .... 83, 105, 191
Osman v United Kingdom (2000) 29 EHRR 245 .... 47, 98–99, 102–3, 105, 124–25,
                                              127–28, 143, 144–45, 146–56, 167–68, 176
Özel and Others v Turkey [2020] ECHR 277 98–99
Plattform 'Ärzte für das Leben' v Austria (1991) 13 EHRR 204 116
Poltoratskiy v Ukraine (2004) 39 EHRR 43 .... 112–13, 157
PS v Germany (2003) 36 EHRR 61 177
Rantsev v. Cyprus and Russia (22 June 2010) Opinion No 6/2010 188
Rantsev v Cyprus and Russia (2010) 51 EHRR 1 .... 2–3, 6, 9–10, 28, 30, 34, 35–37,
                          40, 41, 42–43, 44, 46, 48, 49, 65, 71, 105, 117–18, 119,
                          123–24, 126, 127, 129, 135–37, 141–42, 144, 146, 147, 149–50, 151–52, 153, 154,
                          162–63, 164, 177, 188–89, 190, 191–92, 194–95
Saïdi v France (1993) Series A No 261-C 177–78
Schenk v Switzerland (1988) Series A No 140 ....:...................... 177–78
Siliadin v France (2006) 43 EHRR 16 .... 41, 47, 49, 53–54, 55, 94, 98–99,
                                                                     105, 123–24, 125, 148
Silver v United Kingdom (1983) 5 EHRR 347 111–12

TABLE OF CASES   xi

SM v Croatia App no 60561/14 (ECtHR GC, 25 June 2020) 2–3, 6, 7–8, 17–18,
25, 34–36, 42–43, 46, 59, 71–72, 111, 115, 120–21, 123,
124–26, 127–28, 129–30, 131–32, 135–36, 138–39,
140–42, 144, 147, 151–53, 173–74
SN v Sweden (2004) 39 EHRR 13 177–78
Soering v United Kingdom (1989) 11 EHRR 439 100–1
Stubbings and Others v United Kingdom (1997) 23 EHRR 213 105
Stummer v Austria [GC] (2012) 54 EHRR 11 54–55
Tyrer v United Kingdom (1979–80) 12 EHRR 1 100–1
Van der Mussele v Belgium (1983) 6 EHRR 163 . . . . 49, 54–55, 86
Van Droogenbroeck v Belgium (1982) 4 EHRR 443 53–54
Van Mechelen and Others v Netherlands (1997) 25 EHRR 647 177–78
VCL and AN v United Kingdom [2021] ECHR 132 . . . . 7–8, 36–37, 57–58,
119, 121, 125–26, 132, 144, 149, 150–52, 154–55,
162–63, 165, 169–70, 178–80, 181, 189
X and Y v Netherlands (1986) 8 EHRR 235 105
Young, James and Webster v United Kingdom (1982) 4 EHRR 38 124
Z and Others v United Kingdom (2002) 34 EHRR 3 . . . . 47, 94, 102, 105, 109, 144
Zoletic and Others v Azerbaijan [2021] ECHR 789 . . . . 6, 109, 111, 120–21,
124–26, 127–28, 129, 130, 132, 133, 135–36, 138–39,
140–42, 144, 149, 151–52, 157–58, 162–63

INTERNATIONAL

African Commission on Human and Peoples' Rights

Malawi African Association and Others v Mauritania African Commission
on Human and Peoples' Rights, Communications Nos 54/ 91,
61/ 91, 98/ 93, 164/ 97-196/ 97, and 210/ 98 (2000),
Ruling of 11 May 2000 . . . . 48, 86, 100

Economic Community of West African States

Hadijatou Mani Koraou v Republic of Niger, Judgment No ECW/CCJ/JUD/06/08
of 27 October 2008 . . . . 52, 88
Koraou v Niger Judgment No ECW/CCJ/JUD/06/08 (27 October 2008) 88

Inter-American Court of Human Rights

Castillo Petruzzi and Others v Peru Judgment of 30 May 1999 120–21
González and Others ('Cotton Field') v Mexico (Preliminary Objection, Merits,
Reparations and Costs) IACtHR Series C No 205 (16 November 2009) 102
Favela Nova Brasilia v Brazil (Preliminary Objections, Merits, Reparations and Costs)
IACtHR Series C No 333 (16 February 2017) 102
López Soto v Venezuela (Judgment, Merits, Reparations and Costs) IACtHR
Series C No 318 (26 September 2018) 102, 120, 124–25
Velasquez-Rodriguez v Honduras Inter-American Court of Human Rights
Series C No 4 (29 July 1988) 35, 99, 120–21
Workers of the Hacienda Brasil Verde v Brazil (Preliminary Objections, Merits,
Reparations and Costs) Inter-American Court of Human Rights
Series C No 318 (20 October 2016) 25, 48, 51, 53, 99, 103, 105, 123,
124–25, 127–28, 130, 134–35, 142, 144, 147–48,
149, 154, 157, 159–60, 164–65

International Criminal Tribunal for the Former Yugoslavia

Prosecutor v Kunarac (Trial Chamber) Case No IT-96-23-T & IT-96-23/1-T
  (22 February 2001). 52
Prosecutor v Kunarac, Kovac and Vukovic, Case Nos IT-96-23 and
  IT-96-23/1-A [2002] ICTY 2 (12 June 2002) 42–43, 50, 52
Prosecutor v Kupreškić and Others ICTY Case IT 95 16 T (14 January 2000) 33

International Court of Justice (ICJ)

Democratic Republic of the Congo v Uganda), Judgment of 19 December 2005
  [2005] ICJ Rep 168. 97

NATIONAL COURTS

Australia
Queen v Tang, The [2008] HCA 39 (28 August 2008) M5/2008 . . . . 50–52, 57

Sierra Leone
Prosecutor v Alex Tamba Brima, Brima Bazzy Kamara and Santigie Borbor Kanu,
  The (the AFRC Accused), SCSL-04-16-T, Special Court for Sierra Leone
  (20 June 2007) (Judgment) 52
Prosecutor v Charles Ghankay Taylor, The (SCSL-03-1-T) Trial Chamber II,
  Special Court for Sierra Leone (26 April 2012) (Judgment) 52

United States
United States of America v Oswald Pohl and Others, The (Case No 4)
  United States Military Tribunal II 88

United Kingdom
Minh, R (on the application of) v The Secretary of State for the Home
  Department [2015] EWHC 1725 (Admin) (18 June 2015) 149–50, 169–70
R v LM and Others [2010] EWCA Crim 2327 192–93
R v N; R v LE (2012) EWCA Crim 189 57–58
R v SK [2011] EWCA Crim 1691 53–54

Table of Legislation

UK STATUTES

Criminal Justice Act 1988
   s 134 34
Modern Slavery Act 2015 32
   s 1 63
   s 2 63

EUROPEAN UNION

Charter of Fundamental Rights of the
   European Union (18 December 2000)
   2000/C 364/01 (EU Charter) 48
   art 5 .... 3–4, 32, 48, 64–65
   art 5(3) 25–26
European Convention for the Protection
   of Human Rights and Fundamental
   Freedoms (4 November 1950)
   ETS 5 (ECHR) 10, 26, 93–94, 123,
                    164, 165–66
   art 1 101–2
   art 2 .... 41–42, 47, 94,
            102–3, 113, 114, 117, 128,
            140–41, 143, 144, 146, 147–48, 159
   art 3 .... 41–42, 47, 94,
        102–3, 108, 112, 113, 114, 115, 117–18,
          128, 131, 138–39, 140–41, 142, 144,
              145, 146, 147–48, 159, 185
   art 4 .... 2–3, 7–8, 28, 30,
         34–35, 36–37, 40, 41–44, 45, 46, 47,
        48–63, 64–65, 71–72, 82, 86, 92, 94, 99,
          109, 115, 123, 124, 125–26, 127–28,
          129, 130, 131, 132, 133, 134, 135, 137,
        138, 140–42, 144, 146, 147, 148, 149–
       50, 152, 153, 154–55, 156, 157–58, 159,
          162–63, 164, 165, 176, 178–80, 181,
            185, 186, 188–89, 190–92
   art 4(1) 47, 102–3
   art 4(2) 141
   art 5 .... 41–42, 176
   art 5(1) 94, 159
   art 6 .... 141–42, 176–78, 179–80
   art 6(1) 130, 186
   art 6(2) 130
   art 7 .... 47, 62, 102–3
   art 8 .... 176, 178–79
   art 13 .... 109–10, 111, 112,
                113–14, 117–18, 157–58
   Protocol 1
      art 1 141
      art 2 191
      art 3 101
   Protocol 4, art 2 141
Directive 2011/36/EU of the European
   Parliament and of the Council on
   Preventing and Combating Trafficking
   in Human Beings and Protecting
   its Victims, and Replacing Council
   Framework Decision 2002/629/
   JHA (5 April 2011) (Anti-Trafficking
   Directive) 1–2, 32–33,
                     49–50, 57–58
   Recital 21 149
   Preamble, para 7 24
   art 2 .... 45, 172–73
   art 2(2) 84
   art 2(3) 57–58
   art 8 .... 36–37, 165, 172, 179
   art 10(2) 151
   art 11 181–82
   art 11(2) 147–48
   art 11(3) 106–7, 182
   art 11(5) 181–82
   art 12 .... 175, 181–82
   art 15 175

CONVENTIONS, PROTOCOLS AND AGREEMENTS

African Charter of Human and Peoples'
   Rights CAB/LEG/67/3 rev.5, 21 ILM
   58 (1982) (27 June 1981) (African
   Charter)
   art 5 .... 2–3, 64–65, 86, 100
Arab Charter on Human Rights (adopted
   22 May 2004, entered into force 15
   March 2008) (Arab Charter)

art 10 .... 3–4, 25–26, 32, 48, 64–65
ASEAN Convention against Trafficking in
  Persons, Especially Women
  and Children (22 November
  2015) 1–2, 24–25
art 16(7)....................... 175
Association of Southeast Asian Nations
  (ASEAN) Human Rights Declaration
  (adopted 18 November 2012) (ASEAN
  Declaration)
  para 13 .... 3–4, 48, 64–65
Convention for the Suppression of
  the Traffic in Persons and of the
  Exploitation of the Prostitution of
  Others (adopted 2 December
  1949, entered into force
  25 July 1951) 96 UNTS 271
  (1949 Convention) 21–22
  arts 1–3 21–22
  art 1 67
  arts 8–11 21–22
  art 14 21–22
  art 14(7).................... 165, 172
  art 19 21–22
Convention on Action against Trafficking
  in Human Beings (adopted 16 May
  2005, entered into force 1 February
  2008) CETS 197 (Anti- Trafficking
  Convention) 1–2, 24,
                                119, 164, 195
  Ch III 10, 148
  Ch VII 92, 174–75
  art 1(1)(b) 173
  art 2 149
  art 3 149
  art 4 .... 45, 67, 146
  art 4(a) 42–43, 146, 151–52
  art 5(3)........................ 171
  art 8 149
  art 10 148
  art 10(2)....................... 148
  art 11 .... 148, 183
  art 12 148
  art 12(1)...... 148, 151, 181–83, 188–89
  art 12(1)(d) 182–83
  art 12(1)(e) 182–83
  art 12(2)............... 148, 151, 169,
                                181–83, 188–89
  art 12(3).................... 170, 185
  art 12(4).................... 170, 185
  art 12(6).................. 106–7, 184

art 12(7)....................... 149
art 13 .... 148, 169, 181–82
art 13(1)....................... 182
art 14 .... 170, 184, 186
art 15 .... 148, 186, 187
art 15(2)....................... 186
art 15(3)....................... 186
art 16 148
art 16(2)....................... 185
art 19 .... 173, 174–75
art 18 172–73
art 20 174–75
art 21 173
art 22 173
art 23 173
art 26 .... 7–8, 36–37, 165, 172, 179
art 27 173
art 28 175
art 29 173
art 29(1).................... 174–75
art 30 .... 175–76, 183
art 32 173
Explanatory Report
  para 8 24
  paras 28–37....................24
  para 32 170–71
  para 51 24
  para 83 82–83
  para 87 .... 2–3, 31
  para 127 .... 149, 151–52, 169–70
  para 138..................... 183
  paras 146–147 183–84
  para 147..................... 182
  para 149.................. 183–84
  para 151.................. 183–84
  para 158..................... 183
  para 160..................... 183
  para 164..................... 183
  para 175..................... 182
  para 176..................... 182
  paras 183–84 184–85
  para 192..................... 187
  para 196..................... 186
  para 197..................... 187
  para 198..................... 186
  para 203..................... 185
  para 234..................... 173
  para 275..................... 172
  para 286..................... 175
  para 288..................... 175
  paras 306–26 175

Convention on the Elimination of All
    Forms of Discrimination against
    Women (adopted 18 December 1979,
    entered into force 3 September 1981)
    1249 UNTS 13 (CEDAW)
    art 6 . . . . 3–4, 25–26
Convention on the Rights of the Child
    (adopted 20 November 1989, entered
    into force 2 September 1990) 1577
    UNTS 3 (CRC) 3–4
    art 2(1) 101–2
    art 19(1) 67
    art 35 25–26
Council of Europe Convention against
    Trafficking in Human Organs (2014)
    CETS 2016 . . . . 61, 88–89
    art 4(1) 61
    art 7(1) 61
Council of the European Union,'
    Brussels Declaration on Preventing
    and Combating Trafficking in
    Human Beings' 14981/02
    (29 November 2002) 29–30
Inter-American Convention on Human
    Rights (adopted 22 November 1969,
    entered into force 18 July 1978) 1144
    UNTS 143 OASTS No 36 (American
    Convention)
    art 1 101–2
    art 1(1) 99, 101–2, 157
    art 6 . . . . 2–3, 64–65, 99, 105,
                                    160, 164–65
    art 6(1) 25–26
    art 8(1) 134
    art 25 160
    art 25(1) 134, 159–60
    art 63(1) 160
International Agreement for the
    Suppression of the White Slave Traffic
    (adopted 4 May 1904, entered into
    force 18 July 1905) 1 LNTS 83 20
International Convention for the Suppression
    of the Traffic in Women of Full Age
    (adopted 11 October 1933, entered into
    force 24 August 1934) 150 LNTS 431
    (1933 Convention) 20–21
    art 1 20–21
International Convention for the
    Suppression of the White Slave Traffic
    (adopted 4 May 1910, entered into
    force 8 August 1912) 3 LNTS 278
    art 1 20

art 2 20
International Convention for the
    Suppression of Traffic in Women
    and Children (adopted
    30 September 1921, entered
    into force 15 June 1922) 9 LNTS
    415 (1921 Convention) 20–21
    art 2 20–21
International Convention on the Protection
    of the Rights of All Migrant Workers
    and Members of their Families 1990,
    2220 UNTS 3 67
International Covenant on Civil and
    Political Rights (adopted 16 December
    1966, entered into force 23 March
    1976) 999 UNTS 171 (ICCPR)
    art 2 102
    art 2(1) 101–2
    art 8 . . . . 2–3, 64–65
International Labour Organization (ILO)
    Convention No 29 (Forced Labour
    Convention) 31, 49
    art 2(1) 54–55
International Law Commission, 'Draft
    Articles on Responsibility of States
    for Internationally Wrongful Acts'
    Doc A/56/10 (2001) 95
    art 2 96
    art 8 96
Optional Protocol to the Convention on
    the Rights of the Child on the Sale of
    Children, Child Prostitution and Child
    Pornography 2000, 2171 UNTS 227
    art 3(1) 67
Protocol of 2014 to the Forced Labour
    Convention, 1930 (adopted 11
    June 2014, entered into force 9
    November 2016)
    Preamble 59
    art 4(2) 7–8, 36–37
Protocol to Prevent, Suppress and Punish
    Trafficking in Persons Especially
    Women and Children, Supplementing
    the United Nations Convention against
    Transnational Organized Crime
    (adopted 15 November 2000, entered
    into force 25 December 2003)
    2237 UNTS 319 (Palermo
    Protocol) 1, 15, 49, 65, 164
    Preamble 23
    art 2 166–67
    art 3 . . . . 4–6, 30, 45, 61, 67, 167–68

art 3a 30, 35–36, 146, 151–52
art 5 . . . . 166–68, 172–73
arts 6–8 166–67
art 6(1) 167–68
art 6(3) 166–68
art 6(5) 167–68
art 8 166–67
art 9 166–67
art 9(3) 166–67
art 10 166–67
arts 11–13 166–67
Rome Statute of the International
    Criminal Court
    art 7 33
    art 7(1)(k) 33
Slavery Convention (25 September 1926)
    212 UNTS 17 . . . . 49, 50–51
    art 1(1) 50
Supplementary Convention on the
    Abolition of Slavery, the Slave Trade
    and Institutions and Practices Similar
    to Slavery (adopted 7 September 1956,
    entered into force 30 April 1957) 266
    UNTS 3 . . . . 49, 58–59
    art 1 58–59
UN Convention Against Transnational
    Organized Crime and the Protocols
    Thereto
    art 24 167–68
    art 25 167–68
    art 25(1) 167–68
UN Human Right Committee, 'General
    Comment No 31: The Nature of the
    General Legal Obligation Imposed on
    States Parties to the Covenant' (26 May
    2004) CCPR/C/21/Rev.1/Add.13
    para 6 . . . . 98–99, 101–2

UN Protocol Amending the Convention
    for the Suppression of the Traffic
    in Women and Children, and
    Amending the Convention for the
    Suppression of the Traffic in Women
    of Full Age (12 November 1947) 53
    UNTS 13 20–21
UN Protocol Amending the International
    Agreement for the Suppression
    of the White Slave Traffic, and
    Amending the International
    Convention for the Suppression of the
    White Slave Traffic (adopted 4 May
    1949, entered into force 21 June 1951)
    30 UNTS 23 20
United Nations Convention against
    Transnational Organized Crime and
    the Protocols Thereto (adopted 15
    November 2000, entered into force 29
    September 2003), UNGA Res 55/25
    (UN TOC) 22–23, 37
    art 32 33
Universal Declaration of Human Rights
    (10 December 1948) 217 A (III)
    (UDHR) 59
    art 4 . . . . 2–3, 58–59, 64–65

OTHER LEGISLATION

Australia

Australian Modern Slavery Act 2018, No
    153, 2018 63

Netherlands

Dutch Criminal Code
    art 273f 87

List of Abbreviations

ACHPR	African Commission on Human and Peoples' Rights
ACHR	American Convention on Human Rights
ARSIWA	Articles on State Responsibility for Internationally Wrongful Acts
ASEAN	Association of Southeast Asian Nations
CAT	Committee against Torture
CED	Committee on Enforced Disappearances
CEDAW	Convention on the Elimination of All Forms of Discrimination against Women
CERD	Committee on the Elimination of Racial Discrimination
CESCR	Committee on Economic, Social and Cultural Rights
CRC	Committee on the Rights of the Child
CRPD	Committee on the Rights of Persons with Disabilities
ECHR	European Convention on Human Rights
ECtHR	European Court of Human Rights
ECOWAS	Economic Community of West African States
EU Charter	Charter of Fundamental Rights of the European Union
IACHR	Inter-American Convention on Human Rights
IACtHR	Inter-American Court of Human Rights
ICTY	International Criminal Tribunal for the Former Yugoslavia
ILC	International Law Commission
ILO	International Labour Organization
ODIHR	Office for Democratic Institutions and Human Rights
OHCHR	Office of the High Commissioner for Human Rights
OSCE	Organisation for Security and Cooperation in Europe
PACE	Parliamentary Assembly of the Council of Europe
UNHCR	UN High Commissioner for Refugees

1
Introduction

Human trafficking has captured international attention since 2000 when the UN adopted the Palermo Protocol,[1] which contains the first universally agreed definition of the phenomenon reportedly affecting millions of people worldwide.[2] Its legal nature, however, remains contested. While some authors claim that human trafficking is merely a criminal act, 'just like murder, rape and theft',[3] there is a wide consensus that the practice also represents a grave human rights violation. Yet the existing literature fails to portray a convincing account of the relationship between human trafficking and human rights law. The book thus addresses a pertinent question: is there a human right not to be trafficked and if so, what does this right entail? In answering this question in the affirmative, the book paints a more nuanced view emphasising a *hybrid* nature of human trafficking as *both* a crime and a human rights violation with different implications resulting from its operationalisation in the two legal contexts. The book offers a comprehensive account of the right not to be trafficked and the prohibition of 'modern slavery' overall,[4] which includes the analysis of its scope and the rules for assessing states' responsibility under human rights law.

1.1 The Case for a Right Not to Be Trafficked

For an act to represent a human rights *violation* two conditions are necessary. First, it must be determined which human right is engaged and whether a conduct in question falls within its scope. Secondly, it ought to be established whether a state's

---

[1] Protocol to Prevent, Suppress and Punish Trafficking in Persons Especially Women and Children, Supplementing the United Nations Convention against Transnational Organized Crime (adopted 15 November 2000, entered into force 25 December 2003) 2237 UNTS 319 (Palermo Protocol).
[2] International Labour Organization, Global Estimates of Modern Slavery: Forced Labour and Forced Marriage (2017) 9 (claiming that 'an estimated 40.3 million people were victims of modern slavery in 2016 ... modern slavery covers a set of specific legal concepts including ... human trafficking').
[3] Ryszard Piotrowicz, 'International Focus: Trafficking and Slavery as Human Rights Violations' (2010) 84 Australian Law Journal 812, 814; Ryszard Piotrowicz, 'The Legal Nature of Trafficking in Human Beings' (2009) 4 Intercultural Human Rights Law Review 175.
[4] Practices of human trafficking, slavery, servitude, and forced labour are jointly referred to as 'modern slavery' in the second part of the book, being duly aware of the fact that 'modern slavery' is not a legal term and its use has been contested. See Michael Dottridge, 'Eight Reasons Why We Shouldn't Use the Term "Modern Slavery"' *Open Democracy* (17 October 2017) https://www.opendemocracy.net/en/beyond-trafficking-and-slavery/eight-reasons-why-we-shouldn-t-use-term-modern-slavery/ (accessed 19 January 2020).

act or omission with regard to such conduct has breached a duty owed to a victim. The specialised anti-trafficking instruments, which have started to emerge since 2000, impose on states obligations to criminalise human trafficking in their domestic legislation, to prosecute perpetrators, to provide protection for victims, and to design strategies for its prevention.[5] Whereas such international instruments require states to establish a domestic legal and institutional framework to address human trafficking, they do not create a claim for a victim against a state for failing to do so. In other words, specialised anti-trafficking instruments are *not* human rights instruments, even though some of these instruments have a strong victim protection dimension. As such, they do not establish a right of a victim not to be trafficked that gives rise to individual human rights claims against states.

Human rights claims against states for human trafficking have nevertheless been reviewed by international courts, which have ruled that those states have certain human rights obligations towards trafficking victims. Specifically, human trafficking has been conceived as a distinct prohibition under the right to be free from slavery, servitude, and forced labour due to 'its very nature and aim of exploitation'.[6] However, the law resulting from these litigations is often inconclusive as to whether there is a *separate* human right not to be trafficked and the nature and scope of states' human rights obligations towards the victims of human trafficking. Specifically, the existing case law fails to establish with certainty the relationship between human trafficking on the one hand, and slavery, servitude, and forced labour, on the other.[7] This clarification is important because, unlike human trafficking, slavery, servitude, and forced labour are expressly prohibited practices in general human rights instruments.[8] At the same time, these practices represent

---

[5] Palermo Protocol; Convention on Action against Trafficking in Human Beings (adopted 16 May 2005, entered into force 1 February 2008) CETS 197 (Anti-Trafficking Convention); Directive of the European Parliament and of the Council on Preventing and Combating Trafficking in Human Beings and Protecting its Victims, and Replacing Council Framework Decision 2002/629/JHA (5 April 2011) 2011/36/EU (Anti-Trafficking Directive); ASEAN Convention against Trafficking in Persons, Especially Women and Children (22 November 2015).

[6] *Rantsev v Cyprus and Russia* (2010) 51 EHRR 1 [281]. See also *M and Others v Italy and Bulgaria* [2012] ECHR 1967; *CN and V v France* App no 67724/09 (ECtHR, 11 October 2012); *CN v United Kingdom* (2013) 56 EHRR 24; *LE v Greece* [2016] ECHR 107; *Chowdury and Others v Greece* [2017] ECHR 300; *J and Others v Austria* [2017] ECHR 37; *SM v Croatia* App no 60561/14 (ECtHR GC, 25 June 2020).

[7] See generally Vladislava Stoyanova, *Human Trafficking and Slavery Reconsidered: Conceptual Limits and States' Positive Obligations in European Law* (CUP 2017).

[8] Human rights instruments frame this right differently. The Universal Declaration of Human Rights (10 December 1948) 217 A (III), art 4 (UDHR) prohibits only slavery, servitude, and the slave trade but not forced labour. The International Covenant on Civil and Political Rights (adopted 16 December 1966, entered into force 23 March 1976) 999 UNTS 171, art 8 (ICCPR), the European Convention for the Protection of Human Rights and Fundamental Freedoms (4 November 1950) ETS 5, art 4 (ECHR), and the American Convention on Human Rights (adopted 22 November 1969, entered into force 18 July 1978) 1144 UNTS 143 OASTS No 36, art 6 (American Convention) prohibit slavery, servitude, and forced labour (the American Convention also prohibits slave trade and traffic in women). The African Charter of Human and Peoples' Rights CAB/LEG/67/3 rev.5, 21 ILM 58 (1982) (27 June 1981), art 5 (African Charter) prohibits 'all forms of exploitation and degradation of man' and lists explicitly slavery and slave trade alongside torture, cruel, inhuman, or degrading punishment and treatment.

the exploitative end purposes of a human trafficking offence, which is completed *before* intended exploitation has materialised.[9] It is therefore necessary to clarify whether human trafficking amounts to a self-standing prohibition within the right to be free from slavery, servitude, and forced labour, or it is consumed by any of the three explicitly prohibited practices.

The claim that human trafficking represents a distinct human rights violation is substantiated in a two-step process. First, it is established that a human right not to be trafficked is derived from the prohibition of slavery, servitude, and forced labour—and not any other human right—because these practices have a common root in the notion of human exploitation, which justifies their joint prohibition under the same human right. Notably, as a complex social phenomenon, human trafficking often impinges upon a number of human rights including the right to life, the prohibition of torture, the right to private life, and many more.[10] Yet, human trafficking is *inherently* connected with the practices of slavery, servitude, and forced labour because exploitation represents their respective purpose (human trafficking) and effect (slavery, servitude, or forced labour). Exploitation is thus considered 'a large tent'[11] and 'the overarching theme that subsumes all forms of human trafficking, slavery, forced labour, bonded labour, child labour, forced prostitution, economic exploitation, and so on'.[12] The notion of human exploitation thus amounts to distinct *wrong* underlying these diverse practices and bringing them together under an umbrella of the same right. Other rights violations are ancillary, but nonetheless grave.

Having established an inherent link between human trafficking, on the one hand, and practices of slavery, servitude, and forced labour, on the other, the second step demonstrates that human trafficking represents an implied but stand-alone prohibition within the right to be free from slavery, servitude, and forced labour

---

[9] UNODC, 'Legislative Guide for the Implementation of the Protocol to Prevent, Suppress and Punish Trafficking in Persons, Especially Women and Children, Supplementing the United Nations Convention against Transnational Organized Crime' (2004) para 33; Explanatory Report to the Council of Europe Convention on Action against Trafficking in Human Beings (16 May 2005) CETS 197, para 87.

[10] UN Office of the United Nations High Commissioner for Human Rights, Recommended Principles and Guidelines on Human Rights and Human Trafficking—Commentary (2010) 51; UN High Commissioner for Refugees, 'Prevent, Combat, Protect Human Trafficking: Joint UN Commentary on the EU Directive: A Human Rights Based Approach' (November 2011); UN Office of the High Commissioner for Human Rights, *Human Trafficking and Human Rights* (Factsheet 36, 2014). These sources provide a list of key rights engaged in trafficking in human beings together with treaty sources in which those rights have been enshrined.

[11] Jean Allain, *Slavery in International Law: Of Human Exploitation and Trafficking* (Martinus Nijhoff Publishers 2013).

[12] Johannes Koettl, 'Human Trafficking, Modern Day Slavery, and Economic Exploitation' World Bank Discussion Paper No 0911 (May 2009) 4. See also Roger Plant, 'Modern Slavery: the Concepts and Their Practical Implications' ILO Working Paper (5 February 2015) 3; UN Working Group on Trafficking in Persons, 'Key Concepts of the Trafficking in Persons Protocol, with a Focus on the United Nations Office on Drugs and Crime Issue Papers on Abuse of a position of Vulnerability, Consent and Exploitation' (25 August 2015) CTOC/COP/WG.4/2015/4, para 20.

and could not be consumed by any of the three expressly prohibited practices.[13] This is because slavery, servitude, and forced labour represent different *manifestations* of exploitation whereas human trafficking amounts to a *process* leading to such exploitation. Human trafficking is therefore a precursor to slavery and other serious forms of exploitation, aptly described as 'the international supply chain into exploitation'.[14] However, the claim that there is an autonomous right not to be trafficked begs a question. If slavery, servitude, and forced labour are already expressly prohibited in human rights law, what is an added value of including human trafficking—as inchoate slavery, servitude, and forced labour—in its scope?

The prohibition of slavery, servitude, and forced labour, in the same vein as other 'absolute' human rights,[15] imposes on states obligations to pre-empt violations in certain well-defined circumstances. These include: the presence of a real and immediate risk to an identifiable individual; states' awareness of that risk; and that the necessary actions were within the scope of the powers of state authorities which, judged reasonably, might have been expected to avoid such risk.[16] States are therefore obliged to protect against imminent exploitation (slavery, servitude, or forced labour) in the same vein as they are bound to protect against the real and immediate risk of torture or of the violation of the right to life.[17] Given that the trafficking offence (if uninterrupted) always results in exploitation, which is its main purpose, and the offence is complete before any such exploitation has materialised, being subject to human trafficking amounts to a real and immediate risk of being subject to exploitation triggering states' duties to act to prevent severe rights violations.

However, slavery, servitude, and forced labour may take place without a victim being trafficked into such conditions and states would be equally obliged to prevent these practices, subject to the above outlined conditions. One may therefore assume that this would make the inclusion of human trafficking within the scope of this right redundant.[18] This assumption is misguided. On the contrary, if a state is bound to protect against the real and immediate risk of slavery, servitude, and

---

[13] The newer human rights instruments including the Charter of Fundamental Rights of the European Union (18 December 2000) 2000/C 364/01, art 5 (EU Charter); the Arab Charter on Human Rights (adopted 22 May 2004, entered into force 15 March 2008), art 10 (Arab Charter); and the Association of Southeast Asian Nations (ASEAN) Human Rights Declaration (adopted 18 November 2012), para 13 (ASEAN Declaration) explicitly prohibit human trafficking alongside slavery servitude and forced labour (although the ASEAN Declaration does not mention forced labour but includes human smuggling within this right). Human trafficking is also explicitly mentioned in the Convention on the Elimination of All Forms of Discrimination against Women (adopted 18 December 1979, entered into force 3 September 1981) 1249 UNTS 13 (CEDAW), art 6; and the Convention on the Rights of the Child (adopted 20 November 1989, entered into force 2 September 1990) 1577 UNTS 3 (CRC), art 35.
[14] Allain (n 11) 355.
[15] The term 'absolute' rights is contested since it implies the hierarchy of rights that has not been explicitly recognised in international human rights instruments. See Chapter 5, sections 5.1 and 5.3 for a discussion of the term.
[16] See further discussion of these conditions in Chapter 6.
[17] ibid.
[18] As argued by Stoyanova (n 7).

forced labour, there is hardly a better reason for the inclusion of human trafficking within this right. Human trafficking, if uninterrupted, *always* results in exploitation.[19] The elements of a human trafficking act, outlined in its definition, thus serve as indicia of imminent exploitation that states are required to prevent. Thus, the real and immediate risk of exploitation, which is intrinsic to the trafficking situation, brings human trafficking within the realm of the prohibition of slavery, servitude, and forced labour, requiring states to act before any such risk materialised. Accordingly, the inclusion of human trafficking within the scope of the right to be free from slavery increases rather than diminishes its potential to protect against severe forms of exploitation. Specific acts and means, which are the necessary elements of the trafficking definition,[20] serve as indicia of the risk that a person is to be subject to severe forms of exploitation that might otherwise be difficult to establish.

Therefore, human trafficking, as imminent exploitation, and practices of slavery, servitude, and forced labour, as manifestations of exploitation that may but do not always result from human trafficking, are not mutually exclusive nor could they consume each other, unless an act of human trafficking has already progressed into the stage of exploitation. In the latter case, a victim could bring a claim against a state based on its failure to protect either from human trafficking or from slavery, servitude, or forced labour, depending on the concrete facts of the case. Accordingly, it is vital to recognise the distinction between human trafficking as a *process* of bringing people into exploitative conditions and the resulting exploitative *conditions* that represent its end purpose, and which may, but do not always result from trafficking. This *key distinction* has often been overlooked in the attempt to submerge diverse practices under popular umbrella terms such as 'modern slavery'.

1.2 One Definition, Two Legal Contexts: Individual Criminal Responsibility versus State Responsibility under Human Rights Law

As a legal concept, human trafficking represents a point where criminal law and human rights law traverse. Criminal law is focused on punishing a perpetrator while human rights law addresses victims as rights bearers. These rights are inextricably linked to the crime, but they are invoked against a state—not against a perpetrator of such crime. Accordingly, whereas individuals are prohibited from

---

[19] Albeit of potentially different levels of severity, not all of which would amount to slavery, servitude, or forced labour. However, since this could be assessed with certainty only *after* such exploitation materialised, it is posited that the risk of serious exploitation would warrant state intervention at an earlier moment.
[20] Palermo Protocol, art 3. See detailed discussion of this point in Chapter 2.

trafficking people under international and municipal criminal law, states are required to protect people against human trafficking under international human rights law. Such protection warrants different state actions and punishing the offenders is but one of them. Accordingly, different rules govern the assessment of perpetrators' and states' responsibility for human trafficking respectively, although both are anchored in the same international legal definition of the phenomenon—the UN Palermo definition.[21]

For a criminal conviction for human trafficking to succeed, the elements of a crime, as prescribed in the Palermo definition, must be established *beyond reasonable doubt*. These elements of a crime are at the same time factual grounds on which to build a human rights claim against a state. Yet, state responsibility for a human rights violation necessitates three conditions. First, there must be indicia of human trafficking that trigger state obligations. Criminal law standard of proof beyond reasonable doubt is *not* necessary for triggering these obligations.[22] What is required is the presence of *reasonable grounds to believe* (a credible suspicion) that a person has been trafficked.[23] The second condition is the awareness of state officials about these circumstances. Thus, it must be shown that state authorities were 'aware or ought to have been aware' of such individual circumstances, which gave rise to a credible suspicion that a person may have been trafficked.[24] Finally, the imposed obligations do not guarantee absolute protection. They require states to take 'appropriate' measures and must not be interpreted to impose impossible or disproportionate burdens.[25] Based on this tripartite matrix, states would only be responsible for a *violation* of a human right not to be trafficked if it was shown that they had failed to comply with what was reasonably expected from them in the circumstances of a concrete case.

In sum, save for a direct involvement of states' agents in human trafficking, states only violate this right if they fail to comply with their *own* positive obligations towards trafficking victims arising out of it—obligations which are not contingent upon prior establishing of a criminal offence in the course of a criminal trial. This is true not just for human trafficking but also for slavery, servitude, and forced labour, or for any other rights infringement by non-state actors. These rules for establishing states' responsibility in situations when rights are infringed upon by non-state actors have long been recognised in the jurisprudence of human rights courts.[26]

---

[21] Palermo Protocol, art 3. See detailed discussion of this point in Chapter 2.
[22] *Rantsev v Cyprus and Russia* (n 6) [288]; *SM v Croatia* (n 6) [324] ('The Court ... must examine whether, in the circumstances of a particular case, the applicant made an arguable claim or whether there was prima facie evidence (*commencement de preuve*) of her having been subjected to such prohibited treatment').
[23] *CN v United Kingdom* (n 6) [71]; *Zoletic and Others v Azerbaijan* [2021] ECHR 789 [185].
[24] *Rantsev v Cyprus and Russia* (n 6) [286].
[25] ibid [287]; *Zoletic v Azerbaijan* (n 23) [184], [188].
[26] See the discussion in Chapter 6.

It is therefore clear that the same international definition of human trafficking applies differently in the criminal law and human rights law contexts, which reveals a hybrid legal nature of human trafficking—both as a crime and a human rights violation.

The value of framing human trafficking as a human rights issue, in addition to being a matter of criminal law, is two-fold. First, bringing human trafficking within the realm of human rights law allows victims to claim protection and make states accountable for implementing anti-trafficking actions. Criminal law contains a weak notion of victimhood where a victim is often considered a mere excuse for punishing the offenders.[27] Considering human trafficking purely as a matter of criminal law thus carries a risk of seeing victims as passive beneficiaries of criminal justice actions—protection recipients rather than right bearers. Human rights law remedies this weakness but at the same time draws on criminal law for the conceptualisation of the problem that gives rise to human rights obligations of states.

In addition to enhancing the agency of trafficking victims, the inclusion of human trafficking within the human rights framework allows international human rights bodies to draw directly on obligations established under the specialised anti-trafficking instruments when interpreting positive obligations under the right to be free from slavery, even in cases of *non-trafficked* slavery, servitude, and forced labour. For instance, the Strasbourg Court expressly relies on the Council of Europe Anti-Trafficking Convention to determine the scope of the states' positive obligations under Article 4 ECHR[28] even in situations of forced or compulsory labour that do not involve human trafficking, because of 'the conceptual proximity' between these exploitative practices.[29] Moreover, the principle of non-punishment of trafficking victims for crimes committed in the course of or resulting from human trafficking, first established by the Council of Europe Anti-Trafficking Convention,[30] now applies to victims of forced labour who have not been trafficked into such exploitation.[31] As this book shows in the final chapter, while not all victim protection measures included in the specialised anti-trafficking instruments qualify to become positive human rights obligations, there is a scope for developing these obligations by drawing on a range of international instruments

---

[27] See generally Markus Dubber, *Victims in the War on Crime* (NYU Press 2002); Liora Lazarus, 'Positive Obligations and Criminal Justice: Duties to Protect or Coerce?' in Lucia Zedner and Julian V Roberts (eds), *Principles and Values in Criminal Law and Criminal Justice: Essays in Honour of Andrew Ashworth* (OUP 2012).
[28] *Chowdury and Others v Greece* (n 6) [104], [110]; *VCL and AN v United Kingdom* [2021] ECHR 132 [150], [153].
[29] *SM v Croatia* (n 6) [307].
[30] See art 26. See also Marija Jovanovic, 'The Principle of Non-Punishment of Victims of Trafficking in Human Beings: A Quest for Rationale and Practical Guidance' (2017) 1 Journal of Trafficking and Human Exploitation 1; Ryszard Piotrowicz and Liliana Sorrentino, 'Human Trafficking and the Emergence of the Non-Punishment Principle' (2016) 16 Human Rights Law Review 669.
[31] Protocol of 2014 to the Forced Labour Convention, 1930 (adopted 11 June 2014, entered into force 9 November 2016), art 4(2).

devoted to human trafficking specifically, which in turn strengthens the protection against exploitation guaranteed by the totality of these instruments. It is therefore evident that human trafficking victimhood has two dimensions—human rights law and criminal law—each bearing different implications. The specialised anti-trafficking instruments and human rights instruments draw on and reinforce each other in order to provide fuller protection to individuals affected.

When it comes to the nature and scope of positive human rights obligations, and criteria for assessing states' responsibility for complying with these, the book is premised on four central claims. First, positive obligations arising out of the prohibition of slavery and human trafficking are comparable to those arising out of the prohibition of torture and the right to life when these rights are infringed upon by non-state actors. Thus, in the absence of an extensive jurisprudence on the prohibition of slavery, servitude, and forced labour, principles and standards developed in respect to the prohibition of torture and right to life serve as a useful guidance in articulating positive obligations arising out of the former.

Secondly, positive obligations that stem from these 'absolute' rights are both general and specific. General obligations require states to establish an adequate and effective legal framework that governs private actions and states' responses to rights infringements by private actors. Specific obligations concern actions of state authorities with regard to a concrete victim. These include both operational and procedural obligations. The procedural obligations require states to conduct an effective investigation into a private act alleged to have encroached upon the right. The operational duties require states to remove individuals from a situation that puts them at risk of rights violations by private actors. A distinction should therefore be made between actions required to achieve general prevention of human trafficking by putting in place an adequate and functional legal and institutional framework, on the one hand, and prevention of a specific act that threatens a concrete individual, on the other.

Thirdly, whereas the prohibition of torture, the prohibition of slavery, servitude, and forced labour, and the right to life are considered 'absolute' rights in that they contain an absolute negative prohibition for states not to engage in practices that can infringe these rights, positive obligations in situations of their infringements by non-state actors are not. Rather, appropriate actions required from national authorities must be within the scope of their powers and must not impose an impossible or disproportionate burden on them. These are therefore obligations of means, not ends. This is the second *key distinction* critical for understanding the place of human trafficking within human rights law. Accordingly, in addition to the first *key distinction* between human trafficking as a *process* of bringing people into exploitative conditions and the resulting exploitative *conditions* that represent its end purpose, distinguishing between the scope of the right and the scope of state responsibility helps reconcile the 'absolute' nature of prohibitions contained in these rights with the language of proportionality often used when assessing states' responsibility in situations of private infringements. In other words, whereas the prohibition of slavery is absolute, states' positive obligations and eventual responsibility for private acts of enslavement are not. The book's main task is therefore to articulate and explain the scope of such obligations and the rules for assessing states' responsibility for their breach. This enquiry animates Chapters 5 and 6.

Fourthly, positive human rights obligations arising out of the prohibition of slavery, servitude, forced labour, and human trafficking can be informed by obligations established under the specialised anti-trafficking instruments. However, not all victim protection measures amount to positive human rights obligations of states. The third *key distinction* deployed to explain the dynamics between human trafficking and human rights law is between victim protection measures and victims' human rights. The final chapter of the book demonstrates that victim protection measures contained in the specialised anti-trafficking instruments do not necessarily and automatically translate into (justiciable) human rights of victims. This distinction is relevant for determining the scope of states' positive obligations towards trafficking victims under human rights law and the potential for their further development. It is shown nonetheless that some obligations contained in the specialised anti-trafficking instruments have been recognised as human rights obligations and the book demonstrates a strong potential of other provisions to inform positive obligations in accordance with the well-established principles of interpretation of human rights instruments.[32]

1.3 The Scope of the Book: Human Trafficking and the European Legal Space

The book draws extensively on the jurisprudence of the ECtHR, a human rights court with the most far-reaching impact on the development of international human rights law so far[33] and 'the *de facto* model for developing human rights elsewhere'.[34] Its seminal decision in the *Rantsev* case was the first time an international tribunal established that human trafficking infringes upon the prohibition of slavery. The book, however, does not confine the analysis to the ECtHR case law and draws on examples from other jurisdictions, both international and domestic.

---

[32] Eirik Bjorge, *The Evolutionary Interpretation of Treaties* (OUP 2014).
[33] Alec Stone Sweet and Clare Ryan, 'Introduction and Overview' in Alec Stone Sweet and Clare Ryan (eds), *A Cosmopolitan Legal Order: Kant, Constitutional Justice, and the European Convention on Human Rights* (OUP 2018) 2 ('The Strasbourg Court is the single most active and important rights-protecting body in the world'). See also Laurence R Helfer, 'Redesigning the European Court of Human Rights: Embeddedness as a Deep Structural Principle of the European Human Rights Regime' (2008) 19(1) The European Journal of International Law 125 (describing the Strasbourg Court as 'the crown jewel of the world's most advanced international system for protecting civil and political liberties'); Jonas Christoffersen and Mikael Rask Madsen (eds), *The European Court of Human Rights between Law and Politics* (OUP 2011) 2.
[34] Christoffersen and Madsen (n 33) 2.

The broad choice of jurisdictions beyond the ECtHR is guided by the extent to which these are relevant to, and shed light upon, the legal issues being discussed.

Moreover, the most comprehensive anti-trafficking instrument so far was also adopted within the Council of Europe. The Council of Europe Anti-Trafficking Convention is seen as 'one of the Council of Europe's most important achievements in its 60 years of existence'.[35] The Convention requires states to afford to victims of trafficking a wide range of protection and assistance measures, including appropriate accommodation, medical treatment, or counselling.[36] While these requirements do not amount to victims' human rights, the Anti-Trafficking Convention provides ample opportunity for the Strasbourg Court to draw on its provisions in framing positive obligations within the ECHR, which would be in line with its practice of interpreting the latter as a living instrument.[37]

The extent and pace of legal and juridical developments on this issue therefore justifies the book's focus on the European legal space with a distinct possibility that these developments may well influence law and policy at a global level.

1.4 Book Structure

The book is divided into two parts, each comprising three substantive chapters. Part I establishes that there is a human right not to be trafficked, that this right derives from the prohibition of slavery, servitude, and forced labour, but could not be consumed by practices explicitly listed within this right. Human trafficking is thus shown to represent a self-standing prohibition, which triggers states' positive obligations in certain well-defined circumstances. These positive obligations and the rules that govern state responsibility for violations of this right are then examined in Part II.

Chapter 2 presents a historical evolution of the notion of human trafficking in international law. This analysis reveals the concept's unequivocal grounding in transnational criminal law with human rights law having emerged as a competing legal framework only recently. The chapter further elucidates the *hybrid* legal nature of human trafficking and explains the value of framing it as a human rights issue. Chapter 2 also shows that establishing state responsibility under human rights law is qualitatively different from establishing criminal law responsibility of an individual perpetrator. While the same definition may be used in both criminal

---

[35] Directorate General of Human Rights and Legal Affairs, 'Practical Impact of the Council of Europe Monitoring Mechanisms in Improving Respect for Human Rights and the Rule of Law in Member States' (Council of Europe 2010) 12.
[36] Chapter III of the Convention.
[37] Bernadette Rainey, Pamela McCormick, and Clare Ovey (eds), *Jacobs, White & Ovey: The European Convention on Human Rights* (6th edn, OUP 2014).

law and human rights context, this does not necessarily mean that it applies in the same manner.

Chapter 3 demonstrates that the human right not to be trafficked is an implied but stand-alone prohibition within the right to be free from slavery, servitude, and forced labour because of the underlying notion of exploitation, which represents a distinct wrong this right is meant to protect against. The chapter explores conceptual boundaries of this right, elucidates the meaning and relationships between both expressly prohibited and implied concepts in order to determine situations in which the right is or is not engaged. This analysis exposes common misunderstandings about the relationship between human trafficking and practices of slavery, servitude, and forced labour.

Chapter 4 offers the first comprehensive analysis of the concept of exploitation in human rights law, which is central for the understanding of human trafficking and slavery but has never been defined in international law and has been neglected in human rights scholarship.[38] This chapter thus represents a vital contribution to an understanding of the theoretical foundations of the prohibition of slavery and the right not to be trafficked. Drawing on international legal instruments and jurisprudence, and the literature on moral philosophy, the chapter distils the necessary and sufficient conditions for a conduct to qualify as exploitation of a sufficient gravity thus engaging the right to be free from slavery, servitude, forced labour, and human trafficking.[39] The chapter articulates and explains such necessary and sufficient conditions in the context of *this* right, arguing that they distinguish exploitation from other wrongs, such as abuse, fraud, or extortion. These elements are (a) abuse of vulnerability; (b) excessive (disproportionate) gain acquired through the actions required from an exploited person; and (c) sustained action (the practice is taking place over a prolonged period of time).

Having clarified the scope of the right not to be trafficked and its relationship with the explicit prohibitions of slavery, servitude, and forced labour, the book proceeds to assess positive human rights obligations of states arising out of this right. Part II of the book thus addresses state responsibility for 'modern slavery' in human rights law by examining positive human rights obligations arising out of this right. It draws on the jurisprudence of the ECtHR and other international and domestic courts, international conventions, soft law instruments, policy documents, and academic analysis to flesh out these obligations and clarify the rules of assessing state responsibility in situations where the right is engaged.

---

[38] An adapted version of this chapter has been published as a journal article. See Marija Jovanovic, 'The Essence of Slavery: Exploitation in Human Rights Law' (2020) 20(4) Human Rights Law Review 674.

[39] Notably, the article does not attempt to articulate a general account of exploitation beyond these most severe forms of exploitation, even though it accepts that these forms are not the only types of exploitation that need to be addressed, as argued by Virginia Mantouvalou, 'Legal Construction of Structures of Exploitation' in Hugh Collins, Gillian Lester, and Virginia Mantouvalou (eds), *Philosophical Foundations of Labour Law* (OUP 2018) 189–90.

Chapter 5 elaborates on positive human rights obligations in general, their origins, rationale, nature, and scope. Particular attention is paid to the distinction between positive obligations in situations of rights infringements by state and non-state actors. Positive obligations in the latter cases are classified in two main categories: general and specific. General obligations require states to establish preconditions for effective protection of fundamental rights from private persons. This entails putting in place an adequate legislative and administrative framework capable of providing effective protection of individual rights accompanied by appropriate institutional arrangements to enforce such a legal framework. Specific duties, on the other hand, are concerned with concrete actions required in individual cases to put those legislative provisions in effect and include a range of measures. These entail both procedural and operational measures taken by national authorities when rights of an identifiable individual have been, or are at risk of being infringed by actions of non-state actors.

Chapter 6 conducts a comprehensive analysis of positive obligations arising out of 'absolute' rights, including the prohibition of slavery, the right to life, and the prohibition of torture. The jurisprudence on the right to life and the prohibition of torture is considerably broader and serves to elucidate and inform the analysis of obligations under the right to be free from slavery, servitude, forced labour, and human trafficking. This analysis provides an important contribution to the understanding of the rules that apply to situations where infringements of these 'absolute' rights are committed by non-state actors. The chapter explains that, even though these rights contain an absolute prohibition (negative duty), positive obligations of states in situations when the right is encroached upon by non-state actors are not absolute.

Finally, Chapter 7 evaluates specialised anti-trafficking instruments and their potential to influence the interpretation of positive human rights obligations arising out of the prohibition of slavery and human trafficking. Emphasising the *key distinction* between victim protection measures and victims' human rights, the book explains why this right is not able to accommodate all measures of victim protection prescribed by the specialised anti-trafficking instruments. This chapter presents a coherent normative account of the potential to develop positive human rights obligations arising out of the prohibition of slavery and human trafficking. The book concludes by emphasising the limits of human rights law in providing protection against the exploitation of persons and paves the way for further engagement with this topic.

PART I
HUMAN TRAFFICKING AND HUMAN RIGHTS LAW

2
On the Legal Nature of Human Trafficking

2.1 Human Trafficking as a Complex and Contested Phenomenon

Human trafficking is generally considered as 'both a cause and a consequence' of grave human rights violations.[1] Thus, empirical evidence suggests that people who fall victims to human trafficking have already suffered 'human rights violations associated with (a) poverty and inequality, (b) migration and (c) discrimination'.[2] At the same time, human trafficking involves practices that are 'unambiguously prohibited under international human rights law',[3] including 'arbitrary detention, forced labour, debt bondage, forced marriage, and the sexual exploitation of children and women'.[4] However, is trafficking per se a human rights violation? In other words, is there an independent human right not to be trafficked, and if so, what does such right entail? Alternatively, is human trafficking simply a criminal offence,[5] which engages human rights law only insofar as certain well-established human rights, such as life, liberty, or privacy, have been violated in the course of it? Answers to these questions determine the legal nature of human trafficking and the role of human rights law in addressing it. This chapter shows that human trafficking is *both* a criminal offence and a self-standing human rights violation, and that the same universal definition established by the United Nations Protocol to the Transnational Organized Crime Convention (Palermo Protocol)[6] applies in both legal domains, although in a different manner and for a different purpose.

Human trafficking touches upon a range of important societal issues, including poverty, gender inequality, migration, organised crime, or labour conditions, to

---

[1] United Nations Human Rights Office of the High Commissioner (OHCHR), Recommended Principles and Guidelines on Human Rights and Human Trafficking (20 May 2002) E/2002/68/Add.1, Guideline 1; OHCHR, Interim Report of the Special Rapporteur on Trafficking in Persons, Especially Women and Children, Joy Ngozi Ezeilo (9 August 2010) A/65/288, para 15.
[2] Report of the Special Rapporteur on Trafficking in Persons, Especially Women and Children, Joy Ngozi Ezeilo (1 April 2014) A/HRC/26/37, para 41.
[3] OHCHR, Recommended Principles and Guidelines on Human Rights and Human Trafficking: Commentary (2010) 38.
[4] UN Office of the High Commissioner for Human Rights, *Human Trafficking and Human Rights* Factsheet 36 (2014).
[5] Ryszard Piotrowicz, 'International Focus: Trafficking and Slavery as Human Rights Violations' (2010) 84 Australian Law Journal 812, 814.
[6] Protocol to Prevent, Suppress and Punish Trafficking in Persons Especially Women and Children, supplementing the United Nations Convention against Transnational Organized Crime (adopted 15 November 2000, entered into force 25 December 2003) 2237 UNTS 319 (Palermo Protocol).

name but a few.[7] It is therefore not surprising that the prism through which it is seen critically influences its conceptualisation, and a preferred strategy for addressing it. If trafficking is perceived as primarily a migration or organised crime problem, tougher law enforcement actions and tighter border controls may seem to be an appropriate solution to it.[8] If, however, human trafficking is considered to be a product of the global economic order and rising inequality first and foremost, improving labour conditions and rights at work may appear as a top priority of anti-trafficking actions.[9] And if the problem of human trafficking is observed through the lens of prostitution, the responses may well focus on those measures that seek to either outlaw prostitution altogether or to address the demand side of it.[10]

Different conceptualisations of the trafficking problem also influence the perceptions of its prevalence around the world.[11] How many victims are there globally? What are the trafficking 'hot spots'? Who are the traffickers? These important questions, however, do not animate the enquiry in this book, which primarily deals with conceptual and legal issues raised by the phenomenon of human trafficking and the role of human rights law in addressing it. But before proceeding with such an enquiry, and in order to understand what it is that the law seeks to address, the main features of human trafficking and points of contention among different stakeholders must be outlined.

In a nutshell, human trafficking is a *profit-driven* practice aimed at the exploitation of human beings for economic gain. Women, men, and children are trafficked for many purposes, which include, but are not limited to, forced labour, sexual exploitation, domestic servitude, forced marriage, forced begging, forced criminality, or forced organ removal.[12] A common feature that binds these diverse practices into a unique concept of 'human trafficking' is 'the business around the exploitation of the victims'.[13] The United Nations Office on Drugs and Crime (UNODC) thus observes that:

---

[7] See generally Prabha Kotiswaran (ed), *Revisiting the Law and Governance of Human Trafficking, Forced Labor and Modern Slavery* (CUP 2017).

[8] See generally Maggy Lee, *Trafficking and Global Crime Control* (SAGE Publishing 2011).

[9] Hila Shamir, 'A Labour Paradigm for Human Trafficking' (2012) 60 UCLA Law Review 76; Cathryn Costello, 'Migrants and Forced Labour: A Labour Law Response' in Alan Bogg and others (eds), *The Autonomy of Labour Law* (Hart Publishing 2015).

[10] Janie Chuang, 'Rescuing Trafficking from Ideological Capture: Prostitution Reform and Anti-trafficking Law and Policy' (2010) 158 University of Pennsylvania Law Review 1655.

[11] Sally Engle Merry, 'Counting the Uncountable: Constructing Trafficking through Measurement' in Prabha Kotiswaran (ed), *Revisiting the Law and Governance of Trafficking, Forced Labor and Modern Slavery* (CUP 2017).

[12] Anti-Slavery International, 'What is Human Trafficking?' https://www.antislavery.org/slavery-today/human-trafficking/.

[13] United Nations Office on Drugs and Crime (UNODC), 'Global Report on Trafficking in Persons 2014' (November 2014) 46.

The 'loverboy' who exploits his girlfriend in sexual exploitation is leveraging his power over her for profit. The families exploiting domestic help in Africa or housing *restavek* children in the Caribbean are benefiting from the labour of these children. The debt bondage schemes behind some West African or East Asian trafficking networks are leveraging the migration dream of the victims to exploit them in forced labour or in the commercial sex market. Trafficking in persons is motivated by profit maximisation and organised by traffickers trying to maximise benefits and minimise costs. The higher the profits, the greater the economic incentives to conduct the trafficking crime.[14]

Despite a wide consensus that profit from the exploitation of others is a driving force behind the phenomenon of human trafficking, a number of important questions remain unsettled. These include: the role of organised crime in human trafficking;[15] the range of exploitative practices included under the umbrella of human trafficking;[16] whether human trafficking implies physical *movement* of persons— either across or within national border;[17] its relationship with people smuggling;[18] or whether human trafficking amounts to just a *process* leading to exploitation,[19] or it also covers exploitative *conditions*.[20] Human trafficking has therefore been used both as a shorthand for all forms of 'modern slavery'[21] and, at the very least,

---

[14] ibid 46–47.
[15] See generally Louise Shelley, *Human Trafficking: A Global Perspective* (CUP 2010) 83–111; UNODC, 'Global Report on Trafficking in Persons 2014' (2014).
[16] Jean Allain, 'No Effective Trafficking Definition Exists: Domestic Implementation of the Palermo Protocol' (2014) 7 Albany Government Law Review 111, 122–24. See also Prabha Kotiswaran, 'From Sex Panic to Extreme Exploitation: Revisiting the Law and Governance of Human Trafficking' in Prabha Kotiswaran (ed), *Revisiting the Law and Governance of Trafficking, Forced Labor and Modern Slavery* (CUP 2017) 1, 11–15.
[17] Jennie Chuang, 'Exploitation Creep and the Unmaking of Human Trafficking Law' (2014) 108 American Journal of International Law 609, 630 (showing that the Palermo Protocol's *travaux préparatoires* 'include several indications that delegates assumed that trafficking entails movements'). See also Susan Kneebone and Julie Debeljak, *Transnational Crime and Human Rights: Responses to Human Trafficking in the Greater Mekong Subregion* (Routledge 2012) 127 ('[M]any countries in the [Great Mekong Subregion] understand trafficking as involving the movement and trade of people'). But see US Department of State, Trafficking in Persons Report (2008) 6; European Commission, *EU Strategy Towards the Eradication of Trafficking in Human Beings 2012-2016* (19 June 2012) 2 (suggesting that 'there is no need to cross a border or be physically transported' for an act to constitute human trafficking); *SM v Croatia* App no 60561/14 (ECtHR GC, 25 June 2020).
[18] Paolo Campana and Federico Varese, 'Exploitation in Human Trafficking and Smuggling' (2016) 22 European Journal on Criminal Policy and Research 89.
[19] James Hathaway, 'The Human Rights Quagmire of "Human" Trafficking' (2008) 49 Virginia Journal of International law 1, 10 (describing human trafficking as 'specific forms of dealing which facilitate or lead to exploitation'). See also Jean Allain, *Slavery in International Law: Of Human Exploitation and Trafficking* (Brill 2013) 355 (describing human trafficking as 'the international supply chain into exploitation').
[20] UN Office of the High Commissioner for Human Rights (n 4) 3 ('trafficking does not just refer to the process whereby someone is moved into situations of exploitation; it also extends to the maintenance of that person in a situation of exploitation'); Chuang (n 17) 631 ('[S]tate practice appears to be on a trajectory toward a view of trafficking that deemphasizes movement and that emphasizes exploitation as the core of the harm').
[21] US Department of State, 'Trafficking in Persons Report' (2012) 9. See also Anne T Gallagher, *The International Law of Human Trafficking* (CUP 2010) 47–53; Dominika Borg Jansson, *Modern Slavery: A*

to denote clandestine cross-border movement of people with a view to exploiting them.[22] Competing views on these issues have been shaped by the frameworks deployed to examine this complex phenomenon, bearing directly upon the trafficking statistics. The estimates thus display striking fluctuation ranging from 800,000 to over 40 million people thought to be affected by 'modern slavery' today.[23] Accordingly, despite significant political attention, numerous international and regional initiatives, and 'the torrent of academic and near-academic output' in the past two decades, human trafficking remains a heavily contested and politicised phenomenon.[24]

What has been the role of international human rights law in these developments? Specifically, how has the growing body of law on human trafficking both influenced and been shaped by the doctrines and practices of human rights law? To answer these questions, the following sections explore, first, the evolutional trajectory of human trafficking in international law culminating with the adoption of the Palermo Protocol, which established its first universal legal definition. The subsequent sections then examine the influence of the Palermo Protocol on the successive anti-trafficking instruments, which are believed to have strengthened the 'human rights dimension' of the anti-trafficking action,[25] and the ensuing impact of these developments on human rights law in general. The analysis of the dynamics between instruments developed to address human trafficking specifically and human rights law reveals a nuanced picture of the hybrid legal nature of trafficking and of the role and value of human rights law as a response to it.

Comparative Study of the Definition of Trafficking in Persons (2014) 341. For the critique of the concept of 'modern slavery' see Roger Plant, 'Modern Slavery: The Concepts and Their Practical Implications' ILO Working Paper (5 February 2015); Michael Dottridge, 'Eight Reasons Why We Shouldn't Use the Term "Modern Slavery"' *Open Democracy* (17 October 2017) https://www.opendemocracy.net/en/beyond-trafficking-and-slavery/eight-reasons-why-we-shouldn-t-use-term-modern-slavery/ (accessed 19 January 2020).

[22] Allain (n 16).
[23] Prabha Kotiswaran, 'From Sex Panic to Extreme Exploitation: Revisiting the Law and Governance of Human Trafficking' in Prabha Kotiswaran (ed), *Revisiting the Law and Governance of Trafficking, Forced Labor and Modern Slavery* (CUP 2017) 3–4.
[24] Austin Choi-Fitzpatrick, 'From Rescue to Representation: A Human Rights Approach to the Contemporary Anti-Slavery Movement' (2015) 14(4) Journal of Human Rights 486, 498–99. (It remains unclear what exactly human trafficking is an example of 'since it intersects with a host of issues and agendas and since answers, however provisional, drive policies, funding, advocacy, interventions, and numerous debates'.)
[25] Ryszard Piotrowicz, 'The Legal Nature of Trafficking in Human Beings' (2009) 4 Intercultural Human Rights Law Review 175, 176 (arguing that human trafficking 'is primarily a matter of criminal law, albeit with a human rights dimension').

2.2 A Brief History of Human Trafficking in International Law: From Law Enforcement to Human Rights and Not the Other Way Around

The adoption of the Palermo Protocol in 2000 brought human trafficking to the forefront of international attention and provided both an impetus and a groundwork for legal and political developments that followed worldwide.[26] Despite its well-documented shortcomings,[27] the Palermo Protocol was praised for securing a wide international consensus on the definition of human trafficking that is said to be 'sufficiently broad to embrace all but a very small range of situations in which individuals are severely exploited for private profit.'[28] Yet, its adoption was also interpreted as the process where '[h]uman trafficking, an obscure but jealously guarded mandate of the UN's human rights system, had been ... unceremoniously snatched away from its traditional home.'[29] Such a move was nonetheless defended by claims that '[d]uring the entire twentieth century, when trafficking and its array of associated practices *belonged exclusively to human rights*, states could not even agree on a definition, much less on specific legal obligations.'[30]

While it may well be true that the law enforcement treaty was, at the time, the only way to mobilise wide state support for anti-trafficking action,[31] the statement that prior to the Palermo Protocol human trafficking belonged exclusively to the human rights domain warrants a particular scrutiny. On the contrary, a closer look at the evolutional trajectory of human trafficking in international law reveals that the Palermo Protocol emerged from a steady stream of instruments that were firmly grounded in the crime prevention and law enforcement field. This is not to say that human rights law has been irrelevant for anti-trafficking action and vice versa, but that their interrelationship must be carefully examined rather than assumed.

---

[26] Gallagher (n 21) 42. See also UN Human Rights Council, *Report of the Special Rapporteur on Trafficking in Persons, especially Women and Children*, para 22, A/HRC/26/37 (1 April 2014); Kalen Fredette, 'Revisiting the UN Protocol on Human Trafficking: Striking Balances for More Effective Legislation' (2009) 17 Cardozo Journal of International and Comparative Law 101, 112.

[27] See generally Hathaway (n 19); Jennifer Chacon, 'Tensions and Trade-Offs: Protecting Trafficking Victims in the Era of Immigration Enforcement' (2010) 158 University of Pennsylvania Law Review 1609; Chuang (n 10); Jonathan Todres, 'Widening Our Lens: Incorporating Essential Perspectives in the Fight against Human Trafficking' (2011) 33 Michigan Journal of International Law 53.

[28] Anne Gallagher, 'Human Rights and Human Trafficking: Quagmire or Firm Ground? A Response to James Hathaway' (2009) 49(4) Virginia Journal of International Law 789, 791.

[29] Gallagher (n 27) 790.

[30] ibid 792 (emphasis added).

[31] Elaine Pearson, 'Historical Development of Trafficking: the Legal Framework for Anti-Trafficking Interventions' in Sector Project against Trafficking in Women (eds), *Challenging Trafficking in Persons: Theoretical Debate and Practical Approaches* (Nomos 2005) 23. The Protocol was said to have been developed 'in a context of governments' fear about the rapid growth and power of organised crime worldwide, rather than a particular concern about women in prostitution or slavery-like practices and forced labour'.

2.2.1 Anti-trafficking Instruments before the Palermo Protocol

The notion of human trafficking first surfaced in international law in the instruments concerned with 'white slave traffic' for the purpose of prostitution developed at the turn of the twentieth century. Thus, the International Agreement for the Suppression of the White Slave Traffic from 1904 aimed at securing 'effective protection against the criminal traffic known as the "White Slave Traffic"'.[32] Principally concerned with the coordination of information and state actions in detecting 'criminal traffic', as well as with facilitating repatriation of victims to their states of origins, the 1904 Agreement did not explicitly define the notion of 'white slave traffic'. However, several provisions and statements from the Agreement suggest that the notion of '*criminal* traffic known as white slave traffic' should be understood as 'the procuring of women or girls for immoral purposes abroad'.[33]

The subsequent International Convention for the Suppression of the White Slave Traffic from 1910 prescribed two *offences* the parties undertook to include in their legislation.[34] Article 1 required states to punish a person who 'in order to gratify the passions of another person, has procured, enticed, or led away, even with her consent, a woman or girl under age, for immoral purposes'. Article 2 was concerned with a woman or girl over age and requires that the prohibited action has been committed 'by fraud, or by means of violence, threats, abuse of authority, or any other method of compulsion'.[35] In comparison with the 1904 Agreement, these provisions contained more evolved and better-articulated statements on what exactly states were committed to combat. Notably, notwithstanding their limited focus on trafficking of women and girls for prostitution, both instruments approached human trafficking as a law enforcement matter.[36]

Shortly after these two international instruments came into force, states adopted the International Convention for the Suppression of Traffic in Women and Children in 1921,[37] followed by the International Convention for the Suppression

---

[32] International Agreement for the Suppression of the White Slave Traffic (adopted 4 May 1904, entered into force 18 July 1905) 1 LNTS 83.

[33] Nicole Siller, 'Human Trafficking in International Law Before Palermo' (2017) 64 Netherlands International Law Review 407 (emphasis added).

[34] International Convention for the Suppression of the White Slave Traffic (adopted 4 May 1910, entered into force 8 August 1912) 3 LNTS 278.

[35] Paragraph B of the Final Protocol in the Annex to the Convention specifies that '[f]or the punishment of the offences mentioned in articles 1 and 2, it is agreed that the words "a woman or a girl who is a minor, a woman or a girl of full age" mean women or girls, who are either above or below twenty years of age. A law may, however, establish a higher age for protection on condition that it is the same for women and girls of every nationality.' For full text, see https://treaties.un.org/doc/Treaties/1951/08/19510814%2010-35%20PM/Ch_VII_9p.pdf.

[36] Both instruments were amended and updated by the UN Protocol Amending the International Agreement for the Suppression of the White Slave Traffic, and Amending the International Convention for the Suppression of the White Slave Traffic (adopted 4 May 1949, entered into force 21 June 1951) 30 UNTS 23.

[37] International Convention for the Suppression of Traffic in Women and Children (adopted 30 September 1921, entered into force 15 June 1922) 9 LNTS 415 (1921 Convention).

of the Traffic in Women of Full Age in 1933.[38] Both Conventions[39] broadened the scope of actions required from states, while still being narrowly focused on prostitution. Thus, the 1921 Convention required states to 'take all measures to discover and prosecute persons who are engaged in the traffic in children of *both sexes*'.[40] In addition, the 1933 Convention removed the element of compulsion that was previously required in cases of 'a woman or girl of full age', a threshold lower than the one established by the Palermo Protocol, which differentiates between trafficking of children and adults on the basis of the relevance of consent.[41] Both instruments nonetheless remained focused on law enforcement actions to discover, prosecute, and punish persons who are engaged in the trafficking of women and children.

Finally, in 1949, the Convention for the Suppression of the Traffic in Persons and of the Exploitation of the Prostitution of Others consolidated all the previously described Protocols, Conventions, and Agreements.[42] While the 1949 Convention applied to 'any person' and not only women and children, the focus remained solely on 'prostitution and the accompanying evil of the traffic in persons for the purpose of prostitution', which are said to be 'incompatible with the dignity and worth of the human person'. Despite the fact that this preambular opening statement places trafficking within a human rights paradigm of 'human dignity', Edwards rightly observes that 'its substantive provisions continue to focus on criminal prosecution and punishment'.[43] Accordingly, the 1949 Convention stipulates offences that states were required to punish,[44] regulates extradition and transfer of criminal proceedings,[45] and requires states to establish a service charged with the coordination and centralisation of the results of the investigation of offences referred to in the Convention.[46] Measures related to the protection of victims were linked to pending repatriation arrangements and required states 'to make suitable provisions for their temporary care and maintenance'.[47] Such provisions were only to be implemented 'so far as possible', leaving no doubt as to the central focus of the

---

[38] International Convention for the Suppression of the Traffic in Women of Full Age (adopted 11 October 1933, entered into force 24 August 1934) 150 LNTS 431 (1933 Convention).

[39] They were later consolidated and amended by the UN Protocol Amending the Convention for the Suppression of the Traffic in Women and Children, and Amending the Convention for the Suppression of the Traffic in Women of Full Age (12 November 1947) 53 UNTS 13.

[40] 1921 Convention (n 37) art 2 (emphasis added).

[41] 1933 Convention (n 38) art 1: 'Whoever, in order to gratify the passions of another person, has procured, enticed or led away *even with her consent*, a woman or girl of full age for immoral purposes to be carried out in another country, shall be punished, notwithstanding that the various acts constituting the offence may have been committed in different countries' (emphasis added).

[42] Convention for the Suppression of the Traffic in Persons and of the Exploitation of the Prostitution of Others (adopted 2 December 1949, entered into force 25 July 1951) 96 UNTS 271 (1949 Convention).

[43] See Alice Edwards, 'Traffic in Human Beings: At the Intersection of Criminal Justice, Human Rights, Asylum/Migration and Labor' (2007–2008) 36(1) Denver Journal of International Law and Policy 9, 16.

[44] 1949 Convention (n 42) arts 1–3.

[45] ibid arts 8–11.

[46] ibid art 14.

[47] ibid art 19.

Convention committed to the suppression of criminal activity that occurs across borders. Pearson thus rightly observes that the 1949 Convention 'adopts the migration and crime control perspective as well as the moralist approach to abolish all prostitution'.[48] The UN Special Rapporteur on Violence against Women furthermore categorically concludes that the 1949 Convention 'does not take a human rights approach'.[49] Farrior correctly points out that this was largely due to the fact that 'in 1949, the notion of human rights as a matter of international concern was still relatively new in international law'.[50]

Clearly, the instruments leading up to the Palermo Protocol belong squarely to the law enforcement paradigm, a focus preserved by the latter notwithstanding its broader understanding of human trafficking, which includes trafficking in men, is ambivalent towards prostitution, and covers a range of exploitative practices.[51] Accordingly, a claim that by choosing transnational criminal law as a frame for the international instrument dealing with human trafficking the concept was 'unceremoniously snatched away' from the human rights domain holds no ground. The role and importance of human rights law in addressing human trafficking must be considered in that light.

2.2.2 The Palermo Protocol and the Universalisation of Anti-trafficking Action

The Palermo Protocol accompanies the UN Convention against Transnational Organized Crime, together with the Protocol against the Smuggling of Migrants by Land, Sea and Air and the Protocol against the Illicit Manufacturing of and Trafficking in Firearms, their Parts and Components and Ammunition.[52] Its adoption in 2000 was undoubtedly a landmark moment for the global action against human trafficking because it triggered an avalanche of initiatives, legislation, and research.[53] Within ten years since its entry into force, the number of

---

[48] Elaine Pearson, *Human Rights and Trafficking in Persons: A Handbook* (Global Alliance Against Traffic in Women 2000) 44. See also Barbara Sullivan, 'Trafficking in Women: Feminism and New International Law' (2003) 5(1) International Feminist Journal of Politics 67 (noticing that the complete removal of the compulsion requirement by which any consent of a victim is deemed irrelevant, was a result of the 'feminist impetus' aimed at preventing prostitution altogether).

[49] UN OHCHR, Report of the Special Rapporteur on Violence against Women, its Causes and Consequences, Ms Coomaraswamy, on Trafficking in Women, Women's Migration and Violence against Women, Submitted in Accordance with Commission on Human Rights Resolution 1997/44 (29 February 2000) UN Doc E/CN.4/2000/68, para 22.

[50] Stephanie Farrior, 'The International Law on Trafficking in Women and Children for Prostitution: Making It Live Up to Its Potential' (1997) 10 Harvard Human Rights Law Journal 213, 219.

[51] See further the analysis of the definition of human trafficking in sub-section 2.4.1.

[52] United Nations Convention against Transnational Organized Crime and the Protocols Thereto (adopted 15 November 2000, entered into force 29 September 2003), UNGA Res 55/25 (UN TOC).

[53] Choi-Fitzpatrick (n 24) 498 (describing 'the torrent of academic and near-academic output' since 2000).

countries which did not introduce a specific offence of trafficking in persons in line with the Protocol has dropped from 100 to just nine out of 173 countries reviewed.[54]

As a transnational instrument, the Palermo Protocol was not designed to establish a complete and comprehensive set of rules on how states should address human trafficking domestically. Instead, it gave direction and set a framework for state actions and international cooperation. Central features of this framework are the universal definition of the term 'trafficking in persons'[55] and the 'four Ps' paradigm for conceptualising anti-trafficking actions, which includes: prevention, prosecution of traffickers, protection of victims, and partnerships (co-operation) between different actors involved in anti-trafficking action.[56] These elements have been replicated in the legal instruments across the world,[57] thus creating the *perception* of universality and coherence of the global anti-trafficking action.[58]

Such apparent success of the Palermo Protocol has not deceived the critics. Hathaway thus argues that 'the primary purpose of the Protocol[s] was not (or at least did not remain) to advance the fight against transnational organized crime, but was rather to conscript less developed countries to join the developed world's migration control project'[59] and considers the fight against human trafficking in general as 'fundamentally in tension with core human rights goals'.[60] Even those looking more favourably on the Protocol concede that its law enforcement focus fails to capture victim protection needs placing rather weak demands on states when it comes to assistance and protection measures.[61] Thus, a general consensus that global action against human trafficking warrants a broader set of actions that go well beyond law enforcement actions has influenced international instruments developed after the Palermo Protocol, and those adopted in Europe, in particular.

---

[54] UNODC, *Global Report on Trafficking in Persons 2014* (2014) 52.
[55] The term 'trafficking in persons' is used interchangeably with 'human trafficking' or 'trafficking' throughout the book.
[56] The Palermo Protocol refers in its preamble to a three-pronged approach comprising measures to prevent trafficking, punish traffickers, and protect victims. The fourth 'P', which amounts to 'partnerships' between different actors involved in anti-trafficking action, has been subsequently added and widely accepted. See UN Global Plan, *supra* note 2, Preamble; Jonathan Todres, 'Taking Prevention Seriously: Developing a Comprehensive Response to Child Trafficking and Sexual Exploitation' (2010) 43 Vanderbilt Journal of Transnational Law 1, 41 (suggesting that 'partnerships' should be mainstreamed in each of the original three prongs).
[57] Gallagher (n 21); UNODC (n 54) 52.
[58] This paragraph is largely reproduced from Marija Jovanovic, 'International Law and Regional Norm Smuggling: How the EU and ASEAN Redefined the Global Regime on Human Trafficking' (2020) 68(4) American Journal of Comparative Law 801.
[59] Hathaway (n 19) 56.
[60] ibid 4.
[61] Anne Gallagher, 'Human Rights and the New UN Protocols on Trafficking and Migrant Smuggling: A Preliminary Analysis' (2001) 23 Human Rights Quarterly 975; Shelley (n 15) 10; Choi-Fitzpatrick (n 24).

2.2.3 The Post-Palermo Developments and the Human Rights Dimension of Human Trafficking

The Council of Europe Convention on Action against Trafficking in Human Beings (Anti-Trafficking Convention)[62] sought to strengthen the framework developed by the Palermo Protocol 'in particular in relation to the protection of the human rights of the victims of trafficking'.[63] Its preamble identifies 'respect for victims' rights, protection of victims, and action to combat trafficking in human beings' as its 'paramount objectives'. The subsequent EU Directive mirrors this approach, calling for 'more rigorous prevention, prosecution and protection of victims' rights'.[64] The European anti-trafficking action has therefore, at least nominally, been placed squarely within the victim protection and human rights paradigm.[65]

The language of human rights deployed in anti-trafficking instruments can be interpreted in two ways. On one hand, it could mean that the protection of victims' human rights must be a paramount consideration when devising and implementing anti-trafficking actions. Such an understanding could be discerned, for example, from the statement of the former Council of Europe Secretary General who described the Anti-Trafficking Convention as 'the only international treaty which includes comprehensive protection of the human rights of victims as an integral part of the fight against this criminal activity'.[66] However, human rights of trafficking victims need to be protected in any case, regardless of their status as victims of crime, because that is the idea behind *universal* human rights. Unless the Secretary General referred to some specific rights that apply *only* to trafficking victims in which case it would be questionable whether such rights could be considered human rights rather than simply legally protected interests.

On the other hand, the language used in anti-trafficking instruments could also lend weight to the view that human trafficking is a human rights violation in its own right, much like the expressly recognised human rights violations, such as slavery, servitude, and forced or compulsory labour. Thus, the Preamble of the Anti-Trafficking Convention declares that trafficking in human beings constitutes 'a violation of human rights and an offence to the dignity and the integrity of the

---

[62] CETS 197 (16 May 2005).

[63] Council of Europe, *Explanatory Report to the Council of Europe Convention on Action against Trafficking in Human Beings*, CETS 197 (16 May 2005) paras 8, 30, and 51.

[64] Council Directive 2011/36EU [2011] OJ L101/1 (5 April 2011) preamble, para 7 (EU Trafficking Directive).

[65] European Commission, *EU Anti-Trafficking Action 2012-2016 at a Glance*, at 3 (2017) 3 ('Directive 2011/36/EU ... establishes robust provisions on victim's protection, assistance and support, but also on prevention and prosecution of the crime.' This implies that criminal justice goals are secondary to victim protection). See also Explanatory Report (n 63) paras 28–37. For a critique of this perception see Jovanovic (n 58).

[66] Thorbjørn Jagland, the EU Ministerial Conference 'Towards Global EU Action against Trafficking in Human Beings' (Brussels, 19–20 October 2009). See Chapter 7 for a detailed analysis of the Anti-Trafficking Convention.

human being'. Similarly, the Convention Against Trafficking in Persons adopted by the Association of Southeast Asian Nations (ASEAN)[67] — the only region beyond Europe to have adopted a binding treaty on human trafficking — states in its Preamble that 'trafficking in persons constitutes a violation of human rights and an offence to the dignity of human beings'.[68] This view has also found expression in the jurisprudence of the European Court on Human Rights (ECtHR)[69] and remains the discreet focus of this book.

The two views represent polar opposites when it comes to describing the relationship between human trafficking and human rights law. On the former view, human rights are merely side-constrains[70] for anti-trafficking actions. In other words, states must not infringe upon human rights of victims while implementing their anti-trafficking policy. On the latter view, the practice represents a human rights violation in its own right, with anti-trafficking actions being considered as part of states' positive obligations aimed at upholding that right.

A middle ground perspective might consider human trafficking not as a human rights violation per se, but instead as a practice which, owing to its complex nature, engages a range of human rights, such as life, liberty, freedom from torture, or slavery, to name but a few.[71] In other words, this view would require *translating* the criminal law concept of human trafficking into the language of human rights to match one or more rights from the existing catalogue of human rights—not merely *transplanting* it from one legal domain to another.

The apparent lack of clarity about the relationship between human trafficking and human rights law stems from the two facts. First, human trafficking is not mentioned in most general human rights instruments. Those instruments that expressly refer to it[72] do not, however, specify the meaning of the concept of 'human trafficking' included in their text.[73] This is significant because such instruments, with the exception of the EU Charter and the Arab Charter, were adopted *before* the Palermo Protocol's widely endorsed universal definition of human trafficking. The previous subsection reveals a narrow prostitution-focused understanding of the term 'traffic in persons' in the instruments that preceded the Palermo Protocol,

---

[67] ASEAN Convention against Trafficking in Persons, Especially Women and Children (21 November 2015);
[68] See Jovanovic (n 58).
[69] See further chs 3 and 6.
[70] Robert Nozick, *Anarchy, State, and Utopia* (Blackwell Publishing 1974).
[71] UN Office of the High Commissioner for Human Rights (n 4). See also *Workers of the Hacienda Brasil Verde v Brazil* (Preliminary Objections, Merits, Reparations and Costs) Inter-American Court of Human Rights Series C No 318 (20 October 2016) [306]; *SM v Croatia* (n 17) [241]–[242].
[72] Convention on the Elimination of All Forms of Discrimination against Women (adopted 18 December 1979, entered into force 3 September 1981) 1249 UNTS 13 (CEDAW) art 6; the Convention on the Rights of the Child (adopted 20 November 1989, entered into force 2 September 1990) 1577 UNTS 3 (CRC) art 35; Inter-American Convention on Human Rights (prohibiting trafficking in women only) art 6(1); EU Charter of Fundamental Rights, art 5(3); the Arab Charter of Human Rights, art 10.
[73] Gallagher (n 21) 64–68.

which has been widely dismissed as inadequate. Accordingly, without a firm grounding in general human rights instruments, a claim that human trafficking represents a human rights violation in its own right may appear problematic.

Besides the fact that general human rights instruments do not straightforwardly prohibit human trafficking as defined in the Palermo Protocol, those international instruments developed to address human trafficking specifically are not human rights instruments despite their use of the human rights language. Specialised anti-trafficking instruments developed in the aftermath of the Palermo Protocol undoubtedly contain stronger provisions concerning the assistance and protection of victims but, as Stoyanova rightly points out, 'the principles underlying [the Anti-Trafficking Convention] are different from those underlying the ECHR. When drafting [the Anti-Trafficking Convention], states sought to address criminal activities'.[74] Accordingly, it is incorrect 'to equate the provision of assistance to select victims as establishing a right to assistance', as duly noted by Todres.[75] While this *key distinction* between victim protection measures contained in anti-trafficking instruments and human rights enshrined in general human rights instruments will be explored in greater detail in the final chapter of this book, Todres' reference to US jurisprudence on health rights illustrates it crisply:

> Through programs such as Medicare and Medicaid, the United States has long provided health-related services to individuals in need, but the existence of these programs has not equated to recognition of a 'right to health' under federal law. In short, when a government elects to provide social services, such action does not necessarily rise to the level of establishing a fundamental right to those services.[76]

Therefore, the relationship between instruments developed to address human trafficking specifically and human rights law, and consequently the legal nature of human trafficking, remains unsettled and has been subject to an animated discussion.

2.3 Competing Narratives on the Relationship between Human Trafficking and Human Rights Law

Whereas the post-Palermo instruments and related discussions expressly recognised a human rights *dimension* of human trafficking,[77] little effort has been put

---

[74] Vladislava Stoyanova, *Human Trafficking and Slavery Reconsidered: Conceptual Limits and States' Positive Obligations in European Law* (CUP 2017) 12.
[75] Jonathan Todres, 'Human Rights, Labor, and the Prevention of Human Trafficking: A Response to a Labor Paradigm for Human Trafficking' (2013) 60 UCLA Law Review Discourse 142, 150.
[76] ibid.
[77] UN OHCHR, Recommended Principles and Guidelines on Human Rights and Human Trafficking (20 May 2002) E/2002/68/Add.1. See also Piotrowicz (n 25).

into explaining how the legal concept originating from transnational criminal law squares with the human rights framework. For example, the Factsheet issued by the UN Human Rights Office of the High Commissioner oscillates between the views that 'trafficking *itself* is a serious violation of human rights',[78] that '[d]ifferent human rights will be relevant at different points in the trafficking cycle',[79] and also that *anti-trafficking measures* themselves 'may adversely affect established rights'.[80]

In response to this lack of conceptual and legal clarity, two critical strands of scholarship have crystallised. On the one hand, it is argued that human trafficking and human rights belong to two different legal universes, which are governed by different internal logic and therefore ought to remain separate.[81] According to such views, instead of transplanting the criminal law concept of human trafficking into the realm of human rights law, the concept of human trafficking should be discarded and attention redirected towards well-established human rights violations such as slavery, servitude, and forced or compulsory labour, which should be deployed to address a broad range of practices encapsulated by the term 'modern slavery'. Therefore, whereas enhancing the anti-trafficking action with a human rights dimension was mostly perceived as a welcome development, at least by the civil society, some human rights scholars found the reverse process—the inclusion of human trafficking in the human rights domain—'problematic' and a threat to the internal consistency of human rights law.[82]

On the other hand, human rights law itself is seen as part of the problem and not a solution for addressing human exploitation in general, of which human trafficking and generally practices of 'modern slavery' represent the most egregious examples. Several arguments underpin this claim. First, it is argued that the human rights framework, 'as currently interpreted', is overly reliant on criminal law measures.[83] In addition, the human rights framework is said to be part of the problem because it provides remedies for only the most extreme cases of exploitation.[84] Moreover, it is claimed that the human rights framework focuses on the post-exploitation situation and is oriented towards 'victim rescue rather than on transforming structural causes of worker vulnerability'.[85] In contrast, the labour law approach to trafficking is seen as a forward-looking strategy that 'can help lessen the reliance on *ex post* strategies by reducing the risk of extreme exploitation in the

---

[78] UN Office of the High Commissioner for Human Rights, *Human Trafficking and Human Rights* (Factsheet 36, 2014) 5 (emphasis added).
[79] ibid 4–5.
[80] ibid 50.
[81] See Stoyanova (n 74) Introduction.
[82] ibid.
[83] Costello (n 9) 191.
[84] Shamir (n 9).
[85] ibid 102–103. See also Virginia Mantouvalou, 'Legal Construction of Structures of Exploitation' in Hugh Collins, Gillian Lester, and Virginia Mantouvalou (eds), *Philosophical Foundations of Labour Law* (OUP 2018).

first place'.[86] By reducing vulnerability to trafficking in the first place, the labour law perspective is said to 'offer greater hope of long-term prevention and change'.[87]

There is nonetheless room for a more nuanced perception of the relationship between human trafficking and human rights law—the one which considers human rights law as just one instrument in the legal toolbox available for addressing exploitative practices and which does not compete with, but rather complements, other available tools and frameworks. While it is true that obligations arising out of human right law would often entail criminal law actions, such as police investigations and prosecution, human rights obligations are by no means limited to criminal law. Thus, for example, in the seminal *Rantsev* case, which will be discussed in more detail in Chapters 3 and 6, the Strasbourg Court has ruled that:

> [T]he spectrum of safeguards set out in national legislation must be adequate to ensure the practical and effective protection of the rights of victims or potential victims of trafficking. Accordingly, in addition to criminal law measures to punish traffickers, Article 4 requires member States to put in place adequate measures regulating businesses often used as a cover for human trafficking. Furthermore, a State's immigration rules must address relevant concerns relating to encouragement, facilitation or tolerance of trafficking.[88]

Furthermore, it is wrong entirely to dismiss the relevance of criminal law for addressing practices of 'modern slavery'. Edwards rightly points out that 'treating trafficking as a [solely] labor issue could potentially result in the minimization of the seriousness of the criminal acts, human rights violations and/or violence being committed during the trafficking cycle, especially by governments that see labor issues as requiring regulation, rather than justice and redress'.[89] Criminal law is therefore a necessary but not sufficient aspect of states' obligations under human rights law.[90] In addition, the views that favour the labour approach to human trafficking over the human rights one are said to create a 'false dichotomy' between them, when in fact the two paradigms largely complement one another.[91]

Despite its significance, human rights law should not be seen as the *only* mechanism for tackling exploitation. A range of policy measures and broader structural changes are necessary to address the root causes of both human trafficking and of

---

[86] Chuang (n 17) 645. See also Skrivankova, 'Between Decent Work and Forced Labour: Examining the Continuum of Exploitation' (The Joseph Rowntree Foundation 2010); Shamir (n 9); Todres (n 75).
[87] Chuang (n 17) 644.
[88] *Rantsev v Cyprus and Russia* (2010) 51 EHRR 1 [284].
[89] Edwards (n 43) 4.
[90] Jennifer Collins, 'Exploitation at Work: Beyond a "Criminalization" or "Regulatory Alternatives" Dichotomy' in Alan Bogg and others (eds), *Criminality at Work* (OUP 2020) 105 (arguing similarly that 'there is a need for a multifaceted legal response to serious exploitation in work relations, which may include, but must extend beyond, criminalization').
[91] Todres (n 75).

lesser forms of exploitation. Such a diverse set of measures could not and should not be lumped together under the umbrella of human rights law, even though this often transpires in the scholarship. Choi-Fitzpatrick, for example, argues for the 'expanded version of the human rights approach' that focuses on: [T]he empowerment of enslaved persons in economic, political, and social and cultural systems. This empowerment occurs through access to the political process and representation, economic opportunity and livelihood, and the recognition of individual dignity, regardless of sociocultural background or status.[92]

It is obvious that human rights are invoked in a rhetorical fashion to draw attention to the range of injustices associated with human trafficking, rather than a specific legal tool designed to hold states accountable for securing rights to individuals within their jurisdiction. It is thus important to emphasise that a perspective, which considers human rights law as just one instrument in the legal toolbox for addressing human trafficking and exploitation, rests on a particular conception of human rights. Such a conception considers human rights as a means for the protection of individuals and groups against violations by governments, enshrined in international instruments to which states have acceded.[93]

In that context, the criticism of human rights law as inadequate a framework for tackling structural causes of exploitation is misguided because this is not the primary goal human rights instruments are designed to achieve in the first place. Certainly, human rights law, and especially the jurisprudence of influential human rights bodies, can cast light on such structural problems that lead to and facilitate human rights violations of individuals and can therefore instigate the necessary action. But human rights instruments are not primarily designed to address structural causes of rights violations, or at least not directly. They are designed to enable individuals to assert their rights vis-à-vis the state and demand protection and redress. In other words, while the current human rights mechanisms provide an opportunity to assess whether a state secured adequate protection to an individual victim of human trafficking, it is for that state to decide on specific actions needed to address structural conditions that facilitate human trafficking and other human rights violations.

In that light, a distinction must be drawn between obligations of states to prevent and remedy an *individual* act of human trafficking and exploitation, on the one hand, and *general* prevention, which includes addressing structural causes that lead to or facilitate trafficking and exploitation, on the other.[94] A conflation of the two aspects of prevention creates false expectations and often misjudged criticism of the human rights framework as a solution to the trafficking problem. Therefore,

---

[92] Choi-Fitzpatrick (n 24) 497.
[93] For an overview of different conceptualisations of human rights see Marie-Bénédicte Dembour, 'What Are Human Rights? Four Schools of Thought' (2010) 32 Human Rights Quarterly 1.
[94] See chs 5 and 6 for a comprehensive discussion of individual and general obligations of states in relation to the practices of 'modern slavery'.

a general call for developing 'a comprehensive, multidisciplinary and effectively co-ordinated policy that involves actors from all fields concerned'[95] requires mobilising different legal and policy domains and it would be a mistake to try framing all such efforts as human rights obligations in the traditional sense.

2.4 Human Trafficking as a Hybrid Legal Concept

Adopted within the realm of transnational criminal law, the Palermo definition of human trafficking has since transcended the boundaries of criminal law. Thus, in *Rantsev*, the European Court of Human Rights (ECtHR) has declared that human trafficking, *as defined in Article 3(a) of the Palermo Protocol*, falls within the scope of Article 4 of the ECHR, even though the latter does not expressly prohibit it.[96] This may raise concerns about the appropriateness of simply transplanting the concept from one legal domain to another. In other words, can the same definition be used to ascertain both individual criminal responsibility and state responsibility under human rights law? If so, does it apply differently in these two legal contexts? And ultimately, what is the added value of including human trafficking in human rights law instead of deploying concepts of slavery, servitude, and forced labour that have long existed within this domain? To answer these questions, we first turn to the Palermo definition of human trafficking.

2.4.1 The Universal Definition of Human Trafficking: One Size Fits All

Notwithstanding the criticism for its narrow law enforcement approach, the Palermo Protocol has been commended for introducing the first universal and comprehensive definition of human trafficking, which is broad enough to protect against newly emerging exploitative practices and techniques used by traffickers. Article 3 of the Palermo Protocol thus defines human trafficking in the following terms:

(a) 'Trafficking in persons' shall mean the recruitment, transportation, transfer, harbouring or receipt of persons, by means of the threat or use of force or other

---

[95] Council of the European Union,' Brussels Declaration on Preventing and Combating Trafficking in Human Beings' 14981/02 (29 November 2002). See also European Commission Report of the Experts Group on Trafficking in Human Beings (22 December 2004); Tom Obokata, *Trafficking in Human Beings from a Human Rights Perspective: Towards a Holistic Approach* (Martinus Nijhoff 2006); Edwards (n 43); Skrivankova (n 86); Todres (n 75); Nicola Jägers and Conny Rijken, 'Prevention of Human Trafficking for Labor Exploitation: The Role of Corporations' (2014) 12(1) Northwestern Journal of International Human Rights 47; Plant (n 21) 21.

[96] *Rantsev v Cyprus and Russia* (n 88). For a detailed discussion of this case see Chapter 3.

forms of coercion, of abduction, of fraud, of deception, of the abuse of power or of a position of vulnerability or of the giving or receiving of payments or benefits to achieve the consent of a person having control over another person, for the purpose of exploitation. Exploitation shall include, at a minimum, the exploitation of the prostitution of others or other forms of sexual exploitation, forced labour or services, slavery or practices similar to slavery, servitude or the removal of organs;

(b) The consent of a victim of trafficking in persons to the intended exploitation set forth in subparagraph (a) of this article shall be irrelevant where any of the means set forth in subparagraph (a) have been used.

All three elements—an action, the use of certain means, and the purpose of exploitation—must be present for a human trafficking offence to be established.[97] In the case of trafficking in children, the means element is immaterial. It is important to emphasise that exploitation, as a distinct purpose of human trafficking, needs not to have taken place: the offence is complete when *intended* exploitation could be established.[98] This makes human trafficking clearly distinguishable from the practices of slavery, servitude, or forced labour, which represent different *manifestations* of exploitation that has already begun—a distinction further explored in Chapter 3.

However, the absence of clear parameters of the 'action', 'means' and 'purpose' elements allows for a degree of interpretative liberty,[99] which has often led to the conflation of human trafficking with slavery or forced labour. Thus, the International Labour Organization (ILO) states that 'forced labour takes different forms, including debt bondage, trafficking and other forms of modern slavery',[100] suggesting that trafficking represents but one form of forced labour.[101] The ILO accordingly asserts that 'the definition of forced labour is sufficiently broad to encompass most forms of slavery ... [and] most forms of trafficking including sexual exploitation'.[102] Such conflation is clearly problematic and untenable. Chuang rightly notes that:

---

[97] UNODC, 'Legislative Guide for the Implementation of the Protocol to Prevent, Suppress and Punish Trafficking in Persons, Especially Women and Children, Supplementing the United Nations Convention against Transnational Organized Crime' (2004) (Trafficking Legislative Guide) para 32; Explanatory Report (n 63) para 76.
[98] Trafficking Legislative Guide (n 97) para 33; Explanatory Report (n 63) para 87.
[99] For a discussion of the three elements see Parosha Chandran, 'A Commentary on Interpreting Human Trafficking' in Parosha Chandran (ed), *Human Trafficking Handbook: Recognising Trafficking and Modern-Day Slavery in the UK* (LexisNexis 2011) 5. See also Gallagher (n 21).
[100] http://www.ilo.org/global/topics/forced-labour/lang--en/index.htm (accessed 15 February 2019).
[101] See also Jägers and Rijken (n 95) 49.
[102] ILO, *Forced Labour and Human Trafficking: Casebook of Court Decisions* (A Training Manual for Judges, Prosecutors and Legal Practitioners 2009) 9. Similarly ILO, Report for discussion at the Tripartite Meeting of Experts concerning the possible adoption of an ILO instrument to supplement the Forced Labour Convention 1930 (No 29) Geneva (11–15 February 2013) para 17, claims that: 'For the purposes of this report, and consistent with the comments of the Committee of Experts, the term "trafficking" is understood as being encompassed by the definition of forced or compulsory labour in Convention No 29.'

If trafficking could be so easily conflated with these or any other of the listed exploitative purposes, it is hard to see why States would have invested resources to create a new treaty regime when the target phenomena were already addressed by well-established treaty and customary international law.[103]

A distinction between human trafficking, involving the act-means-purpose matrix (with or without exploitation having materialised), on the one hand, and practices of slavery, servitude, and forced labour, as examples of actual exploitation, on the other, has been expressly recognised in some domestic and international legal instruments. Thus, the EU Charter of Fundamental Rights expressly prohibits human trafficking *alongside* the prohibitions of slavery, servitude, and forced or compulsory labour in Article 5. Article 10 of the Arab Charter on human rights also prohibits human trafficking separately. Furthermore, the 2015 UK Modern Slavery Act includes under the umbrella term 'modern slavery' the offences of slavery, servitude, forced or compulsory labour, and human trafficking.[104]

Leaving aside for a moment the differences and relationship between these practices, which will be explored at length in Chapter 3, the most significant flaw of the Palermo definition of human trafficking is the fact that it leaves open-ended the list of exploitative practices that represent the distinct purpose of a trafficking act. Without clear and specific parameters of the notion of exploitation,[105] the Palermo definition effectively allows for an ever-expanding interpretation of human trafficking. Thus, the EU Trafficking Directive expressly listed in its definition 'newer types of human trafficking such as forced begging, illegal adoption, forced marriage, the exploitation of criminal activities or the removal of organs for the purpose of trafficking', which have not featured in the Palermo Protocol.[106] The problem lies not in including newer practices that fit the definitional boundaries of the concept in question, but in the fact that such boundaries are not clearly set. In other words, the absence of clear parameters of the notion of exploitation embedded in the definition of human trafficking thwarts any attempt to determine the boundaries of such definition and criteria for including newer practices in it. Chapter 4 fills this lacuna by offering a comprehensive analysis of the notion of exploitation—the concept that establishes a direct link between human trafficking and the right to be free from slavery, servitude, and forced labour—and explains

---

[103] Chuang (n 17) 41.

[104] The 2015 MSA, however, considers 'travel' taken to mean 'arrival in or entry into, departure from, or travel within, the United Kingdom' as the essential part of the trafficking offence, which is not universally endorsed view. See n 17.

[105] Plant argues that '[o]f all the concepts now on national and international agendas, certainly the most difficult is that of exploitation. It has never been defined in international law'. See Plant (n 21) 3. Similarly, the ILO noted that 'exploitation is a concept for which there is almost no juridical precedent which prompts questions for both legislators and judges'. See ILO (n 102) Preface.

[106] UN High Commissioner for Refugees, 'Prevent, Combat, Protect Human Trafficking: Joint UN Commentary on the EU Directive: A Human Rights Based Approach' (November 2011) 104.

the necessary and sufficient conditions that must be present for a practice to reach the definitional threshold to be included within this right.

2.4.2 One Definition, Two Legal Contexts: Human Trafficking as *Both* a Crime and Human Rights Violation

The critiques of the Palermo definition outlined in the previous section have mostly focused on the ambiguities concerning the question of which practices ought to be criminalised. Scholars have thus warned that 'even in situations where the Palermo Protocol definition of trafficking in persons is reproduced, it does not necessarily mean the same thing or constitute the same crime'.[107] Yet many legal concepts suffer from similar problems, which is exacerbated in the absence of a body assigned to provide authoritative interpretations. For example, the prohibition of crimes against humanity, which is considered a peremptory norm of international law,[108] is defined in Article 7 of the Rome Statute of the International Criminal Court to include several acts such as murder, extermination, or enslavement. But the final example in Article 7(1)(k) includes 'other inhumane acts'. This clearly invites further specification by the courts interpreting the said provision.

As a transnational instrument, the Palermo Protocol does not envisage a judicial organ in charge of its interpretation. Instead, the Transnational Organized Convention, as a parent instrument, establishes a Conference of the Parties to the Convention to promote and review the implementation of the Convention.[109] The Conference set up a Working Group on Trafficking in Persons to advise and assist in the implementation of its mandate.[110] The latter has tried to assist in interpreting 'those aspects of the definition that are not elsewhere defined in international law or commonly known to the major legal systems of the world', including the notions of 'the abuse of a position of vulnerability', 'consent', and 'exploitation'.[111]

Given that the main rationale for adopting the definition of human trafficking in international law was to 'to support efficient international cooperation in investigating and prosecuting cases'[112] by ensuring some degree of standardisation

---

[107] Allain (n 16) 122–24.
[108] *Prosecutor v Kupreškić and Others* ICTY Case IT 95 16 T (14 January 2000) [520].
[109] UN TOC (n 52) art 32.
[110] Report of the Conference of the Parties to the United Nations Convention against Transnational Organized Crime on its fourth session, held in Vienna from 8 to 17 October 2008 (1 December 2008) CTOC/COP/2008/19, decision 4/4 https://www.unodc.org/unodc/en/treaties/CTOC/working-group-on-trafficking-apr-2009.html.
[111] UN Conference of the Parties to the United Nations Convention against Transnational Organized Crime, Working Group on Trafficking in Persons, 'Key Concepts of the Trafficking in Persons Protocol, with a Focus on the United Nations Office on Drugs and Crime Issue Papers on Abuse of a Position of Vulnerability, Consent and Exploitation' (25 August 2015) CTOC/COP/WG.4/2015/4.
[112] Legislative guide for the Protocol to Prevent, Suppress and Punish Trafficking in Persons, Especially Women and Children (2004) para 35.

of domestic criminal offences, it is understandable that the critique has focused on whether or not such a goal has been accomplished. However, less attention has been paid to explaining how a definition, which outlines the elements of a crime to be transposed into domestic legislation—even if drafted in a crystal-clear manner—fits in the human rights law context. In other words, is such a definition suitable for establishing the responsibility of a state in human rights law—either for its direct involvement in human trafficking or for its inadequate response to practices committed by non-state actors?

While there is no inherent problem with using the same legal definition in both criminal and human rights law contexts, for this has been the case with the definition of torture, for example,[113] the standards for establishing individual criminal responsibility as opposed to responsibility of states in human rights law are different. Therefore, to establish individual criminal responsibility for human trafficking all three elements of the Palermo definition ought to be proved *beyond reasonable doubt*, which is the criminal standard of proof.

But the nature of state responsibility in human rights law is different. It is premised on states' own actions in relation to such a criminal conduct, unless a state is directly involved in trafficking, which does occasionally occur.[114] Most often, therefore, state responsibility for human trafficking in human rights law will arise because of its inadequate *response* to practices committed by non-state actors. In these circumstances, a state violates a human right when it does not discharge its *own* positive obligations towards individuals whose right(s) have been infringed by actions of private individuals. As will be discussed in detail in Chapter 6, such positive obligations are triggered when there are *reasonable grounds to believe* that a person has been trafficked and do not depend on establishing the guilt of a perpetrator, which calls for a much higher 'beyond reasonable doubt' standard.[115] This is expressly confirmed in *Rantsev*, where the Strasbourg Court concluded that:

> [T]here were sufficient indicators available to the police authorities, against the general backdrop of trafficking issues in Cyprus, for them to have been aware of circumstances giving rise to a credible suspicion that Ms Rantseva was, or was at real and immediate risk of being, a victim of trafficking or exploitation.

---

[113] See eg Criminal Justice Act 1988, s 134 (UK).

[114] Leslie Holmes, 'Corruption and Trafficking: Triple Victimisation?' in Cornelius Friesendorf (ed), *Strategies Against Human Trafficking: The Role of the Security Sector* (National Defence Academy and Austrian Ministry of Defence and Sport 2009); Philippa Webb and Rosana Garciandia, 'State Responsibility for Modern Slavery: Uncovering and Bridging the Gap' (2019) 68(3) International and Comparative Law Quarterly 539.

[115] See also UK Home Office, 'Modern Slavery Act 2015: Statutory Guidance for England and Wales' (24 March 2020). The Home Office Guidance expressly notes in para 14.59 that '[i]t is not necessary to prove that an offence has taken place, or for there to be an ongoing criminal investigation to find that an individual is a victim of human trafficking and/or slavery, servitude, and forced or compulsory labour'.

Accordingly, a positive obligation arose to investigate without delay and to take any necessary operational measures to protect Ms Rantseva.[116]

Similarly, the Inter-American Court of Human Rights confirmed that 'the violation can be established even if the identity of the individual perpetrator is unknown'.[117]

Accordingly, on one hand, states have, as a matter of transnational criminal law, a duty to transpose and apply the criminal law definition of trafficking domestically to establish individual criminal responsibility of traffickers. On the other hand, human rights law mandates states to act on early signs before, or even regardless of whether the guilt of the perpetrator has been proved in criminal proceedings. The ECtHR expressly confirmed that:

> Indeed, (potential) victims need support even before the offence of human trafficking is formally established; otherwise, this would run counter to the whole purpose of victim protection in trafficking cases. The question whether the elements of the crime had been fulfilled would have to have been answered in subsequent criminal proceedings.[118]

Therefore, the universal definition of human trafficking applies differently when discussing the potential state responsibility to protect victims in the human rights law context as opposed to establishing the guilt of an individual perpetrator in criminal proceedings. In the former sense, human trafficking would amount to a human rights violation if: (a) a state is directly involved in human trafficking as defined by the Palermo Protocol; or (b) a state fails to discharge its positive duties that arise in circumstances where human trafficking is committed by non-state actors, when it could be established that authorities 'were aware, or ought to have been aware, of circumstances giving rise to a credible suspicion that an identified individual had been, or was at real and immediate risk of being, trafficked or exploited within the meaning of Article 3(a) of the Palermo Protocol'.[119] Evidently, while all three elements of the definition must be proven beyond reasonable doubt to establish criminal responsibility of a trafficker, in the human rights context, 'credible suspicion' with regard to these elements would suffice to trigger positive obligations of states. Distinguishing between 'administrative recognition of the status of

---

[116] See para 296 (emphasis added). In the most recent decision in *SM v Croatia*, the Grand Chamber of the Court held that 'the applicability of the protection under Article 4 in relation to human trafficking' would depend on 'whether, in the circumstances of a particular case, the applicant made an arguable claim or whether there was prima facie evidence (commencement de preuve) of her having been subjected to such prohibited treatment'. *SM v Croatia* (n 17) [324].

[117] *Velasquez-Rodriguez v Honduras* Inter-American Court of Human Rights Series C No 4 (29 July 1988) [173].

[118] *J and Others v Austria*, App no 58216/12 (ECtHR, 17 January 2017) [115]; *SM v Croatia* (n 17) [322]. See also Chapter 6 section 6.3.2.

[119] *Rantsev v Cyprus and Russia* (n 88) [286]. See further discussion in Chapter 3.

a potential victim' for the purpose of their protection and the question of 'whether the elements of the crime are present' for the purpose of criminal conviction of the perpetrator has been clarified in the recent jurisprudence of the Strasbourg Court.[120] With regard to the latter, the Court especially reminded of 'the necessity of the protection of the rights of the suspects or accused, in particular the right to the presumption of innocence and other fair-trial guarantees under Article 6 of the Convention'.[121]

2.5 The Value of the Human Rights Approach to Human Trafficking

It is one thing to argue that human trafficking could be included in the human rights framework as a self-standing prohibition without conceptual difficulties. It is another to claim that this is an appropriate and desirable move. Why should human trafficking be so included when the human rights framework already contains the prohibitions of slavery, servitude, and forced labour, which could be used to address the worst forms of exploitation? Three broad justifications could be offered.

The first is that human trafficking, slavery, servitude, and forced labour are different but overlapping phenomena and therefore could not be consumed by one another. The difference between these practices and their mutual relationship are explained in detail in the following chapter. Suffice it to say here that none of the three expressly mentioned concepts (slavery, servitude, and forced labour) captures the breadth of conducts included in the definition of human trafficking, especially the early phases of the offence, such as recruitment, which ensure early intervention to prevent exploitation.

The second value of bringing human trafficking within the human rights domain is a possibility for human rights tribunals to draw on obligations established by specialised anti-trafficking instruments in instances of non-trafficked exploitation. The best example for this is the principle of non-punishment of victims for unlawful activities committed in the course of, or as a consequence of, being trafficked or exploited.[122] This obligation was first articulated in the Anti-Trafficking Convention,[123] but has been subsequently transposed in the human rights domain to apply to victims of non-trafficked forced labour.[124] Human rights jurisprudence

---

[120] *J and Others v Austria* (n 118) [115]; *SM v Croatia* (n 17) [322].
[121] *SM v Croatia* (n 17) [322].
[122] Marija Jovanovic, 'The Principle of Non-Punishment of Victims of Trafficking in Human Beings: A Human Rights Obligation?' (2017) 1 Journal of Trafficking and Human Exploitation 41.
[123] Anti-Trafficking Convention, art 26. See also EU Trafficking Directive, art 8.
[124] Protocol of 2014 to the Forced Labour Convention 1930, art 4(2). Notably, in *VCL and AN v United Kingdom* [2021] ECHR 132 [113]–[159], the Strasbourg Court emphasised that '[i]t has no competence to interpret the provisions of the Anti-Trafficking Convention or to assess the compliance of the respondent State with the standards contained therein'. However, it specified that 'the prosecution of

on slavery, servitude, and forced labour has been largely undeveloped until human trafficking came to the forefront of international attention. Negotiations of specialised anti-trafficking instruments represented a fresh opportunity for articulating a set of comprehensive and specific obligations of states, which could then be drawn upon by the human rights courts when discussing duties under general human rights law.[125] Such an approach is fully aligned with the living instrument doctrine embraced by the Strasbourg Court[126] and other international human rights bodies.

The third justification for including human trafficking in the human rights domain is concerned with strengthening victims' agency. The possibility of finding states responsible for breaches of human rights law adds further pressure to enforce their commitments undertaken by specialist anti-trafficking instruments. Neither the Palermo Protocol nor the Anti-Trafficking Convention envisage an individual complaints mechanism for holding states accountable for implementing the agreed commitments. Instead, they rely on the Conference of the Parties to the United Nations Convention against Transnational Organized Crime and the Committee of the Parties of the Council of Europe Convention on Action against Trafficking in Human Beings to exert political pressure on non-conforming states. Human rights law and directly enforceable human rights, in particular, thus represent an important tool for victims to attain justice and redress when states fail to give effect to their international obligations. What is more, the ECHR has been used as a vehicle for assessing compliance with obligations arising out of the Anti-Trafficking Convention duties even against states that are *not* signatories to the latter. Thus, in *Ranstev v Cyprus and Russia*, the Strasbourg court expressly drew on obligations enshrined in the Anti-Trafficking Convention to find a breach of Article 4 ECHR against Russia, even though Russia is not a party to the former.[127]

Therefore, obligations established by the specialised anti-trafficking instruments developed over the past two decades concretise and strengthen the protections against the worst forms of exploitation available in human rights law. At

---

victims, or potential victims, of trafficking may, in certain circumstances, be at odds with the State's duty to take operational measures to protect them'. It went on to explain that: 'It is axiomatic that the prosecution of victims of trafficking would be injurious to their physical, psychological and social recovery and could potentially leave them vulnerable to being retrafficked in future. Not only would they have to go through the ordeal of a criminal prosecution, but a criminal conviction could create an obstacle to their subsequent integration into society. In addition, incarceration may impede their access to the support and services that were envisaged by the Anti-Trafficking Convention.'

[125] This has been the case in *Chowdury and Others v Greece* [2017] ECHR 300. See Vladislava Stoyanova, 'Sweet Taste with Bitter Roots: Forced Labour and Chowdury and Others v Greece' (2018) 1 European Human Rights Law Review 67 (noting that 'the obligations imposed by the Council of Europe Convention on Action against Trafficking in Human Beings are of relevance not only to factual circumstances qualified as human trafficking, but to the whole gamut of abuses intended to be captured by Article 4 ECHR').
[126] *Rantsev v Cyprus and Russia* (n 88) [277].
[127] ibid [307]–[309].

the same time, human rights law provides an opportunity for victims of human trafficking to seek justice and hold states accountable for their implementation of anti-trafficking measures, which is not possible under the existing anti-trafficking instruments. Accordingly, the anti-trafficking framework and human rights law are mutually reinforcing rather than in conflict with each other.

2.6 Final Remarks on the Relationship between Human Trafficking and Human Rights Law

Before proceeding to consider how the right not to be trafficked could be framed in positive human rights law, it is worth restating what has been established so far. It is first shown that international law has always approached human trafficking as a law enforcement issue and that the Palermo Protocol merely continued with such tradition. But it became obvious that the law enforcement approach was inadequate for addressing many aspects of this complex phenomenon. The post-Palermo initiatives thus sought to inject a human rights perspective into the global anti-trafficking action, yet it remained unclear how exactly human trafficking engages human rights law and whether it is a human rights violation per se.

This has opened space for competing views about the relationship between human trafficking and human rights law, including critical perspectives that consider human trafficking as an unnecessary and problematic addition to the existing human rights arsenal for tackling inter-personal exploitation and the views that see human rights law itself as inadequate a tool for addressing such exploitation. This chapter has nonetheless shown that a more amiable view of the relationship between human trafficking and human rights law is both possible and desirable.

Notably, different legal and policy frameworks each have a role to play in addressing this complex phenomenon and human rights law is but one instrument in the plethora of legal tools available. Problems in assessing the role of human rights law in addressing human trafficking arise from different conceptions of human rights law, its mission, scope, and the mode of enforcement embraced by different authors. The book proceeds from a positivist conception of human rights, which sees rights as individual claims against a state enshrined in international human rights instruments. Without suggesting that this is the dominant or best conception of human rights, it is important to clarify the perspective from which the human rights analysis is conducted. For the assessment of the capacity of human rights law to successfully address human trafficking hinges on a particular conception of human rights used to anchor such an analysis. Accordingly, the following chapter proceeds to examine the link between human trafficking and the *existing* catalogue of human rights explaining how the latter could be used to secure effective protection of the victims of human trafficking.

Finally, despite competing views on the best legal framework to address human trafficking, the Palermo definition has been universally endorsed as the legal definition of this phenomenon. Although such a definition allows a degree of interpretative liberty in specifying a range of practices that could be included in its ambit, this is neither a unique nor insurmountable obstacle for its application. What is more, it is shown that the concept's hybrid legal nature as both a criminal offence and a human rights violation leads to a different application of the Palermo definition in the human rights and criminal law contexts respectively. Therefore, establishing all three elements of the definition beyond reasonable doubt is an imperative when assessing the perpetrator's responsibility in criminal proceedings. However, when it comes to examining state responsibility under human rights law, the trigger for positive human rights obligations (and resulting responsibility for failing to fulfil such obligations) is a reasonable grounds belief that a person has been trafficked and/or exploited, or is at risk thereof. This assessment does not depend on establishing criminal responsibility of an offender and could be conducted even in situations where the offender is unknown. Having therefore established that there are no conceptual obstacles to conceive human trafficking as a human rights violation, the analysis in the next chapter examines how the right not to be trafficked could be framed within the existing human rights instruments.

3
A Right Not to Be Trafficked?

The previous chapter has shown that human trafficking involves practices that may encroach upon different human rights, such as the right to liberty and security, the right to privacy, and occasionally even the right to life or the prohibition against torture and inhuman or degrading treatment. The UN Special Rapporteur on Trafficking in Persons thus declared that human trafficking 'represents the denial of virtually all human rights'.[1] A decade later, the Rapporteur clarified that 'while there was regular condemnation of the human rights violations associated with trafficking, the practice was rarely linked to the violation of a specific right in a specific treaty'.[2]

The European Court of Human Rights changed this perception by recognising in *Rantsev v Cyprus and Russia* that even though human trafficking was not mentioned in the European Convention on Human Rights (ECHR), it nonetheless violates the prohibition of slavery and forced labour contained in Article 4.[3] The Court's attempt to incorporate human trafficking within the ambit of this right was justified, if incomplete and rigour-free. This is because the Court in *Rantsev* did not clarify whether human trafficking fell within the scope of this right as a stand-alone prohibition, that is, without the need to be interpreted as either one of the three expressly prohibited practices. By failing to explain how the notion of human trafficking, defined in the treaty that belongs to transnational criminal law, translates into the human rights context, the Court is said to have 'failed to demonstrate or set out a clear understanding of the substance or content of Article 4'.[4]

The chapter therefore explores the conceptual boundaries of the prohibition of 'modern slavery' and elucidates the meaning and relationships between both expressly prohibited and implied concepts in order to determine situations in which the right is or is not engaged. Establishing practices that fall within the protective ambit of the human rights prohibition of 'modern slavery' is a precondition for any assessment of the state responsibility for it.

---

[1] UN OHCHR, Report of the Special Rapporteur on Trafficking in Persons, Especially Women and Children, 'Integration of Human Rights of Women and the Gender Perspective' (22 December 2004) UN Doc E/CN.4/2005/71, para 9.

[2] UN OHCHR, Report of the Special Rapporteur on Trafficking in Persons, Especially Women and Children, Joy Ngozi Ezeilo (28 July 2014) A/69/33797, para 46.

[3] *Rantsev v Cyprus and Russia* (2010) 51 EHRR 1 [281]; *J and Others v Austria* [2017] ECHR 37 [104].

[4] Jean Allain, '*Rantsev v Cyprus and Russia*: The European Court of Human Rights and Trafficking as Slavery' (2010) 10(3) Human Rights Law Review 546, 555.

3.1 From Palermo to Strasbourg: The *Rantsev* Case and the Inclusion of Human Trafficking in the Human Rights Framework

The ECHR—the main human rights instrument of the Council of Europe and one of the most successful human rights mechanisms globally—does not explicitly refer to trafficking in human beings. While the Strasbourg Court effectively dealt with the treatment closely related to human trafficking in *Siliadin v France*,[5] it did not in that case engage with the concept as such. Rather, the Court in *Siliadin* decided to address the issue from the perspective of practices expressly prohibited in Article 4 ECHR, namely slavery, servitude, and forced labour. Five years later, the Court delivered a ground-breaking decision in the *Rantsev* case, where it directly addressed the issue of human trafficking.[6]

The case emerged from the application submitted by the father of a victim, a Russian national who arrived in Cyprus on an 'artiste' visa to work as a cabaret dancer. According to subsequently published reports of the Cypriot Ombudsman and the Council of Europe Commissioner for Human Rights, the word 'artiste' in Cyprus has become synonymous with 'prostitute'. It appears that thousands of women have entered the country through this immigration scheme to work as artistes, and many of them were forced by their employers into prostitution.[7] Soon after Ms Rantseva had arrived in Cyprus, she fled the apartment provided by her employer where she lived with several other women. A man who managed the cabaret informed the Immigration Office in Limassol that Ms Rantseva had abandoned her place of work and residence. According to his statement, he wanted her to be arrested and expelled from Cyprus so that he could bring another girl to work. Yet her name was not entered on the list of persons wanted by the police. Several days later he was informed of her presence in a discothèque and he called the police requiring her arrest. He then went to the discothèque himself, apprehended her, and brought her to the local police station. However, having found that Ms Rantseva was not in Cyprus illegally, the police neither arrested nor released her but instead asked him to collect her (together with her passport and other documents) and bring her back the next morning for further investigation. Several hours later, she was found dead on the street below the apartment where she had been taken from the police station.

Ms Rantseva's father brought a case to the Strasbourg Court alleging violations of different human rights contained in Articles 2, 3, 4, and 5 ECHR.[8] The Court decided to focus on Article 4 and its relevance for human trafficking. This case

---

[5] (2006) 43 EHRR 16.
[6] *Rantsev v Cyprus and Russia* (n 3).
[7] ibid [80]–[104].
[8] The right to life, the prohibition of torture, the prohibition of slavery and forced labour, and the right to liberty and security, respectively.

is important because it clarifies for the first time the range of positive obligations imposed upon Member States by this right, which will be subject to a detailed scrutiny in Chapter 6. It is nonetheless equally important to consider the Court's findings on 'why trafficking falls within the parameters of article 4'.[9]

The Court was called to determine two questions—one conceptual and the other more focused on the circumstances of the present case. The first question was whether, and how, human trafficking fits into the scope of Article 4, given that it was not explicitly mentioned in the Convention text. The second question was, whether, and how, the circumstances of the present case amounted to conduct prohibited by Article 4, in whichever form. The conceptual question invites the Court to explain two things: first, *why* trafficking *primarily* violates Article 4 and not some other rights; secondly, whether every case of human trafficking needs to be assessed against standards required for establishing slavery, servitude, or forced labour—concepts explicitly listed in the Convention—or, alternatively, whether trafficking can be read into Article 4 *alongside* these explicitly prohibited practices? This is effectively concerned with the question of *how* trafficking violates Article 4.

The Court first stated that it 'has never considered the provisions of the Convention as the sole framework of reference for the interpretation of the rights and freedoms enshrined therein'.[10] It went on to say that practical and effective protection of individual human rights requires that the Convention is read as a whole and in harmony with other rules of international law, of which it forms part.[11] Furthermore, emphasising the nature of the Convention as 'a living instrument which must be interpreted in the light of present-day conditions' and 'in light of the proliferation of both trafficking itself and of measures taken to combat it', the Court deemed it appropriate to consider the extent to which trafficking *itself* may be considered to run counter to the spirit and purpose of Article 4.[12]

The Court started its analysis by referring to the decision of the International Criminal Tribunal for the Former Yugoslavia (ICTY) in the *Kunarac* case,[13] which held that the traditional concept of 'slavery' has evolved to include various contemporary forms of slavery, which are based on the exercise of powers attaching to the right of ownership. It declared that human trafficking too 'by its very nature and aim of exploitation' is based on the exercise of powers attaching to the right of ownership, thus essentially implying that trafficking is a form of slavery, understood in modern terms.[14] Having said that, it moved on to state that it was not necessary to identify whether the treatment complained of constituted any of the explicitly

---

[9] Anne Gallagher, *The International Law of Human Trafficking* (CUP 2010) 189.
[10] *Rantsev v Cyprus and Russia* (n 3) [273].
[11] ibid [274].
[12] ibid [277]–[279] (emphasis added).
[13] *Prosecutor v Kunarac, Kovac and Vukovic*, Case Nos IT-96-23 and IT-96-23/1-A [2002] ICTY 2 (12 June 2002) [117].
[14] *Rantsev v Cyprus and Russia* (n 3) [280]–[281].

prohibited practices. Instead, it found that 'trafficking itself, within the meaning of Article 3(a) of the Palermo Protocol and Article 4(a) of the Anti-Trafficking Convention' falls within the scope of Article 4 of the ECHR[15]—the formulation consistently repeated in its subsequent jurisprudence.[16]

However, it is not clear whether the Court wanted to say that there was no need to classify the conduct complained of (with strong indicia of trafficking) as either 'slavery', 'servitude', or 'forced labour' *in this particular case* (because, for example, that would not affect the duties of the states) or whether *in general* there was no need to do so (because, again, this would not affect duties owed by states). In the case of the latter, this would imply that trafficking stands *alongside* those three explicitly prohibited activities.

Moreover, apart from not giving the explicit answer on how trafficking violates Article 4, the Court neither gave a definite answer as to whether Ms Rantseva herself was indeed trafficked or exploited.[17] Rather, it moved on quickly to elaborate the duties enshrined in Article 4, whether those duties arose in particular circumstances, and whether and how both states complied with them.

The Court's failing to clarify these matters gave rise to the fierce criticism of the ruling. Many authors have pointed out the Court's apparent equating of trafficking with slavery, thus 'not having truly engaged with the legal distinctions that exist between these two concepts'.[18] The judgment was furthermore criticised for failing 'to demonstrate or set out a clear understanding of the substance or content of Article 4'.[19] The Court's decision to assess whether trafficking could fall within the Article 4 prohibition without considering specifically whether the practice was slavery, servitude, or forced labour was seen as 'weakness and, perhaps, intellectual incoherence'.[20] Declining to say precisely how trafficking of human beings violates Article 4 ECHR, the Court left those critics wondering whether '*all* cases of trafficking potentially violate Article 4'.[21]

---

[15] ibid [282].

[16] *M and Others v Italy and Bulgaria* [2012] ECHR 1967; *CN and V v France* App no 67724/09 (ECtHR, 11 October 2012); *CN v United Kingdom* (2013) 56 EHRR 24; *LE v Greece LE v Greece* [2016] ECHR 107; *Chowdury and Others v Greece* [2017] ECHR 300; *J and Others v Austria* (n 3); *SM v Croatia* App no 60561/14 (ECtHR GC, 25 June 2020).

[17] Vladislava Stoyanova, 'The Relationship between the Concept of Human Trafficking and the Concepts of Slavery, Servitude and Forced Labour' in Vladislava Stoyanova, *Human Trafficking and Slavery Reconsidered Conceptual Limits and States' Positive Obligations in European Law* (CUP 2017).

[18] Allain (n 4). See also Vladislava Stoyanova, 'Dancing on the Borders of Article 4: Human Trafficking and the European Court of Human Rights in the Rantsev Case' (2012) 30 Netherlands Quarterly of Human Rights 163; Ramona Vijeyarasa and José Miguel Bello y Villarino, 'Modern Day Slavery? A Judicial Catchall for Trafficking, Slavery and Labour Exploitation: A Critique of Tang and Rantsev' (2012) 8 Journal of International Law and International Relations 36.

[19] Allain (n 4) 555.

[20] Ryszard Piotrowicz, 'States' Obligations under Human Rights Law towards Victims of Trafficking in Human Beings: Positive Developments in Positive Obligations' (2012) 24(2) International Journal of Refugee Law 181, 196.

[21] ibid.

However, even though the Court's phrasing may not have been the most fortunate, there may be a more favourable reading of the claim that 'trafficking in human beings, by its very nature and aim of exploitation, is based on the exercise of powers attaching to the right of ownership'.[22] Rather than equating trafficking with slavery, it may well be that the Court wished to stress that both practices belong to the ambit of Article 4 due to *their* 'very nature', which aims at the exploitation of another human being. Hence, the following section shows that even though the ruling could have been phrased more clearly, the Court's approach may not necessarily be viewed as 'deeply flawed'.[23]

3.2 Saving *Rantsev*: A Case for the Right Not to Be Trafficked

3.2.1 Process versus Condition

The right to be free from slavery explicitly prohibits practices of slavery, servitude, and forced labour. In *Rantsev*, the Strasbourg Court included human trafficking within its scope, drawing on the definition established by the Palermo Protocol. Borrowing a definition from another international instrument is not a novel or controversial action of the Court for the same was done with concepts of slavery, servitude, and forced labour, neither of which has been defined by any of the general human rights instruments containing this right.[24] However, the Court never fully engaged in explaining the differences between these practices and their mutual relationship.

The discussion of the Palermo definition of human trafficking in the previous chapter reveals that human trafficking represents a *process* that contains a range of interconnected phases such as recruitment, transfer, or harbouring of victims using different means that vitiate their consent. The United Nations Office on Drugs and Crime published a case digest that illustrates this 'chain of trafficking'. For instance, it describes a Colombian Supreme Court case[25] concerning a criminal network behind trafficking of Colombian women to Hong Kong, Singapore, and Indonesia:

> The criminal group recruited the women, arranged for their travel and transported them to the bars where they would subsequently be exploited. The network

---

[22] *Rantsev v Cyprus and Russia* (n 3) [281].
[23] Allain (n 4) 557.
[24] Council of Europe, European Court of Human Rights, 'Guide on Article 4 of the Convention: Prohibition of Slavery and Forced Labour' (2014).
[25] *Garcia et al*, Criminal Appellate Court of the Supreme Court of Justice, Colombia (6 March 2008). The case is available in the UNODC Human Trafficking Case Law Database (UNODC Case No COL005).

included the recruiter, his assistant and other facilitators. Some of the defendants were former victims of trafficking.[26]

Clearly, the aim of these interconnected actions is placing an individual in exploitative *conditions*. If uninterrupted, a human trafficking chain always results in victims' exploitation, which may manifest in different forms. Thus, in his lengthy concurring opinion in *J and Others*, Judge de Albuquerque rightly observes that 'the trafficking process itself is a preparatory stage of the ensuing exploitation and therefore is attached to each of the three proscribed conducts in Article 4'.[27] Exploitative conditions include, but are not limited to, slavery, servitude, and forced labour. Other examples of exploitative practices listed in the Palermo definition include 'at a minimum': 'the exploitation of the prostitution of others or other forms of sexual exploitation', 'practices similar to slavery', 'the removal of organs', 'forced begging', and 'exploitation of criminal activities'.[28]

At the same time, a person can be subject to slavery, servitude, or forced labour without having been trafficked. The Strasbourg Court has recognised this in *CN v United Kingdom*, a case involving domestic servitude of a Ugandan national who worked as a live-in carer for an elderly Iraqi couple.[29] She alleged that she was permanently on call, day and night, that her salary was sent to the agent who had arranged her work with the family, who then passed a percentage of the money to her cousin on the apparent understanding that it would be paid to her. Yet she claimed not to have received any significant payment for her labour. The Court found a violation of Article 4 because the legislative provisions in force at the relevant time and official investigation into her claims were focused only on human trafficking or, in the Court's words, 'criminal offences which often—but do not necessarily— accompany the offences of slavery, servitude and forced or compulsory labour'.[30] As such, they were deemed inadequate to afford practical and effective protection against treatment that the Court qualified as 'domestic servitude'.

---

[26] UNDOC, Evidential Issues in Trafficking in Persons Cases: Case Digest (United Nations 2017) 129. file:///C:/Users/majov/Downloads/Case_Digest_Evidential_Issues_in_Trafficking.pdf.

[27] *J and Others v Austria* (n 3) Concurring Opinion of Judge Pinto de Albuquerque, joined by Judge Tsotsoria [40].

[28] Protocol to Prevent, Suppress and Punish Trafficking in Persons Especially Women and Children, supplementing the United Nations Convention against Transnational Organized Crime (adopted 15 November 2000, entered into force 25 December 2003) 2237 UNTS 319 (Palermo Protocol), art 3; Convention on Action against Trafficking in Human Beings (adopted 16 May 2005, entered into force 1 February 2008) CETS 197 (Anti-Trafficking Convention), art 4; Directive of the European Parliament and of the Council on preventing and combating trafficking in human beings and protecting its victims, and replacing Council Framework Decision 2002/629/JHA (5 April 2011) 2011/36/EU (Anti-Trafficking Directive), art 2.

[29] *CN v United Kingdom* (n 16) [74]–[80].

[30] ibid [76]. See a further discussion of this case in Chapter 6, sections 6.1 and 6.2.

Accordingly, while there is a certain degree of overlap,[31] human trafficking could not be equated with either of the three expressly prohibited exploitative conditions, not least because it exists before any exploitation has materialised. This raises a question of whether it warrants a place on its own within this human right. In other words, does human rights law require states to act before a person has been subject to exploitative conditions? And if so, would this be required even if intended exploitation does not amount to slavery, servitude, or forced labour, but involves other exploitative practices listed in the definition of human trafficking? Reading human trafficking into the prohibition of slavery clearly raises important conceptual questions, which the Court in *Rantsev* left unanswered.

Until the Grand Chamber's ruling in *SM v Croatia* in 2020, the Strasbourg Court never explicitly answered whether human trafficking fell within the scope of this right as a stand-alone prohibition, that is, without the need to be interpreted as either one of the three expressly prohibited practices. In *J and Others v Austria*, for example, the Court stated that 'the identified elements of trafficking ... cut across the three categories set out in Article 4',[32] without specifying whether it amounted to a self-standing violation of this right. In *SM*, the Court declared that 'there are good reasons to accept the assertion in Rantsev that the global phenomenon of trafficking in human beings runs counter to the spirit and purpose of Article 4 and thus falls within the scope of the guarantees offered by that provision'.[33] It went on to proclaim that:

> [F]rom the perspective of Article 4 of the Convention the concept of human trafficking covers trafficking in human beings ... in so far as the constituent elements of the international definition of trafficking in human beings, under the Anti-Trafficking Convention and the Palermo Protocol, are present.[34]

The Court seems to acknowledge in this statement that human trafficking amounts to an independent prohibition within the right to be free from slavery, servitude, and forced labour, yet it fails to explain why this ought to be. While it referred to its earlier decision in *Chowdury and Others v Greece*, which noted 'the intrinsic relationship between forced or compulsory labour and human trafficking',[35] the Court nonetheless failed to elaborate the substance of such intrinsic connection. The Court therefore missed another opportunity to explain the important difference between the concepts of human trafficking, on one hand, and slavery, servitude,

---

[31] In *J and Others v Austria* (n 3) [104] and *SM v Croatia* (n 16) [291], the Strasbourg Court noted that 'the identified elements of trafficking ... cut across these three categories [slavery, servitude, and forced labour]'.
[32] *J and Others v Austria* (n 3) [104].
[33] *SM v Croatia* (n 16) [292].
[34] ibid [296].
[35] *Chowdury and Others v Greece* (n 16) [93].

and forced labour, on the other, which are bound by the notion of exploitation that this right is meant to protect against.

The following section shows that human trafficking triggers protection afforded by the right to be free from slavery, servitude, and forced labour even when intended exploitation has not yet materialised and even when such exploitation involves practices beyond those expressly prohibited by this human right.

3.2.2 Absolute Rights and Imminent Threat: Human Trafficking as a Real and Immediate Risk of Exploitation

Article 4 ECHR, which expressly prohibits slavery, servitude, and forced labour, together with Articles 2 and 3 that guarantee the right to life and freedom from torture respectively, is said to enshrine one of the basic values of the democratic societies making up the Council of Europe.[36] These rights are sometimes called 'absolute' rights[37] and the Court has made it clear that states must act to *prevent* their violations, especially when the threat arises from private actors.[38] For example, in the *Opuz* case concerning the Turkish authorities' failure to protect the applicant and her mother from domestic violence, the Strasbourg Court emphasised the states' duty to ensure that individuals within their jurisdiction are not subjected to torture or inhuman or degrading treatment or punishment, including such ill-treatment administered by private individuals.[39] It found that the authorities failed to 'prevent the recurrence of violent attacks against the applicant, since the applicant's husband perpetrated them without hindrance and with impunity'.[40] Equally, when it comes to the right to life, the Court emphasised 'a positive obligation on the authorities to take preventive operational measures to protect an individual whose life is at risk from the criminal acts of another individual'.[41]

---

[36] *Siliadin v France* (2006) 43 EHRR 16 [82] and [112]; *CN v United Kingdom* (n 16) [65].

[37] The term 'absolute rights' refers to rights contained in arts 2, 3, 4(1), and 7. See Bernadette Rainey, Pamela McCormick, and Clare Ovey (eds), *Jacobs, Ovey, and White: The European Convention on Human Rights* (7th edn, OUP 2017) 219. However, the term 'non-derogable' has been suggested as more accurate by Andrew Ashworth and Mike Redmayne, *The Criminal Process* (4th edn, OUP 2010) 37. See also N Mavronicola, 'What Is an "Absolute Right"? Deciphering Absoluteness in the Context of Article 3 of the European Convention on Human Rights' (2012) 12 Human Rights Law Review 723. G Webber, 'Proportionality and Absolute Rights' in V Jackson and M Tushnet (eds), *Proportionality: New Frontiers, New Challenges* (CUP 2016).

[38] This point is analysed in detail in Chapter 6.

[39] *Opuz v Turkey* (2010) 50 EHRR 28 [159]. See also *Z and Others v United Kingdom* (2002) 34 EHRR 3; *Denizci and Others v Cyprus* [2001] ECHR 351; *E and Others v United Kingdom* (2003) 36 EHRR 31; *M and Others v Italy and Bulgaria* (n 16).

[40] *Opuz v Turkey* (2010) 50 EHRR 28 [159], [169].

[41] ibid [128]; *Osman v United Kingdom* (2000) 29 EHRR 245 [115]; *Kontrová v Slovakia* [2007] ECHR 419 [49]; *Öneryıldız v Turkey* (2004) 39 EHRR 12; *Kilic v Turkey* (2001) 33 EHRR 58; *Calvelli and Ciglio v Italy* [2002] ECHR 3. See also J McBride, 'Protecting Life: A Positive Obligation to Help' (1999) 24 European Law Review 43, 45.

Accordingly, the prohibition of slavery, servitude, and forced labour also requires such pre-emptive protection, in circumstances when authorities are aware or ought to have been aware that an identified individual is subject to, or is at a 'real and immediate' risk of, treatment that impairs the guaranteed rights.[42] The sole purpose of human trafficking process is subjecting people to serious exploitation and, if uninterrupted, will always lead to such exploitation materialising. Being in a situation of human trafficking thus amounts to the real and immediate risk of exploitation, even though the type or extent of such exploitative treatment may not always be clear in advance. However, it would defeat the spirit and purpose of this right to afford protection only to people who have already been subject to exploitative treatment in the form of slavery, servitude, or forced labour. Accordingly, even the earliest stages of a trafficking process, such as recruitment by using certain means, trigger states' protective duties when authorities are aware or ought to have been aware of a 'real and immediate' risk to an identifiable individual of being subject to exploitative treatment.[43] This makes it clear that human trafficking has a specific and independent place within the scope of this right and could not be consumed or replaced by expressly listed practices such as slavery, servitude, or forced labour.

This conclusion is bolstered by the fact that the Charter of Fundamental Rights of the European Union (EU Charter) and the newer human rights instruments expressly prohibit human trafficking *alongside* slavery, servitude, and forced labour in the same provision.[44]

Importantly, reading human trafficking into Article 4 ECHR as a stand-alone prohibition does not preclude invoking slavery, servitude, or forced labour in individual complaints against states, when exploitation has in fact materialised. Thus, when exploitation had already begun, victims may choose either to ground their complaint in the notions of slavery, servitude, or forced labour, or to rely on the prohibition of trafficking, depending on the circumstances of each case. There is no evidence that one option is better than the others in terms of succeeding before the Court.

The problem with reading human trafficking into Article 4 ECHR may nevertheless occur in situations when exploitation has manifested in one of the forms other than slavery, servitude, or forced labour. This raises a question of whether practices

---

[42] *Rantsev v Cyprus and Russia* (n 3) [286]; Inter-American Court of Human Rights, *Workers of the Hacienda Brasil Verde v Brazil*, Preliminary Objections, Merits, Reparations and Costs, Series C No 318 (20 October 2016) [323]–[324]. See also 54/91, 61/91, 98/93, 164/97, 196/97, and 210/98, *Malawi African Association and Others v Mauritania* 13th Annual Activity Report (1999–2000) [132]–[135].

[43] A detailed analysis of these conditions is conducted in Chapter 6.

[44] The Charter of Fundamental Rights of the European Union (18 December 2000) 2000/C 364/01, art 5 (EU Charter); the Arab Charter on Human Rights (adopted 22 May 2004, entered into force 15 March 2008), art 10 (Arab Charter); and the Association of Southeast Asian Nations (ASEAN) Human Rights Declaration (adopted 18 November 2012), para 13 (ASEAN Declaration).

of forced begging[45] or forced marriage[46] are prohibited by Article 4 ECHR, even though a victim has not been *trafficked into* these exploitative conditions? In other words, what is the relationship between 'other' exploitative practices listed in the Palermo Protocol's definition of human trafficking with slavery, servitude, or forced labour respectively and is there a threshold of severity that needs to be met to engage this human right? The following section clarifies this issue.

3.2.3 The Scope of Article 4 ECHR and the Range of Exploitative Practices Included

Article 4 ECHR does not define the three expressly prohibited practices—slavery, servitude, and forced or compulsory labour. Instead, in determining their meaning the Strasbourg Court refers to international instruments that specifically address them guided by the view that the Convention should 'so far as possible be interpreted in harmony with other rules of international law of which it forms part'.[47] In interpreting Article 4 ECHR with regard to the three expressly prohibited practices, the Court has thus relied on the 1926 Slavery Convention,[48] the Supplementary Convention on the Abolition of Slavery, the Slave Trade and Institutions and Practices Similar to Slavery,[49] and the International Labour Organization (ILO) Convention No 29 (Forced Labour Convention).[50] Hence, unsurprisingly, the Court has followed the same approach when reading human trafficking into this right relying on the UN Palermo Protocol and the Council of Europe Anti-Trafficking Convention to determine its meaning.[51]

The definition of human trafficking from the Palermo Protocol, mirrored in the Anti-Trafficking Convention, provides an open-ended list of exploitative purposes that include 'the exploitation of the prostitution of others or other forms of sexual exploitation', 'forced labour or services', 'slavery', or 'practices similar to slavery', and 'servitude' or 'the removal of organs'. The EU Anti-Trafficking Directive has expanded such an open-ended list by explicitly listing 'forced begging' and 'the exploitation of criminal activities' in order to 'keep abreast of the developing forms of trafficking'.[52] However, neither the Palermo Protocol nor the subsequent specialised anti-trafficking instruments define any of these diverse exploitative

---

[45] Anti-Slavery, 'Trafficking for Forced Criminal Activities and Begging in Europe: Exploratory Study and Good Practice Examples' (2014).
[46] UNODC, 'Interlinkages between Trafficking in Persons and Marriage' (Issue Paper 2020).
[47] ECtHR Guide on Article 4 of the Convention (n 24) paras 5–6.
[48] *Siliadin v France* (n 36) [122].
[49] *CN and V v France* (n 16) [90].
[50] *Van der Mussele v Belgium* (1983) 6 EHRR 163 [32].
[51] *Rantsev v Cyprus and Russia* (n 3) [282].
[52] UN High Commissioner for Refugees, 'Prevent, Combat, Protect Human Trafficking: Joint UN Commentary on the EU Directive: A Human Rights Based Approach' (November 2011) 104.

purposes. Instead, their definitions are scattered across a myriad of international instruments and further refined through the practice of international and domestic tribunals. Thus, a conclusive answer as to their meaning and mutual relationship requires a meticulous conceptual analysis of different international instruments and jurisprudence.[53] The central question for the discussion here is the relationship between slavery, servitude, and forced labour as expressly prohibited practices in Article 4 ECHR, on the one hand, and these other exploitative practices enumerated in the Palermo definition of human trafficking, on the other.

Slavery, servitude, and forced labour as express prohibitions under Article 4 ECHR

Slavery was defined in the 1926 Convention as 'the status or condition of a person over whom any or all of the powers attaching to the right of ownership are exercised'.[54] This traditional concept of slavery, often referred to as 'chattel slavery', is said to have evolved to encompass 'various contemporary forms of slavery which are also based on the exercise of any or all of the powers attaching to the right of ownership'.[55] However, Allain is critical of 'attempts ... to obfuscate the term "slavery" and to distance its legal definition from a definition that might instead be consonant with any type of exploitation'.[56] Thus, he argues that:

> Individuals interested in ending exploitation in the guise of forced, bonded, or indentured labor or sexual exploitation have muddied the waters of what slavery means and sought to intimate that slavery persisted beyond the 1926 Convention's definition, even where the 'powers attaching to the right of ownership' were not at issue.[57]

The Australian High Court similarly stressed that it is important not to 'banalise crimes against humanity' by giving slavery a meaning that extends beyond the limits set by the text, context, and purpose of the 1926 Slavery Convention and 'to recognise that harsh and exploitative conditions of labour do not of themselves amount to slavery'.[58] Slavery in other words is seen as a pinnacle of exploitation

---

[53] For a detailed analysis of concepts of slavery, servitude and forced labour see David Weissbrodt and Anti-Slavery International, Abolishing Slavery and its Contemporary Forms (UN OHCHR 2002); Jean Allain, 'Definition of Slavery in International Law' (2009) 52 Howard Law Journal 239; Jean Allain, 'R v Tang: Clarifying the Definition of "Slavery" in International Law' (2009) 10 Melbourne Journal of International Law 246; Jean Allain, 'On the Curious Disappearance of Human Servitude from General International Law' (2009) 11 Journal of the History of International Law 303; Andrea Nicholson, 'Reflections on Siliadin v. France: Slavery and Legal Definition' (2010) 14(5) The International Journal of Human Rights 705.

[54] The Slavery Convention (25 September 1926) 212 UNTS 17, art 1(1).

[55] *Prosecutor v Kunarac, Kovac and Vukovic*, Case Nos IT-96-23 and IT-96-23/1-A [2002] ICTY 2 (12 June 2002) [117]; *The Queen v Tang* [2008] HCA 39 (28 August 2008) M5/2008 [21].

[56] Allain, 'Definition of Slavery in International Law' (n 53) 242.

[57] ibid.

[58] *The Queen v Tang* (n 55) [32].

that ought to be reserved for the most severe practices. The existing jurisprudence suggests that such a high threshold has rarely been satisfied.

Thus, in the first case before the Inter-American Court of Human Rights to address this issue, the Court ruled that the situation to which the 85 workers rescued from a cattle farm in Brazil were subjected met 'the strictest criteria of the definition of slavery established by the Court ... in particular, the exercise of the powers attaching to the right of ownership'.[59] The Court specified the factors that led to such a finding:

> In this regard, the Court notes that: (i) the workers were subject to the control of the gatos, foremen, and armed guards of the hacienda and ultimately, of its owner; (ii) in a way that restricted their personal liberty and autonomy; (iii) without their free consent; (iv) by means of threats, and physical and psychological violence, (v) in order to exploit their forced labor in inhumane conditions. Furthermore, the circumstances of the escape undertaken by Antônio Francisco da Silva and Gonçalo Luiz Furtado and the risks they faced until they were able to report what had happened to the Federal Police reveal: (vi) the vulnerability of the workers, and (vii) the environment of coercion that existed in the hacienda, which (viii) did not allow the workers to change their situation and recover their liberty. Based on all the foregoing, the Court concludes that the situation verified in Hacienda Brasil Verde in March 2000 constituted a situation of slavery.[60]

The violation of the prohibition of slavery was also established by the High Court of Australia in the *Tang* case.[61] The trial court in that case found the defendant guilty of possessing and using slaves in relation to five women of Thai nationality who were used as sex workers in a brothel.[62] It established that the women were 'financially deprived and vulnerable upon arriving in Australia', having entered the country 'on visas that were obtained illegally' and their passports and return airfares were retained by the accused.[63] While they appear to have been 'well-provisioned, fed, and provided for' and 'were not kept under lock and key', the trial judge noted that they were 'effectively restricted to the premises'.[64] Deciding the case on appeal, the High Court of Australia confirmed the conviction and clarified the legal parameters of the notion of slavery for the purpose of *criminal law*. In the High Court's interpretation, 'powers attaching to the right of ownership' should be interpreted to include 'the capacity to make a person an object of purchase, the capacity to use a person and a person's labour in a substantially unrestricted manner,

---

[59] *Workers of the Hacienda Brasil Verde v Brazil* (n 42) [304].
[60] ibid.
[61] *The Queen v Tang* (n 55).
[62] ibid [14].
[63] ibid [15]–[16].
[64] ibid.

and an entitlement to the fruits of the person's labour without compensation commensurate to the value of the labour'.[65] The High Court found that:

> On the evidence it was open to the jury to conclude that each of the complainants was made an object of purchase (although in the case of one of them the purchaser was not the respondent); that, for the duration of the contracts, the owners had a capacity to use the complainants and the complainants' labour in a substantially unrestricted manner; and that the owners were entitled to the fruits of the complainants' labour without commensurate compensation.[66]

In *Kunarac*, the Trial Chamber of the International Tribunal for the Former Yugoslavia found the accused guilty of 'enslavement' as a crime against humanity.[67] The Trial Chamber noted that like slavery 'enslavement as a crime against humanity in customary international law consisted of the exercise of any or all of the powers attaching to the right of ownership over a person'.[68] It then identified factors to be taken into consideration in determining whether enslavement was committed to include: '[C]ontrol of movement, control of physical environment, psychological control, measures taken to prevent or deter escape, force, threat of force or coercion, duration, assertion of exclusivity, subjection to cruel treatment and abuse, control of sexuality and forced labour'.[69]

This somewhat more expansive interpretation is said to be largely due to the fact that the ICTY focused on interpreting the notion of 'enslavement' in international criminal law which, unlike international human rights law, does not make 'the normative distinction between slavery and other lesser servitudes'.[70] Accordingly, the ICTY clarified that 'this definition may be broader than the traditional and sometimes apparently distinct definitions of either slavery, the slave trade and servitude or forced or compulsory labour found in other areas of international law'.[71]

---

[65] ibid [26].
[66] ibid.
[67] *Prosecutor v Kunarac* (Trial Chamber) Case No IT-96-23-T & IT-96-23/1-T (22 February 2001).
[68] ibid [539].
[69] *Prosecutor v Kunarac* (Trial Chamber) (n 67) [543]. The Appeals Chamber largely agreed with these factors. *Prosecutor v Kunarac* (Appeals Chamber) Case No IT-96-23 & IT-96-23/1-A (12 June 2002) 35–36 [117]–[119]. This approach is followed by the Special Court for Sierra Leone in *Prosecutor v Charles Ghankay Taylor* (SCSL-03-1-T) Trial Chamber II, Special Court for Sierra Leone (26 April 2012) (Judgment); *The Prosecutor v Alex Tamba Brima, Brima Bazzy Kamara and Santigie Borbor Kanu* (the AFRC Accused), SCSL-04-16-T, Special Court for Sierra Leone (20 June 2007) (Judgment) [539]––[749].
[70] Allain, '*R v Tang*' (n 53). However, relying on the indicia of enslavement identified by the Trial Chamber in *Kunarac*, the ECOWAS Community Court of Justice ruled that Niger had not upheld its legal responsibility to protect the applicant from slavery under international law in *Hadijatou Mani Koraou v Republic of Niger*, Judgment No ECW/CCJ/JUD/06/08 of 27 October 2008, [72]–[89] (unofficial translation by INTERRIGHTS).
[71] *Prosecutor v Kunarac* (Trial Chamber) (n 67) [541].

While there might be good reasons to interpret the term slavery conservatively,[72] the Strasbourg Court has been criticised for its overly narrow approach which referred to slavery as 'a genuine right of legal ownership' over an individual in *Siliadin v France*—the first case where the Court considered positive obligations of states under Article 4 ECHR.[73] The Court was criticised for failing to distinguish between 'powers attaching to the right of ownership' as opposed to 'right of ownership',[74] the difference that captures slavery de jure and slavery de facto, both covered by the 1926 definition. Whether the Strasbourg Court genuinely holds this view about the notion of slavery, or its *Siliadin* ruling represents yet another example of unfortunate choice of wording is unclear, but the reality is that the Court has never found a violation of the prohibition of slavery.

In contrast, in addition to finding the violation of the prohibition of slavery in the *Hacienda Brasil Verde* case, the Inter-American Court of Human Rights (IACtHR) noted that 'the absolute prohibition of traditional slavery and its interpretation have evolved so that it also includes certain analogous forms of this phenomenon'.[75] The IACtHR thus considered that 'servitude is a practice analogous to slavery and should receive the same protection and involve the same obligations as traditional slavery'.[76]

Unlike slavery, servitude has not been expressly defined in any international instrument and has been given content through the pronouncements of bodies supervising human rights treaties.[77] According to Allain, servitude should be understood as human exploitation falling short of slavery. Similarly, the Strasbourg Court has seen servitude as 'a particularly serious form of denial of liberty',[78] which

---

[72] Suzanne Miers, *Slavery in the Twentieth Century: The Evolution of a Global Problem* (AltaMira Press 2003) 453 (arguing that very expansive notion of slavery renders the concept 'virtually meaningless'). But see AY Rassam, 'Contemporary Forms of Slavery and the Evolution of the Prohibition of Slavery and the Slave Trade under Customary International Law' (1999) 39 Virginia Journal of International Law 303, 309 (arguing that, 'although multilateral treaties on slavery: (1) historically circumscribe the definition of "slavery" to narrow circumstances where people involved in coercive labor practices do not possess, to some degree, a juridical personality under domestic law; and (2) distinguish the issue of sex trafficking and the resulting forced prostitution from other forms of slavery; international opinio juris of the term "slavery" has evolved under U.N. practice to include sex trafficking, forced prostitution, debt bondage, forced labor, and exploitation of immigrant domestic workers').

[73] *Siliadin v France* (n 36) [122].

[74] Allain, 'Definition of Slavery in International Law' (n 53) 261–62.

[75] *Workers of the Hacienda Brasil Verde v Brazil* (n 42) [276].

[76] ibid.

[77] Allain, 'On the Curious Disappearance of Human Servitude from General International Law' (n 53) 304. He argues that 'the "practices similar to slavery" are no different than "servitude" in their nature, but in law they have been divided, with the former forming part of general international law as manifest in the 1956 Supplementary Convention, the latter in international human rights law as "servitude" left undefined'. Similarly, during the negotiations of the Palermo Protocol, the United Nations High Commissioner for Human Rights commenting on one of the initial drafts noted that 'the term "servitude", when used in this context, should be understood to include practices that have been defined elsewhere as "contemporary forms of slavery", such as forced prostitution'. See Fourth session of the Ad Hoc Committee on the Elaboration of a Convention against Transnational Organized Crime Vienna (28 June–9 July 1999) Informal Note by the High Commissioner for Human Rights A/AC.254/16 (1 June 1999) [12].

[78] *Van Droogenbroeck v Belgium* (1982) 4 EHRR 443 [78]–[80].

means 'an obligation to provide one's services that is imposed by the use of coercion, and is to be linked with the concept of "slavery"'.[79] Moreover, the Strasbourg Court held that 'in addition to the obligation to perform certain services for others, the notion of servitude embraces the obligation for the "serf" to live on another person's property and the impossibility of altering his condition'.[80] Thus, it established that that servitude corresponds to a special type of forced or compulsory labour or, in other words, 'aggravated' forced or compulsory labour,[81] where the fundamental distinguishing feature between servitude and forced or compulsory labour lies in the victim's feeling that their condition is permanent and that the situation is unlikely to change. Consequently, the Strasbourg Court is said to have 'retained the classic distinction between slavery and forced labour, allowing the concept of servitude to fill any gap between the two'.[82] This way the Court seems to have created a hierarchy between the three explicitly prohibited practices.[83]

The lowest rung in such a hierarchy is reserved for forced labour, which is defined in Article 2(1) of ILO Convention No 29 of 1930 as 'all work or service which is exacted from any person under the menace of any penalty, against the will of the person concerned and for which the said person has not offered himself voluntarily'. The Strasbourg Court has taken this definition as a starting point for its interpretation of Article 4 ECHR.[84] The Court, thus, clarified that there has to be work 'exacted ... under the menace of any penalty' and also performed against the will of the person concerned, that is work for which the said person 'has not offered himself voluntarily'.[85] When it comes to the notion of 'penalty', the Court considered that it is used in the broad sense, as confirmed by the use of the term 'any penalty'. Thus, it noted that the 'penalty' may go as far as physical violence or restraint, but it can also take subtler forms, of a psychological nature, such as threats to denounce victims to the police or immigration authorities when their employment status is illegal.[86] As to the second criteria, in deciding whether the applicant offered herself voluntarily for the work in question, the Court took into account, but did not give a decisive weight to the element of the applicant's prior consent to the tasks required.[87] Rather, it is said that the Court would have regard to all the

---

[79] *Siliadin v France* (n 36) [124].

[80] *Van Droogenbroeck v Belgium* (n 78) [69]; *CN and V v France* (n 16) [90].

[81] *CN and V v France* (n 16) [91].

[82] Holly Cullen, '*Siliadin v France*: Positive Obligations under Article 4 of the European Convention on Human Rights' (2006) 6 Human Rights Law Review 585, 592.

[83] The Court of Appeal of England and Wales suggested that practices prohibited by art 4 ECHR represent 'a hierarchy of denial of personal autonomy' in *R v SK* [2011] EWCA Crim 1691 [24], [39]. See also Stoyanova (n 18) 181.

[84] *Graziani-Weiss v Austria* App no 31950/06 (ECtHR, 18 October 2011) [36]–[43]; *Stummer v Austria* [GC] (2012) 54 EHRR 11 [118].

[85] *Van der Mussele v Belgium* (n 50) [34].

[86] ECtHR Guide on Article 4 of the Convention (n 24) para 25. See also *CN and V v France* (n 16) [55]; ILO, 'The Cost of Coercion' International Labour Conference 98th Session (2009).

[87] *Van der Mussele v Belgium* (n 50) [36]; *Graziani-Weiss v Austria* (n 84) [40].

circumstances of the case in the light of the underlying objectives of Article 4 when deciding whether a service required to be performed falls within the prohibition of forced or compulsory labour.[88]

While the above outlined conceptual differentiation between practices expressly prohibited by Article 4 ECHR spelled out by the Strasbourg Court appears sound, the analysis of factual scenarios does not always support such neat delineations. For example, the applicant in *Siliadin* had been brought to France from Togo by a relative of her father and was subsequently made to work as a maid for some considerable time for fifteen hours a day, seven days a week. She had no personal resources, her papers had been confiscated, she was afraid of contacting the authorities because of her irregular immigration status, and was vulnerable and isolated. The Court considered that the applicant could not be said to be owned by the couple in the strict sense, but her lack of freedom and the requirement that she work such long hours on every day of the week meant that she had been held in servitude.

The subsequent case of *CN and V v France* concerned allegations of servitude and forced or compulsory labour by two sisters from Burundi who arrived in France to live with their uncle and aunt after their parents had been killed in the civil war.[89] They slept in the basement of the house and alleged that they were obliged to carry out all 'all the housework and domestic chores necessary for the upkeep of the house and the M family of nine' without remuneration or any days off.[90] They also complained that they lived in unhygienic conditions, were not allowed to share family meals, and were subjected to daily physical and verbal harassment. Distinguishing between the situations of the two sisters, the Strasbourg Court found that the older one had indeed been forced to work without having offered herself for it voluntarily. In addition, she is said to have been obliged to work 'so hard that without her aid Mr and Mrs M would have had to employ and pay a professional housemaid'.[91] However, the Court did not reach such a conclusion with regard to the younger sister, who was said not to have contributed 'in any excessive measure to the upkeep of Mr and Mrs M's household'.[92] Similarly, the Court found that the older sister was kept in servitude because of her belief that she could not escape from Mr and Mrs M's guardianship without finding herself in an illegal situation, her understanding that, without vocational training, she would be unable to find external employment, and the fact that this situation had lasted for four years. Yet, it ruled that this was not the case with respect to the younger sister because:

---

[88] ECtHR Guide on Article 4 of the Convention (n 24) para 29.
[89] *CN and V v France* (n 16).
[90] ibid [12].
[91] ibid [75].
[92] ibid.

Unlike her elder sister she attended school and her activities were not confined to Mr and Mrs M's home. She was able to learn French, as witnessed by her good marks at school. She was less isolated than her sister, which is why she was able to alert the school nurse to her situation. Lastly, she had time to do her homework when she got home from school.[93]

This distinction and the findings that the younger sister, who had been between ten and fourteen years old at the material time, was neither subject to servitude nor forced labour is entirely unconvincing. As she rightly pointed out, as a minor placed in the care of her aunt and uncle, she had had no choice but to live in their home, and no means of escape from the situation imposed on her. It is striking that the Court used the fact that she had done reasonably well at school as evidence that she had *not* been subject to exploitation, despite the fact that both sisters had been obliged to live and work without pay on another person's property. What is more, even though it was undisputed that the younger sister 'was the victim of ill-treatment by her aunt', the Court asserted that 'it has not been established that the said violence was directly linked to the alleged exploitation, that is, to the housework in question'.[94] In fact, the Court placed the burden of establishing sufficient proof that she contributed in excessive measure to the upkeep of Mr and Mrs M's household squarely on the victim.[95]

In the case concerning Bangladeshi migrants who worked on the strawberry farm in Greece without pay and in particularly harsh living and working conditions, the Court found a violation of the prohibition of forced labour but not servitude. Despite accepting that the workers 'laboured under extreme physical conditions and for exhaustingly long working hours and were subjected to constant humiliation',[96] that 'they were in a situation of vulnerability as irregular migrants without resources and at risk of being arrested, detained and deported',[97] and that 'the employer informed the workers that he would not pay them and that he would kill them if they did not continue to work for him',[98] the Court found that their situation could not be characterised as servitude. The Court based this finding on the assumption that the workers could not have had a feeling that their condition was 'permanent' and that the situation was 'unlikely to change' because 'they were all seasonal workers recruited to pick strawberries'.[99] This appears to suggest that, as long as exploiters keep exploiting individuals in a limited period of

---

[93] ibid [93].
[94] ibid [75].
[95] ibid.
[96] ibid [98].
[97] ibid [97].
[98] ibid [98].
[99] ibid [99].

time, they can reasonably expect to escape the accusations of slavery and servitude, regardless of the extreme nature of treatment imposed.

What transpires from this overview of the Strasbourg Court jurisprudence is that, even though the parameters of the three expressly prohibited practices appear reasonably clear, their application to the specific circumstances of each case is often haphazard and unprincipled.

Article 4 ECHR and 'other' types of exploitation listed in the Palermo definition of human trafficking

Beyond the practices expressly prohibited by Article 4 ECHR, it is unclear whether and how the remaining examples of exploitation from the Palermo definition engage this right on their own. In other words, are 'the exploitation of the prostitution of others or other forms of sexual exploitation', 'practices similar to slavery', 'the removal of organs', 'forced begging', or 'the exploitation of criminal activities' prohibited by Article 4 in and of themselves, or must they be interpreted as either slavery, servitude, or forced labour to trigger protections under this right?

The analysis so far has demonstrated that Article 4 is engaged in two situations. The first is when such 'other' exploitative practices form part of the human trafficking process because the risk of exploitation in trafficking situations is real, but it is, nonetheless, impossible to establish in advance what form it would take. As noted by the High Court of Australia in *The Queen v Tang*, 'those who engage in the traffic in human beings are unlikely to be so obliging as to arrange their practices to conform to some convenient taxonomy'.[100] Therefore, rather than waiting for exploitation to materialise to consider whether it would engage protections afforded by Article 4 (or any other human right), the risk of such exploitation embodied in the trafficking process requires immediate action. Secondly, Article 4 is engaged in situations of non-trafficked slavery, servitude, and forced labour as currently interpreted by the Court, however confusing this appears to be, as shown above.

When it comes to the remaining exploitative purposes *alone*, the situation is unclear. It could be argued that some of these practices represent manifestations of slavery, servitude, or forced labour, which means that they ought to meet the definitional criteria of the three expressly prohibited practices to trigger protections under *this* human right.[101] For instance, 'forced begging', which does not feature in the Palermo definition of human trafficking, but was added to the list of exploitative purposes by the EU Anti-Trafficking Directive, is classified in the latter as a type of forced labour or services.[102] Similar reasoning applies to 'exploitation

---

[100] *The Queen v Tang* (n 55) [29].
[101] There may well be other rights that are triggered alongside or alone, when the circumstances do not reach the level of severity required by art 4.
[102] Anti-Trafficking Directive, art 2(3). See also Iveta Cherneva, 'Human Trafficking for Begging' (2011) 17 Buffalo Human Rights Law Review 25.

of criminal activities' (also referred to as 'forced criminality' or 'criminal exploitation').[103] The practices of Vietnamese minors working in cannabis production in the UK support this view. Thus, research reveals that a significant number of 'minors and vulnerable young adults' from Vietnam have been deployed to cultivate cannabis in the UK, while confined within private houses or premises.[104] The exploiters are said to use them because such individuals 'are easy to manipulate and/or coerce, and they do not pay them'.[105] Instead of protection, they often face criminal prosecutions for their involvement in illegal cannabis production.[106] Such convictions are sometimes quashed by the courts which recognise that 'the decision to prosecute was flawed on the basis that the appellant was a victim of forced labour'.[107] The UK Independent Anti-Slavery Commissioner similarly emphasised that 'it is troubling that some Vietnamese individuals who go on to be recognised as victims of forced labour are still criminalised first'.[108]

Accordingly, 'forced begging' and 'criminal exploitation' would engage Article 4 ECHR if they satisfied *at minimum* the definitional criteria of forced labour identified above,[109] even though they may well meet the legal parameters of servitude or slavery too.

Furthermore, when it comes to 'practices similar to slavery', these are defined in the 1956 Supplementary Convention to include debt-bondage, serfdom, servile marriage, and child exploitation.[110] Allain argues persuasively that these practices represent, in fact, servitude.[111] According to him, the reason why states avoided

---

[103] RACE in Europe, 'Victim or Criminal? Trafficking for Forced Criminal Exploitation in Europe: UK Chapter' (2013); Anti-Slavery, 'Trafficking for Forced Criminal Activities and Begging in Europe: Exploratory Study and Good Practice Examples' (2014).

[104] Daniel Silverstone and Claire Brickell, 'Combating Modern Slavery Experienced by Vietnamese Nationals en Route to, and Within, the UK' Independent Anti-Slavery Commissioner (2017). See also A Kelly and M McNamara, '3,000 Children Enslaved in Britain after Being Trafficked into Britain' *The Guardian Online* (25 May 2015)http://www.theguardian.com/global-development/2015/may/23/vietnam-children-trafficking-nail-bar-cannabis (accessed 15 January 2021).

[105] Silverstone and Brickell (n 104) 45.

[106] Marija Jovanovic, 'The Principle of Non-Punishment of Victims of Trafficking in Human Beings: A Human Rights Obligation?' (2017) 1 Journal of Trafficking and Human Exploitation 41.

[107] *R v N; R v LE* (2012) EWCA Crim 189, para 89. See also *VCL and AN v United Kingdom* [2021] ECHR 132.

[108] Silverstone and Brickell (n 104) 49.

[109] *J and Others v Austria* (n 3) Concurring Opinion of Judge Pinto de Albuquerque [9] (noting that 'Forced labour thus includes forced prostitution, forced begging, forced criminal activity, forced use of a person in an armed conflict, ritual or ceremonial servitude, forced use of women as surrogate mothers, forced pregnancy and illicit conduct of biomedical research on a person').

[110] Supplementary Convention on the Abolition of Slavery, the Slave Trade, and Institutions and Practices Similar to Slavery (adopted 7 September 1956, entered into force 30 April 1957) 266 UNTS 3, art 1.

[111] Allain, 'On the Curious Disappearance of Human Servitude from General International Law' (n 53) 312. In analysing the drafting history of art 4 of the Universal Declaration of Human Rights and its impact on the negotiations of the 1956 Supplementary Convention on the Abolition of Slavery, the Slave Trade and Institutions and Practices Similar to Slavery, he points out that the latter instrument was originally drafted in 1954 as the Draft Supplementary Convention on Slavery and *Servitude*.

using the term 'servitude' in the 1956 Supplementary Convention, calling them 'institutions or practices similar to slavery' was because they:

> [w]ere unwilling to go as far as the 1948 Universal Declaration of Human Rights which stated that 'no one shall be held in servitude'. Instead, they wished to act 'progressively and as soon as possible' to abolish servitude. As a result, and so as not to be seen as back-tracking on their pledge that no one should be held in servitude, States avoided using the term 'servitude' in the 1956 Supplementary Convention, instead calling debt-bondage, serfdom, servile marriage and child exploitation 'institutions or practices similar to slavery'.[112]

On this view, a range of 'practices similar to slavery' would be assessed against the definitional criteria for servitude, as interpreted by the Court, in order to trigger protection Article 4 ECHR.[113]

When it comes to 'the exploitation of the prostitution of others or other forms of sexual exploitation', this exploitative practice has not been defined in any international instrument. The preamble to the recent Protocol to the 1930 Forced Labour Convention expressly recognised that sexual exploitation falls within trafficking in persons for the purposes of forced or compulsory labour,[114] which would imply that, for the purpose of human rights law, and Article 4 ECHR in particular, such practices should be evaluated against the definitional criteria of forced labour. This was confirmed in the recent decision of the Grand Chamber of the Strasbourg Court, which clarified that:

> [T]he notion of 'forced or compulsory labour' under Article 4 of the Convention aims to protect against instances of serious exploitation, such as forced prostitution, irrespective of whether, in the particular circumstances of a case, they are related to the specific human-trafficking context. Moreover, any such conduct may have elements qualifying it as 'servitude' or 'slavery' under Article 4, or may raise an issue under another provision of the Convention.[115]

It appears, finally, that 'organ removal' is the only exploitative purpose specifically mentioned in the Palermo definition,[116] which sits uneasily with either of the three

---

[112] ibid.
[113] It is of course possible that these practices would trigger other human rights or meet the definition of slavery or forced labour.
[114] The preamble to the Protocol of 2014 to the Forced Labour Convention 1930 (Geneva, 103rd ILC session, 11 June 2014) (entered into force 9 November 2016). See also ILO, *Forced Labour and Human Trafficking, Casebook of Court Decisions* (A Training Manual for Judges, Prosecutors and Legal Practitioners 2009) 9.
[115] *SM v Croatia* (n 16) [300].
[116] Notably, the first EU instrument on human trafficking, adopted two years after the Palermo Protocol excluded organ removal from its definition of trafficking. Council Framework Decision of 19

practices expressly prohibited by Article 4 ECHR. This view has been been spelled out in the recent UNODC study, which concludes that ' "[r]emoval of organs" is unique among the stipulated forms of exploitation in that unlike slavery, servitude, exploitation of prostitution and sexual exploitation, *it does not constitute a practice that may be considered inherently exploitative*'.[117] Instead, human trafficking for organ removal is to be considered as a subset of trafficking in human organs, which squares better with the notions of inhuman or degrading treatment rather than slavery.

Despite attempts to separate trafficking in persons for organ removal and trafficking in human organs,[118] it has been noted that the two crimes are difficult to distinguish in practice.[119] Hence, the European Parliament noted recently that: 'The term "trafficking in organs" groups together a whole range of illegal activities that aim to commercialise human organs and tissues for the purpose of transplantation. It *encompasses* the trafficking of persons with the intent to remove their organs.'[120] Similarly, the joint study by the Council of Europe and United Nations noted earlier that 'trafficking in human beings for the purpose of organ removal was a small part of the bigger problem of trafficking in [organs, tissues and cells]'.[121] The study nonetheless insists on distinguishing between the two phenomena but its explanation remains largely unpersuasive. Thus, it purports that in the case of trafficking in organs, 'the object of the crime is the organs', whereas in the case of human trafficking for organ removal, the object of the crime is 'the trafficked person'.[122] While such distinction might possibly be maintained in the context of criminal law, it becomes largely irrelevant in the human rights setting where the focus is on a victim—in both instances the organ donor.

July 2002 on combating trafficking in human beings (2002/629/JHA) [2002] OJ L203. The subsequent EU directive nonetheless does contain a reference to it.

[117] UNODC, 'The Concept of Exploitation in The Trafficking in Persons Protocol' (2015) 8 (emphasis added).

[118] Arthur Caplan and others, *Trafficking in Organs, Tissues and Cells and Trafficking in Human Beings for the Purpose of the Removal of Organs*, Joint Council of Europe/United Nations Study (2009) 11; Organization for Security and Co-operation in Europe (OSCE), *Trafficking in Human Beings for Purposes of Organ Removal in the OSCE Region: Analysis and Findings*, Occasional Paper Series No 6 (2013) 11–12.

[119] UNODC, *Assessment Toolkit: Trafficking in Persons for the Purpose of Organ Removal* (2015) 19. See also D Marty, *Inhuman Treatment of People and Illicit Trafficking in Human Organs in Kosovo*, Council of Europe Parliamentary Assembly, Committee on Legal Affairs and Human Rights (Draft Report), AS/Jur (2010) 46 (12 December 2010). Even though the latter addresses the issue of 'illicit trafficking in human organs', what it describes fits more into the definition of trafficking in people for organ removal. Thus, paragraphs 3 and 4 state that 'numerous concrete and convergent indications confirm' that people were 'held prisoner in secret places of detention in northern Albania, were subjected to inhuman and degrading treatment, before ultimately disappearing and that organs were removed from some of them to be taken abroad for transplantation'.

[120] European Parliament, Policy Department, Director General for External Policies, *Trafficking in Human Organs* (2015) 8 (emphasis added).

[121] Caplan and others (n 118) 11.

[122] ibid.

The adoption of the Council of Europe Convention against Trafficking in Human Organs[123]—the first international treaty addressing organ trafficking and providing its definition—further collapses the distinction between human trafficking for the purpose of organ removal and trafficking in organs. Article 4(1) of the new Convention requires States to criminalise 'the removal of human organs from living or deceased donors' when 'the removal is performed without the free, informed and specific consent of the living or deceased donor' or when 'in exchange for the removal of organs, the living donor, or a third party, has been offered or has received a financial gain or comparable advantage'. Moreover, Article 7(1) requires states to punish 'the solicitation and recruitment of an organ donor or a recipient, where carried out for financial gain or comparable advantage for the person soliciting or recruiting or for a third party'. On this basis, it is difficult to see how human trafficking for the purpose of organ removal is any different from the removal of organs by 'the solicitation and recruitment' of the donor and 'without [his] free, informed and specific consent'. This is because the tripartite definition of human trafficking recognises 'recruitment' as one of the 'acts' of human trafficking, and vitiated consent as one of the 'means' of human trafficking, with exploitation (in this case organ removal) being the third and final element.[124]

It is therefore questionable whether, in light of the newly adopted Convention against Trafficking in Human Organs, organ removal should still be seen as a form of exploitation. Instead, it could be argued that even though *tactics* (*means*) used to subject people to illicit removal of organs may well be the same as in the cases of trafficking for other purposes, *conceptually* the former represents a distinctive practice that fits better with the notion of inhuman or degrading treatment rather than exploitation. Thus, widely reported practices of forced organ harvesting from non-consenting prisoners of conscience in the People's Republic of China[125] are deemed a violation of the freedom from torture and other cruel, inhuman, or degrading treatment or punishment.[126] Furthermore, in his report on Inhuman Treatment of People and Illicit Trafficking in Human Organs in Kosovo, Dick Marty refers to 'allegations of inhuman treatment, including those relating to possible organ trafficking', making a direct link between the two.[127]

In sum, based on the premises that human trafficking for the purpose of organ removal is a subset of trafficking in human organs, and that illicit organ removal and trafficking amount to inhumane or degrading treatment, it is questionable

---

[123] Council of Europe Convention against Trafficking in Human Organs (2014) CETS 2016.
[124] Palermo Protocol, art 3.
[125] Independent Tribunal into Forced Organ Harvesting from Prisoners of Conscience in China, Final Judgment and Summary Report 2019 (17 June 2019).
[126] NW Paul and others, 'Human Rights Violations in Organ Procurement Practice in China' (2017) 18(11) BMC Medical Ethics 1, 7.
[127] Marty (n 119) para 12.

whether organ removal as a purpose of human trafficking should be examined within the purview of Article 4 ECHR.

In light of the forgoing analysis, it is plausible to conclude that the scope of Article 4 ECHR is determined by the reference to either one of the three explicitly prohibited practices, or to human trafficking, as a process leading to exploitation. However, it remains unclear why, if all exploitative practices were to be qualified as slavery, servitude, or forced labour, the Palermo definition did not use only these terms. An answer to this question lies in the fact that the definition (developed for the purpose of transnational criminal law) does not distinguish between examples of exploitative practices that form part of a *criminal offence*, on the one hand, and their legal reflections in *human rights law*, on the other. Accordingly, examples of exploitative practices such as forced begging or forced criminality considered alone need to satisfy the definitional criteria of slavery, servitude, or forced labour (which they usually would) to trigger protection guaranteed by Article 4 ECHR. If, however, these practices are part of the trafficking process, but have not yet materialised, this situation too would engage Article 4 because of the real and immediate risk of serious exploitation. Certainly, states are entitled to create different *criminal offences* to ensure that the prohibitions required by Article 4 are effectively enforced in domestic law. What is more, the principle of legality enshrined in Article 7 ECHR requires crimes to be clearly defined.[128] As noted in Chapter 2, the issue with human trafficking and exploitative practices is that scholars, policymakers, and activists often do not recognise their dual legal nature as crimes as well as human rights violations.

3.3 The Notion of 'Modern Slavery' in Human Rights Law

Despite not being expressly prohibited by the majority of general human rights instruments, human trafficking does potentially engage a number of rights. Nonetheless, the chapter has explored the approach of the ECtHR, which established that *conceptually* human trafficking violates the prohibition of slavery, servitude, and forced labour due to their common nature and aim of exploitation—the notion that will be analysed in detail in Chapter 4. And while human trafficking is complete before such exploitation has materialised, slavery, servitude, and forced labour represent actual manifestations of exploitation. This *key distinction* between trafficking as a *process* leading to exploitative conditions, and slavery, servitude, and forced labour as exploitative *conditions* alone justifies the inclusion of human

---

[128] The UNODC Model Law against Trafficking in Persons (2009) 28 explains that under the Protocol, '[t]he definition of exploitation covers the forms of exploitation that, according to the Protocol, shall be included "at a minimum" ... The principle of legality, however, requires crimes to be clearly defined. Additional forms of exploitation will have to be spelled out in the law ... States may consider including also other forms of exploitation in their criminal law. In that case these should be well defined'.

trafficking within the scope of this fundamental right as a stand-alone prohibition. This is because rights that protect against the most severe violations of individual autonomy such as the right to life, freedom from torture, and the prohibition of slavery (often referred to as 'absolute' rights) warrant pre-emptive action of states to prevent such violations. Human trafficking epitomises the imminent threat of exploitation, thus triggering state obligations to protect individual victims. The chapter finally clarifies that exploitative practices included in the Palermo definition, such as forced criminality or forced begging, need to satisfy the definitional criteria of slavery, servitude, or forced labour to trigger the protection offered by Article 4 ECHR.

The discussion so far has focused on establishing the right not to be trafficked as an independent prohibition within the right to be free from slavery, servitude, and forced labour. After addressing the notion of exploitation that underpins all practices included within this right in Chapter 4, the analysis in the second part of the book considers state obligations and criteria of responsibility for violations of this right *as a whole*—and not just the right not to be trafficked. Being duly aware of the controversy surrounding the term 'modern slavery',[129] which is not the legal term per se, the book nonetheless deploys it as an umbrella term for the practices of human trafficking, slavery, servitude, and forced or compulsory labour included in this right.[130]

---

[129] Jean Allain, *Slavery in International Law: Of Human Exploitation and Trafficking* (Martinus Nijhoff Publishers 2013) 272–89; JA Chuang, 'Exploitation Creep and the Unmaking of Human Trafficking Law' (2014) 108 The American Journal of International Law 609; JA Chuang, 'The Challenges and Perils of Reframing Trafficking as "Modern-Day Slavery"' (2015) 5 Anti-Trafficking Review 146; Mike Dottridge, 'Trafficked and Exploited: The Urgent Need for Coherence in International Law' in Prabha Kotiswaran, *Revisiting the Law and Governance of Trafficking, Forced Labour and Modern Slavery* (CUP 2017) 76–77. But see Rassam (n 72) 320 (arguing that 'While not meeting all of the criteria of the classical definition of slavery, the practices of sex trafficking, forced prostitution, debt bondage, forced labor, and exploitation of immigrant domestic workers do share similar elements that deem them obvious candidates for inclusion in the term "modern forms of slavery"').

[130] In the same vein, according to the UK Modern Slavery Act 2015, ss 1 and 2, 'modern slavery' encompasses the offences of human trafficking, slavery, servitude, and forced or compulsory labour. Practices that constitute 'modern slavery' under the Australian Modern Slavery Act 2018, No 153, 2018 include: human trafficking, slavery, servitude, forced labour, debt bondage, forced marriage, and the worst forms of child labour. Notably, both acts consider *criminal offences* and, as explained in Chapter 1, their interpretation and application will differ from the assessment conducted within the auspices of international human rights law.

4
The Notion of Exploitation: Theoretical Foundations of the Human Rights Prohibition of 'Modern Slavery'

The notion of exploitation is central for an understanding of the practices prohibited by Article 4 ECHR and the general human rights prohibiton against slavery.[1] It is said to be 'a large tent'[2] and 'the overarching theme that subsumes all forms of human trafficking, slavery, forced labour, bonded labour, child labour, forced prostitution, economic exploitation, and so on'.[3] However, it has never been defined in international law. The chapter[4] thus represents a pioneering effort in articulating and interpreting the legal parameters of the notion of exploitation for the purposes of human rights law, and the prohibition of slavery, servitude, forced labour, and human trafficking specifically.[5] This analysis contributes to a better

---

[1] Human rights instruments differ in how they define this right. Article 4 of the Universal Declaration of Human Rights 1948, GA Res 217 A(III), A/810 at 71 prohibits only slavery, servitude, and slave trade but not forced labour. Like art 4 ECHR, art 8 of the International Covenant on Civil and Political Rights 1966, 999 UNTS 171 and art 6 of the American Convention on Human Rights 1969, 1144 UNTS 123 prohibit slavery, servitude, and forced labour (the American Convention also prohibits slave trade and traffic in women). Article 5 of the African Charter of Human and Peoples' Rights 1981, 1520 UNTS 217 prohibits 'all forms of exploitation and degradation of man' and lists explicitly slavery and slave trade alongside torture, cruel, inhuman, or degrading punishment and treatment. The newer human rights instruments, including art 5 of the Charter of Fundamental Rights of the European Union 2000, 2000/C 364/01 (the EU Charter), art 10 of the Arab Charter on Human Rights 2004, 12 IHRR 893 (the Arab Charter), and para 13 of the Association of Southeast Asian Nations (ASEAN) Human Rights Declaration 2012 (the ASEAN Declaration), explicitly prohibit human trafficking alongside slavery servitude and forced labour (the ASEAN Declaration does not mention forced labour but it includes human smuggling).

[2] Jean Allain, *Slavery in International Law: Of Human Exploitation and Trafficking* (Brill 2013) 369.

[3] Johannes Koettl, *Human Trafficking, Modern Day Slavery, and Economic Exploitation* The World Bank Social Protection and Labor Policy and Technical Notes 49802 (2009) 4. See also Roger Plant, *Modern Slavery: The Concepts and Their Practical Implications* International Labour Organization (5 February 2015) 3; Working Group on Trafficking in Persons, *Key Concepts of the Trafficking in Persons Protocol, with a Focus on the United Nations Office on Drugs and Crime Issue Papers on Abuse of a Position of Vulnerability, Consent and Exploitation*, Conference of the Parties to the United Nations Convention against Transnational Organized Crime, CTOC/COP/WG.4/2015/4 (25 August 2015) para 20.

[4] The chapter has been previously published as an article: Marija Jovanovic, 'The Essence of Slavery: Exploitation in Human Rights Law' (2020) 20(4) Human Rights Law Review 674.

[5] Virginia Mantouvalou, 'Legal Construction of Structures of Exploitation' in Hugh Collins, Gillian Lester, and Virginia Mantouvalou (eds), *Philosophical Foundations of Labour Law* (OUP 2018) 189–90. Mantouvalou's discussion of exploitation is different in two major respects. First, it is primarily concerned with 'structural accounts of exploitation' rather than interpersonal relations, which is the main focus of this chapter. Secondly, she focuses on exploitation in the context of labour relations and workers' rights, a conception which is both broader and narrower than exploitation that underpins

understanding and interpretation of this under-theorised and under-adjudicated right. Exploitation is shown to be a distinct wrong, which binds together a range of practices that this right protects against.

The need for articulating the legal parameters of exploitation in human rights law has become pressing with an increased international engagement with human trafficking following the adoption of the Palermo Protocol, which provided its universal definition discussed previously in Chapter 2. Exploitation is an essential part of this definition and represents the sole purpose of a trafficking act. But neither the Palermo Protocol nor any other international instrument explain the meaning of exploitation. Instead, the Palermo definition contains an open-ended list of exploitative practices without specifying criteria for deciding which other practices may qualify. Chapter 3 showed that human trafficking, as defined by the Palermo Protocol, was then brought within the scope of the right to be free from slavery, servitude, and forced labour through the teleological interpretation of this right by the Strasbourg Court.[6] The same view is reflected in the human rights instruments adopted after the Palermo Protocol, which expressly list human trafficking alongside practices of slavery, servitude, and forced labour, such as the EU Charter of Fundamental Rights,[7] the Arab Charter,[8] and the ASEAN Declaration.[9] But the open-ended nature of the defintion of human trafficking with regard to the exploitative practices included in its scope has obfuscated the boundaries of this right because it is unclear which practices reach the definitional threshold of exploitation.[10] The need for specifying the parameters of exploitation in this context is thus evident and pressing.

The present analysis of the concept of exploitation is grounded in international legal instruments and jurisprudence, and in the literature on moral philosophy. These sources are consulted in order to distil the necessary and sufficient conditions[11] for a practice to qualify as exploitation of a sufficient gravity to engage

---

practices of 'modern slavery'. Accordingly, her conception does not take into account, for example, exploitation in the context of trafficking for forced begging or for criminal activities while at the same time includes a broader spectrum of conducts that go well beyond the instances of 'modern slavery'. See also Jean Allain, 'Conceptualizing the Exploitation of Human Trafficking' in Bryson Clark and Sasha Poucki (eds), *The SAGE Handbook on Human Trafficking and Modern Day Slavery* (SAGE Publications 2018) 3.

[6] *Rantsev v Cyprus and Russia* (2010) 51 EHRR 1.
[7] Charter of Fundamental Rights of the European Union (18 December 2000) 2000/C 364/01, art 5 (EU Charter).
[8] Arab Charter on Human Rights (adopted 22 May 2004, entered into force 15 March 2008), art 10 (Arab Charter).
[9] Association of Southeast Asian Nations (ASEAN) Human Rights Declaration (adopted 18 November 2012), para 13 (ASEAN Declaration).
[10] Jean Allain, '*Rantsev v Cyprus and Russia*: The European Court of Human Rights and Trafficking as Slavery' (2010) 10 Human Rights Law Review 546; Vladislava Stoyanova, 'Dancing on the Borders of Article 4: Human Trafficking and the European Court of Human Rights in the Rantsev Case' (2012) 30 Netherlands Quarterly of Human Rights 163.
[11] The construction 'necessary and sufficient conditions' is commonly used in the traditional conceptual analysis in legal philosophy. See Kenneth Einar Himma, 'Reconsidering a Dogma: Conceptual Analysis, the Naturalistic Turn, and Legal Philosophy' in Michael Freeman and Ross Harrison (eds),

the right to be free from slavery, servitude and forced or compulsory labour. The chapter thus articulates such necessary and sufficient conditions in the context of *this* right,[12] arguing that these conditions distinguish exploitation from other wrongs, such as abuse, fraud, or extortion.

This study has both a practical and theoretical value. Setting the parameters of exploitation helps determine which practices meet the criteria of the open-ended list of exploitative purposes within the definition of human trafficking, as a distinct prohibition under the right to be free from slavery, servitude and forced or compulsory labour. This contributes to the legal certainty while leaving enough room for a further refinement of the concept in domestic jurisprudence. Beyond such a practical value, the analysis of the concept of exploitation represent one of the pioneering attempts at elucidating the very core of the prohibition of slavery, servitude, forced or compulsory labour, and human trafficking in human rights law.

The following section describes the insufficient engagement with the notion of exploitation in international law, focusing specifically on the legal frameworks developed to address human trafficking and the prohibition of slavery, servitude and forced or compulsory labour. The subsequent discussion of moral philosophy literature provides guidance as to the possible common elements of the general concept of exploitation, while the last section elaborates on such elements in the context of the human rights prohibition of modern slavery.

4.1 The Insufficient Engagement with the Notion of Exploitation and International Law

Susan Marks rightly wonders:

> When activists invoke international law to challenge exploitation, when lawyers advise on rights and duties regarding exploitation under international law, and

---

Law and Philosophy (OUP 2007) 6 (noting that traditional conceptual analysis 'seeks to identify the content of the sense of the relevant word—eg the meaning of "law"; and it does this by identifying properties that distinguish things that fall under the relevant concept from things that do not. These properties are usually thought expressible in the form of necessary and sufficient conditions for applying the concept'); Andrew Brennan, 'Necessary and Sufficient Conditions' in Edward N Zalta (ed), *The Stanford Encyclopedia of Philosophy* (Summer 2017 Edition) https://plato.stanford.edu/archives/sum2017/entries/necessary-sufficient/ (accessed 24 March 2020) (pointing out that '[a] handy tool in the search for precise definitions is the specification of necessary and/or sufficient conditions for the application of a term, the use of a concept, or the occurrence of some phenomenon or event'). See also Matthew Kramer, *Where Law and Morality Meet* (OUP 2008) (especially ch 3: 'On Morality as a Necessary or Sufficient Condition for Legality'); HLA Hart, *The Concept of Law* (2nd edn, OUP 1994) 116.

[12] Notably, the chapter does not purport to provide a general account of exploitation beyond these most severe forms of exploitation, even though it accepts that these forms are not the only types of exploitation that need to be addressed, as argued by Mantouvalou (n 5) 192.

when academics discuss the theme of exploitation in international legal writing, what is it that they have in mind?[13]

She observes that international legal instruments refer to exploitation in both the 'positive or neutral sense' and in a 'pejorative sense', to name a problem and to secure the redress of something considered bad.[14] Those positive or neutral references concern exploitation of a thing whereas negative examples usually refer to exploitation of human beings.[15] In the latter sense, Marks notices that exploitation features most prominently in international legal provisions concerning children,[16] instruments associated with human trafficking,[17] and in the work of International Labour Organization (ILO) focused on preventing the exploitation of different categories of vulnerable workers (indigenous people,[18] people with disabilities,[19] or migrants[20]). Lastly, she observes that '[a] final category of international norms and standards which is widely understood to touch on issues of exploitation, even if... the term is not actually used, has to do with slavery, forced labour and pay and conditions at work'.[21]

These diverse references to exploitation in international law, however, fail to supply any meaning of the concept as such, prompting a conclusion that a new kind of engagement with the problem of exploitation needs to be developed in international law.[22]

The focus here is exploitation in the context of the human rights prohibition of slavery, servitude, forced or compulsory labour, and human trafficking. The following subsections first explore the conceptualisation of exploitation in human trafficking instruments and subsequently examines its relationship with the prohibition of slavery, servitude, and forced or compulsory labour in human rights instruments and jurisprudence.

---

[13] Susan Marks, 'Exploitation as an International Legal Concept' in Susan Marks (ed), *International Law on the Left: Re-examining Marxist Legacies* (CUP 2008) 293.
[14] See also Judy Pearsall and Bill Trumble (eds), *Oxford English Reference Dictionary* (2nd edn, OUP 1996).
[15] Allain (n 2) 2.
[16] Convention on the Rights of the Child 1989, 1577 UNTS 3 (CRC), art 19(1); Optional Protocol to the Convention on the Rights of the Child on the Sale of Children, Child Prostitution and Child Pornography 2000, 2171 UNTS 227, art 3(1).
[17] Convention for the Suppression of the Traffic in Persons and of the Exploitation of the Prostitution of Others 1950, 96 UNTS 271, art 1; Palermo Protocol, art 3; Convention on Action against Trafficking in Human Beings 2005, CETS 197, art 4 (Anti-Trafficking Convention).
[18] ILO, Indigenous and Tribal Populations Recommendation, R104 (1957) para 36(g).
[19] ILO, Vocational Rehabilitation and Employment (Disabled Persons) Recommendation, R168 (1983) para 11(m).
[20] ILO, Employment Policy (Supplementary Provisions) Recommendation, R169 (1984) para 43(b); International Convention on the Protection of the Rights of All Migrant Workers and Members of their Families 1990, 2220 UNTS 3.
[21] Marks (n 13) 298.
[22] ibid 299.

4.1.1 Exploitation and Human Trafficking Instruments

While the Palermo Protocol's definition of human trafficking identifies exploitation of another human being as the sole purpose of a trafficking act, instead of defining it, it provdes a non-exhaustive list of *examples* of exploitative practices. However, what something refers to is distinct from what it means.[23] Wolff explains this pertinently:

> To give a complete explanation of how a term is to be used is to fix the reference: it is to give an infallible way of picking out that object or those objects to which the term refers. In itself doing this may convey little understanding, or only partial understanding. Another task is to give, or we might better say explain, the meaning of the term.[24]

The Palermo Protocol's reference to exploitation fails to deliver on both accounts. Not only does it fail to offer any insight into the nature and meaning of exploitation itself, but it also fails to provide a 'reference-fixing' definition as 'a way of picking out all and only cases of where exploitation takes place'.[25] In other words, the open-ended list of exploitative practices does not provide an obvious way of selecting other acts that may be classified as such in future. According to the interpretative notes of the negotiation of the Palermo Protocol, this concern was raised during negotiations by one (unnamed) delegation, which 'felt that any definition of exploitation needed careful examination and restriction', whereas another delegation 'expressed its concern that a definition might end up being too broad, which in turn might hamper the implementation of the protocol'.[26] However, these concerns were not given further consideration during negotiations and the final definition of human trafficking remained open-ended. Accordingly, Heide Uhl is right to conclude that in the absence of a definition of the term 'exploitation' in international law the Palermo definition of trafficking 'lacks terminological clarity'.[27]

Allain, by contrast, argues that this taxonomical account of exploitation is sufficient and that any attempts to uncover the meaning of the concept itself is not necessary.[28] He purports that:

---

[23] Saul Kripke, *Naming and Necessity* (Harvard UP 1980) 53–59 (emphasising a difference between how a word is to be used and how it is to be understood).
[24] Jonathan Wolff, 'Marx and Exploitation' (1999) 3 The Journal of Ethics 105, 108.
[25] ibid 118.
[26] UNODC, *Travaux préparatoires of the Negotiations for the Elaboration of the United Nations Convention against Transnational Organized Crime and the Protocols Thereto* (2006) 352.
[27] Bärbel Heide Uhl, 'Lost in Implementation? Human Rights Rhetoric and Violations: A Critical Review of Current European Anti-trafficking Policies' (2010) 2 Security and Human Rights 119, 125.
[28] Allain (n 2) 350.

It would be a mistake to attempt to deduce common characteristics from these various activities and to then seek to establish in law what might be considered exploitation. The manner in which the provision is laid out is not definitional but categorical ... exploitation should, in the legal context of the definition of trafficking in persons, be understood as the sum of its parts.[29]

This view nonetheless would only hold if the Palermo definition provided a *definite* list of exploitative practices. In the circumstances where such a list is left open-ended and the meaning of exploitation is left undefined, it is virtually impossible to predict what other practices are deemed exploitative without allowing for a high degree of arbitrariness.[30]

The Working Group on Trafficking in Persons rightly emphasised the importance of clearly defining 'either the term exploitation or individual forms of exploitation in order to ensure uniformity of interpretation'.[31] The United Nations Office on Drugs and Crime (UNODC) has subsequently published a study on the concept of exploitation in the Palermo Protocol.[32] The study represents the third in a series of studies aimed at addressing 'the risk that important concepts contained in the [Palermo] Protocol are not clearly understood and, therefore, are not consistently implemented and applied'.[33] It includes an overview and analysis of the international legal and policy framework around exploitation with a particular focus on the Palermo Protocol, a survey of national law and practice of states representing different regions and legal traditions, and a guidance on policy and practice for further consideration. The study first noted that the concept of exploitation, as it appears in the Palermo Protocol, did not arise in a vacuum with a range of disciplines—from law to philosophy, from economics to politics—having long been occupied with examining and seeking to establish what it means, or should

---

[29] ibid. However, in his recent publication, Allain changed his position, arguing that 'the time is ripe to move away from an understanding of exploitation based on various types ... and to start thinking of exploitation as a concept'. See Allain (n 5) 3.

[30] In his insightful analysis of the human rights prohibition of 'inhuman and degrading treatment', Jeremy Waldron criticises the recent practice of the Strasbourg Court of creating precedents to supply these terms with the meaning. He points out that '[n]either judges nor scholars spend much time reflecting on the meaning of the predicates that are incorporated in the Article 3 standard—"inhuman" and "degrading"—and explaining how the Court is guided by their meanings in generating its principles, presumptions and benchmarks. The Court simply announces its finding that certain practices are inhuman or degrading while others are not'. Waldron argues that such an approach is not helpful when a court is confronted with an unprecedented practice alleged to be inhuman or degrading: 'How should a court approach the task of establishing a new precedent in this area? How should counsel in such a case frame their arguments? Should they proceed by a process of analogy with the list of practices already condemned as violations of the standard? Or should they go back to the original standard and reflect on the fundamentals of its application to this new set of circumstances?' He strongly advocates for the latter. See Jeremy Waldron, 'The Coxford Lecture Inhuman and Degrading Treatment: The Words Themselves' (2010) 23 Canadian Journal of Law & Jurisprudence 269, 273–74.

[31] Working Group on Trafficking in Persons (n 3) para 23.

[32] UNODC, *The Concept of Exploitation in the Trafficking in Persons Protocol* Issue Paper (2015).

[33] ibid 6.

mean. However, it observes that 'this has not resulted in agreement and the concept remains ambiguous'.[34]

Despite its promising title, the UNODC study is overly focused on explaining the *examples* of exploitation, at the expense of elucidating the elements of the *concept* itself, for which, according to the study, 'there was no apparent appetite' to be defined during the negotiations of the Palermo Protocol. Instead, the study claims that 'the forms of exploitation listed in the Trafficking in Persons Protocol are an integral part of its substantive content'.[35] Consequently, it is claimed that the substance and scope of these forms of exploitation, taken together, ought to provide the minimum parameters of the notion of exploitation. While this is an interesting proposal, the study does not proceed to distil such parameters that characterise all the examples of exploitation it had meticulously described. Thus, the only reference to the meaning of the concept itself states that exploitation, as it relates to trafficking, 'appears to be broadly consistent with its general meaning of one person taking unfair advantage of another person, their vulnerability or their situation'.[36] Furthermore, while the UNODC study notes that member states were concerned 'to not unduly narrow the exploitative purpose of trafficking' by providing a non-exhaustive list of exploitative purposes, it acknowledged that there are limits in terms of the potential for expansion. These limits 'may potentially include a *threshold of seriousness* that operates to prevent the expansion of the concept of trafficking to less serious forms of exploitation such as labour law infractions'.[37] However, the study concludes that the Palermo Protocol does not clearly establish any such threshold. Similarly, Gallagher argues that 'most activists and scholars appear to accept the validity of some kind of a "seriousness" threshold',[38] but does not provide any reference to support her claim. Thus, in the absence of the severity threshold, the open-ended list of exploitative practices from the Palermo definition does not provide any guidance for defining the concept itself.

Therefore, one of the 'key findings' of the study is '[t]he absence of clear definitions in the law (both of exploitation and of stipulated forms of exploitation) ... providing individuals with a measure of interpretative discretion that can lead to inconsistency'.[39] While the study is useful in elucidating these problems, it does very little to offer specific guidance as to how the concept ought to be framed in international law and national legislation. Rather, it questions whether there could be a universal understanding of what constitutes exploitation for purposes of trafficking and whether it would be possible to provide guidance that could be

---

[34] ibid 21.
[35] ibid 27.
[36] ibid 39.
[37] ibid 8 (emphasis added).
[38] Anne Gallagher, *The International Law of Human Trafficking* (CUP 2010) 49.
[39] ibid 11.

useful for all states and national contexts in the light of substantial differences between states.[40]

However, it may well be argued that such universal guidance needs not establish definite and uniform *rules* for deciding when a situation would constitute exploitation. Instead, it could identify the necessary and sufficient conditions for the use of the concept that would serve as a frame of reference to be further specified on a national level. Thus, whereas international law and human rights law, in particular, are well-placed to articulate such necessary and sufficient conditions in order to provide the universal parameters of the concept of exploitation, it is for national legislatures and judiciaries to give them a specific expression in a domestic context.

4.1.2 Exploitation and the Human Rights Prohibition of 'Modern Slavery'

Previous chapters explored the relationship between the regime created to address human trafficking and the general human rights law and explained the hybrid legal nature of human trafficking, which represents both a criminal offence and a human rights violations. While the Strasbourg Court was the first international tribunal to expressly recognise the link between human trafficking and the prohibition of slavery and forced labour, specifying that the former was prohibited under the this right *in and of itself*,[41] the Court has not yet explained the *meaning* of exploitation, which binds together human trafficking and expressly prohibited practices.[42]

The critics argued that by absorbing the definition of human trafficking the right to be free from slavery 'the material scope of article is enlarged to cover any exploitation'.[43] A concern about the potential expansion of the material scope of Article 4 has proven well founded. Thus, in the most recent case of *SM v Croatia*, the Strasbourg Court extended the scope of Article 4 beyond human trafficking (and the express prohibition of slavery, servitude and forced labour) by adding 'exploitation of prostitution' as a self-standing prohibition within this right.[44] This is

---

[40] See also Allain (n 2) 369.
[41] *Rantsev v Cyprus and Russia* (n 6) [282]; *SM v Croatia*, App no 60561/14 (ECtHR GC, 25 June 2020) [56].
[42] Beyond the ECtHR, which emphasised exploitation as *raison d'être* for including human trafficking within the scope of the prohibition of slavery, servitude and forced or compulsory labour, but failed to elaborate on its meaning, the limited jurisprudence of other regional human rights bodies has avoided addressing this challenge. The jurisprudence of other international tribunals concerning the prohibition of slavery in general is extremely limited. For a good overview of such case law see Helen Duffy, 'Litigating Modern Slavery in Regional Courts: A Nascent Contribution' (2016) 14 Journal of International Criminal Justice 375.
[43] Vladislava Stoyanova, *Human Trafficking and Slavery Reconsidered: Conceptual Limits and States' Positive Obligations in European Law* (CUP 2017) 301. See also James Hathaway, 'The Human Rights Quagmire of "Human Trafficking"' (2008) 49 Virginia Journal of International Law 1 (criticising the inclusion of human trafficking within the human rights framework).
[44] *SM v Croatia* (n 41) [54].

criticised by the dissenting judge Koskelo as a 'significant and obscure' enlargement of Article 4, which is introduced 'without any real analysis, without proper discussion or explanation, and without clarity or openness'.[45]

It is thus clear that the notion of exploitation, which underpins practices prohibited (expressly or implicitly) by Article 4 ECHR has a key role in defining the boundaries of this right. Yet, as observed by Judge De Albuquerque in *J and Others*, 'exploitation itself is not defined in law',[46] resulting in a failure of the international jurisprudence to explain the *fundamental wrong* underpinning this absolute human right. In such circumstances, articulating and explaining the legal parameters of exploitation would significantly strengthen the interpretation of this right and the following sections offer important guidance in that respect.

4.2 Exploitation in Moral Philosophy

The lack of engagement with the notion of exploitation in international human rights law justifies turning to the philosophical debates, which seek to elucidate its meaning. These philosophical discussions provide a groundwork for articulating the necessary and sufficient conditions for the concept of exploitation in the context of the prohibition of slavery, servitude, forced or compulsory labour, and human trafficking.

4.2.1 Moralised and Non-moralised Exploitation

In everyday discourse, it is frequently claimed that some act, practice, or transaction is exploitative and the concept of exploitation is typically invoked without much analysis or argument, 'as if its meaning and moral force were self-evident'.[47] Yet, the term itself does not necessarily carry a negative connotation. Thus, exploitation may refer to 'the action of extracting or harvesting natural resources from a place'[48] and it may also mean 'taking advantage of something or someone in an unfair or unethical manner'.[49]

Wood has blamed philosophers who reflect on the concept of exploitation for providing a 'moralised' account of exploitation because they tend to follow the practice of dictionaries, distinguishing a 'non-moral' sense of exploitation from a

---

[45] ibid, Dissenting Opinion of Judge Koskelo [18] and [21].
[46] *J and Others v Austria* [2017] ECHR 37, Concurring Opinion of Judge Pinto de Albuquerque [43].
[47] Matt Zwolinski and Alan Wertheimer, 'Exploitation' in Edward Zalta (ed), *The Stanford Encyclopedia of Philosophy* (Summer 2015 Edition) http://plato.stanford.edu/archives/sum2015/entries/exploitation/ (accessed 24 March 2020).
[48] Oxford English Dictionary https://www.oed.com/ (accessed 24 March 2020).
[49] ibid.

'moral' sense, and taking the latter to involve the idea of making use of someone or something unjustly or unethically. Hence, he claims that since these philosophers suppose that only the latter or 'pejorative' meaning of the term is of interest for social critics, they provide a so-called 'moralised' account of exploitation that 'already has wrongfulness or moral badness built into its very meaning'.[50] By contrast, he suggests that, in spite of a popular belief, exploitation is 'not unjust' by definition, although it 'is nearly always a bad thing'.[51] He further claims that a non-moralised account of exploitation would not necessarily preclude using the term pejoratively. It would merely deny that the moral wrongness was built into the very meaning of the term 'exploitation'. Accordingly, Wood argues that there is no semantic distinction between 'pejorative' and 'non-pejorative' senses of exploitation, 'any more than the words seizure and payment mean something different when the seizure is wrongful or the payment involves a breach of ethics'.[52] What is more, he claims that a moralised account of exploitation results in labelling actions 'wrongful because [they are] exploitative'.[53]

Furthermore, Wood argues that 'exploitation consists in the exploiter's using something about the person for the exploiter's ends by playing on some weakness or vulnerability in that person'.[54] This 'basic idea behind all exploitation involving human objects' is said to apply equally to cases where exploitation is commonly considered unfair, wrongful, or unethical and to cases where it is not. Accordingly, he claims that nobody thinks it is wrong or unethical for a chess player to exploit her opponent's inattention in order to win the game. Therefore, he wonders why we should suppose that exploitation has a special meaning when applied to cases of injustice or wrongdoing.[55] Feinberg, by contrast, argues that it is precisely the element of 'wrongfulness' that distinguishes the term 'exploitation' from 'nonexploitative utilization'.[56]

Nevertheless, Wood acknowledges that even on his own account of exploitation, which 'applies equally to cases where exploitation is commonly considered unfair, wrongful, or unethical and to cases where it is not', exploitation would, nevertheless, be 'morally objectionable', not because of the meaning of the word itself, but because of moral convictions which most of us hold.[57] Thus, he contends that, while there is no *semantic* distinction between 'pejorative' and 'non-pejorative' senses of exploitation, 'what there may be is a distinction between some cases in which exploitation is (or is taken to be) morally innocent, and other cases in which, *on the basis of substantive moral principles* exploitation is taken to be morally

---

[50] Allen Wood, 'Exploitation' (1995) 12(2) Social Philosophy and Policy 136, 137.
[51] ibid 136.
[52] ibid 147.
[53] ibid 141.
[54] ibid 147.
[55] ibid 138.
[56] Joel Feinberg, *The Moral Limits of the Criminal Law*, vol 4: *Harmless Wrongdoing* (OUP 1990) 199.
[57] Wood (n 50) 152.

objectionable'.[58] These substantive moral principles, which he claims most of us hold, and which make exploitation objectionable, are based on the moral belief 'that when people are weak or vulnerable, others should not use their weakness or seek to benefit from it, but instead should seek to help them and rescue them from their bad situation'.[59] Thus, 'it is an affront to people's human dignity to have their weaknesses used, and shameful to use the weaknesses of others'.[60] This moral belief, he submits, is widely shared, and it is why the term 'exploitation' seems to refer to something bad, unfair, or unethical, which he argues, has nothing to do with the meaning of the word itself.

This is an important question for the discussion of exploitation in the context of the human rights prohibition of slavery because it is argued that exploitation represents a distinct *wrong* underpinning this right. If exploitation as a term is neutral, we may well need to reconsider what is wrong with slavery and human trafficking and why they ought to be outlawed. However, even though exploitation as a general term does not necessarily carry a negative connotation, exploitation of a certain kind or quality may well do so. What distinguishes (morally innocent) exploitation of a chess player from (morally objectionable) exploitation of a child in a sweatshop—both satisfying Wood's semantically neutral definition of exploitation as 'using something about the person for the exploiter's ends by playing on some weakness or vulnerability in that person'—is the understanding of weakness or vulnerability that are being used for the exploiter's ends, and also the manner in which they are being used.

Hence, the account of exploitation ultimately depends on the meaning of its constitutive elements. Further refining and specifying such elements does not undermine the definition itself. Therefore, an action may be rightly labelled wrongful 'because exploitative', provided that the conditions that qualify an action as exploitative are clearly established. However, the concept of exploitation lacks clearly defined necessary and sufficient conditions that govern its application.[61]

Furthermore, it is argued that in addition to establishing the true conditions for an exploitation claim, a theory of exploitation needs to consider the moral force of exploitation. In other words, what, if anything, should be done in response? Thus, it was noted that 'the wrongness of exploitation does not dictate the way in which these moral questions should be answered'.[62] The following two sections examine philosophers' views on both the necessary and sufficient conditions for the application of the term and on its moral force.

---

[58] ibid 147.
[59] ibid 150.
[60] ibid 158.
[61] John Lawrence Hill, 'Exploitation' (1994) 79 Cornell Law Review 631, 635.
[62] Zwolinski and Wertheimer (n 47).

4.2.2 The Necessary and Sufficient Elements of the Concept of Exploitation in Moral Philosophy

Philosophical discussions of the concept of exploitation are mainly associated with Marxist thought.[63] In essence, Marxist theory sees exploitation as a structural feature of capitalism where capital accumulation depends on labour exploitation, which is a function of the inequalities of bargaining power that arise from class divisions.[64] There are variations of this account but they generally engage with the question of the extent to which, and the ways in which, one section of society had prospered at the expense of another.[65]

The focus of human rights law in modern slavery cases is not on such *structural* or *systemic* but *interpersonal* exploitation.[66] Nonetheless, Marks rightly questions whether structural or systemic exploitation can be so neatly separated from interpersonal exploitation. In other words, it is doubtful whether the latter could truly materialise without being embedded in larger structural formations. Thus, she concludes that 'despite the very different context in which we study capitalism today, Marx's account of exploitation still remains relevant'.[67] In fact, the moral core of the Marxist view of exploitation is not unique to Marxism. Thus, the Marxist account is said to employ 'the ordinary notion that one party exploits another when it gets unfair and undeserved benefits from its transactions or relationships'.[68]

Beyond Marxist thought, contemporary political and moral philosophy is said to have been largely unconcerned with exploitation. Wertheimer, therefore, notes that:

> John Rawls's *A Theory of Justice* has virtually nothing to say about exploitation, as such. Nozick discusses the Marxian account of exploitation in *Anarchy, State, and Utopia*, but, not surprisingly, only to reject it as a basis for interfering with (most) transaction ... Although the American Society for Political and Legal Philosophy's annual NOMOS volumes ... have covered many of the important concepts in political philosophy, there is no volume on exploitation.[69]

Notwithstanding this criticism, there has been a decent amount of literature on exploitation, both of non-Marxist and Marxist orientation, which may be useful for

---

[63] Allen Wood, 'The Marxian Critique of Justice' (1972) 1 Philosophy and Public Affairs 244; Nancy Holmstrom, 'Exploitation' (1977) 7 Canadian Journal of Philosophy 353; Wolff (n 24) 105.
[64] Marks (n 13) 281.
[65] ibid.
[66] For a difference between interpersonal and structural exploitation see Jonathan Wolff, 'Structures of Exploitation' in Hugh Collins, Gillian Lester, and Virginia Mantouvalou (eds), *Philosophical Foundations of Labour Law* (OUP 2018).
[67] Marks (n 13) 289.
[68] Zwolinski and Wertheimer (n 47).
[69] Alan Wertheimer, *Exploitation* (Princeton UP 1995) 6–7.

identifying a plausible account of exploitation in the context of the prohibition of slavery, servitude, forced or compulsory labour, and human trafficking.

These different philosophical accounts of exploitation overlap in many respects. Therefore, most accept that exploitation involves, at minimum, some *gain* for the exploiter,[70] which is sometimes called a benefit[71] or advantage.[72] Furthermore, they generally agree that such gain is obtained by *using* another party's *vulnerability* or *weakness*.[73] What they tend to disagree on, however, is whether such weakness or vulnerability is simply taken advantage of (the opportunistic use),[74] or it was generated by the exploiter using *coercion*. Accordingly, some accounts insist on the coercion element arguing that the exploited are forced to benefit others,[75] whereas others claim that coercion and exploitation are two different wrongs.[76] Wolff holds that, on the one hand, 'exploitation is typically a matter of using another person's vulnerability to your own advantage. Coercion, on the other hand, typically proceeds by first creating another's vulnerability and then exploiting it'.[77] Accordingly, not all exploitation is coercion. Similarly, Wood explains that:

> Perhaps it will be said that people in such desperate straits are forced or coerced into making such deals ... This is often true in the sense that the exploited have no acceptable alternative to the arrangement under which they are exploited. But it does not follow that the exploiters themselves are coercing the exploited. (This is true only if the exploiters themselves are the ones who put the exploited in their vulnerable situation).[78]

---

[70] Robert Mayer, 'What's Wrong with Exploitation?' (2007) 24 Journal of Applied Philosophy 137.
[71] Mikhail Valdman, 'A Theory of Wrongful Exploitation' (2009) 9(6) Philosophers' Imprint 1.
[72] Wertheimer (n 69).
[73] Mayer (n 70); Robert Goodin, 'Exploiting a Situation and Exploiting a Person' in Andrew Reeve (ed), *Modern Theories of Exploitation* (SAGE Publications 1987); Wood (n 63).
[74] Mayer (n 70).
[75] Allen Buchanan, 'Exploitation, Alienation, and Injustice' (1979) 9 Canadian Journal of Philosophy 121; Jeffrey Reiman, 'Exploitation, Force, and the Moral Assessment of Capitalism: Thoughts on Roemer and Cohen' (1987) 16 Philosophy & Public Affairs 3; George Panichas, 'Vampires, Werewolves, and Economic Exploitation' (1981) 7 Social Theory and Practice 125; Justin Schwartz, 'What's Wrong with Exploitation?' (1995) 29 Noûs 158.
[76] Mayer (n 70) 146–48. Observing an important distinction between taking unfair advantage and putting at a disadvantage, for example by coercing another agent. He explains that 'while exploiters prey upon the vulnerable, often they have not created the vulnerabilities of which they take unfair advantage'. Instead, many who gain at the expense of others are said to be simply opportunists who exploit the disadvantages, which they encounter.
[77] Wolff (n 24) 11. Mayer (n 70) 143 explains this vividly: 'A master who exploits a slave fails to benefit her as fairness dictates and thus gains at her expense. The master also oppresses the slave, but this is a separate wrong. The oppression makes the exploitation possible by putting the slave at a disadvantage, but putting at a disadvantage is not the same as taking unfair advantage ... The coercion is only instrumental, and exploitation is the aim of the perpetrators, but without the disadvantage which the coercion inflicts the exploitation could not happen.'
[78] Wood (n 50) 149.

Furthermore, some authors require at least a defect in the quality of the consent by using fraud, manipulation, or other means, while others maintain that exploitation can be fully voluntary.[79] Wertheimer, nevertheless, notes that it might be objected that perfectly rational and (otherwise) uncoerced choices are not appropriately consensual if made under conditions of desperation or from an inequality of bargaining power, or under unjust background conditions.[80] However, he refuses to classify such transactions as non-consensual, because 'we would still have to contrast the cases that are nonconsensual because of coercion or fraud and those that are allegedly nonconsensual in other ways'.[81]

Furthermore, in the course of taking advantage of other's vulnerability or weakness, the exploited person[82] may well be *harmed*. While no one disputes that possibility, philosophers disagree on whether such harm is a necessary condition of wrongful exploitation. Munzer, for example, thinks that 'persons are exploited if (1) others secure a benefit by (2) using them as a tool or resource so as to (3) cause them serious harm'.[83] Others tend to disagree, claiming that moral wrongness of harmful exploitation is not difficult to explain. Thus, it is argued that:

> It is trivially true that it is wrong for A to gain from an action that unjustifiably harms or coerces B. And even a libertarian will grant that some harmful exploitation may be legitimately prohibited by the state, if only because it is harmful (or rights violating) rather than because it is exploitative.[84]

Instead, it is more intriguing to examine those instances where exploitation is mutually beneficial, where an exploited person too gains from the transaction or an act. In fact, Wertheimer claims that it is precisely the fact that an exploitee has much to gain from the exploitative relation that he wants to be exploited.[85] Similarly, Wood argues that:

> Since being benefited and being exploited are often merely two sides of the same coin, and people may often be in dire need of the benefits in question, they can often be eager to be exploited. The point is that it goes along with being vulnerable, or in a weak bargaining position, that you should have a lot to gain from being taken advantage of, and a lot to lose if you cannot find someone able and willing to take advantage of your vulnerability.[86]

---

[79] Zwolinski and Wertheimer (n 47).
[80] ibid.
[81] ibid.
[82] The term 'exploitee' also features in philosophical discussions.
[83] Stephen Munzer, *A Theory of Property* (CUP 1990) 171.
[84] Zwolinski and Wertheimer (n 47).
[85] Alan Wertheimer, 'Two Questions about Surrogacy and Exploitation' (1992) 21 Philosophy and Public Affairs 211, 223. See also Valdman (n 71) 3.
[86] Wood (n 50) 148–49.

Accordingly, while exploitation often harms an exploited person, it may not necessarily do so. Furthermore, there are different understandings of what constitutes harm. Those philosophers who invoke the Kantian notion that one wrongfully exploits when one treats another merely as a means to an end argue that the instrumental use of one person is a distinctive harm on its own.[87] Mayer, on the other hand, sees 'a failure to benefit others as some norm of fairness requires' as the fundamental wrong of exploitation in every case. Accordingly, 'as an exploiter, the master inflicts losses and thus *harms* by failing to benefit his victim as fairness requires'.[88]

In sum, while philosophical accounts of exploitation are not settled on the question of whether harm and coercion are necessary elements of wrongful exploitation, most of them agree that the exploitative practice represents a *wrongful gain* for the exploiter by taking advantage of some *weakness* or *vulnerability* on the part of an exploited person. Thus, even if the transaction does not leave an exploited person worse off than before, it leaves him worse off than he *might* or *ought to be* judging from the standpoint of fairness.[89] Mayer, thus, uses an example of a sweatshop noticing that while sweated labourer is better off than before, he is still insufficiently compensated. What fairness requires is, however, difficult to discern. Mayer admits that 'conceptions of desert drive this concept and make exploitation the most contentious form of wrongful gain'.[90] It has been said that there will be 'as many competing conceptions of exploitation as theories of what persons owe to each other by way of fair treatment'.[91]

Exploitation, then, according to Mayer, becomes 'a thoroughly politicized concept' because contestable ideas about what fairness requires determine whether taking unfair advantage is recognised or not. He gives an example of Aristotle who did not view slavery as exploitative because he did not think slaves suffered a loss from the standpoint of fairness. Today, however, we tend to view slavery as 'paradigmatically exploitative because slaves are thought to receive much less than they deserve'.[92]

Valdman offers a plausible account of exploitation that explains both a wrongful gain for the exploiter and weakness or vulnerability of an exploited person that has been taken advantage of, which are the conditions on which most philosophers agree. This account is used to frame the notion of exploitation in the context of the

---

[87] Immanuel Kant, 'Groundwork of the Metaphysics of Morals' in HJ Paton (tr), *The Moral Law* (Hutchinson University Library 1948) 90–91. According to Kant, 'to exploit someone is to treat that person purely as a means to your own ends, and not as an "end in themself"'. See also Allen Wood, 'What Is Kantian Ethics?' in Allen Wood (ed), *Rethinking the Western Tradition* (Yale UP 2002); Wolff (n 24).
[88] Mayer (n 70) 142.
[89] ibid 141. See also Wertheimer (n 69).
[90] Mayer (n 70) 144.
[91] Richard Arneson, 'Exploitation' in Lawrence Becker and Charlotte Becker (eds), *Encyclopedia of Ethics* (Routledge 1992) 350.
[92] Mayer (n 70) 144.

prohibition of slavery, servitude, forced or compulsory labour, and human trafficking canvassed in section 4.

According to Valdman, the deepest wrong of exploitation lies in 'our moral obligation not to extract excessive benefits from people who cannot, or cannot reasonably, refuse our offers'.[93] On this view, there are two necessary conditions for an exploitation claim: first, that one extracts excessive benefits, and second, that these benefits are extracted from someone who is unable to reasonably refuse an offer. As for the latter condition—being unable to reasonably refuse an exploitative offer—Valdman emphasises the difference between 'being wrongly exploited' and 'let oneself being used' where the former refers to situations where a person has little control over her actions and choices. On the contrary, 'when a rational person has acceptable options but nevertheless allows someone to extract excessive benefits from her, she may be a victim of exploitation but she is also complicit in her victimhood'.[94] Thus, he claims 'to wrongly exploit someone is to extract excessive benefits from him—it is to use the fact that his back is to the wall, so to speak, to get him to accept lopsided and outrageous terms of exchange'.[95] However, Valdman doubts that a clear demarcation exists between being wrongly exploited and letting oneself be used. Whether someone has 'acceptable options' depends on one's perceptions and not only on objective conditions and it is not clear which of these two Valdman has in mind.

In elaborating the first element—the extraction of excessive benefits—Valdman argues that extracted benefits are excessive 'insofar as they deviate from the benefits we would expect A to receive were he transacting with someone who was rational, informed, and could reasonably refuse his offer'.[96] However, he admits that 'because it is not always possible to tell whether extracted benefits are excessive or whether one is in no position to refuse an offer, my theory will not always deliver a clear verdict'.[97] In principle, Valdman's theory is useful for setting the parameters of the concept of exploitation underpinning the practices prohibited by the right to be free from slavery, servitude, forced or compulsory labour, and human trafficking, but it requires further refinement to be suitable for practical application. Thus, it requires specifying conditions in which people 'cannot, or cannot reasonably, refuse our offers' as well as clarifying the meaning of 'excessive'. Yet, once international law supplies the definition of exploitation, which articulates its parameters, it will be a task for domestic legislators and judiciary to specify these conditions taking into consideration local circumstances.

In sum, philosophical discussions of the concept of exploitation point out to a number of conditions that explain a specific wrong inherent in this notion. These

---

[93] Valdman (n 71) 1.
[94] ibid 10.
[95] ibid 13.
[96] ibid 12.
[97] ibid 13.

include: the use of another, harm, coercion, fairness, abuse of vulnerability, a failure of reciprocity, or the combination thereof. However, two conditions—*abuse of vulnerability* of an exploited person to acquire an *excessive gain* from her—appear as common denominators of all these accounts. Accordingly, a further elaboration of these conditions may well represent the first step towards a workable concept of exploitation in the context of modern slavery.

4.2.3 The Moral Force of Exploitation

In addition to establishing the true conditions for an exploitation claim, a theory of exploitation needs also to consider the *moral force* of exploitation.[98] In other words, what, if anything, should be done in response? This is important in order to determine the rationale and scope of the human rights provisions that prohibit slavery, servitude, forced or compulsory labour, and human trafficking as a means of addressing such exploitation.

Wertheimer argues that the questions as to what agreements should be treated as invalid and what behaviours should be prohibited will be settled by moral argument informed by empirical investigation rather than conceptual analysis.[99] Regardless of the approach to resolving this question, it is important to notice that philosophers tend to recognise different levels of severity of exploitation ranging from 'non-consensual or harmful' to 'consensual and mutually advantageous'.[100] Wolff, for example, explicitly notes there are different dimensions of strength, or moral seriousness, of exploitation. These range from 'a paradigm case of the deepest type of exploitation' that involves the employment of young children at very low wages in extremely hazardous and life-shortening jobs, to 'shallow exploitation' that refers to a trader who, purely as a matter of brute good fortune, has large stocks during a temporary shortage, and who hikes the price simply because local consumers now have no alternative but to pay up.[101]

In light of this sliding scale approach, an appropriate state intervention in exploitative practices may well require the use of different means and strategies for different levels of severity, ranging from criminal law to social policy measures or warrant no intervention at all. Furthermore, Wolff warns that by interfering with exploitative arrangements, we may prevent one person from taking advantage of another's weakness, but in doing so we also risk consigning the vulnerable person to an even worse fate than being exploited.[102] Therefore, a line between what ought

---

[98] Zwolinski and Wertheimer (n 47).
[99] Wertheimer, 'Remarks on Coercion and Exploitation' (1996-97) 74 Denver University Law Review 889, 890.
[100] Zwolinski and Wertheimer (n 47).
[101] Wolff (n 24) 114–15.
[102] ibid 113.

to be prohibited by criminal law and what is best to be dealt by other legal instruments or measures of social policy should be drawn carefully. Thus, the UNODC report points out that:

> The literature review confirmed support for understanding exploitation—in the sense of taking unfair advantage—as a continuum, albeit one that is poorly defined and highly contested.... From a legal perspective, the idea of a continuum is particularly useful because points on that continuum can be set with reference to the legal regime they fall within (and vice-versa).[103]

Accordingly, the term 'modern slavery' encompasses practices that represent the most abhorrent cases of exploitation, which states ought to criminalise, leaving aside practices that could or should be dealt with by other means. Importantly, state intervention by means of criminal law is a *minimum safeguard* necessary to secure this 'absolute' right and should not be considered as the only or even predominant method of dealing with the most egregious cases of exploitation.[104]

4.3 The Emerging Contours of the Concept of Exploitation in Human Rights Law

The philosophical accounts of exploitation discussed in the previous section coalesce around two common elements—the abuse of vulnerability of an exploitee and excessive gain for an exploiter. These common elements serve as a starting point for sketching out the account of exploitation in the context of the human rights prohibition of slavery, servitude, forced or compulsory labour, and human trafficking. The remaining sections thus elaborate the necessary and sufficient conditions for the notion of exploitation that bounds together practices listed in the definition of human trafficking[105] (including slavery, servitude, and forced or compulsory labour).[106] These are: (a) abuse of vulnerability of an exploitee;

---

[103] UNODC (n 32) 21–22.
[104] For a criticism of the excessive reliance on criminal law to respond to exploitation of persons see Cathryn Costello, 'Migrants and Forced Labour: A Labour Law Response' in Alan Bogg and others (eds), *The Autonomy of Labour Law* (OUP 2015); Jennifer Collins, 'Exploitation of Persons and the Limits of the Criminal Law' (2017) 3 Criminal Law Review 169.
[105] See below in subsection 4.3.3 a discussion of organ removal as one of the purposes of human trafficking, which is argued to represent an anomaly among other exploitative practices listed in the definition of human trafficking.
[106] For the excellent analysis of these concepts see David Weissbrodt and Anti-Slavery International, *Abolishing Slavery and its Contemporary Forms*, United Nations High Commissioner for Human Rights (OHCHR), HR/PUB/02/4 (2002); Jean Allain, 'R v Tang: Clarifying the Definition of "Slavery" in International Law' (2009) 10 Melbourne Journal of International Law 246; Jean Allain, 'On the Curious Disappearance of Human Servitude from General International Law' (2009) 11 Journal of the History of International Law 303.

(b) excessive (disproportionate) gain acquired through the actions of an exploitee; and (c) sustained action (the practice takes place over a period of time). The three necessary and sufficient conditions help distinguish exploitation from other, often related wrongs, such as abuse, fraud, or extortion, which are commonly observed in the cases of human trafficking but are not inherent in its notion. Furthermore, these necessary and sufficient conditions distinguish exploitation in the context of modern slavery from those practices that may well be considered exploitative in the general meaning of the term but do not reach a level of severity necessary to trigger protection afforded by this 'absolute' right.

4.3.1 Abuse of Vulnerability

It is generally accepted that vulnerability and its abuse are 'central to any understanding of trafficking'[107] and 'the common feature of all forms of exploitation' contained in Article 4 ECHR.[108] Thus, it is said that 'to a large extent [human trafficking] is about exploiting vulnerable individuals'.[109] Human traffickers 'prey on people who are poor, isolated and weak'.[110] The UNODC observes that 'in both politics and philosophy, "exploitation", when attached to a person, is commonly understood as being linked to some weakness or vulnerability, which becomes the object of exploitation'.[111]

Vulnerability is described as 'a social condition of powerlessness ascribed to individuals with certain characteristics that are perceived to deviate from those ascribed to the prevailing definitions of a national'.[112] The term 'vulnerable victim' is used to refer to 'a victim who is unusually vulnerable due to age, physical or mental condition, or who is otherwise particularly susceptible to criminal conduct'.[113] The explanatory report to the Council of Europe Anti-Trafficking Convention notes that:

> The vulnerability may be of any kind, whether physical, psychological, emotional, family-related, social or economic. The situation might, for example, involve

---

[107] UNODC, *Abuse of a Position of Vulnerability and Other "Means" within the Definition of Trafficking in Persons* (Issue Paper 2013) 5.
[108] *Chowdury and Others v Greece* App no 21884/15 (ECtHR, 30 March 2017) [82].
[109] Council of Europe Parliamentary Assembly, 'Trafficking of Migrant Workers for Forced Labour' Doc 13086 Report (4 January 2013) para 1.
[110] UNODC, *An Introduction to Human Trafficking: Vulnerability, Impact and Action* Background paper (2008)3.
[111] UNODC (n 32) 21.
[112] Jorge Bustamante, 'Immigrants' Vulnerability as Subjects of Human Rights' (2002) 36 International Migration Review 333, 340.
[113] Mohamed Mattar, 'Incorporating the Five Basic Elements of a Model Anti-Trafficking in Persons Legislation in Domestic Laws: From the United Nations Protocol to the European Convention' (2005) 14(2) Tulane Journal of International and Comparative Law 29, 30.

insecurity or illegality of the victim's administrative status, economic dependence or fragile health. In short, the situation can be any state of hardship in which a human being is impelled to accept being exploited.[114]

The notion of vulnerability is thus associated with a set of victims' personal characteristics, such as a person's age, disability, immigration or socio-economic status. For example, in the Dutch jurisprudence, 'a person is in a "vulnerable position" if there is a combination of illegal residence, a poor economic situation and being unable to speak the Dutch language'.[115] Furthermore, it is noted that, 'people that are vulnerable to exploitation are people that reside illegally in the Netherlands, especially minors, and members of closed migrant communities in the Netherlands'.[116] Irregular migration status is said to create vulnerability 'in the sense of disadvantage both factual and legal, engendering openness to exploitation or abuse'.[117]

In addition to irregular migrants and migrant workers who are declared 'a particularly vulnerable group and therefore deserve specific attention from States',[118] the Strasbourg Court has recognised other groups as vulnerable including children,[119] Roma minority,[120] persons with mental disabilities,[121] women subject to domestic violence,[122] and asylum-seekers.[123]

Importantly, it is the *abuse of vulnerability*, not vulnerability per se, that is a necessary condition for the notion of exploitation. It is thus noted that 'to exploit a person is to use a weakness in order to gain substantial control over the person's life or labour'.[124] Wolf similarly argues that 'one's vulnerability is exploited if the other person uses this weakness to obtain agreement to, or at least acquiescence in, a course of action that one would not have accepted had there not been this asymmetry in power'.[125]

The notion of 'abuse of a position of vulnerability' figures as one of the means of human trafficking in its tripartite definition, which invalidates victims' consent.[126]

---

[114] Explanatory Report to the Council of Europe Convention on Action against Trafficking in Human Beings, CETS 197 (16 May 2005) para 83.
[115] M Heemskerk and Conny Rijken, 'Combating Trafficking in Human Beings for Labour Exploitation in the Netherlands' in Conny Rijken (ed), *Combating Trafficking in Human Beings for Labour Exploitation* (Wolf Legal Publishers 2011) 77.
[116] ibid 89.
[117] Mark Freedland and Cathryn Costello, 'Migrants at Work and the Division of Labour Law' in Cathryn Costello and Mark Freedland (eds), *Migrants at Work: Immigration and Vulnerability in Labour Law* (OUP 2014) 1.
[118] Council of Europe Committee of Ministers, Reply to Parliamentary Assembly Recommendation 2011, Doc 13287 (16 July 2013) para 2.
[119] *A v United Kingdom* (1999) 27 EHRR 611 [22].
[120] *Oršuš and Others v Croatia* [GC] (2011) 52 EHRR 7 [147].
[121] *Alajos Kiss v Hungary* (2013) 56 EHRR 38 [42].
[122] *Opuz v Turkey* (2010) 50 EHRR 28 [160].
[123] *MSS v Belgium and Greece* [GC] (2011) 53 EHRR 2 [232]–[233] and [252].
[124] Allen Wood, 'Exploitation' in Ted Honderich (ed), *The Oxford Companion to Philosophy* (2nd edn, OUP 2005).
[125] Wolff (n 24) 111.
[126] UNODC, *Abuse of a Position of Vulnerability* (n 107) 78–9.

Arguably, the abuse of vulnerability represents the least coercive means of inducing consent 'without relying upon direct physical abuse, threats or fraud'.[127] But the abuse of vulnerability is instrumental to both human trafficking as a process leading to exploitation and to manifestations of such exploitation in the form of slavery, servitude and forced or compulsory labour. Thus, the International Labour Organisation and the European Commission list separately indicators for 'recruitment by abuse of vulnerability' as one of the means of human trafficking, and indicators of 'abuse of vulnerability at destination' (at the exploitation stage).[128] Specific indicators may well differ between the recruitment and exploitation stages or between different countries without affecting the fact that 'abuse of vulnerability' is integral to such practices.

Overall, the term 'abuse of vulnerability', according to the *travaux préparatoires* to the Palermo Protocol, is understood to refer to 'any situation in which the person involved has no real and acceptable alternative but to submit to the abuse involved'.[129] The EU Anti-Trafficking Directive mirrors this statement.[130]

Clearly, the abuse of vulnerability requires, first, recognising specific traits as constituting vulnerability and, secondly, explaining the dynamics in which such vulnerability is played upon to ensure control over a victim. Hence, the notion of control (power) is inherent in this element and it is contingent upon a number of circumstances, which may not always stem from coercion. For instance, when a child is in a dependant position with respect to her carers, or in cultures where male family members have the power over female family members, control over an individual creates or exacerbates their vulnerability, which may then be abused to exploit that person.[131]

The ILO study thus observes that vulnerability can result from some *innate characteristic* of the victim (physical or mental deficiency, ill health, or youth) or may develop due to the *situation* the victim finds him/herself in within a destination country (poverty, precarious administrative status).[132] Significantly, the study notes that actions of a trafficker could also either *create* or *worsen* a victim's vulnerability (extremely poor wages causing poverty, restricted movement causing isolation, seizure of identity documents causing fear of deportation). This allows an exploiter to extract disproportionate gains from a person by abusing such vulnerability (innate or constructed).

---

[127] Rohit Malpani, *Legal Aspects of Trafficking for Forced Labour Purposes in Europe* (ILO Working Paper, 04 January 2006) 4.
[128] ILO and European Commission, *Operational Indicators of Trafficking in Human Beings: Results from a Dephi Survey implemented by the ILO and the European Commission* (2009).
[129] UNODC, *Travaux préparatoires of the negotiations for the elaboration of the United Nations Convention against Transnational Organized Crime and the Protocols thereto* (2006) at 347.
[130] EU Anti-Trafficking Directive art 2(2).
[131] Collins, 'Exploitation of Persons and the Limits of the Criminal Law' (n 104) 11 (drawing attention to recent research on grooming, which examines how exploiters seek to set themselves in positions of domination over vulnerable persons).
[132] Malpani, *Legal Aspects of Trafficking for Forced Labour Purposes* (n 127) 5.

As discussed in Section 3, most philosophers do not treat coercion as a necessary condition for exploitation, although they do accept that it would often be present in exploitative situations.[133] When it is present, coercion serves to either create or exacerbate vulnerability.

Therefore, both intrinsic and created vulnerability can be subject to abuse in order to induce control over a victim, making her susceptible to 'agree' to exploitation. However, the difference between coercion alone and the abuse of vulnerability (intrinsic or created) is that the latter is an integral part of the notion of exploitation. Namely, a person may be coerced by one individual while being exploited by others. Whether or not exploiters also coerce a victim, they always abuse victim's vulnerability that was either given or created/exacerbated by the use of coercion. Thus, the abuse of vulnerability, as a means of vitiating consent, is the minimum necessary condition of exploitation in the context of modern slavery.

The existence and abuse of vulnerability is said to be 'contextually relative' and is thus best assessed on a case-by-case basis.[134] However, determining in which instances there was an abuse of a vulnerable position is challenging, especially in situations where irregular migrants approach predatory employers themselves. This was the case in the seminal 'Chinese restaurant workers case' by the Dutch Supreme Court concerning the exploitation of Chinese workers with irregular migration status in the Netherlands.[135] The workers were employed in a restaurant under very poor conditions. Large numbers of them slept together in the same room, they worked long hours and had no days off. However, they had come to the Netherlands voluntarily and approached the restaurant owners themselves. The Supreme Court ruled that 'to prove misuse of a vulnerable position, for example, it is enough that the perpetrator recognises the vulnerable position and takes advantage of this position'.[136] It established that 'a certain initiative and positive act by the perpetrators is presumed, by which they consciously misuse the weaker or vulnerable position of the victims'.[137]

Establishing that a person had no realistic alternative due to the abuse of vulnerability might be a weighty task that requires assessing factual circumstances, but it is the one that national courts engage with on a daily basis. Thus the UNODC study reviewed national legislations across the world and concluded that 'a number of countries have integrated abuse of vulnerability into their understanding of exploitation'[138] noting that specific vulnerability factors were remarkably similar across very different countries of origin, transit and destination.

---

[133] See text with (n 75)—(n 78).
[134] UNODC, *Abuse of a Position of Vulnerability* (n 107) 72.
[135] Supreme Court of the Netherlands, LJN: BI7099, 27 October 2009, cited in Linda van Krimpen, 'The Interpretation and Implementation of Labour Exploitation in Dutch Case Law' in Conny Rijken (ed), *Combating Trafficking in Human Beings for Labour Exploitation* (Wolf Legal Publishers 2011) 500–02.
[136] ibid 499.
[137] ibid 498.
[138] UNODC, *Abuse of a Position of Vulnerability* (n 107) 4.

4.3.2 Disproportionate Gain

The second element of the notion of exploitation requires that an exploiter gains excessively from the actions of an exploited person. It is shown that most philosophers use a reference to an unfair or excessive gain, advantage, or benefit acquired by using another (vulnerable) individual to describe the situations of morally wrongful exploitation. It is also considered that an exploited person may sometimes 'benefit' from being exploited.[139] Such benefit, however, is always significantly less then 'what it might or ought to be', judged from the stand-point of fairness.[140]

Exploitation, thus, always implies the notion of excess—an unfair gain at the expense of an exploited person—distinguishing this type of wrong from others. In all situations of exploitation, an exploitee gives significantly more than she receives in return. Thus, in the case of *Van der Mussele v Belgium*, the Strasbourg Court made use of the notion of a 'disproportionate burden' to determine whether a lawyer had been subjected to compulsory labour when required to defend clients free of charge.[141] In this case, a pupil-advocate complained of the lack of remuneration and of reimbursement of expenses arguing that these constituted forced and compulsory labour under Article 4 ECHR. However, the Court held that such prejudice 'went hand in hand with advantages and had not been shown to be *excessive*'.[142] Thus, the Court concluded that, while remunerated work may also qualify as forced or compulsory labour, 'the lack of remuneration and of reimbursement of expenses constitutes a relevant factor when considering what is *proportionate* or in the normal course of business'.[143] Similarly, the African Commission on Human and Peoples' Rights established a clear link between exploitation and the lack of 'just and favourable remuneration' and ruled that Mauritania violated Article 5 of the African Charter on Human and Peoples' Rights that protects against 'all forms of exploitation and degradation of man'.[144]

Furthermore, what counts as an excessive (disproportionate) gain is not necessarily expressed in monetary terms. Thus, the Strasbourg Court recently considered allegations of servitude and forced or compulsory labour by two orphaned Burundi sisters aged sixteen and ten years, on the basis of their unremunerated domestic chores in their aunt and uncle's home.[145] The Court noted that 'the type and amount of work involved ... help distinguish between "forced labour" and a

---

[139] Wertheimer, 'Two Questions about Surrogacy and Exploitation' (n 85) 223; Mayer (n 70) 3; Wood (n 59) 148–9.
[140] Mayer (n 70) 141.
[141] *Van der Mussele v Belgium* (1983) 6 EHRR 163 [34]–[41].
[142] ibid [40].
[143] ibid.
[144] 54/91, 61/91, 98/93, 164/97, 196/97 and 210/98, *Malawi African Association and Others v Mauritania* 13th Annual Activity Report (1999-2000) para 135.
[145] *CN and V v France* App no 67724/09 (ECtHR, 11 October 2012).

THE NOTION OF EXPLOITATION   87

helping hand which can reasonably be expected of other family members or people sharing accommodation'.[146] Distinguishing between the situations of the two sisters, the Strasbourg Court found that the older one was forced to work 'so hard that without her aid Mr and Mrs M. would have had to employ and pay a professional housemaid'.[147] The second sister, by contrast, was said not to have contributed 'in any *excessive* measure to the upkeep of Mr and Mrs M's household'.[148]

It is clear that all circumstances of the case need to be taken into account when assessing whether actions required from an individual were disproportionate to the benefits she received in return. Like the assessment of 'no realistic alternative' for the element of abuse of vulnerability, this is a factual question for the courts. Hence, in the previously discussed 'Chinese restaurant workers case', the Dutch Supreme Court held that a finding of exploitation depends heavily on the circumstances of the case. It ruled that in the case before them, relevant factors include 'the nature and duration of the employment, the restrictions to the employee resulting from such employment, and the financial gain of the employer'.[149] Importantly, it noted that standards in Dutch society should be adopted as the frame of reference for weighing those factors. In the concrete case, it was proven that the Chinese workers were put to work on an average of eleven to thirteen hours a day, six days a week, for a wage far below the minimum wage. Similarly, the explanatory report to Article 273f of the Dutch Criminal Code noted that an extremely long working week for disproportionately low pay under poor working conditions represents an example of exploitation.[150] It is therefore clear that the economic benefit of an exploiter together with other conditions of work play a decisive role in establishing exploitation.

Furthermore, the requirement of an excessive gain distinguishes exploitation from abuse—wrongs which are different in nature while often interrelated. The difference is best explained using the examples of sexual exploitation and sexual abuse. Accordingly:

> The term 'sexual exploitation' means any actual or attempted *abuse of a position of vulnerability*, differential power, or trust, for sexual purposes, including, but not limited to, *profiting* monetarily, socially or politically from the sexual exploitation of another. Similarly, the term 'sexual abuse' means the actual or threatened *physical intrusion* of a sexual nature, whether by force or under unequal or coercive conditions.[151]

---

[146] ibid [74].
[147] ibid [75].
[148] ibid (emphasis added).
[149] Heemskerk and Rijken (n 115) 80.
[150] Cited in The Dutch National Rapporteur on Trafficking in Human Beings, *Trafficking in Human Beings: Case law on Trafficking in Human Beings 2009-2012—An Analysis*, BNRM (2012) 85.
[151] United Nations Secretariat, *Special Measures for Protection from Sexual Exploitation and Abuse*, ST/SGB/2003/13 (9 October 2003) section 1 (emphasis added).

This distinction, nevertheless, has not always been recognised. Thus, Amar argues that child abuse should be seen as slavery under the Thirteenth Amendment of the US Constitution.[152] However, this confuses the distinctive wrongs of exploitation, which represents the core of practices such as slavery or human trafficking, and abuse. Thus, while victims of exploitation are also nearly always abused, the same cannot be said for the opposite. The case of *Hadijatou Mani Koraou* decided by the Economic Community of West African States (ECOWAS) Court of Justice illustrates this difference.[153] The Court endorsed the position of the Nuremberg Military Tribunals, which held that:

> Slaves may be well fed, well clothed, and comfortably housed, but they are still slaves.... We might eliminate all proof of ill-treatment, overlook the starvation, beatings, and other barbarous acts, but the admitted fact of slavery—*compulsory uncompensated labour*—would still remain.[154]

4.3.3 Sustained Action

Inherent in the notion of exploitation is the idea of repetitiveness. Exploitation takes place (or is intended to) over a period of time. One-off situations may qualify as fraud or abuse but exploitation in the context of modern slavery involves sustained activity. Bales thus notes that 'indeterminate temporal nature is one of the defining characteristics of the crime of slavery'.[155] According to him, 'it is fundamental to the conceptualization of slavery that, once enslaved, a person cannot affect the period of their bondage'.[156] Similarly, inherent in the notion of servitude is a victim's feeling that her condition is permanent and that the situation is unlikely to change.[157] When it comes to the concept of forced labour, it is evident that 'labour' implies work that stretches over a period of time—not a one-off transaction.

This view, nonetheless, might not square with human trafficking for the purpose of organ removal, which is considered as a one-off venture. The previous chapter nonetheless expxlained that human trafficking for the purpose of organ removal is a unique form of mistreatment that does not share many similarities with other exploitative practices listed in the Palermo Protocol's definition of human trafficking.

---

[152] Akdzil Reed Amar and Daniel Widawsky, 'Child Abuse as Slavery: A Thirteenth Amendment Response to Deshaney' (1992) 105(6) Harvard Law Review 1359.
[153] *Koraou v Niger* Judgment No ECW/CCJ/JUD/06/08 (27 October 2008) [79].
[154] *The United States of America v Oswald Pohl and Others* (Case No 4) United States Military Tribunal II, Trials of Major War Criminals before the Nuremberg Military Tribunals under Control Council Law No 10, vol V (1950) 970 (emphasis added).
[155] Monti Narayan Datta and Kevin Bales, 'Slavery in Europe: Part 1, Estimating the Dark Figure' (2013) 35 Human Rights Quarterly 817, 821.
[156] ibid 822.
[157] *CN and V v France* (n 145) [91].

THE NOTION OF EXPLOITATION   89

Instead, it ought to be considered a subset of trafficking in human organs, which is addressed through a separate treaty regime within the Council of Europe.[158]

This illustrates the urgency of defining exploitation, especially because of the increasing number of practices that have been deemed 'exploitative'.[159] Thus, Van Krimpen criticises a new development in the Dutch case law, which concerns 'rather "new" types of forced services as exploitation. A characteristic in these cases is that the services are only performed over a short period of time, sometimes only once'.[160] For example, she points out the cases involving 'exploitation by forced subscribing to phone contracts' (after which victims had to give the phones to the suspect). In one of these cases, the domestic court declared the suspect guilty of fraud, while the latter cases led to a conviction for human trafficking.[161] In one of the latter examples, however, in spite of convicting the accused of human trafficking, the court noted that the term 'fraud' did better fit common parlance and the public perception of the facts of this case.[162] Van Krimpen condemns the courts for 'overstepping the mark' since these rulings imply that almost every case of deception or fraud to induce victims to make themselves available for performing services, could now be defined as human trafficking. She rightly concludes that cases such as those involving forced subscription to phone contracts 'do rather remind of a form of fraud'.[163] Accordingly, what distinguishes exploitation from mere fraud or extortion is the fact that an exploited person is required to perform an action over a period of time—to offer her work or services of some kind—that benefit another disproportionately in a situation where she has no acceptable alternatives.

To conclude, this section has articulated an account of exploitation in the context of the human rights prohibition against practices of 'modern slavery', which is grounded in the philosophical debates and jurisprudence of international and domestic courts. On this view, to exploit is *to acquire disproportionate gains from the actions of an individual by abusing her position of vulnerability over a sustained period of time*. The discussion has demonstrated that all three identified conditions ('abuse of vulnerability', 'excessive gain', and 'sustained action') are factual, which leaves room for domestic courts to use national parameters when interpreting potentially exploitative practices, while preserving the universality of the definition itself. The proposed definition of exploitation thus serves both to distinguish exploitation from other wrongs and to separate practices that trigger protection under the right to be free from slavery, servitude, forced labour, and human trafficking from lesser forms of exploitation, which are to be dealt by other means. In the latter sense, it provides the severity threshold that has been missing from the

---

[158] Council of Europe Convention against Trafficking in Human Organs 2014, CETS 2016.
[159] Allain (n 2).
[160] Van Krimpen (n 135) 502–506 (emphasis added).
[161] Dordrecht District Court, LJN: BM1743 (20 April 2010), cited in Van Krimpen (n 135) 504.
[162] Haarlem District Court, LJN: BO8985 (8 December 2010), cited in Van Krimpen (n 135) 505.
[163] Van Krimpen (n 135) 506–507.

jurisprudence on modern slavery. This definition is not, however, intended to replace the existing definitions of slavery, servitude, forced labour, and human trafficking, but to explain why these practices are prohibited under the same right, to elucidate their theoretical and normative grounding, and to offer guidance to national adjudicators and policy makers when applying the relevant instruments.

PART II
STATE RESPONSIBILITY FOR 'MODERN SLAVERY' IN HUMAN RIGHTS LAW

What does human rights law offer to individuals subject to human trafficking, slavery, servitude, or forced labour practices commonly referred to as 'modern slavery'? What obligations do states owe to them under human rights law and how are these enforced? And what does 'state responsibility' imply in the context of 'modern slavery' perpetrated by private individuals? These are the questions that animate the discussion in the second part of the book, which explores the jurisprudence of human rights tribunals dealing with cases of 'modern slavery'. While such jurisprudence has been growing steadily worldwide since the beginning of the twenty-first century, the European Court of Human Rights (ECtHR) remains the most prolific in its engagement with this issue.[1] For this reason, its case law represents the focal point of the analysis.

As explained in the first part of the book, although human trafficking undeniably raises a range of human rights issues, it only amounts to a human rights *violation*[2] if states owed to victims some duties in the first place, which they failed to discharge. Hence, it is essential to know what these obligations are, when they arise, and what standards are to be used to assess state compliance. Tom Obokata thus invites the human rights community 'to move beyond reporting the cases of human rights violations pertinent to trafficking and to articulate human rights obligations'.[3]

---

[1] One of the important pieces of work analysing its jurisprudence is the book by Vladislava Stoyanova, *Human Trafficking and Slavery Reconsidered: Conceptual Limits and States' Positive Obligations in European Law* (CUP 2017).
[2] For a useful distinction between the situations when rights are: *fulfilled* ('when the correlative duty is being carried out'); *infringed* ('when the correlative duty is not carried out, ie when the required action is not performed or the prohibited action is performed'); *violated* ('when it is unjustifiably infringed, ie when the required action is unjustifiably not performed or the prohibited action is unjustifiably performed'); and *overridden* ('when it is justifiably infringed, so that there is sufficient justification for not carrying out the correlative duty, and the required action is justifiably not performed or the prohibited action is justifiably performed) see Alan Gewirth, 'Are There Any Absolute Rights' (1981) 31(122) The Philosophical Quarterly 1, 2.
[3] Tom Obokata, *Trafficking in Human Beings from a Human Rights Perspective: Towards a Holistic Approach* (Martinus Nijhoff Publishers 2006) 172.

However, many studies of human trafficking, which emphasise its human rights dimension and seek to clarify state obligations arising out of different international instruments, tend to label measures aimed at victim protection as human rights *obligations* of states. For example, Chaudary argues that 'many if not all of the victim-protection provisions in the [Council of Europe Anti-Trafficking Convention] are also covered by the positive obligations States owe victims (or possible victims) of human trafficking under Article 4 [ECHR]'.[4] The former President of GRETA—an expert body established by the Council of Europe Anti-Trafficking Convention to monitor state compliance with this treaty[5]—similarly contends that the requirements enshrined in the Convention concerning 'identification, assistance, recovery and reflection period, compensation, protection against reprisals and non-punishment for illegal acts which victims are compelled to commit by traffickers' represent the set of the victims' 'fundamental rights'.[6]

These accounts gloss over the distinction between the different nature of international instruments relevant for 'modern slavery' and thus conflate obligations of states concerning victim protection measures with states' *human rights obligations*. Such conflation is conceptually imprecise and legally untenable. It also undermines attempts at articulating a set of justiciable rights that victims do have under the existing human rights law. Clearly articulating obligations that stem from human rights law is important because it allows victims to demand accountability of states before international *fora*. As already noted, specialised anti-trafficking instruments do not offer such a possibility, although they may well inform the interpretation of obligations of states under general human rights law, as explained in Chapter 7.

It is thus conceivable that a comprehensive and rigorous analysis of the specialised international anti-trafficking instruments and general human rights law might result in the latter being developed to accommodate many specific measures that stem from the global anti-trafficking regime. However, international and domestic courts, unlike academics or activists, are cautious to engage in such a creative interpretation of human rights law. One reason for that might be the fact that many victim protection measures contained in the anti-trafficking instruments warrant some sort of material support, which creates demands on state resources with policy implications that extend beyond the remit of courts.[7] Moreover, some of these requirements can interfere with states' immigration policies.[8] Both the

---

[4] Saadiya Chaudary, 'Trafficking in Europe: An Analysis of the Effectiveness of European Law' (2011) 33(77) Michigan Journal of International Law 77, 94.

[5] Anti-Trafficking Convention, ch VII.

[6] Third GRETA Report, Introduction by the President of GRETA (emphasis added). The President adds to this list the right to compensation and non-punishment for illegal acts which victims are compelled to commit by traffickers.

[7] Alastair Mowbray, *The Development of Positive Obligations under the European Convention on Human Rights by the European Court of Human Rights* (Hart Publishing 2004); Andrew Clapham, *Human Rights in the Private Sphere* (Clarendon Press 1993) 345.

[8] UN High Commissioner for Refugees (UNHCR) 'Guidelines on International Protection: The application of Article 1A (2) of the 1951 Convention and/or 1967 Protocol relating to the Status of

question of resource allocation and immigration policy raise hotly debated issues of the courts' 'democratic deficit',[9] which is even more acute when it comes to international courts. The courts are finally also limited to discussing specific questions raised in the cases brought before them, which has led to the incremental development of positive obligations over the last couple of decades. Accordingly, while there is evidently further scope for their continuing evolution, the question of the outer limits of states' obligations under international human rights law remains a point of contention among human rights scholars, activists, and politicians.[10]

There is therefore a strong and urgent need to clarify and distinguish human rights of victims of 'modern slavery' and correlative state obligations, on one hand, from duties that stem from other international law domains which do not confer any justiciable rights on victims, on the other. Such analysis must acknowledge that victim protection measures and human rights of victims are not necessarily the same thing—the key distinction to draw upon in the remaining chapters of the book.[11] Whereas the boundary between them is not impermeable, further evolution of human rights obligations through the jurisprudence of the international human rights tribunals must be based on scrupulous analysis rather than wishful thinking.

Before proceeding with the assessment of the relevant human rights jurisprudence concerning states' obligations towards victims of 'modern slavery', it is important to remember that the impact of these jurisprudential developments on the overall suppression of 'modern slavery' is not to be overstated. The Strasbourg Court, or any other international judicial or quasi-judicial body, has neither the capacity nor mandate to set up a comprehensive anti-slavery strategy. They are instead established to rule on individual complaints and provide redress to specific applicants. Moreover, the number of cases that reach these adjudicating bodies is small, which means that they will not bring relief to a substantial number of individuals. Notwithstanding this, the existence of clearly articulated human rights obligations of states and the real possibility of being found in breach of these by a binding decision of a supranational court will arguably provide a strong impetus for compliance and create the environment conducive of stronger victim protection.

Refugees to victims of trafficking and persons at risk of being trafficked' (7 April 2006) HCR/GIP/06/07; Ryszard Piotrowicz, 'The UNCHR's Guidelines on Human Trafficking' (2008) 20(2) International Journal of Refugee Law 242. This particular question is addressed in sections 4.1–4.3.

[9] Sandra Fredman, *Human Rights Transformed: Human Rights Transformed: Positive Rights and Positive Duties* (OUP 2008) ch 4.
[10] For a criticism of 'judicial overreach' see eg Jonathan Sumption, *Trials of the State: Law and the Decline of Politics* (Profile Books 2019); John Finnis and Simon Murray, *Immigration, Strasbourg, and Judicial Overreach* (Policy Exchange 2021).
[11] In the context of constitutional rights and the case law of the German Federal Constitutional Court, Alexy similarly points out to the distinction between 'subjective rights to protection' and 'norms which require the state to protect individuals, without giving these individuals rights'. Robert Alexy, *A Theory of Constitutional Rights* (OUP 2002) 301.

This might not be true for obligations arising from other international instruments, with different enforcement mechanisms.[12] Therefore, human rights tribunals have an important role in the global action against 'modern slavery' consolidating and reinforcing obligations established under specialised anti-trafficking instruments. Human rights obligations articulated by such tribunals set requirements that states owe to any victim of 'modern slavery' within their jurisdiction. They thus represent the minimum core obligations owed by states. With that in mind, the book proceeds to offer a comprehensive, systematic, and in-depth analysis of the existing human rights law and jurisprudence on this issue and the potential for their further development.

Chapter 5 clarifies the mechanism for establishing state responsibility for 'modern slavery' in human rights law, which is grounded in the doctrine of positive obligations. It explains how positive obligations apply in the context of rights which are considered 'absolute'—rights that enshrine some of 'the most fundamental values of a democratic society',[13] especially when the interference with such rights stem from a non-state actor. Chapter 6 then analyses the relevant jurisprudence cataloguing and clarifying obligations of states vis-à-vis victims of 'modern slavery'. Chapter 7 finally considers how the specialised international anti-trafficking instruments could inform and assist the interpretation of human rights law pertaining to the prohibition of 'modern slavery', thus providing a roadmap for future development of human rights law on this subject.

---

[12] This was pointed out by Durieux, who compared the attitudes of the EU Member States towards the 1951 Refugee Convention and towards the European Convention on Human Rights. Jean-François Durieux, 'The Vanishing Refugee' in Hélène Lambert, Jane McAdam, and Maryellen Fullerton (eds), *The Global Reach of European Refugee Law* (CUP 2013) 254–55.

[13] *Z and Others v United Kingdom* (2002) 34 EHRR 3 [73]; *E and Others v United Kingdom* (2003) 36 EHRR 31 [88]; *Siliadin v France* (2006) 43 EHRR 16 [80]–[84]; *Giuliani and Gaggio v Italy* [GC] [2009] ECHR 23458/02 [174]. The Strasbourg Court has referred to the rights contained in Arts 2, 3, 4, or 5 (1) of the Convention, guaranteeing respectively the right to life, the prohibition of torture, inhuman, or degrading treatment or punishment, the prohibition of slavery, and the right to liberty and security of person, as the 'core rights'. See European Court of Human Rights, 'The Court's Priority Policy' (22 May 2017). For a discussion about whether there are any 'absolute' rights and what they entail see Gewirth (n 2); Alan Gewirth, 'There Are Absolute Rights' (1982) 32 Philosophical Quarterly 348; Steven Greer, 'Is the Prohibition against Torture, Cruel, Inhuman and Degrading Treatment Really "Absolute" in International Human Rights Law?' (2015) 15(1) Human Rights Law Review 101; John Finnis, 'Absolute Rights: Some Problems Illustrated' (2016) 61 American Journal of Jurisprudence 195.

5
Positive Obligations as a Means of Establishing State Responsibility for 'Modern Slavery' in Human Rights Law

The discussion of state responsibility for 'modern slavery' must consider how the rules that govern state responsibility in general international law apply in the human rights law context, especially in situations when rights infringements result from non-state actors. The notion of 'state responsibility' traditionally governs the relationship between states as the only subjects of international law. The Articles on State Responsibility for Internationally Wrongful Acts (ARSIWA), articulated by the International Law Commission (ILC) in 2001, thus contain the rules used by states to hold each other to account for the breach of obligations which they undertook by signing international agreements.[1] The ARSIWA therefore make it clear that '[t]he Articles do not deal with the possibility of the invocation of responsibility by persons or entities other than States'.[2]

This traditional approach to state responsibility, embodying 'the classic system of international law, which centred exclusively on sovereign states', is deemed unfit for 'the international system of the twenty-first century'.[3] It is said to ignore 'a wide range of contemporary situations where individuals, other non-state entities, and international organizations invoke state responsibility by initiating judicial or other formal complaint proceeding'.[4] Such situations where state responsibility is invoked by individuals and other non-state entities usually involve international human rights law,[5] and especially the mechanisms which allow for individual petition to the judicial and quasi-judicial bodies.[6]

---

[1] International Law Commission, 'Draft Articles on Responsibility of States for Internationally Wrongful Acts' Doc A/56/10 (2001).
[2] James Crawford, The International Law Commission's Articles on State Responsibility: Introduction, Text and Commentaries (CUP 2002) art 33, para 4.
[3] Edith Brown Weiss, 'Invoking State Responsibility in the Twenty-First Century' (2002) 96(4) The American Journal of International Law 798, 798–99.
[4] ibid.
[5] ibid 809. Weiss suggests that '[t]hree areas illustrate the significant role of individuals and nonstate entities in invoking state responsibility before international dispute settlement bodies: human rights, environmental protection, and foreign investor protection'.
[6] Within the United Nations system of human rights protection, eight of the human rights treaty bodies may, under certain conditions, receive and consider individual complaints or communications from individuals. These are: the Human Rights Committee (CCPR), the Committee on Elimination of Discrimination against Women (CEDAW), the Committee against Torture (CAT), the Committee

However, it is important to distinguish between the rules that govern state responsibility from the rules that govern 'the possibility of the invocation of responsibility by persons or entities other than States'.[7] The commentary to the ARSIWA expressly notes that 'State responsibility extends, for example, to human rights violations and other breaches of international law where the primary beneficiary of the obligation breached is not a State'.[8] Accordingly, state responsibility in both general international law and human rights law is determined with reference to the two basic questions identified in Article 2 ARSIWA: whether state conduct is attributable to the state under international law, and whether it constitutes a breach of an international obligation of the State.

When it comes to state responsibility for the acts of non-state actors, such acts too must be attributable to the state. Thus, Article 8 ARSIWA prescribes that: 'The conduct of a person or group of persons shall be considered an act of a State under international law if the person or group of persons is in fact acting on the instructions of, or under the direction or control of, that State in carrying out the conduct.' This may appear to pose a challenge for human rights law in situations when rights infringements originate from acts of private persons that could not be attributed to a state. In such cases, human rights tribunals have relied on the doctrine of positive obligations as a jurisprudential tool to hold states answerable for rights infringements. In doing so, rather than seeking to stretch the doctrine of attribution, they have worked under the second limb of Article 2 ARISWA, expanding the scope of what constitutes 'an international obligation of the State'. Crawford and Keene note that even in cases where relevant acts could be attributable to the state, such as the actions of police officers constituting wrongful detention, the Strasbourg Court instead went on to find a breach of positive obligations.[9] Garciandia similarly draws attention to a palpable trend in the jurisprudence of the Strasbourg Court towards 'a broad interpretation of many ECHR rights as giving rise to positive obligations as the Court avoids the application of some ARSIWA provisions, and the departure from some of the ARSIWA principles'.[10]

---

on the Elimination of Racial Discrimination (CERD), the Committee on the Rights of Persons with Disabilities (CRPD), the Committee on Enforced Disappearances (CED), the Committee on Economic, Social and Cultural Rights (CESCR), and the Committee on the Rights of the Child (CRC). For further details about how these different mechanisms operate see https://www.ohchr.org/EN/HRBodies/TBPetitions/Pages/HRTBPetitions.aspx. On the regional level, the European Court of Human Rights, the Inter-American Court of Human Rights, and the African Court On Human and People's Rights allow for individual petition against states for violations of human rights.

[7] Crawford (n 2) art 33, para 4.
[8] ibid art 28, para 3.
[9] James Crawford and Amelia Keene, 'The Structure of State Responsibility under the European Convention on Human Rights' in Anne van Aaken and Iulia Motoc (eds), *The European Convention on Human Rights and General International Law* (OUP 2018) 182.
[10] Rosana Garciandia, 'State Responsibility and Positive Obligations in the European Court of Human Rights: The Contribution of the ICJ in Advancing Towards More Judicial Integration' (2020) 33(1) Leiden Journal of International Law 177, 178.

However, even though human rights tribunals may not expressly rely on the ARSIWA, the logic underpinning their decisions on state responsibility for rights infringements by private actors using the doctrine of positive duties is the same. This is because in such cases states are responsible for their *own* conduct and not the original conduct of a non-state actor infringing upon a human right. As expressly noted by the ARSIWA, state conduct can consist of both acts or omissions.[11] In the context of rights infringements by private actors, positive obligations represent the primary rule—'an international obligation of the State'—which demands state action. By not performing the required action, the state is in breach of its own international obligation, and such conduct (omission) is clearly attributable to the state. The ICJ decision in *Congo v Uganda* is one of the rare instances where the courts made explicit the distinction between the responsibility attributed to a state for the human rights violations committed by non-state actors and its responsibility for failing to fulfil its own positive obligations.[12]

Therefore, the challenge for establishing state responsibility for human rights infringements by non-state actors does not lie solely with 'the application of the "effective control" test' under the rules of attribution, as suggested by Garciandia.[13] In most cases it lies instead with the uncertainty about the scope of positive obligations as primary rules arising out of substantive rights, because most positive obligations are not imposed expressly by the language of the international human rights instruments; they are implied in their text by international tribunals through the case law, which is constantly evolving.[14] Accordingly, as noted by Milanovic, the cases that deal with state responsibility for human rights violations by corporate actors[15] 'from the standpoint of positive obligations, where the conduct being attributed is the State's omission to protect an individual against the corporate actor ... raise no issues of inconsistency with the [ARSIWA]'.[16] The same applies to all other instances of rights infringements by non-state actors.

Positive obligations therefore play a central role in shaping states' accountability for 'modern slavery' in human rights law, because instances where state agents are directly engaged in exploitation are extremely rare.[17] The vast majority of states are accountable because they fail to comply with their duties to prevent or adequately

---

[11] Crawford (n 2) art 2, para 4.
[12] Armed Activities on the Territory of the Congo (*Democratic Republic of the Congo v Uganda*), Judgment of 19 December 2005 [2005] ICJ Rep 168.
[13] Garciandia (n 10) 180–81.
[14] The former President of the European Court of Human Rights Jean-Paul Costa noted that the Court's approach 'leaves Governments in a situation of uncertainty over the scope and nature of their legal responsibilities'. See Jean-Paul Costa, 'The European Court of Human Rights: Consistency of Its Case-Law and Positive Obligations' (2008) 33(5) NJCM Bulletin 719.
[15] The same is true for other private actors.
[16] Marko Milanovic, 'Special Rules of Attribution of Conduct in International Law' (2020) 96 International Law Studies 295.
[17] Philippa Webb and Rosana Garciandia, 'State Responsibility for Modern Slavery: Uncovering and Bridging the Gap' (2019) 68(3) International and Comparative Law Quarterly 539.

respond to actions of private individuals who engage in trafficking and exploitation. The nature and scope of such duties, as well as the methodology used by international tribunals to assess state responsibility in these situations are analysed and explained in Chapter 6.

5.1 Non-state Actors and Human Rights Law: A Doctrine of Positive Obligations

The challenge with conceiving practices of 'modern slavery' as a *prima facie* human rights *violation* and attributing responsibility for such a violation to states, stems from the 'private' nature of these practices, which makes it difficult to establish a clear link between the original harm and state conduct. This link is important because, despite recent trends towards greater accountability of private actors for human rights protection,[18] only states can be held *responsible* for their violation under the existing international mechanisms.

However, the nature and scope of such responsibility have fundamentally changed throughout the years. It is now uncontroversial that the effective enjoyment of human rights requires more than just respect or non-interference on the part of a state. Fredman argues that 'the basic values behind human rights, namely freedom, equality, solidarity, and democracy, support the need to ensure that human rights are not just formal entitlements but can in fact be enjoyed by all rights-holders'.[19] Therefore, regardless of whether the threat to human rights emanates from state or non-state actors,[20] dangerous activities and natural disasters,[21] or even socio-economic conditions in other countries,[22] states have a duty to secure their effective enjoyment to individuals within their jurisdiction. As a result, 'the artificial distinction'[23] between negative duties—mainly associated with civil and political rights, and positive duties—linked with socio-economic rights and described as indeterminate, programmatic, resource intensive, and thus non-justiciable, is firmly rejected both in theory and in the practice of human rights bodies.[24]

---

[18] Andrew Clapham, *Human Rights Obligations of Non-State Actors* (OUP 2006).
[19] Sandra Fredman, *Human Rights Transformed: Human Rights Transformed: Positive Rights and Positive Duties* (OUP 2008) 65.
[20] *Osman v United Kingdom* (2000) 29 EHRR 245; *A v United Kingdom* (1999) 27 EHRR 611; *Siliadin v France* (2006) 43 EHRR 16.
[21] *Öneryıldız v Turkey* [GC] (2005) 41 EHRR 20; *Budayeva and Others v Russia* [2008] ECHR 216; *Özel and Others v Turkey* [2020] ECHR 277.
[22] *D v United Kingdom* (1997) 24 EHRR 423.
[23] Fredman (n 19).
[24] UN Human Right Committee, 'General Comment No 31: The Nature of the General Legal Obligation Imposed on States Parties to the Covenant' (26 May 2004) CCPR/C/21/Rev.1/Add.13, para 6.

Accordingly, all human rights give rise to both negative and positive duties.[25]

While the jurisprudence of the Strasbourg Court has been instrumental for this paradigm shift, it was not the first international tribunal expressly to articulate the doctrine of positive obligations.[26] It was the ruling of the Inter-American Court of Human Rights that expressly recognised states' obligations to prevent and respond to acts that threaten individual rights even when they are committed by a private person:

> An illegal act which violates human rights and which is initially not directly imputable to a State (for example, because it is the act of a private person or because the person responsible has not been identified) can lead to international responsibility of the State, not because of the act itself, but because of the lack of due diligence to prevent violation or to respond to it as required by the Convention.[27]

In the context of the human rights prohibition of slavery, one of the first cases to address the issue of positive obligations arising out of this right was *Siliadin v France*, decided by the Strasbourg Court in 2005. The Court recognised that 'restricting the application of Article 4 only to direct actions of state authorities that breached the obligations enshrined in the relevant international instruments would have deprived that provision of its substance'.[28] In the similar vein, the Inter-American Court of Human Rights ruled that:

> States have the obligation to ensure the creation of the conditions required to guarantee that violations of this inalienable right do not occur and, in particular, the duty to prevent its agents as well as private individuals from violating it. Compliance with Article 6, in relation to Article 1(1) of the American Convention, not only supposes that no one may be subjected to slavery, servitude, trafficking or forced labor, but also requires States to adopt all appropriate measures to end such practices and prevent violations of the right not to be subjected to such conditions pursuant to the obligation to ensure the free and full exercise of their rights to every person subject to their jurisdiction.[29]

---

[25] Henry Shue, *Basic Rights: Subsistence, Affluence, and U.S. Foreign Policy* (2nd edn, Princeton UP 1996); Alastair Mowbray, *The Development of Positive Obligations under the European Convention on Human Rights by the European Court of Human Rights* (Hart Publishing 2004); Fredman (n 19).

[26] The Strasbourg Court first recognised implied positive obligations in *Belgian Linguistic (No 2)* (1968) 1 EHRR 252. However, it was noted that such '[t]he implied positive obligations recognised in Belgian Linguistics, did not make an immediate impact. They were not relied on in any judgment over the next decade.' See Hugh Tomlinson, 'Positive Obligations Under the European Convention on Human Rights' Matrix Chambers (21 July 2012); *Marckx v Belgium* (1979) 2 EHRR 330 [31].

[27] Inter-American Court of Human Rights, *Velasquez-Rodriguez v Honduras*, Series C No 4 [1988] IACHR 1 (29 July 1988). See also Tara Melish and Ana Aliverti, 'Positive Obligations in the Inter-American Human Rights System' (2006) 15(3) Interights Bulletin: Positive Obligations 120.

[28] (2006) 43 EHRR 16 [89].

[29] , *Workers of the Hacienda Brasil Verde v Brazil* (Preliminary Objections, Merits, Reparations and Costs) Inter-American Court of Human Rights Series C No 318 (20 October 2016) [317].

Also, the African Commission on Human and Peoples' Rights found a violation of Article 5 of the African Charter on Human and Peoples' Rights safeguarding against '[a]ll forms of exploitation and degradation of man particularly slavery, slave trade, torture, cruel, inhuman or degrading punishment and treatment' on the basis of the Mauritania's failure to prevent practices similar to slavery in its territory.[30]

Yet, the scope of these positive duties has not been firmly set and a number of important questions with regard to their application remain unanswered. Notably, the distinction between the nature and scope of obligations depending on whether the infringement stems from state conduct or that of non-state actors has escaped scrutiny. This results in the conflation of positive obligations with remedies for their breach and further confusion about what states owe to victims of 'modern slavery' in the first place. There is furthermore a need to clarify the nature and scope of positive obligations that stem from 'absolute' rights and whether different standards apply when reviewing state's compliance with these duties. These broader points concerning the operation of positive obligations shall be addressed in the following parts of this chapter, while Chapter 6 explores in detail the relevant jurisprudence of international tribunals pertaining to this budding area of human rights law.

5.2 The Rationale, Legal Basis, and Scope of Positive Obligations

Positive obligations arose out of the need to provide 'practical and effective' protection of fundamental rights.[31] The principle of effectiveness has been one of the general principles of interpretation of the ECHR.[32] Alongside the 'living instrument' doctrine,[33] the Convention's object and purpose,[34] and the evolving European consensus,[35] it is one of the key interpretative tools which has enabled the Strasbourg Court to keep pace with social, moral, legal, and political developments across

---

[30] *Malawi African Association and Others v Mauritania* African Commission on Human and Peoples' Rights, Communications Nos 54/91, 61/91, 98/93, 164/97-196/97, and 210/98 (2000), Ruling of 11 May 2000 [134].

[31] JG Merrills, *The Development of International Law by the European Court of Human Rights* (Manchester UP 1993) 102–103.

[32] *Airey v Ireland* (1979–80) 2 EHRR 305 [24]; *Artico v Italy* (1981) EHRR 1 [33]. Jacobs, White and Ovey (eds), *The European Convention on Human Rights* (5th edn, OUP 2010) 74. See also Georghios Serghides, 'The Principle of Effectiveness as Used in Interpreting, Applying and Implementing the European Convention on Human Rights (Its Nature, Mechanism and Significance)' in Iulia Motoc, Paulo Pinto de Albuquerque, and Krzysztof Wojtyczek (eds), *New Developments in Constitutional Law: Essays in Honour of András Sajó* (Eleven International 2018) 389–98.

[33] *Tyrer v United Kingdom* (1979–80) 12 EHRR 1 [31]; *Christine Goodwin v United Kingdom* (2002) 35 EHRR 18 [75]; *Soering v United Kingdom* (1989) 11 EHRR 439 [102].

[34] *Soering v United Kingdom* (1989) 11 EHRR 439 [87].

[35] *Dudgeon v United Kingdom* (1982) 4 EHRR 149 [60]; *Marckx v Belgium* (n 26) [41].

Europe and ensure the Convention's continuing relevance.[36] This has resulted in the expansion of the Court's remit and review of state conduct—both in terms of scope and intensity.[37] Such perceived 'judicial activism' has attracted strong criticism by some states and parts of legal academia, who argue that that the courts have significantly enlarged the scope of duties initially undertaken by states.[38] Similar trend has been observed with regard to the Inter-American Court of Human Rights, which is said to have used 'interpretive tools as a means to expand its jurisdiction into new areas of international law which were originally thought to fall outside the domain of human right'.[39]

Positive human rights obligations are thus seen as part of the expansive approach to rights interpretation. However, it is important to note that not all positive obligations are implied. Some provisions in human rights treaties are expressed in terms that clearly demand action from states, such as the right to fair trial or the right to free elections.[40] Article 3 of Protocol 1 of the ECHR thus imposes a duty 'to hold free elections at reasonable intervals by secret ballot', which clearly warrants state action. The right to a fair trial presupposes the duty of states to establish and maintain a network of courts and other mechanisms of adjudication.

While the teleological method of interpretation of human rights treaties has been used as a jurisprudential tool for developing positive obligations, their legal basis is found in a general obligation to secure to everyone within the state's jurisdiction the rights and freedoms stipulated in a specific instrument.[41] Such a duty requires states to both 'respect and to ensure' the rights,[42] which 'is both negative and positive in nature'.[43] General Comment No. 31 of the UN Human Rights

---

[36] Another motivation is said to be the Court's institutional needs in light of the increasing case load and 'the Court's desire to minimise the use of time-consuming and expensive fact-finding missions to examine specific complaints', which are said to have given rise to positive obligations to conduct effective investigations. See Alastair Mowbray, *The Development of Positive Obligations under the European Convention on Human Rights by the European Court of Human Rights* (Hart Publishing 2004) 222.

[37] Jacobs, White and Ovey (n 32) 73; David Feldman, *Civil Liberties and Human Rights in England and Wales* (2nd edn, OUP 2002) 55; Alastair Mowbray, 'Creativity of the European Court of Human Rights' (2005) 5(1) Human Rights Law Review 57.

[38] Paul Mahoney, 'Judicial Activism and Judicial Self-Restraint in the European Court of Human Rights: Two Sides of the Same Coin' (1990) 57 Human Rights Law Journal 66. For the positions that welcome this judicial creativity see George Letsas, 'The ECHR as a Living Instrument: Its Meaning and Legitimacy' in Geir Ulfstein, Andreas Follesdal, and Birgit Schlütter (eds), *The European Court of Human Rights in a National, European and Global Context* (CUP 2012).

[39] Lucas Lixinski, 'Treaty Interpretation by the Inter-American Court of Human Rights: Expansionism at the Service of the Unity of International Law' (2010) 21(3) The European Journal of International Law 585, 586.

[40] Hugh Tomlinson, 'Positive Obligations under the European Convention on Human Rights' Matrix Chambers (21 July 2012).

[41] ECHR, art 1. See also ICCPR, art 2(1); CRC, art 2(1); ACHR, art 1.

[42] ICCPR, art 2(1); IACHR, art 1(1).

[43] UN Human Right Committee, General Comment No 31 (26 May 2004) CCPR/C/21/Rev.1/Add. 13, para 6.

Committee is instructive in clarifying the nature of the legal obligation imposed on State Parties to the ICCPR:

> [T]he positive obligations on States Parties to ensure Covenant rights will only be fully discharged if individuals are protected by the State, not just against violations of Covenant rights by its agents, but also against acts committed by private persons or entities that would impair the enjoyment of Covenant rights in so far as they are amenable to application between private persons or entities. There may be circumstances in which a failure to ensure Covenant rights as required by article 2 would give rise to violations by States Parties of those rights, as a result of States Parties' permitting or failing to take appropriate measures or to exercise due diligence to prevent, punish, investigate or redress the harm caused by such acts by private persons or entities.[44]

Accordingly, although 'once considered to be the exception rather than the rule,'[45] the doctrine of positive obligations now applies to all human rights and has been widely deployed by all international judicial and quasi-judicial bodies.

However, even though positive obligations are now part of the mainstream human rights discourse and practice, their scope and extent have not been firmly settled. In general, it is said that positive duties oblige states 'to do something'[46] but the content and limits of such duties are usually determined on a case-by-case basis. The jurisprudence thus reveals a broad range of actions that may be required from states to fulfil their duty to secure rights: from the adoption of adequate legislation[47] to ensuring protection against acts of private violence.[48] In the context of the prohibition of 'modern slavery' specifically, the next two chapters will map out and elucidate the incremental expansion of positive obligations and the potential of their future development.

5.3 Positive Obligations and 'Absolute' Rights

Positive obligations pose a challenge to the interpretation of the so-called 'absolute' rights. A right is considered absolute 'when it cannot be overridden in any

---

[44] ibid para 8.
[45] Jacobs, White, and Ovey (n 32) 100.
[46] Dissenting Opinion of Judge Martens in *Gul v Switzerland* (1996) 22 EHRR 93.
[47] *Marckx v Belgium* (n 26).
[48] *Osman v United Kingdom* (n 20) [115]; *A v United Kingdom* (n 20); *Z and Others v United Kingdom* (2002) 34 EHRR 3 [73]; *E and Others v United Kingdom* (2003) 36 EHRR 31 [88]; *MC v Bulgaria* (2005) 40 EHRR 20 [149]; *Opuz v Turkey* (2010) 50 EHRR 28 [128], [159]. See also *González and Others ('Cotton Field') v Mexico* (Preliminary Objection, Merits, Reparations and Costs) IACtHR Series C No 205 (16 November 2009) [258]; *Favela Nova Brasilia v Brazil* (Preliminary Objections, Merits, Reparations and Costs) IACtHR Series C No 333 (16 February 2017) [243]; *López Soto v Venezuela* (Judgment, Merits, Reparations and Costs) IACtHR Series C No 318 (26 September 2018) [131].

circumstances, so that it can never be justifiably infringed and it must be fulfilled without any exceptions'.[49] It is not entirely clear how this principle extends to states' positive obligations, which are often indeterminate and constantly evolving.[50] For instance, one of the positive obligations commonly associated with rights considered 'absolute' is a duty to take 'preventive operational measures' to protect an individual from 'the criminal acts of another'.[51] Does that mean that states need to guarantee to everyone absolute protection from the acts of private violence? International courts have been clear that this was not the case; they have maintained that the obligation to protect must be interpreted 'in a way which does not impose an impossible or disproportionate burden on the authorities'.[52] This was explained crisply by the Inter-American Court of Human Rights, which noted that:

> [T]he State's treaty-based obligations of guarantee do not entail the unlimited responsibility of the State for every fact or act involving private individuals, because its duty to adopt measures of prevention and to protect private individuals in their relations among themselves is conditioned by the awareness of a situation of a real and immediate risk for a specific individual or group of individuals and the reasonable possibilities of preventing or avoiding that risk.[53]

A further challenge for explaining the character and scope of positive obligations is posed by situations where two 'absolute' rights clash with each other. Greer examined this question with reference to the prohibition of torture where a state' negative obligation to not inflict torture or inhuman or degrading treatment conflicts with its positive obligation to protect individuals from torture inflicted by private actors.[54] He suggested that in order to protect an individual at risk of being tortured or killed by a private actor, a state might be justified in threatening such a private actor with (or even inflicting upon them) torture or inhuman or degrading treatment. This, in his view, dispels a myth that any right could be considered absolute.

However, Mavronicola refutes this argument explaining that we:

> [m]ust acknowledge that distinct types of duties are at play. On the one hand, there is the negative obligation of the State to refrain from subjecting individuals to torture or CIDT ... on the other, there is the positive obligation on the State to

---

[49] Alan Gewirth, 'Are There Any Absolute Rights' (1981) 31(122) The Philosophical Quarterly 1. Other authors have suggested using the term 'non-derogable' as more accurate. See Andrew Ashworth and Mike Redmayne, *The Criminal Process* (4th edn, OUP 2010) 37. In the context of the ECHR, the terms 'absolute' or 'non-derogable' rights refers to the rights contained in arts 2, 3, 4(1), and 7.

[50] Dimitris Xenos, *The Positive Obligations of the State Under the European Convention of Human Rights* (Routledge 2011) 3.

[51] See n 48.

[52] *Osman v United Kingdom* (n 20) [116].

[53] *Workers of the Hacienda Brasil Verde v Brazil* (n 29) [323].

[54] Steven Greer, 'Is the Prohibition against Torture, Cruel, Inhuman and Degrading Treatment Really "Absolute" in International Human Rights Law?' (2015) 15(1) Human Rights Law Review 101.

take all reasonable measures to protect individuals from being subjected to CIDT at the hands of third parties. It is very hard to argue that the positive obligation on the State is boundless.[55]

The distinction between positive and negative obligations thus plays a critical role in delimiting the scope of states' responsibility for human rights violations, and 'absolute' rights are no exception in this regard. Such a distinction is premised on the understanding of negative obligations as rules and positive obligations as principles, put forward by a legal philosopher Robert Alexy.[56] According to Alexy, 'every norm is either a rule or a principle'.[57] While rules and principles 'both say what ought to be the case' they differ in that rules are 'norms which are always either fulfilled or not'[58] whereas principles are 'norms which require that something be realized to the greatest extent possible given the legal and factual possibilities'.[59] Principles are therefore seen as 'optimisation requirements', which 'can be satisfied to varying degrees'.[60]

Alexy then distinguishes between 'rights to negative actions' or 'defensive rights of the citizen against the state' and 'rights to positive action' or 'protective rights' by which he means 'rights which a right holder has against the state that it protect him from interferences by third parties'.[61] He posits that because the former contain 'a *prohibition* on destroying or adversely affecting something, then *every* act which represents or brings about destruction or an adverse effect is prohibited'.[62] By contrast, 'if there is a *command* to protect or support something, then *not every* act which represents or brings about protection or support is required'.[63] He illustrates this by a reference to the right to life: '[t]he prohibition on killing implies, at least prima facie, the prohibition of every act of killing, whereas the command to rescue does not imply a command to carry out every possible act of rescuing'.[64] This implies a certain level of discretion on the part of a duty-holder as to the choice of a method to satisfy the duty. Accordingly, Alexy characterises protective duties arising out of 'rights to positive actions' as principles because 'they require maximally extensive protection relative to what is factually and legally possible'.[65] The

---

[55] Natasa Mavronicola, 'Is the Prohibition against Torture and Cruel, Inhuman and Degrading Treatment Absolute in International Human Rights Law? A Reply to Steven Greer' (2017) 17 Human Rights Law Review 483.
[56] Robert Alexy, *A Theory of Constitutional Rights* (OUP 2002). See also Fredman (n 19).
[57] Alexy (n 56) 48.
[58] ibid.
[59] ibid 47.
[60] ibid 47–48.
[61] ibid 288, 300.
[62] ibid 308.
[63] ibid.
[64] ibid.
[65] ibid 308–309.

extent of protective duties will therefore depend on the factual circumstances of each case as well as competing principles and rules.

This view corresponds to the approach of international tribunals when interpreting positive obligations, which afford a certain latitude to States to select the means to fulfil obligations arising out of human rights law. The Strasbourg Court thus emphasises that 'where the State is required to take positive measures, the choice of means is in principle a matter that falls within the Contracting State's margin of appreciation'.[66] This is because:

> The choice as to the most appropriate means of achieving [the effective implementation of the Convention] is in principle a matter for the domestic authorities, who are in continuous contact with the vital forces of their countries and are better placed to assess the possibilities and resources afforded by their respective domestic legal systems.[67]

The question, however, is whether the assessment of states' compliance with positive obligations involves different standards or the intensity of review when it comes to 'absolute' rights. The jurisprudence of international human rights courts suggest that it does. The ECtHR thus continuously emphasises that violations of 'absolute' rights, which enshrine 'one of the basic values of the democratic societies making up the Council of Europe'[68] require protection through criminal law.[69] Violations of the right to life, the prohibition of torture, or slavery (as well as certain aspects of the right to liberty and security and of the right to respect for private and family life) are deemed 'serious human rights violations' in respect of which states have an obligation to enact and enforce criminal law.[70] Similarly, The Inter-American Court of Human Rights (IACtHR) noted that the obligation to ensure freedom from slavery, guaranteed in Article 6 of the American Convention, requires States to 'define such offenses under criminal law, with severe penalties' and to 'open, ex officio and immediately, an effective investigation that permits the identification, prosecution and punishment of those responsible'.[71]

In addition, the protection of vulnerable individuals has been given special priority in human rights jurisprudence.[72] Thus, it is pointed out that:

---

[66] *Fadeyeva v Russia* (2007) 45 EHRR 10 [96].
[67] *DJ v Croatia* [2012] ECHR 1642 [93].
[68] *Siliadin v France* (2006) 43 EHRR 16 [82], [112]; *Rantsev v Cyprus and Russia* (2010) 51 EHRR 1.
[69] *Rantsev v Cyprus and Russia* (n 68) [218]. The Court relied on previous rulings in *Osman v United Kingdom* (n 20) [115]; *Medova v Russia* [2009] ECHR 70 [95]; *Opuz v Turkey* (n 48) [128].
[70] The Council of Europe, Committee of Ministers, 'Guidelines of the Committee of Ministers of the Council of Europe on Eradicating Impunity for Serious Human Rights Violations' 1110th Meeting (30 March 2011) II.3. *MC v Bulgaria* (n 48) [150].
[71] *Workers of the Hacienda Brasil Verde v brazil* (n 29) [319].
[72] *X and Y v Netherlands* (1986) 8 EHRR 235 [23]; *Stubbings and Others v United Kingdom* (1997) 23 EHRR 213 [64]; *A v United Kingdom* (n 20) [22]; *Z v United Kingdom* (2002) 34 EHRR 3 [73]; *E v United Kingdom* (2003) 36 EHRR 31 [88]; *MC v Bulgaria* (n 48) [150]; *Siliadin v France* (n 68) [143]; *Bevacqua*

[C]hildren, and other vulnerable individuals, are owed a duty of special protection by the state, and the [Strasbourg] Court will be particularly demanding in its supervision of a state's existing measures designed to protect these individuals from private violence. In other words, the Court will allow states a narrower margin of appreciation regarding the adequacy of the measures taken in such contexts.[73]

Accordingly, due to the significance of interests protected by 'absolute' rights and special protection afforded to vulnerable individuals, the margin given to states to choose the means of complying with their positive obligations is narrower and the scrutiny over their choices is more intensive. This is crucial for 'modern slavery' cases which always involve vulnerable victims and serious forms of abuse and exploitation.

It is important to note, however, that states' obligations to deploy the criminal justice mechanism to secure and redress the infringements of 'absolute' rights by private actors stand in sharp contrast with another set of states' positive obligations concerning the operation of the criminal justice system—obligations aimed at protecting those charged with criminal offences from the excessive exercise of state power.[74] Human rights scholars have warned against a potential 'coercive overreach' of the former obligations—the duties that require states to mobilise criminal law against individuals whose actions encroach upon the human rights of others.[75]

It must be emphasised, however, that even though criminal justice measures might be necessary and appropriate means for securing the interests protected by the 'absolute' rights, positive obligations arising out of these rights are by no means limited to criminal law.[76] As the following chapter demonstrates, obligations concerning law enforcement are just one aspect of state obligations arising out of the prohibition of 'modern slavery' and other 'absolute' rights. In many cases, the perpetrators of such acts will remain unknown or unreachable, while victims will still

---

and S v Bulgaria [2008] ECHR 498 [64]; *Opuz v Turkey* (n 48) [159]; *Oršuš and Others v Croatia* [GC] (2011) 52 EHRR 7 [147]; *MSS v Belgium and Greece* [GC] (2011) 53 EHRR 2 [251].

[73] Clapham (n 18) 357. See eg *MC v Bulgaria* (n 48) [150].
[74] Mowbray (n 25) 222 (Mowbray notes that in general 'the dominant group of positive obligations expressly imposed upon states, by the text of the Convention ... were concerned with different stages of the criminal justice system').
[75] Liora Lazarus, 'Positive Obligations and Criminal Justice: Duties to Protect or Coerce?' in Julian Roberts and Lucia Zedner (eds), *Principled Approaches to Criminal Law and Criminal Justice: Essays in Honour of Professor Andrew Ashworth* (OUP 2012); Laurens Lavrysen and Natasa Mavronicola (eds), *Coercive Human Rights: Positive Duties to Mobilise the Criminal Law under the ECHR* (Hart Publishing 2020).
[76] The same logic underpins the establishment of international criminal law, where severe human rights violations often occurring on a large scale, have been articulated as international crimes, such as genocide or crimes against humanity. This, however, does not imply that international and domestic criminal law are the only means for preventing these atrocities and securing the interests and values protected.

need protection and assistance. For that reason, victim protection has been decoupled from any criminal proceedings against perpetrators of 'modern slavery'.[77]

To sum up, whereas the negative prohibition against 'modern slavery' is 'absolute' for a state, in that a state can never be excused for subjecting individuals to 'modern slavery', positive obligations in situations where private actors engage in these practices are context specific and depend on a range of factors. These factors and the reasoning of the international tribunals in deciding whether states have discharged their positive obligations are examined and explained in detail in the following chapter.

5.4 Positive Obligations versus Remedies when Rights Are Infringed by Non-state Actors

It has already been explained that State's human rights obligations exist irrespective of the type or the source of conduct that threatens rights. States therefore have a duty to secure rights against infringements that stem from the conduct of their own agents and that of non-state actors, but also from dangerous activities, environmental disasters, and even the risks of rights violations in other countries.[78] While it has been acknowledged in the literature that a threat to rights may emanate from different sources, this was done with the intention of showing the irrelevance of such distinction for framing human rights obligations. For instance, Andrew Clapham criticises the traditional state/non-state distinction, which he argues 'risks obfuscating the real violators; to insist on the exclusive applicability of human rights law to governments generates a dangerous sense of impunity for those who are undermining people's rights'.[79] He thus rejects 'the prevalent assumption' that 'that public international law is inoperative outside established enforcement regimes such as international tribunals'[80] suggesting that: '[A] non-state

---

[77] *J and Others v Austria* [2017] ECHR 37 [115]. Anti-Trafficking Convention, art 12(6); Directive of the European Parliament and of the Council on Preventing and Combating Trafficking in Human Beings and Protecting its Victims, and Replacing Council Framework Decision 2002/629/JHA (5 April 2011) 2011/36/EU (Anti-Trafficking Directive), art 11(3); Office of the High Commissioner for Human Rights (OHCHR) Recommended Principles and Guidelines on Human Rights and Human Trafficking (2002) E/2002/68/Add.1, guideline 6.1; UNODC 'Legislative Guide for the Implementation of the Protocol to Prevent, Suppress and Punish Trafficking In Persons, Especially Women and Children, Supplementing the United Nations Convention Against Transnational Organized Crime' (2004) (Trafficking Legislative Guide) para 62. Also, it is suggested that providing unconditional protection to victims contributes to criminal justice goals. See Anne Gallagher, *The International Law of Human Trafficking* (CUP 2010) 297.
[78] See n 20 and n 22) above. In *L v Lithuania* (2008) 46 EHRR 22 [46] the Strasbourg Court expressly noted that 'Article 3 entails a positive obligation on the part of the State to protect the individual from acute ill-treatment, whether physical or mental, whatever its source. Thus if the source is a naturally occurring illness, the treatment for which could involve the responsibility of the State, but is not forthcoming or patently inadequate, an issue may arise under this provision' (emphasis added).
[79] Clapham (n 18) 54.
[80] ibid 29.

actor such as a corporation can still be the bearer of international duties outside the context of international courts and tribunals. Lack of international jurisdiction to try a corporation does not mean that the corporation is under no international legal obligations.'[81]

While these arguments are not without merit, and can pave the way for adapting the human rights system to new demands and new needs *de lege ferenda*, in the context of the *existing* mechanisms for human rights protection, which are the focus of this book, ignoring the difference between the source of the threat to rights leads to a conflation of positive obligations with remedies for human rights violations. This in turn results in the confusion about what *states* owe to victims of 'modern slavery' and the available mechanisms and procedures for holding them accountable for securing guaranteed rights. Accordingly, leaving aside the views about whether it is preferable for non-state actors to bear human rights obligations overall, it is still sensible to distinguish between obligations of states owed to victims of 'modern slavery' from obligations of private actors emanating either directly from international law or from domestic legislation.

Therefore, it is commonly acknowledged in the human rights scholarship and practice that when a human right is unjustifiably infringed[82] by a conduct of the state agent, the state is obliged to provide a remedy for such violation.[83] For example, in *Aydin v Turkey*, the applicant was detained by the security forces, and while in custody, she was raped and subjected to various forms of ill-treatment in violation of Article 3 ECHR.[84] The Court explained that:

> [W]here an individual has an arguable claim that he or she has been tortured by agents of the State, the notion of an 'effective remedy' entails, in addition to the payment of compensation where appropriate, a thorough and effective investigation capable of leading to the identification and punishment of those responsible.[85]

If, on the other hand, a similar act was committed by a non-state actor, the responsibility of a state would only be engaged once it was shown that the state was aware of such a situation (or ought to have been) and it failed to comply with specific positive obligations that arose in such circumstances.[86] These obligations do not, however, amount to a remedy for the said human rights infringement by a

---

[81] ibid 31.
[82] Gewirth (n 49) 2 explains a distinction between rights infringements and violations, the latter being unjustified infringements.
[83] *Aksoy v Turkey* (1997) 23 EHRR 553; *Aydin v Turkey* (1998) EHRR 251.
[84] *Aydin v Turkey* (1998) EHRR 251.
[85] ibid [103].
[86] *Opuz v Turkey* (n 48); *Beganovic v Croatia* [2009] ECHR 992.

non-state actor, but rather self-standing positive obligations arising out of the substantive right (the breach of which results in the separate right to remedy).

In other words, remedies are concerned with rectifying *state's wrongdoing* while positive duties arise with respect to an initial act that causes harm, which is not attributable to a state. However, the action required in both cases may well be the same. For example, on one hand, in cases where a state has either directly contributed to death or ill treatment[87] or it has failed to prevent these,[88] thus violating a self-standing positive obligation, the investigation of these allegations would amount to a remedy for such omission. On the other hand, when the right to life, or the prohibition of torture are infringed upon by actions of private individuals,[89] the duty to conduct an investigation would represent a self-standing positive obligation within the substantive article, provided that state authorities had the required knowledge of such infringement. A failure to discharge such self-standing obligation to investigate private infringements of rights would in turn create a separate duty to provide a remedy for *that* violation.

Therefore, as the following chapter shows, a state's failure to investigate reports of 'modern slavery' by private individuals amounts to the breach of its positive procedural obligation.[90] This in turn gives rise to a separate obligation to remedy such omission. Unfortunately, the Strasbourg Court has failed to explain what counts as an appropriate remedy in these cases, the goal of such remedies, and the distinction between domestic remedies and those afforded by an international tribunal.[91] In rare instances where it reflected on this issue, the Court declared that 'in principle, for complaints concerning treatment contrary to Article 4, the adequate remedy to be pursued is a criminal complaint'.[92] This reveals the lack of appreciation of the difference between positive obligations and remedies, in situations of private infringements of human rights. It also confuses remedies for the original harm inflicted by private actors with remedies for states' failing to comply with their own positive human rights obligations.

The right to remedy requires states to afford access to domestic mechanisms and procedures that can establish *a failure of the state* to act in accordance with its *own* negative or positive obligations and provide appropriate redress.[93] This was made clear in a recommendation adopted by the Committee of Ministers of the

---

[87] *Aksoy v Turkey* (n 83); *Aydin v Turkey* (n 83).
[88] *Z v United Kingdom* (n 72); *E v United Kingdom* (n 72).
[89] *Menson and Others v United Kingdom (Admissibility)* (2003) 37 EHRR CD220; *MC v Bulgaria* (n 48); *Opuz v Turkey* (n 48); *Denis Vasilyev v Russia* [2009] ECHR 2078; *Beganovic v Croatia* (n 86).
[90] *Zoletic and Others v Azerbaijan* [2021] ECHR 789. See the discussion of the procedural obligations in Chapter 6, section 6.2.
[91] See the discussion in Chapter 6, section 6.4.
[92] *Zoletic v Azerbaijan* (n 90) [175].
[93] For an excellent overview of the sources of the right to remedy in human rights law see Kent Roach, *Remedies for Human Rights Violations: A Two-Track Approach to Supra-national and National Law* (CUP 2021) section 1.6.

Council of Europe in 1984,[94] which 'sought to reinforce Article 13 [ECHR]'[95] containing the right to a remedy. The Recommendation calls on all Council of Europe member states to provide remedies for '*governmental wrongs*'[96] and expressly states that '[r]eparation should be ensured for damage caused by an act due to *a failure of a public authority to conduct itself in a way which can be expected from it in law* in relation to the injured person'.[97]

It is therefore apparent that the notion of remedy in human rights law does *not* imply a remedy for the *original harm* which results from actions of non-state actors that infringe upon a right, but for the harm that results from the conduct of a state that has a duty to secure rights against private infringements. This distinction has not always been clearly maintained in the scholarship on human trafficking. For example, while Gallagher correctly distinguishes between two ways the obligation to provide remedies could arise—first, as a result of the state 'being found to be directly responsible for the violation of a human right' and, secondly, 'when the State is not directly implicated in the initial harm, but has failed to discharge its obligation to prevent the harm and/or to respond appropriately'[98]—she goes on to argue that: '[T]he right to a remedy for gross violations of human rights, a term that would incorporate egregious cases of trafficking, includes the rights of access to justice, *reparation for harm suffered*, and access to information concerning violations and reparation mechanisms'.[99]

Similarly, the Special Rapporteur on trafficking in persons acknowledges, on one hand, that 'States are under an obligation to provide remedies for trafficked persons where they fail to exercise due diligence to prevent and combat trafficking in persons or to protect the human rights of trafficked persons'.[100] However, on the other hand, she proceeds to discuss the issues of 'compensation … recovery, restitution, satisfaction and guarantees of non-repetition' without any reference to how these types of remedies are related to the *state's wrongdoing* (as opposed to the

---

[94] Council of Europe, Committee of Ministers, Recommendation No R(84)5 of the Committee of Ministers to Member States Relating to Public Liability (18 September 1984).

[95] Dinah Shelton, *Remedies in International Human Rights Law* (OUP 2015).

[96] Council of Europe, Committee of Ministers, Recommendation No R(84)5 of the Committee of Ministers to Member States Relating to Public Liability (18 September 1984) (emphasis added).

[97] ibid (emphasis added). Council of Europe, Committee of Ministers, Recommendation No R(84)5 of the Committee of Ministers to Member States Relating to Public Liability (18 September 1984) (emphasis added).

[98] Anne Gallagher, 'The Right to an Effective Remedy for Victims of Trafficking in Persons: A Survey of International Law and Policy' Paper submitted for the expert consultation convened by the UN Special Rapporteur on Trafficking in Persons, especially women and children, Ms Joy Ngozi Ezeilo on 'The Right to an Effective Remedy for Trafficked Persons' Bratislava, Slovakia (22—23 November 2010) 3.

[99] ibid 6 (emphasis added).

[100] Report of the Special Rapporteur on trafficking in persons, especially women and children; Joy Ngozi Ezeilo, 'The Right to an Effective Remedy for Trafficked Persons' Doc A/66/283 (9 August 2011) para 12.

original harm suffered at hands of traffickers).[101] When it comes to compensation, the Special Rapporteur elaborates that:

> Compensation should be provided for economic assessable damage to the extent that such damage cannot be made good by restitution. It may be provided *as payment for a wide range of injury, loss or damage caused by the offender*, including, for example: costs of the medical, physical, psychological or psychiatric treatment required by the victim; lost income and due wages; legal fees and other similar costs; and payment for non-material damages, resulting from moral, physical or psychological injury, emotional distress, pain and suffering.[102]

In addition to conflating remedies for the original harm and those for a state's failure to respond adequately to such harm or the risk thereof, the distinction between positive duties and remedies (and the underlying distinction between the source of the threat to human rights) is not always made clear cut in literature or human rights jurisprudence. Stoyanova thus argues that 'criminal conviction of the perpetrators could be a form of remedy'.[103] Yet, this would only be true in situations where state agents are directly involved in 'modern slavery', which is a disproportionately small number of overall cases of 'modern slavery'.[104] In contrast, in situations where 'modern slavery' is inflicted by non-state actors, their criminal conviction would amount to a state's discharging its positive procedural obligation, provided that other conditions are met.

As already noted, the Strasbourg Court struggles with the distinction between positive obligations and remedies for the breach of the ECHR rights, especially in cases where rights are infringed by acts of non-state actors. The Court requires that an applicant demonstrates an 'arguable claim' to be the victim of a *violation* of Convention rights in order to trigger a duty to provide an effective domestic remedy.[105] It flows from this that if the original act infringing upon a specific right was performed by private individuals, there would be no *violation* of the right

---

[101] ibid para 13. The same approach is followed by the subsequent Special Rapporteur on trafficking in persons. See Report of the Special Rapporteur on trafficking in persons, especially women and children, Maria Grazia Giammarinaro, Report of the United Nations High Commissioner for Human Rights, Summary of the consultations held on the draft basic principles on the right to effective remedy for victims of trafficking in persons, Doc A/HRC/26/18 (May 2014).

[102] ibid para 18 (emphasis added).

[103] ibid 411. She later acknowledges on page 412 that 'the procedural limb of Article 4 and the investigative duties under Article 13 are meant to target different types of harm'.

[104] The Strasbourg Court expressly notes that: 'Cases relating to human trafficking under Article 4 typically involve an issue of the States' positive obligations under the Convention. Indeed, the applicants in these cases are normally victims of trafficking or trafficking-related conduct by another private party, whose actions cannot attract the direct responsibility of the State.' See eg *Zoletic v Azerbaijan* (n 90) [181]; *J and Others v Austria* (n 77) [108]–[109]; *SM v Croatia* App no 60561/14 (ECtHR GC, 25 June 2020) [304].

[105] *Silver v United Kingdom* (1983) 5 EHRR 347 [113].

stricto sensu, but only an *infringement* that might trigger positive duties of a state to act in a certain way.

Some cases acknowledge this distinction and correctly frame the obligation to investigate private infringements of the ECHR rights as part of the positive obligations under the substantive article.[106] For instance, in *Denis Vasilyev v Russia*, the applicant and his friend were assaulted and robbed by an unknown person and, even though police officers attended the scene, they assumed that the applicant and his friend were intoxicated, leaving them without conducting an investigation into the circumstances of the assault. The Strasbourg Court explained that Article 3, which prohibits inhuman and degrading treatment or punishment, required that 'the authorities conduct an effective official investigation into the alleged ill-treatment even if such treatment has been inflicted by private individuals'.[107] It thus held that Russia had violated Article 3 under its procedural limb in that the investigation into the assault on the applicant was ineffective.

In addition to Russia's failing to investigate the original assault on the applicant by an unknown perpetrator, in breach of its procedural obligation under Article 3 ECHR, the Court found that the State authorities were responsible for the inhuman treatment of the applicant resulting from the police officers' failure to render him assistance at the time when he had been in a life-threatening state. Being abandoned by the police without assistance while lying unconscious on the ground amounted to the state's direct infringement of Article 3, and the Court correctly framed a failure to investigate allegations against police officers (as opposed to the original offence) as a separate violation of the applicant's right to an effective remedy guaranteed in Article 13 ECHR.

Similarly, in *Aksoy v Turkey*, which addressed applicant's ill-treatment in police custody, the Court expressly noted with regard to Article 13 ECHR that:

> [W]here an individual has an arguable claim that he has been tortured by agents of the State, the notion of an 'effective remedy' entails, in addition to the payment of compensation where appropriate, *a thorough and effective investigation* capable of leading to the identification and punishment of those responsible and including effective access for the complainant to the investigatory procedure.[108]

Again, the Court rightly framed a duty to investigate an arguable claim that the right has been infringed by state agents as part of the right to remedy.

However, other examples from the Strasbourg case law reveal the inconsistency in the Court's approach to grounding the procedural obligation to investigate acts

---

[106] *Beganovic v Croatia* (n 86) [74]–[88]; *Denis Vasilyev v Russia* (n 89) [123]–[129].
[107] *Denis Vasilyev v Russia* (n 89) [99].
[108] *Aksoy v Turkey* (n 83) [98] (emphasis added). See also *Aydin v Turkey* (n 83) [103]–[109]; *İlhan v Turkey* [GC] (2002) 34 EHRR 36 [121].

that infringe upon human rights. In several cases where the rights infringement was a result of actions of state agents, the deficiencies in investigating such allegations were considered a breach of the procedural duty under substantive articles.[109] For example, in Hugh Jordan v United Kingdom, where the applicant alleged that his son had been unjustifiably shot and killed by a police officer, and that there was no effective investigation into, or redress for, his death, the Court ruled that:

> The obligation to protect the right to life under Article 2 of the Convention ... also requires by implication that there should be some form of effective official investigation when individuals have been killed as a result of the use of force ... The essential purpose of such investigation is to secure the effective implementation of the domestic laws which protect the right to life and, *in those cases involving State agents or bodies*, to ensure their accountability for deaths occurring under their responsibility.[110]

Similar reasoning was deployed in *Poltoratskiy v Ukraine*,[111] which concerned the allegations of ill-treatment of the applicant in prison and the failure to carry out an effective official investigation into these allegations. The decision to frame the deficiencies in the required official investigation into the applicant's allegations of ill-treatment as a violation of the procedural aspect of Article 3 ECHR was criticised by the dissenting Judge Nicolas Bratza, who noted that:

> I would have preferred that the complaint relating to the failure of the prison authorities to carry out an effective official investigation into the applicant's allegations of ill-treatment in Ivano-Frankivsk Prison had been examined under Article 13 of the Convention rather than under the so-called 'procedural aspects' of Article 3.[112]

Unfortunately, the explanation provided for this preference, which relied on the reasoning of the Grand Chamber in *İlhan v Turkey* is far from convincing. In *Ilhan*, the Grand Chamber correctly grounded the duty to investigate allegations of ill-treatment by state officials in Article 13, which guarantees the right to remedy, instead of a substantive article that prohibits torture and inhuman or degrading treatment or punishment. However, the Court did not use the distinction between infringements of rights by private individuals and state agents as the basis for

---

[109] *McCann and Others v United Kingdom* [1995] ECHR 18984/91; *Hugh Jordan v United Kingdom* (2001) 37 EHRR 52; *Poltoratskiy v Ukraine* (2004) 39 EHRR 43; *Assenov and Others v Bulgaria* (1999) 28 EHRR 652.
[110] *Hugh Jordan v United Kingdom* (n 109) [105].
[111] *Poltoratskiy v Ukraine* (n 109) [125].
[112] ibid, Dissenting Opinion of Judge Nicolas Bratza.

determining whether a duty to investigate should be considered as part of the substantive right or the right to remedy. Instead, the Grand Chamber held that:

> The obligation to provide an effective investigation into the death caused by, inter alios, the security forces of the State was for this reason implied under Article 2 which guarantees the right to life ... This provision does, however, include the requirement that the right to life be 'protected by law'. It may also concern situations where the initiative must rest on the State for the practical reason that the victim is deceased and the circumstances of the death may be largely confined within the knowledge of State officials.
>
> Article 3, however, is phrased in substantive terms. Furthermore, although the victim of an alleged breach of this provision may be in a vulnerable position, the practical exigencies of the situation will often differ from cases of use of lethal force or suspicious deaths. The Court considers that the requirement under Article 13 of the Convention that a person with an arguable claim of a violation of Article 3 be provided with an effective remedy will generally provide both redress to the applicant and the necessary procedural safeguards against abuses by State officials.[113]

While arriving to the correct conclusion, the explanation provided by the Court in *Ilhan*, which relied on the text of the Convention and the fact that in the right to life cases a victim is deceased to distinguish the legal basis for a duty to investigate in Article 2 and Article 3 cases, is entirely unpersuasive. What is more, in the subsequent case brought by thirteen Turkish nationals who alleged that they had been subject to various forms of ill-treatment while in police custody and that the relevant authorities did not carry out an effective investigation into their complaints of ill-treatment in breach of Article 3, the Court merely noted that:

> [It] considers it appropriate to examine these complaints under Article 13 of the Convention, it being understood that, *since the Court is master of the characterisation to be given in law to the facts of the case*, it does not consider itself bound by the characterisation given by an applicant or a Government.[114]

Refusing to offer a clear criterion for choosing to examine a complaint under the right to remedy instead of the procedural limb of the substantive article reveals the Court's lack of attention to the distinction between state and private infringements, and the implications of this distinction for the framing of positive obligations and remedies for human rights violations.[115]

[113] *İlhan v Turkey* (n 108) [91]–[92].
[114] *Bati and Others v Turkey* [2008] ECHR 246 [127] (emphasis added).
[115] Mowbray suggests that 'the Article 3 duty may well be restricted to cases where the Court, due to a lack of conclusive evidence, is unable to reach a finding in respect of the applicants' substantive

However, one might rightly wonder—is this a distinction without a difference? Is a remedy in the form of effective investigation for the state's direct breach of human rights different from the state's positive obligation to investigate infringements of rights by private actors? Or are these two types of investigation essentially the same?[116] Moreover, if a state fails to comply with its positive procedural duty to investigate alleged infringements of rights by private actors, what is the appropriate remedy for that omission? And if a state then fails to provide such an appropriate remedy, would the finding of the international tribunal be different, than in cases where a state fails to provide a remedy in the form of effective investigation for its own direct breaches of human rights? These questions require a comprehensive engagement with the questions of the nature, scope, and aim of appropriate remedies for human rights violations—violations of both positive and negative obligations.

However, the existing scholarship and jurisprudence fail to explain whether and how the scope of remedies differ depending on whether the conduct infringing upon human rights is attributed to state agents or private parties. Thus, both Dinah Shelton[117] and Kent Roach[118] provide a comprehensive and insightful analysis of remedies in human rights law, yet neither author addresses the question of the nature and scope of remedies in cases where rights infringements emanate from non-state actors and the critical distinction between states' positive obligations to address private infringements and the duty to provide adequate remedy for a failure to comply with such obligations. In several cases concerning rights enshrined in Articles 3 and 4 ECHR, the Strasbourg Court ruled that 'the general scope of the State's positive obligations might differ between cases where the treatment contrary to the Convention has been inflicted through the involvement of State agents and cases where violence is inflicted by private individuals'.[119] While the Court never explained why and how positive obligations in these cases differ, it is plausible to imply from this statement that the scope of remedies also differs depending on the source of the threat to human rights, and the nature of the duty that has been violated.

The jurisprudence of the ECtHR on the issue of remedies has been deemed 'unsatisfactory'[120] and the Strasbourg Court's approach to awards described as 'inconsistent and difficult to rationalize'.[121] Similarly, even though the Inter-American

complaints (ie whether they had been subject to torture or inhuman treatment etc. in violation of Article 3)'. Mowbray (n 25) 63.

[116] In *Denis Vasilyev v Russia* (n 89) [100] the Court noted that '[e]ven though the scope of the State's positive obligations might differ between cases where treatment contrary to Article 3 has been inflicted through the involvement of State agents and cases where violence is inflicted by private individuals ... the requirements as to an official investigation are similar'.
[117] Shelton (n 95).
[118] Roach (n 93).
[119] *SM v Croatia* (n 104) [312]. See also *Beganovic v Croatia* (n 86) [69]; *Denis Vasilyev v Russia* (n 89) [100].
[120] Shelton (n 95) 238.
[121] Roach (n 93) 245.

Court has been praised for its 'innovative remedies'[122] and is considered 'more generous to litigants', it is said to have 'suffered from inconsistency'.[123] There is accordingly a pressing need for human rights tribunals to engage with the issue of remedies in a more rigorous and comprehensive way, and to clarify and explain the relationship between remedies and positive obligations.

Given the discreet focus of this book, it will not seek to offer a general answer to the question of whether and how remedies differ depending on whether the conduct infringing upon the right is performed by state agents or private parties. This requires a comprehensive doctrinal, empirical, and normative enquiry, which exceeds the scope of this book.

5.5 The Range and Classification of Positive Obligations: General and Specific Duties

Henry Shue provided a persuasive and influential account of human rights obligations arguing that every human right gives rise to three types of duties: to respect, to protect, and to aid (provide).[124] He was, however, careful to note that this 'very simple tripartite of duties' was only provisory and should by no means lead to some conceptual obsession. Human rights tribunals appear to have followed this advice and avoided elaborating a 'general theory of positive obligations'.[125] Instead, they opted for a casuistic approach, which led to an incremental development of positive obligations. Despite this, certain categories of positive obligations have crystallised in practice and these categories represent a useful analytical lens for examining the evolution of positive obligations through case law.

Several taxonomies of positive obligations have been proposed in the literature but neither seems to capture the matrix espoused in the existing case law. For instance, drawing on Shue's tripartite classification, Mowbray conducted a 'detailed examination ... of the key positive obligations developed by the [Strasbourg] Court under the major substantive Articles'[126] and identified certain broad types. Mowbray first identifies 'the duty to take reasonable measures *to protect* individuals from infringement of their rights by other private persons' as one of 'the most prevalent types of positive obligation'.[127] This duty, according to Mowbray, can be satisfied by having adequate 'domestic legal provisions criminalizing the conducts'

---

[122] ibid 531. See also Jo Pasqualucci, *The Practice and Procedure of the Inter-American Court of Human Rights* (CUP 2013).

[123] Shelton (n 95) 238.

[124] Shue (n xx) 160. See also Final Report by Asbjørn Eide, 'The Right to Adequate Food as a Human Right' (UN Sub-Commission for the Promotion and Protection of Human Rights, UN Doc E/CN4/Sub2/1987/23 (7 July 1987) paras 112–15.

[125] *Plattform 'Ärzte für das Leben' v Austria* (1991) 13 EHRR 204 [31].

[126] Mowbray (n 25) 225.

[127] ibid.

which threaten another's Convention rights.[128] He furthermore adds that 'a more onerous form of this positive obligation demands that states deploy personnel to provide "physical measures of security" for potential victims known to be facing immediate threats of violence'.[129]

The next broad collection of positive obligations, which according to Mowbray also falls within Shue's general duty to protect, is concerned with the manner in which states treat persons detained under the authority of their criminal justice systems. He examines a range of situations in which this obligation arises under the rights to life, the right to liberty and security, and the prohibition of torture and other ill-treatment.[130]

There are three problems with Mowbray's assessment of the positive duty to protect. First, he appears to restrict the scope of a duty to protect individuals against non-state violations only to those situations where a threat arises from private individuals, although such a duty exists regardless of the source of the threat.[131] For example, the case of *Budayeva v Russia* concerned the failure of Russian authorities to protect rights to life and property from the mudslides that hit the town.[132] The Strasbourg Court ruled that '[t]he fundamental importance of the right to life requires that the scope of the positive obligations under Article 2 includes a duty to do everything within the authorities' power in the sphere of disaster relief for the protection of that right'.[133] Secondly, he seems to limit the scope of states' duties only to the requirements related to criminalisation and application of criminal law, even though this is but one of their obligations, as shown in detail in the next chapter. Thirdly, in arguing that the duty to protect can be satisfied by having adequate 'domestic legal provisions criminalizing the conducts' which threaten another's Convention rights, Mowbray conflates a *general* obligation of states 'to put in place an appropriate legislative and administrative framework' to secure rights within their jurisdiction[134] with *specific* duties 'to take preventive operational measures to protect an individual' from acts of private violence of which the authorities had or ought to have had knowledge[135]—a distinction to be explained further below.

Mowbray's final 'significant group of positive obligations' is concerned with the duty of states to conduct effective *investigations* into credible claims of rights violations.[136] He places this duty under Shue's third category of duties—to aid. But the overview of case law presented to illustrate this group of obligations suggests

---

[128] ibid.
[129] ibid.
[130] ibid chs 2–5.
[131] See text with nn 20 to 22 and n 78.
[132] *Budayeva and Others v Russia* (n 21).
[133] ibid [175].
[134] This obligation has been recognised with regards to most Convention rights. See eg *Rantsev v Cyprus and Russia* (n 68) [285]; *Öneryıldız v Turkey* (n 71) [89]; *Centro Europa 7 SRL and Di Stefano v Italy* [GC] [2012] ECHR 974 [134].
[135] *Opuz v Turkey* (n 48) [148].
[136] Mowbray (n 25) 226.

that such duties mainly concern investigations related to breaches by states. Thus, he explains that '[t]he duty to conduct investigations under Article 3 ... arises when there is an arguable claim that a person has been seriously ill-treated *by state agents*'.[137] The obligation to investigate credible claims of rights infringements by private actors is acknowledged only with respect to the right to life even though such a duty exists with regard to the prohibition of torture, slavery, and the right to private life too.[138] Moreover, his analysis of states' investigative duties confuses positive duties arising out of substantive rights with remedies, which is arguably the consequence of a failure explicitly to acknowledge the distinction between private and state infringements of rights. Accordingly, Mowbray fails to distinguish between situations where an infringement of a human right results from a state action as opposed to that of non-state actor, and views the obligation to investigate the former cases as a positive duty arising out of a substantive article.[139] As explained in the previous subsection, when a violation of the right results from state action, the duty to investigate is to be considered as a remedy for such unjustified infringements.

Mowbray's study therefore does not offer a satisfactory account of the types, structure, and principles that apply to assessing positive human rights obligations in general, and in the context of 'absolute' human rights in particular. His analysis furthermore fails to account for positive obligations in the cases concerning the prohibition of slavery, which is unsurprising given that such duties were expressly recognised by the Strasbourg Court only in 2005—a year after the publication of Mowbray's book.

Other authors have suggested the classification of positive obligations 'based on identifying the nature of actions the state is required to take'.[140] Stoyanova thus identifies the following 'categories of positive obligations':

> [O]bligation to criminalize; obligation to adopt substantive criminal law of a certain quality; obligation to investigate and potentially apply the relevant criminal law framework by prosecuting and punishing; obligation to put in place effective regulatory frameworks; obligation to take protective operational measures; obligation to provide an effective remedy.[141]

---

[137] ibid 227 (emphasis added).
[138] ibid 28, 62. See eg *MC v Bulgaria* (n 48); *Opuz v Turkey* (n 48); *Rantsev v Cyprus and Russia* (n 68).
[139] Mowbray (n 25) 227. Mowbray argues that: 'The Court needs to ... adopt a policy of requiring effective investigations under Article 3 when states have received credible complaints that persons have been subject to ill-treatment (violating the substantive prohibitions of Article 3) by state agents ... Requiring such investigations under Article 3, rather than Article 13, will reflect the seriousness with which the Court characterises this type of ill-treatment.'
[140] Vladislava Stoyanova, *Human Trafficking and Slavery Reconsidered: Conceptual Limits and States' Positive Obligations in European Law* (CUP 2017) 329.
[141] ibid.

While this account accurately enumerates several positive obligations identified in the Strasbourg jurisprudence, it could not be said to offer their *categorisation*. A categorisation or classification involves grouping obligations into classes 'according to shared characteristics or perceived affinities'.[142] Thus, Stoyanova's 'obligation to criminalize', 'obligation to adopt substantive criminal law of a certain quality' and 'obligation to put in place effective regulatory frameworks' all belong to one category: a duty of states 'to put in place a legislative and administrative framework to prevent and punish trafficking and to protect victims' within their jurisdiction.[143] They represent states' *general* obligations, which concern the preconditions for the effective enjoyment of human rights. It is a starting point in every assessment of states' compliance with positive obligations, but also a means for the Court to address broader structural issues and flaws in national legal systems.

For example, in the *Rantsev* case the Court found that the Cypriot immigration policy and legislative shortcomings were encouraging the trafficking of women to Cyprus, and that its regime of artiste visas did not afford to the applicant's daughter practical and effective protection against trafficking and exploitation.[144] The Council of Europe noted that following this judgment '[c]hanges were also made to Cypriot visa rules' and that 'the Cypriot authorities ratified the Council of Europe's Convention on Action against Trafficking in Human Beings' thus illustrating the impact of the Court's jurisprudence on broader structural reforms.[145] Similarly, following a judgment against Greece concerning hundreds of Bangladeshi workers subject to human trafficking and forced labour on a farm, the Council of Europe observed that:

> Greece later ratified the Council of Europe convention on human trafficking, passed EU anti-trafficking legislation and created a National Rapporteur to address the issue. The Rapporteur prepared a national action plan for the years 2018-2023, including measures to prevent forced labour, protect victims, investigate allegations and punish wrongdoers.[146]

These examples illustrate that even though the Strasbourg Court does not have capacity 'to examine in abstracto the compatibility of national legislative or constitutional provisions with the requirements of the Convention',[147] its mandate being restricted to deciding individual petitions, general obligations provide an

---

[142] Oxford English Dictionary (2021).
[143] *VCL and AN v United Kingdom* [2021] ECHR 132 [151].
[144] *Rantsev v Cyprus and Russia* (n 68) [290]–[293].
[145] The Council of Europe, 'Examples of the Impact of the European Convention on Human Rights by Theme: Freedom From Slavery and Human Trafficking' https://www.coe.int/en/web/impact-convention-human-rights/freedom-from-slavery-and-human-trafficking (accessed 25 March 2022).
[146] ibid.
[147] *McCann and Others v United Kingdom* (n 109) [153].

opportunity for the Court to exercise a broader quasi-constitutional role by addressing systemic deficits in national legal systems.[148]

In contrast with such *general* obligations, Stoyanova's 'obligation to investigate and potentially apply the relevant criminal law framework by prosecuting and punishing' individual perpetrators, alongside an 'obligation to take protective operational measures' represent *specific* duties. They are specific because they concern situations of concrete identifiable individuals whose rights have been infringed by actions of non-state actors and apply only when certain conditions are met. As the next chapter examines in detail, such conditions involve state's actual or presumed knowledge of the relevant circumstances. This difference could be illustrated by the recent ruling of the Inter-American Court of Human Rights involving torture and sexual enslavement by private actors. The Court explained that in order to establish the responsibility of the state for acts of gender-based violence by private actors:

> [T]he Court assesses, on the one hand, those [actions implemented by the State] that address the problem of violence against women *in general* and, on the other, those adopted *in the specific case* once the State became aware of the risk of serious harm to the physical, sexual and/or psychological integrity of the woman, and even to her life, which activates the duty of strict or enhanced due diligence.[149]

Finally, when it comes to an 'obligation to provide an effective remedy', the previous section explained that this duty only arises when states have failed to comply with their own positive obligations in situations when rights infringements originate from non-state actors, or when state agents are directly involved in rights violations. Given the prevalence of cases where 'modern slavery' is inflicted by private actors, the right to remedy would only arise when states fail to prevent or investigate such infringements, in line with their specific obligations.

This discussion therefore illustrates that a more pertinent classification of positive obligations should begin with two main categories: general and specific.[150] As

---

[148] Wojciech Sadurski, 'Quasi-constitutional Court of Human Rights for Europe? Comments on Geir Ulfstein' (2021) 10(1) Global Constitutionalism 175 (discussing 'constitutional ambitions of the Strasbourg Court' and its role in the judicial review of national laws or decisions).

[149] Inter-American Court of Human Rights, *López Soto v Venezuela*, Judgment, Merits, Reparations and Costs, Series C No 318 (26 September 2018) [141] (emphasis added).

[150] For an overview of different classifications see Richard Clayton and Hugh Tomlinson (eds), *The Law of Human Rights* (OUP 2009) 366. In the recent case concerning forced prostitution, the Strasbourg Court suggested that there are 'two aspects of the positive obligations' under art 4 of the Convention: 'the duty to put in place a legislative and administrative framework and the duty to take operational measures—can be denoted as substantive, whereas the third aspect concerns the procedural obligation to investigate (*SM v Croatia* (n 104) [306]). The Court failed to elaborate on this proposed distinction. It is nonetheless clear from the case law overview in the following chapter that a duty to investigate and standards of effective investigation are often inextricably linked to an operational duty to protect the individual concerned from a harmful situation. Thus in *J and Others v Austria* (n 77) [107] the Court noted that 'the investigation must fulfil the requirements of . . . urgency where there is a possibility of removing the individual concerned from a harmful situation'.

already noted, international tribunals have avoided articulating any general theory or taxonomy of positive duties in express terms,[151] yet these two broad groups are easily discernible from both the text of, and especially the case law on specific human rights instruments. General obligations thus entail the preconditions for the effective enjoyment of human rights and require states 'to adopt, in accordance with their constitutional processes and the provisions of this Convention, such legislative or other measures as may be necessary to give effect to those rights or freedoms'.[152] This involves, in the words of the Inter-American Court of Human Rights, the obligation of states 'to organize the governmental apparatus and, in general, all the structures through which public power is exercised, so that they are capable of juridically ensuring the free and full enjoyment of human rights'.[153] Notably, the IACtHR emphasises that this obligation is twofold: it requires 'on the one hand, elimination of any norms and practices that in any way violate the guarantees provided under the Convention; on the other hand, the promulgation of norms and the development of practices conducive to effective observance of those guarantees'.[154]

Specific duties relate to concrete steps that states have taken in individual cases to enforce this general framework in practice.[155] They entail both operational and procedural measures taken by authorities to prevent and respond to the infringements of rights in individual cases. While the duty to protect usually arises when the infringement stems from non-state actors, they equally apply to situations where state agents interfere with protected rights. Thus in *VCL and AN v United Kingdom*, concerned the prosecution and punishment of two Vietnamese minors for producing cannabis despite both being recognised as victims of trafficking, the Strasbourg Court noted that such prosecution was at odds with the State's duty to protect them.[156] Similarly, procedural obligations to investigate flow from both state and private infringements of rights, although the previous section explained that in the former cases these should be correctly labelled as remedies rather than positive obligations.

It is worth emphasising that while in the majority of cases both operational and procedural duties concern measures taken within the law enforcement framework,

---

[151] Notably, in its most recent judgment concerning the prohibition of 'modern slavery', the Strasbourg Court expressly articulated '[t]he general framework of positive obligations under Article 4' to include '(1) the duty to put in place a legislative and administrative framework to prohibit and punish trafficking; (2) the duty, in certain circumstances, to take operational measures to protect victims, or potential victims, of trafficking; and (3) a procedural obligation to investigate situations of potential trafficking'. The court referred to the first two positive obligations as substantive, whereas the third was deemed a 'procedural obligation'. See *Zoletic and Others v Azerbaijan* (n 90) [182].
[152] The Inter-American Convention of Human Rights, art 2.
[153] *Velasquez-Rodriguez v Honduras* (n 27) [166].
[154] Inter-American Court of Human Rights, *Castillo Petruzzi and Others v Peru* Judgment of 30 May 1999 [207].
[155] *Zoletic and Others v Azerbaijan* (n 90) [185].
[156] *VCL and AN v United Kingdom* (n 143) [159].

those specific obligations sometimes involve purely protective measures, taken outside the scope of criminal prosecution and irrespective of any action directed against the alleged perpetrator.[157] Hence, in 'modern slavery' cases, neither procedural nor practical duties will *always* require the coercion of potential perpetrators, although their conviction is certainly one of the important aims of the broader anti-trafficking framework.

Accordingly, the following chapter deploys the matrix comprising general and specific obligations, with the latter divided in operational and procedural duties, as an analytical lens for examining the evolving jurisprudence on state responsibility to address 'modern slavery' in human rights law.

---

[157] See eg *E v United Kingdom* (n 72) [88]–[101].

6
Human Rights Obligations of States to Address 'Modern Slavery'

Building on the previous chapter, which considered the theoretical and legal basis of positive obligations in human rights law in general, the present chapter examines the human rights jurisprudence that has fleshed out these obligations in 'modern slavery' cases. Such jurisprudence has developed incrementally and it keeps expanding the outer limits of states' responsibility to tackle serious forms of exploitation. The prohibition of slavery has been one of the least invoked provisions of the European Convention on Human Rights (ECHR), with the Strasbourg Court pointing out in 2010 that it 'is not regularly called upon to consider the application of art.4'.[1] However, both the Strasbourg and San José courts have since engaged in an increasingly robust interpretation of the scope of positive obligations arising out of the prohibition of slavery and standards for assessing states' compliance with such duties. Notably, even though human rights tribunals acknowledge the distinction between various practices that fall within the ambit of the prohibition of slavery, such a distinction only serves to establish the basis on which that right is engaged in a concrete case. It has no relevance for the nature and scope of positive obligations or the standards for evaluating state conduct, which are the same 'in relation to the prohibition of slavery, servitude, trafficking in persons and forced labor'.[2]

In shaping such obligations, the Strasbourg Court drew inspiration from the rich case law concerning the prohibition of torture and other ill-treatment as well as the right to life, because it held that these rights enshrine 'the fundamental values of the democratic societies'.[3] While it has been noted that the full extent of positive obligations 'has yet to be fully established with the Court continuing to add to their number',[4] in all cases involving state responsibility for private acts that

---

[1] *Rantsev v Cyprus and Russia* (2010) 51 EHRR 1 [279].
[2] *Workers of the Hacienda Brasil Verde v Brazil* (Preliminary Objections, Merits, Reparations and Costs) IACtHR Series C No 318 (20 October 2016) [293]; *SM v Croatia* App no 60561/14 (ECtHR GC, 25 June 2020) [307]. In *SM*, the Strasbourg Court explained that because of 'the conceptual proximity' between various practices that fall within the ambit of this provision, the relevant principles articulated in the *Rantsev* case with regard to human trafficking apply equally to other prohibited practices.
[3] *Siliadin v France* (2006) 43 EHRR 16 [112]; *Rantsev v Cyprus and Russia* (n 1) [283]. Despite often repeating this mantra, the Strasbourg Court has never quite explained what such 'basic values' are.
[4] David Harris, Michael O'Boyle, and Ed Warbrick, *Law of the European Convention on Human Rights* (2nd edn, OUP 2009)20.

encroach upon 'absolute' rights, the established state obligations could be classified as either general or specific duties. In a similar vein, when evaluating states' compliance with the Inter-American Convention on Human Rights (IACHR), the Inter-American Court of Human Rights (IACtHR) considers:

> [O]n the one hand, those [actions implemented by the State] that address the problem of violence against women *in general* and, on the other, those adopted *in the specific case* once the State became aware of the risk of serious harm to the physical, sexual and/or psychological integrity of the woman, and even to her life, which activates the duty of strict or enhanced due diligence.[5]

The following sections therefore discuss the methods and reasoning used by international human rights tribunals to establish violations of the general and specific obligations arising out of the prohibition of 'modern slavery'. They offer a close inspection of the testes deployed by the courts and nuances that appear in applying these tests in different cases.

6.1 General Obligation to Establish an Effective Legal Framework

The obligation to develop an appropriate legal framework which provides the effective protection of fundamental rights is said to represent 'the minimum obligation of contracting states'.[6] The Strasbourg Court explained that 'if a violation of one of those rights and freedoms is the result of non-observance of that obligation in the enactment of domestic legislation, the responsibility of the State for that violation is engaged'.[7] In *CN v United Kingdom*, the Court found a violation of Article 4 ECHR on the basis of 'the lack of specific legislation criminalising domestic servitude', which in turn 'prevented the domestic authorities from properly investigating the applicant's complaints'.[8]

As already explained, when the most important interests are at stake, human rights tribunals insists on the protection through criminal law.[9] Therefore, with respect to the right to life, states are required to take appropriate steps to safeguard the lives of those within its jurisdiction by 'putting in place effective criminal law provisions to deter the commission of offences against the person, backed up by

---

[5] *López Soto v Venezuela* (Judgment, Merits, Reparations and Costs) IACtHR Series C No 318 (26 September 2018) [141] (emphasis added).
[6] Keir Starmer, *European Human Rights Law* (Legal Action Group 1999)196.
[7] *Young, James and Webster v United Kingdom* (1982) 4 EHRR 38 [49].
[8] *CN v the United Kingdom* (2013) 56 EHRR 24 [78]–[81].
[9] *MC v Bulgaria* (2005) 40 EHRR 20; *Workers of the Hacienda Brasil Verde v Brazil* (n 2) [319]; *López Soto v Venezuela* (n 5) [250].

law enforcement machinery for the prevention, suppression and punishment of breaches of such provisions'.[10] Similarly, in cases concerning the prohibition of torture and ill-treatment, the Strasbourg Court ruled that 'effective deterrence against grave acts such as rape, where fundamental values and essential aspects of private life are at stake, requires efficient criminal-law provisions'.[11] The same approach has been followed in the 'modern slavery' cases where the Court insisted that 'the States must set in place a legislative and administrative framework that *prohibits and punishes* forced or compulsory labour, servitude and slavery'.[12]

The first case to recognise positive obligations in the context of Article 4 ECHR in general, and the obligation 'to adopt criminal-law provisions which penalise the practices referred to in Article 4 and to apply them in practice' in particular,[13] concerned a 16-year-old Togolese girl who was brought to France under a false promise that her immigration status would be regularised and that she would be sent to school once she paid off her travel costs by working as a housemaid. Instead, she was required to work 'without respite and against her will for about fifteen hours per day, with no day off, for several years, without ever receiving wages or being sent to school, without identity papers and without her immigration status being regularised'.[14] The finding of a violation against France was based on the inadequacy of its criminal legislation, which, at the time, did not specifically address the rights guaranteed by Article 4, but related, in a much more restrictive manner, to the exploitation of labour and subjection to living or working conditions incompatible with human dignity.[15]

Although the Strasbourg jurisprudence usually restricts the scope of the general obligation to set up a legislative and administrative framework to the criminal-law mechanisms put in place 'to prohibit and punish' conduct contrary to Article 4 ECHR, in *Chowdury and Others v Greece* the Court required states to put in place 'a legislative and administrative framework providing *real and effective protection of the rights of victims of* ["modern slavery"]'.[16] In *J v Austria* decided the same year, the Strasbourg Court also altered its usual statement that states are duty bound to 'set in place a legislative and administrative framework that prohibits and punishes forced or compulsory labour, servitude and slavery',[17] stating that states are under an obligation 'to put in place a legislative and administrative framework to prohibit

---

[10] *Osman v The United Kingdom* (2000) 29 EHRR 245 [115]; *Menson and Others v United Kingdom* (Admissibility) (2003) 37 EHRR CD220; *Opuz v Turkey* (2010) 50 EHRR 28 [128]; *Kontrova v Slovakia* [2007] ECHR 419 [49].

[11] *MC v Bulgaria* (n 9) [150]. See also *López Soto v Venezuela* (n 5).

[12] *CN and V v France* App no 67724/09 (ECtHR, 11 October 2012) [105] (emphasis added). See also *CN v the United Kingdom* (n 8) [66]; *Chowdury and Others v Greece* [2017] ECHR 300 [105]; *SM v Croatia* (n 2) [306]; *Zoletic and Others v Azerbaijan* [2021] ECHR 789 [183].

[13] *Siliadin v France* (n 3) [89].

[14] ibid [110].

[15] *CN v the United Kingdom* (n 8) [73]–[82].

[16] *Chowdury and Others v Greece* (n 12) [87] (emphasis added).

[17] *CN and V v France* (n 12) [105]; *SM v Croatia* (n 2) [306]; *Zoletic v Azerbaijan* (n 12) [183].

and punish trafficking, *as well as* to take measures to protect victims, in order to ensure a comprehensive approach to the issue'.[18] Similarly, in *VCL and AN v United Kingdom*, decided in 2021, the European Court of Human Rights (ECtHR) ruled that 'Member States are required to put in place a legislative and administrative framework to prevent and punish trafficking *and to protect victims*'.[19]

A broader interpretation of the general obligation to establish an adequate legislative and administrative framework to address 'modern slavery' is preferable and in line with the Court's express ruling in the seminal *Rantsev* case that the duty to penalise and prosecute trafficking requires the 'spectrum of safeguards' set out in national legislation.[20] In that case, although the Cypriot criminal legislation was generally described as 'satisfactory' and 'suitable', a number of weaknesses were found with respect to 'the general legal and administrative framework and the adequacy of Cypriot immigration policy.[21] *Chowdury* similarly emphasised that 'States' domestic immigration law must respond to concerns regarding the incitement or aiding and abetting of human trafficking or tolerance towards it.[22]

However, despite this progressive development of the general obligation to establish an adequate legal and administrative framework to address practices of 'modern slavery', the most recent judgment has reverted to a narrow view that this obligation primarily concerns the responsibility to 'prohibit and punish' such practices. Therefore, in *Zoletic and Others v Azerbaijan*, the Strasbourg Court reiterated the earlier pronouncement of the Grand Chamber in *SM v Croatia*[23] concerning '[t]he general framework of positive obligations under Article 4', which is said to include:

> (1) the duty to put in place a *legislative and administrative framework to prohibit and punish trafficking*; (2) the duty, in certain circumstances, to take operational measures to protect victims, or potential victims, of trafficking; and (3) a procedural obligation to investigate situations of potential trafficking.[24]

It is therefore imperative for the ECtHR to clarify the breadth of the duty to establish an adequate legislative and administrative framework to address 'modern slavery'. The approach in *J and Others v Austria* is instructive and could be used to model the Court's general approach to this obligation. In that case, the ECtHR considered two *specific* obligations: 'whether the Austrian authorities complied with their positive obligation to identify and support the applicants as (potential)

---

[18] *J and Others v Austria* [2017] ECHR 37; [106] (emphasis added).
[19] *VCL and AN v United Kingdom* [2021] ECHR 132 [151].
[20] *Rantsev v Cyprus and Russia* (n 1) [284]–[285].
[21] ibid [290]–[293].
[22] *Chowdury and Others v Greece* (n 12) [87].
[23] *SM v Croatia* (n 2) [306].
[24] *Zoletic and Others v Azerbaijan* (n 12) [182] (emphasis added).

victims of human trafficking, and whether they fulfilled their positive obligation to investigate the alleged crimes'.[25] Accordingly, the *general* obligation to put in place a legislative and administrative framework had two dimensions: it concerned both the framework established 'to prohibit and punish trafficking, as well as to take measures to protect victims, in order to ensure a comprehensive approach to the issue'.[26] It flows from this that, in examining states' compliance with the two specific duties—the duty to protect and the procedural duty to investigate—the Court is meant to consider the adequacy of the legislative and administrative framework pertaining to each. The ECtHR regrettably failed to articulate this in express terms, although it concluded that 'the legal and administrative framework in place concerning the protection of (potential) victims of human trafficking in Austria appears to have been sufficient'.[27] In doing so, it clearly departed from its usual approach to reviewing only the criminal law mechanisms established to prohibit and punish the acts of trafficking.

When it comes to assessing state compliance with this general obligation, such review is only triggered by a concrete case of the alleged rights violation. Accordingly, the Strasbourg Court noted that 'it is not the role of the Convention institutions to examine *in abstracto* the compatibility of national legislative or constitutional provisions with the requirements of the Convention'.[28] Therefore, the review of state compliance with this obligation is inevitably tied to the analysis of specific duties owed to a concrete victim; it represents the first step in the Court's assessment. Furthermore, rather than establishing universal standards for evaluating states' compliance with this obligation, its scope and the intensity of review depend on the particular circumstances of each case. For instance, in *Rantsev v Cyprus and Russia*, the legal and institutional framework in Russia was subject to less intense scrutiny than the Cypriot one, because the majority of impugned actions occurred in Cyprus as a destination state of the alleged trafficking of Ms Rantseva.[29]

6.2 Specific Obligations: A Procedural Duty to Investigate 'Modern Slavery'

The mere existence of an adequate legal and institutional framework is not sufficient to absolve states from the responsibility to provide practical and effective protection of rights to individuals within their jurisdiction.[30] The IACtHR thus

---

[25] *J and Others v Austria* (n 18) [109].
[26] ibid [106]. This duty also required States 'to provide relevant training for law-enforcement and immigration officials.'
[27] ibid [111].
[28] *McCann and Others v United Kingdom* [1995] ECHR 18984/91 [153]; *Klass and Others v Germany* (1980) 2 EHRR 214 [33].
[29] *Rantsev v Cyprus and Russia* (n 1) [301]–[303].
[30] *Osman v United Kingdom* (n 10) [115]; *Kontrova v Slovakia* (n 10) [49]; *Opuz v Turkey* (n 10) [128].

stipulates that: 'States should have an appropriate legal framework and enforce it effectively, as well as prevention policies and practices that allow them to take effective measures when complaints are received.'[31] The Strasbourg Court similarly distinguishes between 'the positive obligation to penalise and effectively prosecute actions in breach of Article 4' and 'the procedural obligation to investigate situations of potential exploitation when the matter comes to the attention of the authorities'.[32] The former duty essentially relates the relevant legal or regulatory framework in place effectively to combat practices of 'modern slavery', while the procedural obligation to investigate situations of potential exploitation concerns 'the domestic authorities' duty to apply in practice the relevant criminal law mechanisms put in place to prohibit and punish conduct contrary to that provision'.[33] In line with that, the responsibility for complying with the duty to investigate primarily falls on the law-enforcement and judicial authorities: '[w]here those authorities establish that an [individual perpetrator] has had recourse to human trafficking and forced labour, they should act accordingly, within their respective spheres of competence, pursuant to the relevant criminal-law provisions.[34]

As to the content of the procedural obligation in 'modern slavery' cases, the Strasbourg Court expressly noted that this duty 'draws largely on the Court's well-established case-law ... developed under Articles 2 and 3 of the Convention' given that these rights enshrine 'one of the basic values of the democratic societies'.[35] Yet, in their joint concurring opinion in *SM v Croatia*, Judges O'Leary and Ravarani criticised such 'blanket transposition' of the duty to investigate under Articles 2 and 3 because it 'fails to take into account the specificity of the type of investigation' required in Article 4 cases, 'as well as the nature of the facts' that constitute an arguable claim required to trigger procedural obligations under these different Convention articles.[36] The judges rightly note that:

> In an article 2 case, to put matters bluntly, there is generally physical evidence of a death, or concrete elements pointing to the risk thereof. Similarly, in Article 3 cases, the authorities are confronted with allegations of ill-treatment, more often than not including physical manifestations on the body of the alleged victim of the treatment of which they complain.[37]

In contrast, the circumstances and available evidence in 'modern slavery' cases are less clear-cut. In the *SM* case, these included:

---

[31] *Workers of the Hacienda Brasil Verde v Brazil* (n 2) 2016 [320].
[32] *CN and V v France* (n 12) [104].
[33] *Zoletic and Others v Azerbaijan* (n 12) [185]; *SM v Croatia* (n 2) [308].
[34] *Chowdury and Others v Greece* (n 12) [116]; *Zoletic and Others v Azerbaijan* (n 12) [190].
[35] *SM v Croatia* (n 2) [309]–[310].
[36] ibid, Joint Concurring Opinion of Judges O'Leary and Ravarani.
[37] ibid.

[A] first connection via Facebook, social drinks, the search for employment, an alleged attempt to coerce into prostitution, continued social contact, a physical relationship carried on over months which may or may not have been consensual or which may have ceased to be consensual with time, allegations of threats and domestic violence, the renting and payment of a flat by the complainant who had been able to leave the flat on certain occasions and who retained use of her identity documents, mobile phone and part of the money earned from the alleged forced prostitution. It also involved, crucially, evidence of a friend of the complainant, with whom she had lived, confirming the threats to which she had been subject but also testifying that her involvement in prostitution had been voluntary[38].

It is therefore clear that the police and the prosecution service are faced with a difficult task to decide both the kind and amount of evidence necessary to trigger the duty to conduct investigation into allegations of 'modern slavery' and the appropriate scope of such an enquiry.

Therefore, two critical questions must be answered with regard to the procedural obligations of states in 'modern slavery' cases: which circumstances trigger the duty to investigate; and what are the scope of this duty and standards of assessing state compliance with it?

6.2.1 The Circumstances that Engage the Duty to Investigate 'Modern Slavery'

The procedural obligation to investigate situations of potential infringements of the prohibition of 'modern slavery' is said to arise 'once the matter has come to the attention of the authorities'.[39] Notably, the authorities must act on their own motion without the need for the victim or next-of-kin to raise a complaint. This rule, first applied in the context of 'modern slavery' in the *Rantsev* case, has been reiterated in all subsequent cases before the Strasbourg Court.[40] However, the Court specified this requirement in the subsequent cases to include 'a credible suspicion' that an individual's rights under Article 4 ECHR have been violated.[41] In other words, the Court explained that:

[W]hen an applicant's complaint is essentially of a procedural nature as in the present case, it must examine whether, in the circumstances of a particular case,

---

[38] ibid.
[39] *Rantsev v Cyprus and Russia* (n 1) [288].
[40] *CN and V v France* (n 12) [104]; *CN v the United Kingdom* (n 8) [69]. *Chowdury and Others v Greece* (n 12) [116]; *J and Others v Austria* (n 18) [107]; *Zoletic and Others v Azerbaijan* (n 12) [185].
[41] *CN v United Kingdom* (n 8) [69].

the applicant made an arguable claim or whether there was prima facie evidence (commencement de preuve) of her having been subjected to such prohibited treatment.[42]

San José Court similarly imposed an obligation on states to:

> [O]pen, *ex officio* and immediately, an effective investigation that permits the identification, prosecution and punishment of those responsible, when a report has been filed or there is justified reason to believe that persons subject to their jurisdiction are subjected to one of the offenses established in Article 6(1) and 6(2) of the Convention.[43]

However, what constitutes a 'credible suspicion' or 'arguable claim', and when such an arguable claim is 'sufficiently drawn' to the attention of the relevant domestic authorities[44] is not immediately obvious from the jurisprudence. Judges O'Leary and Ravarani correctly emphasised in their separate opinion in *SM* that 'clarity on the trigger for the procedural obligation to investigate is so important' not least because once triggered it becomes an own motion obligation for the domestic authorities.

The majority in *SM v Croatia* ruled that the procedural obligation 'does not depend on an initiative of the applicant to take responsibility for the conduct of any investigatory procedures' and that 'any action or lack of action on the part of the victim cannot justify a lack of action on the part of the prosecuting authorities'.[45] This is a welcome development compared to the Court's approach in *M and Others v Italy and Bulgaria*, one of the early decisions in Article 4 cases. That case concerned a minor of Roma ethnic origin from Bulgaria who claimed to have been trafficked to Italy by a Roma man of Serbian nationality, where she was forced to steal and was subject to ill-treatment, including rape and beatings.[46] The Strasbourg Court held that it 'cannot exclude that the circumstances of the present case, as reported by the first applicant to the Italian authorities ... *had they been proved*, could have amounted to human trafficking'.[47] However, it concluded that:

> [F]rom the evidence submitted there is not sufficient ground to establish the veracity of the applicants' version of events ... It follows that the applicants' allegation that there had been an instance of actual human trafficking has not been proved and therefore cannot be accepted by the Court.[48]

---

[42] *SM v Croatia* (n 2) [324].
[43] *Workers of the Hacienda Brasil Verde v Brazil* (n 2) [219].
[44] *Zoletic and Others v Azerbaijan* (n 12) [169].
[45] *SM v Croatia* (n 2) [336].
[46] *M and Others v Italy and Bulgaria* [2012] ECHR 1967.
[47] ibid [106] (emphasis added).
[48] ibid [154].

It justified its opinion that the circumstances did not raise any issue under Article 4 ECHR by an observation that the applicant 'had not testified that she had not consented to [marriage] and ... emphasised that Y had not forced her to have sexual intercourse with him'.[49] Therefore, despite acknowledging that 'it took the authorities less than a full day to reach their conclusions' about 'the applicant's serious allegations of treatment contrary to Articles 3 and 4',[50] the Court placed the burden of proving such allegations squarely on the applicant in order to trigger the procedural obligation of the Italian authorities to determine the veracity of the applicant's allegations.

This finding is particularly striking in light of the Court's earlier jurisprudence in domestic violence cases, where it obliged domestic authorities to take action even when a victim withdraws their complaint. For instance, in *Opuz v Turkey* the applicant and her mother had lodged several criminal complaints before domestic authorities against her husband, complaining of death threats, grievous bodily harm, and attempted murder.[51] On each occasion the applicant and her mother subsequently withdrew their complaints. Eventually, the applicant's husband shot and killed the applicant's mother and, following his release from prison, she requested the authorities to take measures to protect her as he had started to threaten her. She filed an application to the Strasbourg Court claiming that the authorities had failed to safeguard the right to life of her mother and had been negligent in the face of the repeated death threats and acts of violence to which she had been subjected. The Court particularly focused on the question of the pursuance of criminal prosecution against perpetrators of domestic violence when the victim withdraws her complaint. Although the comparative analysis of legislation and practice did not reveal any general consensus among Member States, the Court nevertheless identified certain factors that could be taken into account in deciding to pursue the prosecution.[52] As a general rule, it concluded that 'the more serious the offence or the greater the risk of further offences, the more likely that the prosecution should continue in the public interest, even if victims withdraw their complaints'.[53] This is particularly significant for 'modern slavery' cases, where victims tend to provide incomplete or misleading information about their experiences, usually because of a lack of trust towards the authorities or the instruction from traffickers to provide

---

[49] ibid [165].
[50] ibid [104]. The dissenting Judge Kalaydjieva's remarks are illustrative of the problems in the way domestic authorities approached this case: 'What I find even more striking in the present case is the fact that having raided the villa, where the first applicant was allegedly held against her will, and released her seventeen days after obtaining information that the mother feared that her daughter might be subjected to forced prostitution, the authorities decided not only to dismiss these complaints without any further enquiries, but also to immediately institute criminal proceedings against the seventeen-year-old girl and her mother for perjury and false accusations.'
[51] *Opuz v Turkey* (n 10).
[52] ibid [138].
[53] ibid [139].

an untrue account.[54] This was recognised in *SM*, where the Court expressly relied on the work of GRETA and other expert bodies to conclude that:

> [T]here may be different reasons why victims of human trafficking and different forms of sexual abuse may be reluctant to cooperate with the authorities and to disclose all the details of the case. Moreover, the possible impact of psychological trauma must be taken into account. There is thus a risk of overreliance on the victim's testimony alone, which leads to the necessity to clarify and—if appropriate—support the victim's statement with other evidence.[55]

While it is welcome that the Court expressly acknowledged that domestic authorities must be cautious to base their conclusions on the victims' statements or actions, the questions posed by the concurring judges were left unanswered:

> What will an arguable claim that treatment contrary to Article 4 has taken place look like in practice and of what, in the absence of a complaint, will prima facie evidence consist? What concretely will either require of the police and subsequently the prosecution service?[56]

The most recent judgment concerning Article 4 may give some indication of the correct approach. *Zoletic v Azerbaijan* concerned the allegations of cross-border human trafficking and forced labour by thirty-three nationals of Bosnia and Herzegovina who worked on high-profile construction projects commissioned by the Azerbaijani government. The ECtHR concluded that the applicants in this case had an 'arguable claim', which was 'sufficiently drawn' to the attention of the relevant domestic authorities, 'even though the applicants themselves had not lodged a formal criminal complaint'.[57] Accordingly, the procedural obligation was triggered. The conclusion that the applicants had an arguable claim was based on their allegations before the domestic *civil* courts that:

> [T]heir passports had been taken away from them for the period of their stay in Azerbaijan, that no work permits had been obtained for them, that their living conditions had been poor and unsanitary, that they had no access to adequate medical care, that their freedom of movement had been restricted by their

---

[54] The Anti-Trafficking Monitoring Group (ATMG), 'Wrong Kind of Victim? One Year on: an Analysis of UK Measures to Protect Trafficked Persons' (June 2010) 27.

[55] *SM v Croatia* (n 2) [344]. See also *VCL and AN v United Kingdom* (n 19) [171] ('trafficked children could be reluctant to disclose the circumstances of their exploitation either for fear of reprisals, out of misplaced loyalty to their traffickers, or because they have been coached. They could also be subject to more psychological coercion or threats, such as threatening to report them to the authorities, threatening their families, or by keeping them socially isolated').

[56] *SM v Croatia* (n 2), Joint Concurring Opinion of Judges O'Leary and Ravarani.

[57] *Zoletic and Others v Azerbaijan* (n 12) [193]–[194].

HUMAN RIGHTS OBLIGATIONS   133

employer, that they had not been paid their wages and that they had been subjected to punishments in the form of fines, beatings and detentions.[58]

While the ECtHR noted that the applicants' factual submissions before the domestic courts and the Court were 'generally brief', they 'pointed to several indicators of potential treatment contrary to Article 4 of the Convention', which were corroborated by the report of the NGO ASTRA. The Court pointed out that the NGO report 'provided more details and additional information concerning the allegations raised by the applicants' and concluded that 'the existence and contents of the ASTRA Report was sufficiently brought to the attention of the domestic courts'.[59] Furthermore, the Court considered:

> [O]ther information referred to by the applicants or otherwise apparently brought to the attention of the domestic courts and other authorities, such as the letter by the Danish Refugee Council ..., information contained in the AMC's letters to the law-enforcement authorities ... the witness statement of the AMC representative before the Baku Court of Appeal ... and the information contained in the legal assistance requests by the Prosecutor's Office of Bosnia and Herzegovina ... All of the above provided corroborating information concerning workers who had reportedly been in the same or similar situation as the applicants during the same time period.[60]

This ruling clarifies that the question of whether there is an arguable claim of the treatment contrary to Article 4 ECHR, which triggers the procedural obligation, is factual and 'must be examined in the light of all the relevant circumstances of a case'.[61] Notably, a conclusion as to whether the domestic authorities' procedural obligation arose 'has to be based on the *circumstances prevailing at the time* when the relevant allegations were made or when the prima facie evidence of treatment contrary to Article 4 was brought to the authorities' attention.[62]

The decision in *Zoletic* suggests that the Court will draw on circumstantial evidence and various reports concerning the general context in the specific country when establishing whether the procedural duty arose in a particular case. It held that:

> [T]he Azerbaijani authorities were aware of the ECRI report of 2011 whose findings were later developed in the GRETA Report ... according to which many employers employing migrant workers in Azerbaijan, including in the construction

---

[58] ibid [159].
[59] ibid [161]–[162].
[60] ibid [165].
[61] ibid [157].
[62] ibid [156] (emphasis added).

sector, had recourse to illegal employment practices and, as a result, migrants employed illegally often found themselves vulnerable to serious forms of abuse. Furthermore, the GRETA Report later observed that law-enforcement officials in Azerbaijan reportedly had a tendency to see potential cases of human trafficking for labour exploitation as mere labour disputes between the worker and the employer and there seemed to be a confusion between cases of human trafficking for labour exploitation and disputes concerning salaries and other aspects of working conditions. In the Court's view, while far from being conclusive, the general context described in those reports is relevant in the assessment of the facts of the case.[63]

This statement is significant, because depending on the general situation in a particular country, as highlighted in the reports of the relevant bodies, the decisions of domestic authorities on whether to initiate or continue with investigation will be subject to a greater or lesser scrutiny. It also shows that the findings of the relevant institutions involved in anti-slavery action and states' compliance with other international instruments serve as circumstantial evidence in cases concerning their compliance with Article 4 ECHR.

In the similar vein, in the first case where the IACtHR found a violation of the prohibition of slavery with regard to eighty-five workers in a cattle ranch in Brazil, who were rescued in March 2000 following a complaint made by two workers who managed to escape the estate, the Court established 'a series of shortcomings' in Brazil's response to the situation of slavery.[64] The Court's reasoning is worth setting out in full:

> Since 1988, the Comissão Pastoral da Terra has filed various complaints concerning the existence of a situation similar to slavery in the state of Pará and, specifically, in Hacienda Brasil Verde. These complaints identified a modus operandi for the recruitment and exploitation of workers in the specific area in the south of the state of Pará. The State was aware of this situation because, as a result of these complaints, inspections of Hacienda Brasil Verde were conducted in 1989, 1992, 1993, 1996, 1997, 1999 and 2000. During several of these inspections, labor law violations were verified, together with degrading living and working conditions, and situations similar to slavery. These verifications resulted in the opening of labor and criminal proceedings; however, such proceedings were ineffective to prevent the situation verified in March 2000. Also, given the frequent complaints, the seriousness of the facts denounced, and the special obligation of prevention

---

[63] ibid [195].
[64] The Court analysed such procedural flaws as part of the obligation of prevention, while it also considered separately the victims' right of access to justice under arts 8(1) (right to a fair trial) and 25(1) (right to judicial protection) of the American Convention.

imposed on the State in relation to slavery, the State should have increased the inspections in this hacienda in order to eradicate the practice of slavery in this establishment. Moreover, in addition to the known risk described above, the actual situation of risk was verified when the youths Antônio Francisco da Silva and Gonçalo Luiz Furtado were able to escape from Hacienda Brasil Verde and went to the Marabá Federal Police. On that occasion, after receiving the report of the adolescents about the offenses that were occurring in this hacienda, the fact that Antônio Francisco da Silva was still a minor, and the seriousness of the facts reported, the police merely indicated that they not could assist them because it was carnival time, and advised them to return two days later. This attitude was in open contradiction to the obligation of due diligence, especially considering that the reported facts referred to an offense as serious as slavery. On receiving information of the occurrence of slavery and violence against a child, the State had the obligation to take every possible measure to deal with these human rights violations.[65]

Overall, given the seriousness of practices prohibited by Article 4 ECHR and the victims' situation of vulnerability, the threshold for engaging the state's obligation to investigate is low, and it neither solely depends on the applicants' allegations nor on the authorities' own assessment of the facts, but is contingent on the evidence available at the time and the general context discernible from the work of relevant institutions and organisations.

6.2.2 The Scope of the Duty to Investigate 'Modern Slavery'

The key principles applicable to the procedural duty to investigate allegations of treatment contrary to Article 4 ECHR were originally laid down in *Rantsev*[66] and have been recently consolidated and further developed in the *SM* and *Zoletic* cases.[67] Therefore the obligation to conduct an effective investigation into the circumstances that gave rise to the credible allegations of the treatment in breach of Article 4 ECHR includes the following principles:

First, as already discussed, the duty to investigate does not depend on a complaint from the victim or next-of-kin. Instead, the authorities must act of their own motion once the matter has come to their attention.[68] Secondly, for an investigation to be effective, it must be independent from those implicated in the events.[69]

---

[65] *Workers of the Hacienda Brasil Verde v Brazil* (n 2) [326]–[327].
[66] *Rantsev v Cyprus and Russia* (n 1) [288].
[67] *SM v Croatia* (n 2) [311]–[320].
[68] See the discussion in section 6.2.1.
[69] *Rantsev v Cyprus and Russia* (n 1) [288]; *CN v the United Kingdom* (n 8) [69]; *LE v Greece* [2016] ECHR 107 [68]; *Zoletic and Others v Azerbaijan* (n 12) [187].

Thirdly, the victim or the next-of-kin must be involved in the procedure to the extent necessary to safeguard their legitimate interests.[70] Fourthly, the requirement of promptness and reasonable expedition is implicit in all cases, but where the possibility of removing the individual from the harmful situation is available, the investigation must be undertaken as a matter of urgency.[71] Fifthly, effective investigation must be capable of leading to the establishment of the facts of the case and to the identification and punishment of individuals responsible,[72] which is an obligation not of result but of means.[73] This means that:

> [T]he procedural obligation must not be interpreted in such a way as to impose an impossible or disproportionate burden on the authorities. Nevertheless, the authorities must take whatever reasonable steps they can to collect evidence and elucidate the circumstances of the case. In particular, the investigation's conclusions must be based on thorough, objective and impartial analysis of all relevant elements. Failing to follow an obvious line of inquiry undermines to a decisive extent the investigation's ability to establish the circumstances of the case and the identity of those responsible.[74]

Finally, in addition to the obligation to conduct a domestic investigation into events occurring on their own territories, states are also subject to a duty in cross-border trafficking cases to cooperate effectively with the relevant authorities of other states concerned in the investigation of events which occurred outside their territories.[75] The Court in *Rantsev* reminded the respondent states that such a duty results from trafficking-specific instruments and is also consistent with international agreements in which both states participate. It emphasised the importance of a full and effective investigation covering all aspects of trafficking allegations, from recruitment to exploitation. Therefore, the Court found Russia in breach of a procedural duty on the basis of the failure of domestic authorities to investigate the recruitment aspect of alleged trafficking.[76] Such a failure was 'all the more serious in light of Ms Rantseva's subsequent death and the resulting mystery surrounding the circumstances of her departure from Russia'.[77] On the other hand, precisely because of the fact that a victim had died, the Court did not elaborate on the procedural requirements placed on Cyprus, as a destination state, to investigate trafficking

---

[70] ibid.
[71] ibid.
[72] *Rantsev v Cyprus and Russia* (n 1) [288]; *SM v Croatia* (n 2) [313]; *Denis Vasilyev v Russia* [2009] ECHR 2078 [100].
[73] *Hugh Jordan v United Kingdom* (2001) 37 EHRR 52 [107]; *Menson and Others v United Kingdom* (n 10); *Denis Vasilyev v Russia* (n 72) [100].
[74] *Zoletic and Others v Azerbaijan* (n 12) [188]. See also *J and Others v Austria* (n 18) [107].
[75] *Rantsev v Cyprus and Russia* (n 1) [289].
[76] ibid [307]–[309].
[77] ibid [307].

allegations. Instead, the analysis of procedural duties in that respect was subsumed by the obligation to investigate her death.[78]

The Court had an opportunity to revisit the question of the procedural obligation in cross-border trafficking cases in the case concerning two Filipino nationals, who worked as maids or au pairs in the United Arab Emirates and claimed that that their employers had taken their passports away from them and exploited them.[79] They claimed that this treatment had continued during a short stay in Vienna where their employers had taken them and where they had eventually managed to escape. The applicants maintained that they had been subjected to forced labour and human trafficking, and at the Austrian authorities had failed to carry out an effective and exhaustive investigation into their allegations. They argued in particular that what had happened to them in Austria could not be viewed in isolation, and at the Austrian authorities had a duty under international law to investigate also those events which had occurred abroad.

While the public prosecutor's office initiated an investigation following the applicants' report to the police, which occurred approximately one year after leaving their employers, this investigation was discontinued because the prosecutor held that the applicants' employers' alleged conduct on Austrian territory did not fulfil the elements of crime under domestic criminal law. The Strasbourg Court confirmed that such conclusion 'does not appear to be unreasonable' because the reported events 'which had taken place over a maximum of three days in Vienna did not in themselves amount to any of the criminal actions exhaustively listed in Article 104a of the CC ... No ill-treatment in Austria was reported by the applicants'.[80]

When it comes to events abroad, the Court ruled that:

> Article 4 of the Convention, under its procedural limb, does not require States to provide for universal jurisdiction over trafficking offences committed abroad ... The Court therefore cannot but conclude that, in the present case, under the Convention, there was no obligation incumbent on Austria to investigate the applicants' recruitment in the Philippines or their alleged exploitation in the United Arab Emirates.[81]

As to the applicants' argument that the events in the Philippines, the United Arab Emirates and Austria could not be viewed in isolation, the Court concluded that 'even if the alleged events were taken together ... there is no indication that the authorities failed to comply with their duty of investigation'.[82] The Court justified

---

[78] ibid [300].
[79] *J and Others v Austria* (n 18).
[80] ibid [116].
[81] ibid [114].
[82] ibid [117].

such a conclusion by the following arguments. It first noted that the Austrian authorities were only alerted approximately one year after the events in Vienna, when the applicants' employers had long left Austria and had presumably returned to Dubai. Based on the information available, the Court considered that the authorities could not have had any reasonable expectation of even being able to confront the applicants' employers with the allegations made against them, as no mutual legal assistance agreement exists between Austria and the United Arab Emirates. Therefore, it held that the options available to the authorities (requesting legal assistance from the United Arab Emirates; attempting to question the applicants' employers by means of letters of request; and issuing an order to determine their whereabouts) had no reasonable prospects of success. Moreover, the Court emphasised that, under Austrian law, the public prosecutor had a certain margin of appreciation when deciding which cases to pursue and which to discontinue, that it was not possible to conduct criminal proceedings in the absence of the accused, and that the public prosecutor could only reopen and continue the investigation into the applicants' allegations if there are legal and factual grounds to do so. The foregoing considerations allowed the Court to conclude that the investigation conducted by the Austrian authorities in the applicants' case was sufficient for the purposes of Article 4 of the Convention.[83]

These six principles of effective investigation are interrelated and 'taken jointly, enable the degree of effectiveness of the investigation to be assessed'.[84] They apply to the proceedings as a whole, including the trial stage.[85] However, the Court reminded that it is not possible to reduce the variety of situations which might occur 'to a bare checklist of acts of investigation or other simplified criteria',[86] emphasising that any defects in the relevant proceedings and the decision-making process must amount to 'significant flaws' in order to raise an issue under Article 4.[87]

The Strasbourg Court has therefore repeatedly emphasised that 'it must be cautious in taking on the role of a first-instance tribunal of fact'.[88] Its approach to the level of scrutiny over domestic proceedings was explained in *Beganovic v Croatia*, which concerned a physical attack on the applicant by seven individuals. The Court considered the applicant's allegations of ill-treatment 'arguable' and 'capable of "raising a reasonable suspicion" so as to attract the applicability of Article 3 of the Convention'.[89] In reviewing whether the authorities' response to the situation

---

[83] ibid [117].
[84] *Zoletic and Others v Azerbaijan* (n 12) [189].
[85] *Ali and Ayse Duran v Turkey* [2008] ECHR 289 [61]–[62]; *Beganovic v Croatia* [2009] ECHR 992 [77]; *Öneryıldız v Turkey* (2004) 39 EHRR 12 [95].
[86] *SM v Croatia* (n 2) [318].
[87] *Zoletic and Others v Azerbaijan* (n 12) [189]; *SM v Croatia* (n 2) [319]–[320]; *MC v Bulgaria* (n 9) [167]–[168].
[88] *SM v Croatia* (n 2) [317]; *Zoletic and Others v Azerbaijan* (n 12) [188];
[89] *SM v Croatia* (n 2) [317].

was in line with their positive obligations flowing from Article 3 ECHR, the Court outlined its approach:

> [I]t is not the Court's task to verify whether the domestic courts correctly applied domestic criminal law; what is in issue in the present proceedings is not individual criminal-law liability, but the State's responsibility under the Convention. The Court must grant *substantial deference* to the national courts in the choice of appropriate measures, while also maintaining a certain power of review and the power to intervene in cases of *manifest disproportion* between the gravity of the act and the results obtained at domestic level.[90]

However, in recent cases involving 'modern slavery', the Court has stressed that 'where this is not rendered unavoidable by the circumstances of a particular case, it has to apply a "particularly thorough scrutiny"'.[91] In practice, this has often meant substituting its own assessment for the evaluation of facts by domestic authorities.

For instance, in *CN v United Kingdom*, which concerned allegations of domestic servitude by a Ugandan woman who complained that she had been forced into working as a live-in carer, the Strasbourg Court found that 'the investigation into the applicant's complaints of domestic servitude was ineffective due to the absence of specific legislation criminalising such treatment'.[92] The reason for this finding was the investigating officers' 'heavy focus' on the offence of human trafficking instead of domestic servitude as a 'specific offence, distinct from trafficking and exploitation'.[93] The Government contested the claim that the lack of specific legislation criminalising domestic servitude prevented the domestic authorities from properly investigating the applicant's complaints arguing that: '[T]he reason no action was taken following investigation of the applicant's complaints was not the absence of appropriate legislation but rather the absence of evidence to support the facts alleged by her. In short, the domestic authorities simply did not believe the applicant's account.'[94]

While the Court paid lip service to the principle that 'it is not its task to replace the domestic authorities in the assessment of the facts of the case',[95] it nonetheless rejected their explanation maintaining that the deficiencies in domestic investigation resulted from the absence of specific offence of domestic servitude. In particular, the Court explained that:

---

[90] *Beganovic v Croatia* (n 85) [78] (emphasis added).
[91] *Zoletic and Others v Azerbaijan* (n 12) [188]; *SM v Croatia* (n 2) [315]–[317].
[92] *CN v the United Kingdom* (n 8) [81].
[93] ibid [80].
[94] ibid [78].
[95] ibid.

[D]omestic servitude is a specific offence, distinct from trafficking and exploitation, which involves a complex set of dynamics, involving both overt and more subtle forms of coercion, to force compliance. A thorough investigation into complaints of such conduct therefore requires an understanding of the many subtle ways an individual can fall under the control of another. In the present case, the Court considers that due to the absence of a specific offence of domestic servitude, the domestic authorities were unable to give due weight to these factors.[96]

This reasoning is problematic for two reasons. First, the Court failed to explain how 'a complex set of dynamics, involving both overt and more subtle forms of coercion, to force compliance' in domestic servitude cases differs from the similar dynamics found in human trafficking cases. Such a difference is all but evident not least because the abuse of the position of vulnerability, as one of the means of human trafficking, arguably covers 'such subtle forms of coercion' pointed out by the Court.[97] For instance, the Court pointed out that:

[N]o attempt appears to have been made to interview S. despite the gravity of the offence he was alleged to have committed ... For the Court, the lacuna in domestic law at the time may explain this omission, together with the fact that no apparent weight was attributed to the applicant's allegations that her passport had been taken from her, that S. had not kept her wages for her as agreed, and that she was explicitly and implicitly threatened with denunciation to the immigration authorities, even though these factors were among those identified by the ILO as indicators of forced labour.[98]

It is difficult to accept that the flaws In investigation that the Court had identified are unique to the offence of domestic servitude, when circumstances such as taking away the passport, the threats of denunciation to the immigration authorities, or the withdrawal of wages are well-known indicia of human trafficking, which the Court expressly acknowledged in the subsequent cases.[99] In *J and Others v Austria*, the Court explained that: 'The identified elements of trafficking—the treatment of human beings as commodities, close surveillance, the circumscription of movement, the use of violence and threats, poor living and working conditions, and little or no payment—cut across these three categories.'[100]

Secondly, this finding directly contradicts the Court's subsequent ruling in *SM*, where it explained that 'the relevant principles relating to human trafficking are accordingly applicable in cases concerning forced prostitution',[101] as well as its

---

[96] ibid [80].
[97] See a detailed discussion of this element in Chapter 4.
[98] *CN v United Kingdom* (n 8) [80].
[99] *J and Others v Austria* (n 8) [104]; *Zoletic and Others v Azerbaijan* (n 12) [159].
[100] *J and Others v Austria* (n 8) [104].
[101] *SM v Croatia* (n 2) [307].

general position that '[t]he procedural obligation under the converging principles of Articles 2 and 3 of the Convention informs the specific content of the procedural obligation under Article 4 of the Convention'.[102] In that light, it would appear illogical that a different set of requirements applies to investigating domestic servitude as opposed to human trafficking, as the Court suggests in *CN*.

The more plausible explanation is that Court used the absence of a specific offence of domestic servitude from domestic legislation as a mere excuse, while engaging in its own evaluation of the factual circumstances and operational choices. Similarly, the Court in *SM* spent a great deal of time outlining what the authorities should have done to determine the true nature of the applicant's and the defendant's relationship and whether the applicant had been exploited by him as she alleged.[103] The suggestions included specific actions such as conducting an inquiry into the circumstances of the applicant's and the alleged perpetrator's contact via Facebook, identifying and interviewing the owner of the flat where the applicant lived, as well as the applicant's neighbours, or interviewing the applicant's parents and even the mother and boyfriend of the applicant's friend.[104] The striking level of detail of such instruction sits uneasily with the Court's proclamation in *Beganovic* quoted earlier that it 'must grant *substantial deference* to the national courts in the choice of appropriate measures'.[105] As rightly warned by the concurring Judges O'Leary and Ravarani, 'the risk of the Court too easily assuming the role of a first-instance tribunal (of fact) is clear'.[106]

Such a proactive approach to reviewing states' compliance with one of the 'absolute' rights is also evident in *Zoletic*, where the Court decided to examine the case under Article 4 ECHR *proprio motu*, even though the applicants themselves did not invoke this provision in their initial application to the Court.[107] The Court clarified that: '[B]y virtue of the *jura novit curia* principle, the Court considers that the applicants' submissions in their initial application form, in substance, amounted to a complaint under Article 4 §2 of the Convention, even though the applicants did not expressly refer to that provision.'[108]

Notwithstanding such a robust approach to reviewing states' compliance with Article 4 ECHR, the Court has stopped short of granting victims the right to have third parties prosecuted or sentenced for criminal offences.[109] Given that the Court is tasked with reviewing states' responsibility under the ECHR and not individual criminal law liability, it emphasised that 'there is no absolute right to

---

[102] *Zoletic and Others v Azerbaijan* (n 12) [185]. See also *SM v Croatia* (n 2) [309].
[103] *SM v Croatia* (n 2) [336]–[347].
[104] ibid.
[105] *Beganovic v Croatia* (n 85) [78] (emphasis added).
[106] *SM v Croatia* (n 2), Joint Concurring Opinion of Judges O'Leary and Ravarani.
[107] The applicants relied instead on art 6 (right to a fair trial), art 1 of Protocol No 1 (protection of property), and art 2 of Protocol No 4 (freedom of movement) to the Convention.
[108] *Zoletic and Others v Azerbaijan* (n 12) [128].
[109] *Öneryıldız v Turkey* (n 85) [96].

obtain the prosecution or conviction of any particular person where there were no culpable failures in seeking to hold perpetrators of criminal offences accountable'.[110] Furthermore, demands that human rights law places on the states to ensure practical and effective protection against 'modern slavery' by no means absolve them from observing the established rights of offenders. Accordingly, in the case concerning the convicted trafficker complaining that his Article 6 rights had been violated because he was convicted solely on the basis of the statements of victims whom he had no opportunity to cross-examine, the Court held that 'the *Rantsev* judgment did not indicate that the positive obligation of States to prosecute traffickers go as far as infringing the defence rights of persons charged with trafficking'.[111] The Grand Chamber in *SM* echoed this position by emphasising 'the necessity of the protection of the rights of the suspects or accused, in particular the right to the presumption of innocence and other fair-trial guarantees under Article 6 of the Convention'.[112]

Finally, it is important to note that the states' procedural obligation usually arises after the original act that potentially violates the right had taken place, with the aim of establishing the facts and eventually punishing the perpetrator. However, in situations of ongoing abuse, such as cases of exploitation or domestic violence cases that engage Article 3, the aim of such investigative duties is also prevention of further harm.[113] For instance, in the previously discussed the *Hacienda Brasil Verde* case, the IACtHR articulated the obligation to 'open, *ex officio* and immediately, an effective investigation that permits the identification, prosecution and punishment of those responsible, when a report has been filed'.[114] It nonetheless found that 'when it received the report of violence and subjection to a situation of slavery, the State failed to react with the due diligence required' by the seriousness of the facts, the victims' situation of vulnerability, and its international obligation to prevent slavery.[115] Also in *Rantsev*, the obligation of the police to make an inquiry into the circumstances which gave rise to a credible suspicion of her potential status as a trafficked victim was inexorably linked to a duty to protect her.[116]

Overall, it is important to emphasise that even though the procedural obligation is mainly focused on the criminal justice process against the perpetrators, it is instrumental for victim protection by both preventing further harm and securing justice and redress for the harm already suffered. While the Strasbourg Court rightly distinguishes between this and the obligation to protect, noting that '(potential) victims need support even before the offence of human trafficking is

---

[110] *SM v Croatia* (n 2) [315]; *Zoletic and Others v Azerbaijan* (n 12) [188].
[111] *Breukhoven v The Czech Republic* [2011] ECHR 1177 [55]. See further discussion of this case in Chapter 7, section 3.
[112] *SM v Croatia* (n 2) [322].
[113] See also *Opuz v Turkey* (n 10); *Kontrova v Slovakia* (n 10).
[114] *Workers of the Hacienda Brasil Verde v Brazil* (n 2) [319].
[115] ibid [328].
[116] *Rantsev v Cyprus and Russia* (n 1) [296] (emphasis added).

formally established',[117] this does not imply that when a victim has received adequate protection, conducting criminal proceedings against the perpetrators is less significant or superfluous.

6.3 Specific Obligations: A Duty to Protect Victims of 'Modern Slavery'

The obligation to protect individuals from the threats that originate from non-state actors involves taking operational measures to prevent harm or its recurrence. While these measures mainly concern police action,[118] the obligation rests on all authorities who have the required knowledge and are in a position to take actions to avert the threat.[119]

The test for assessing states' compliance with this duty was set out by the Strasbourg Court in the landmark *Osman* case, which examined whether the authorities had taken reasonable steps to protect the lives of the Osman family under Article 2 ECHR.[120] Ahmet Osman and his father, Ali Osman, were shot by Ahmet's former teacher who developed a problematic attachment to the boy. Mr Osman died as a result of the shooting, while Ahmet was seriously wounded. The complaints before the Strasbourg Court concerned the alleged failure of the authorities to protect them because the teacher had already threatened the applicant and his family before the fatal accident. The applicants argued that the police had been given information which should have made it clear that the former teacher posed a danger. The Strasbourg Court famously established that Article 2 implies 'in certain well-defined circumstances a positive obligation on the authorities to take preventative operational measures to protect an individual whose life is at risk from the criminal acts of another individual'.[121] Therefore, the Court ruled that:

> [W]here there is an allegation that the authorities have violated their positive obligation to protect the right to life ... it must be established ... that the authorities knew or ought to have known at the time of the existence of a real and immediate risk to the life of an identified individual or individuals from the criminal acts of a

---

[117] *J and Others v Austria* (n 18) [115].
[118] In *Kontrova v Slovakia* (n 10) [52], the Court noted that 'it is one of the main tasks of the police to serve to protect fundamental rights and freedoms, life and health'.
[119] In *E and Others v United Kingdom* (2003) 36 EHRR 31, the responsibility was primarily placed on the social services, who failed to discover the exact extent of the problem and, potentially, to prevent further abuse taking place. In *Öneryıldız*, it concerned the relevant administrative and municipal departments responsible for supervising and managing the rubbish tip that was the source of the risk to the of the people living near the tip.
[120] Jeremy McBride, 'Protecting Life: A Positive Obligation to Help' (1999) 24 European Law Review 43.
[121] *Osman v United Kingdom* (n 10) [115].

third party and that they failed to take measures within the scope of their powers which, judged reasonably, might have been expected to avoid that risk.[122]

Since then, the Court has applied this test to a number of situations engaging Articles 2,[123] 3,[124] and 4.[125] The IACtHR too referred to *Osman* when declaring that:

> [The State's] duty to adopt measures of prevention and to protect private individuals in their relations among themselves is conditioned by its awareness of a situation of real and immediate risk for a specific individual or group of individuals and the reasonable possibilities of preventing or avoiding that risk ... in order to establish the State's responsibility it is necessary to establish whether "at the time of the facts, the State authorities were aware or should have been aware of the existence of a situation that involved a real and immediate risk to the life of an individual or a group of individuals, and failed to take the necessary measures that fell within the scope of their authority to prevent or avoid that risk."[126]

It is therefore important to unpack and examine the three part test developed in *Osman* and the ways in which it has been deployed in 'modern slavery' cases.

6.3.1 The Three-part Test for Assessing State Compliance with the Duty to Protect Individuals from the Acts of Private Violence

The *Osman* test consists of three parts. The first is concerned with the applicant's situation (or victim's situation, since in some cases, the applicants would be victim's relatives) and the risk he or she is facing. At this stage, the Court is invited to rule on whether there was *objectively* a real and immediate risk to an identifiable individual from criminal acts of a third party. The existence of such a risk is independent of the question of whether authorities knew or ought to have known of it, which is the next step in the evaluation of a state's conduct.

The second part of the test therefore relates to the *official awareness* of these circumstances or the inexcusable lack of it. This was said to be 'a discrete precondition for [states] responsibility'.[127] Here, it must be demonstrated that the authorities

---

[122] ibid [116].
[123] *Calvelli and Ciglio v Italy* [2002] ECHR 3 [55]; *Öneryıldız v Turkey* (n 85) [63]; *Opuz v Turkey* (n 10) [128]–[129]; *Kontrova v Slovakia* (n 10) [49]–[50]; *Kilic v Turkey* (2001) 33 EHRR 58 [62]; *Denizci and Others v Cyprus* [2001] ECHR 351 [375]–[376].
[124] *E and Others v The United Kingdom* (n 119) [88]; *Z and Others v United Kingdom* (2002) 34 EHRR 3 [73].
[125] *Rantsev v Cyprus and Russia* (n 1) [286]–[287]; *Chowdury and Others v Greece* (n 12) [88]; *SM v Croatia* (n 2) [305]–[306]; *VCL and AN v United Kingdom* (n 19) [152]; *Zoletic v Azerbaijan* (n 12) [184].
[126] *Workers of the Hacienda Brasil Verde v Brazil* (n 2) [323]–[324].
[127] McBride (n 120) 45.

'knew or ought to have known at the time' of the existence of the real and immediate risk to life. Such awareness may result from the victim's own attempts to draw it to their attention[128] or from other information available to authorities.[129] The Court's task is to scrutinise the way authorities dealt with information known to them at the time. However, it has been noted that states' obligations are not restricted to situations where the risk is effectively staring at their face.[130] Accordingly, the Court expressly rejected an argument that the failure to perceive the risk (or to take preventative measures to avoid that risk) must be tantamount to gross negligence or wilful disregard of the duty to protect life.[131] However, any conclusion as to whether authorities knew or ought to have known of the risk can only be answered with reference to the specific circumstances of the case.

Finally, the last part of the test is concerned with *measures* that were within the scope of the powers of state authorities which, judged reasonably, might have been expected *to avoid that risk*. In other words, it prompts the question of whether the authorities did all that could be reasonably expected of them to avoid a real and immediate risk to life. Such a question requires consideration of three points: first, whether the required measure was *within the state powers*; secondly, whether this could be *reasonably* expected from the state, and lastly, whether it would have had a *capacity* to avert the risk. Clearly, the obligation to protect life is not absolute and different considerations play a role when assessing its scope. As to the second point, the Court ruled that the required action must not impose 'an impossible or disproportionate burden' on the authorities. The limits to the required action are set by 'difficulties involving policing modern societies, the unpredictability of human conduct and the operational choices which must be made both in terms of priorities and resources'.[132]

With respect to the third point, the action required from the state must have had the *potential* to make a genuine difference. In the context of Article 3, the Court explained that this:

> [D]oes not require it to be shown that 'but for' the failing or omission of the public authority ill-treatment would not have happened. A failure to take reasonably available measures which could have had a real prospect of altering the outcome or mitigating the harm is sufficient to engage the responsibility of the State.[133]

Furthermore, the Court clarified that the choice of the measures that are 'necessary and sufficient' to protect individuals[134] primarily rests with national authorities.[135]

---

[128] *Opuz v Turkey* (n 10).
[129] *Öneryıldız v Turkey* (n 85).
[130] McBride (n 120) 47.
[131] *Osman v United Kingdom* (n 10) [116].
[132] ibid.
[133] *E and Others v United Kingdom* (n 119) [99].
[134] *Öneryıldız v Turkey* (n 85) [101].
[135] ibid [107]; *Opuz v Turkey* (n 10) [165].

Thus, it held that 'it is not for the Court to replace the national authorities and to choose in their stead from among the wide range of possible measures that could be taken to secure compliance with their positive duties'.[136] Nevertheless, it reminded of its ultimate power to provide a final authoritative interpretation of the rights and freedoms and, according to the principle of practical and effective protection of the rights, to ensure that states discharge their obligation to protect rights in an adequate manner.[137]

As noted above, the *Osman* test has been used for assessing states' obligations in a variety of contexts—from domestic violence and cases of child abuse and neglect, to environmental disasters and, finally, allegations of 'modern slavery'. While most of the time the Court has replicated the exact wording in *Osman*, it slightly modified the test when applying it to a (potential) trafficking situation. The Court has been criticised for not offering any explanation for this change.[138] However, such adaptation is not without merit given that situations of human trafficking differ from life-threatening situations (although, as seen in *Rantsev*, they may sometimes converge). It is therefore necessary to examine the approach to the operational duty in 'modern slavery' cases and the nuances of the test designed to assess states' compliance with this obligation.

6.3.2 The *Osman* Test in 'Modern Slavery' Cases

Drawing a parallel with Articles 2 and 3, the Strasbourg Court ruled in *Rantsev v Cyprus and Russia* that Article 4 too 'may, in certain circumstances, require a state to take operational measures to protect victims, or potential victims, of trafficking'.[139] The test outlined by the Strasbourg Court reads as follows:

> In order for a positive obligation to take operational measures to arise in the circumstances of a particular case, it must be demonstrated that the state authorities were aware, or ought to have been aware, of circumstances giving rise to a *credible suspicion that an identified individual had been, or was at real and immediate risk of being, trafficked or exploited* within the meaning of art.3(a) of the Palermo Protocol and art.4(a) of the Anti-Trafficking Convention. In the case of an answer in the affirmative, there will be a violation of art.4 of the Convention where the authorities fail to take *appropriate measures within the scope of their powers to remove the individual from that situation or risk*.[140]

---

[136] *Opuz v Turkey* (n 10) [163]–[165].
[137] ibid.
[138] Vladislava Stoyanova, 'Dancing on the Borders of Article 4: Human Trafficking and the European Court of Human Rights in the *Rantsev* Case' (2012) 30(2) Netherlands Quarterly of Human Rights 163, 192.
[139] *Rantsev v Cyprus and Russia* (n 1) [286].
[140] ibid (emphasis added).

The *Rantsev* test and its application in the subsequent cases reveal differences with respect to all three parts of the *Osman* test and the relevant criteria for assessing states' compliance with this duty. The Court has never offered offer any explanation for this change, although it usually provides reasons when seeking to depart from its earlier practice in cases that raise similar considerations.[141] However, this is not to say that such a departure is unjustified, taking into account the nature of human trafficking situations, as opposed to life threatening situations.[142] It nonetheless deserves careful scrutiny.

First part of the test: objective circumstances
With respect to the objective circumstances that should alert authorities to take an action, instead of 'the *existence* of a real and immediate risk to the life', the Court used the phrase '*circumstances giving rise to a credible suspicion* that an identified individual had been, or was at real and immediate risk of being, trafficked or exploited'.[143] Two issues deserve attention: the factual aspect of the test and the evidential standard set out in it.

As for the factual requirement, the test requires that there was a credible suspicion *either* that an identifiable individual *had been trafficked or exploited* or that she was *at real and immediate risk of being trafficked or exploited*. While the first part of the requirement rightly establishes an obligation with respect to victims who have arguably already been subject to trafficking (with or without exploitation having taken place), the second part invites a more detailed consideration. In particular, the phrase 'at real and immediate risk of being trafficked' is too broad. This is because, as already noted in Chapter 2, the definition of trafficking is broad enough to include even those acts that are quite remote from any exploitative practice, such as recruitment, for example. In such circumstances, being 'at real and immediate risk of trafficking' as opposed to having already been trafficked but not yet subject to exploitation (which in turn means being at real and immediate risk of exploitation), seems too distant a moment for imposing protective duties on states. Such a requirement would disproportionately interfere with both the victim's and the potential perpetrator's rights, given the low evidential threshold (i.e. a credible suspicion). The only context where this statement could be relevant are deportation cases, when there is a risk that one might be re-trafficked if deported back to the state of origin. Nevertheless, the basis for such a claim would be the fact that a person has already been trafficked in the past.

Accordingly, the more appropriate phrasing of the requirement with respect to the factual aspect would be that an identifiable individual had been trafficked in

---

[141] *Christine Goodwin v United Kingdom* (2002) 35 EHRR 18 [73]–[74].
[142] Similarly, in the context of a procedural obligation, the concurring judges in *SM v Croatia* (n 2) emphasised a difference between the nature of the facts that constitute an 'arguable claim and the type of investigation necessary to investigate treatment in breach of Article 4, as opposed to Articles 2 and 3'.
[143] *Rantsev v Cyprus and Russia* (n 1) [286].

the past or is currently in the situation of trafficking, regardless of whether any exploitation had occurred.[144] That is because all trafficked victims are indeed at real and immediate risk of being exploited, because that is the sole purpose of the act of trafficking. On the other hand, if the exploitation had already begun, the victim may also rely on one of the explicitly prohibited practices or alternatively, on the protection provided by other Convention articles.[145]

It is important to note that the Court did not seek to establish conclusively that Ms Rantseva had been trafficked or exploited, neither was this necessary, at least with respect to the duty to conduct further enquiries into her circumstances. In fact, contrary to the situation in *Siliadin*, the Court here was not concerned with the question of whether the judicial system provided sufficient protection through prosecuting and penalising those clearly established to have been responsible for the situation. Instead, a *credible suspicion* that she might have been the victim was sufficient to engage Article 4 protection.[146]

Turning to the evidential requirement, it is noteworthy that the standard wording concerning 'the existence of a real and immediate risk' was replaced by 'circumstances giving rise to a credible suspicion'.[147] Stoyanova criticises the Court for 'softening' the *Osman* test, suggesting that the new approach was borrowed from the Anti-Trafficking Convention, namely, the reasonable grounds test for victims' identification contained in article 10(2) of that convention. Apart from expressing regret for the Court's failure to substantiate and explain this modification of the *Osman* test, she also asks whether this 'less stringent' test is of relevance only to persons who are allegedly victims of human trafficking for the purpose of prostitution or it has a wider application. In addition, she is concerned that the test may apply 'irrespective of whether [the victims] want to be saved or whether there is something to be saved from'.[148]

---

[144] Both the Anti-Trafficking Convention and Anti-Trafficking Directive require protection when there are reasonable grounds to believe that a person 'has been victim of trafficking in human beings' (Anti-Trafficking Convention, art 10(2)) or that she 'might have been subjected to any of the offences referred to in Articles 2 and 3' (Anti-Trafficking Directive, art 11(2)).

[145] *M and Others v Italy and Bulgaria* (n 46). Notably, in *Workers of the Hacienda Brasil Verde v Brazil* (n 2) [306], in response to the applicants' claim that, in addition to slavery and human trafficking, the situation in *Hacienda Brasil Verde* constituted violations of the rights to juridical personality, personal integrity, personal liberty, honour, and dignity, and to freedom of movement and residence, the IACtHR explained that 'due to the nature of slavery as a crime that violates multiple norms, when a person is subjected to this condition, various individual rights are violated to a greater or lesser extent depending on the specific factual circumstances of each case. Nevertheless, owing to the specific and complex definition of the concept of slavery, when verifying a situation of slavery, such rights are subsumed in the Convention under Article 6 [IACHR]'.

[146] This, however, inevitably results in a different level of protection and measures required to provide it, which is evident in the Anti-Trafficking Convention. Namely, some of the provisions to protect and assist victims contained in Chapter III of the Convention apply to all victims (arts 10, 11, 12, 15, and 16), while others apply to persons not yet formally identified as victims but whom there are reasonable grounds for believing to be victims. See arts 10(2), 12(1), 12(2), and 13.

[147] Stoyanova (n 138) 193.

[148] ibid.

While the analogy with the Anti-Trafficking Convention is all too obvious, the concerns expressed with respect to the 'weakening' of the *Osman* test are unfounded. In fact, the low evidential threshold is primarily related to the state's duty to conduct necessary enquires and to provide immediate assistance and protection, which should enable the correct identification of victims, 'which is often tricky and necessitates detailed enquiries'.[149] As already noted when discussing the *Opuz* case,[150] the Court places a special emphasis on investigating situations of potential grave abuses of individual rights, not only in the absence of the victim's initiative, but also even *despite* her ostensible opposition. However, in deciding the course of action in such situations, states must strike a proper balance between victim's Article 2, 3 and 8 rights.[151] However, even if such reasonable grounds to believe existed, any measure of victim protection would apply exclusively on a 'consensual and informed basis'.[152] Therefore, the argument about paternalistic protection clearly does not hold.

Furthermore, apart from the victims' reluctance to reveal their ordeal, the lower threshold for state intervention is justified by a difference in the nature of the trafficking act and life-threatening situations. In the latter cases, the question relates to the *future risk*, which, even if eventually materialised, invites a careful consideration of the requirements imposed on states, especially if these involve the coercion of a potential perpetrator. Conversely, in trafficking situations, the question for national authorities is rather that of *uncertainty* about past and present facts, which in turn justifies placing stricter obligations to enquire and establish the facts.

Second part of the test: the official awareness of the objective circumstances
It has already been noted that for a positive obligation to protect to arise, it must also be demonstrated that the objective circumstances were known to the authorities, or ought to have been known to them at the time. In *Rantsev* and the subsequent cases discussing this obligation, the Court used the phrase 'aware or ought to have been aware', which in substance does not differ from the *Osman* test.[153]

Importantly, the Court recognised a range of standards that might be used in assessing states' awareness, many of which flow directly from trafficking-specific instruments. With respect to Cyprus, the seriousness of the trafficking problem

---

[149] Explanatory Report to the Council of Europe Convention on Action against Trafficking in Human Beings (16 May 2005) CETS 197 (Explanatory Report) para 127. See also Jessica Elliott, '(Mis) Identification of Victims of Trafficking: The Case of R v. O' (2009) 21 International Journal of Refugee Law 727, 732; Parosha Chandran, 'The Identification of Victims of Trafficking' in Parosha Chandran (ed), *Human Trafficking Handbook: Recognising Trafficking and Modern-Day Slavery in the UK* (2011) 45–46.
[150] See text with nn 51–53.
[151] *Opuz v Turkey* (n 10) [138].
[152] Anti-Trafficking Convention, art 12(7); Anti-Trafficking Directive, recital 21.
[153] *Chowdury and Others v Greece* (n 12) [88]; *V VCL and AN v United Kingdom* (n 19) [152]; *Zoletic and Others v Azerbaijan* (n 12) [184]. See also *Workers of the Hacienda Brasil Verde v Brazil* (n 2) [323]–[324].

in general, clearly depicted in the reports of the Cypriot Ombudsman and the Council of Europe Commissioner for Human Rights, was instrumental in setting higher expectations from authorities. Hence, they were expected to pay heightened attention and carefully examine every situation that raised a concern with respect to the possibility of trafficking.[154] This ought to be read together with the *general obligation* of states to ensure adequate training for law enforcement and immigration officials, which draw on the relevant provisions of the Palermo Protocol and the Anti-Trafficking Convention.[155] Therefore, the magnitude of the trafficking problem in general, coupled with specific circumstances of the case clearly revealing the indicia of trafficking (especially the fact that her 'employer' was in possession of her passport and other documents'), created a credible suspicion that Ms Rantseva was, or was at real and immediate risk of being, trafficked or exploited, which the authorities ought to have been aware of.[156] In other words, the circumstances of the case were such as to raise a credible suspicion that she might have been a trafficking victim, which adequately trained and diligent authorities would have been aware of and would have had a duty to act upon. Accordingly, authorities were obliged to investigate these circumstances and to take any necessary operational measures to protect her. Instead, they did not even take a statement from her nor did they make any further inquiries into the background facts, which together with the multitude of other failures, resulted in the finding of a violation of Article 4 in this respect.[157]

In *Chowdury and Others v Greece*, the Court observed that 'the situation in the strawberry fields of Manolada was known to the authorities, whose attention had been drawn to it by reports and press articles'.[158] It pointed out to the 'debates held in Parliament on this subject', the fact that 'the Ombudsman alerted a number of State ministries and agencies and the public prosecutor's office to this situation' and 'the Amaliada police station appeared to be aware of the refusal of the applicants' employers to pay their wages'.[159] The problems encountered by the applicants were therefore endemic and widely known.

In *VCL and AN*, the applicants were two Vietnamese minors charged and convicted with drug production. Despite concerns raised by social services and assessments made by the competent authorities regarding their potential status as victims of trafficking they were prosecuted and convicted for the offences. They argued that by prosecuting them, the state failed in its duty to protect them as victims of trafficking. In ruling that 'the prosecution of victims, or potential victims,

---

[154] For a national approach see *Minh, R (on the application of) v The Secretary of State for the Home Department* [2015] EWHC 1725 (Admin) (18 June 2015).
[155] *Rantsev v Cyprus and Russia* (n 1) [296].
[156] ibid.
[157] ibid [298].
[158] *Chowdury and Others v Greece* (n 12) [111].
[159] ibid [111]–[114].

of trafficking may, in certain circumstances, be at odds with the State's duty to take operational measures to protect them',[160] the Court pointed out that both applicants were discovered on or near cannabis factories, and that at the time:

> Both the guidance published by the CPS in December 2007 and its Guidance on Human Trafficking and Smuggling ... highlighted the 'cultivation of cannabis plants' as an offence likely to be carried out by child victims of trafficking... Moreover, the first 'scoping report' of the Child Exploitation and Online Protection Command ('CEOP'), which was published in June 2007, identified Vietnamese boys and girls as a specific vulnerable group. It noted that some of these children had been found being exploited in cannabis factories while others were suspected to have been trafficked for the purposes of sexual exploitation.[161]

There was accordingly no doubt for the Court that 'from the very outset the police and subsequently the CPS should have been aware of the existence of circumstances giving rise to a credible suspicion that he had been trafficked'.[162]

The question of a state's awareness of a potential trafficking situation is evidently closely linked to the issue of victim identification. This duty is set out in Article 10 of the Anti-Trafficking Convention and places a demand on state parties to establish a legal and institutional framework necessary to identify victims and to ensure that:

> [I]f the competent authorities have reasonable grounds to believe that a person has been a victim of trafficking in human beings, that person shall not be removed from its territory until the identification process ... has been completed by the competent authorities and shall likewise ensure that that person receives the assistance provided for in Article 12, paragraphs 1 and 2.[163]

The Explanatory Report to the Convention clarifies that 'a failure to identify a trafficking victim would mean that his or her fundamental rights will continue to be denied and the prosecution will be denied the necessary witness in criminal proceedings'.[164] It is important to note that the Anti-Trafficking Convention affords protection to individuals who are either already recognised as trafficking victims or where there are reasonable grounds to believe that they are.[165] However, as already pointed out, the *Rantsev* test seems to suggest that even persons who are at risk of being trafficked *in future* would qualify for protection under the ECHR.

---

[160] *VCL and AN v United Kingdom* (n 19) [159].
[161] ibid [117].
[162] ibid [118].
[163] Anti-Trafficking Directive, art 10(2).
[164] Explanatory Report, para 127.
[165] See further discussion in Chapter 7, section 4.

While the Court's reference to 'actual or potential victims',[166] seems to indicate the uncertainty about one's victim's status rather than future risk of trafficking, the test used to trigger operational duties which requires that 'an identified individual had been, or *was at real and immediate risk of being, trafficked* or exploited within the meaning of Article 3(a) of the Palermo Protocol and Article 4(a) of the Anti-Trafficking Convention'[167] would benefit from further clarity.

In *Chowdury and Others v Greece*, the Strasbourg Court confirmed that the ECHR duty to protect includes an obligation to identify a person as a victim of trafficking, drawing expressly on the Council of Europe's Anti-Trafficking Convention:

> The Court observes that the Council of Europe's Anti-Trafficking Convention calls on the member States to adopt a range of measures to prevent trafficking and to protect the rights of victims. The preventive measures include measures to strengthen coordination at national level between the various anti-trafficking bodies and to discourage the demand, which promotes all forms of exploitation of persons, including border controls to detect trafficking. Protection measures include facilitating the identification of victims by qualified persons and assisting victims in their physical, psychological and social recovery.[168]

Similarly, in *J and Others v Austria*, the Court considered 'whether the Austrian authorities complied with *their positive obligation to identify and support* the applicants as (potential) victims of human trafficking'.[169] Finally, in *VCL and AN*, the crux of the decision concerned the correct identification of the victim with the Court emphasising that the early identification 'by individuals trained and qualified to deal with victims of trafficking' is of 'paramount importance' for the prosecution of such a victim to demonstrate respect for the freedoms guaranteed by Article 4.[170] The Court nonetheless explained that 'the potential scope of this obligation extends beyond their identification as victims of trafficking'.[171] The breadth of requirements imposed on states by this specific obligation will be discussed in the following sub-section and in the final chapter of the book.

Overall, the assessment of a state's awareness of the objective circumstances, which triggers the obligation to identify a victim, represents the first step in the Court's analysis of the obligation to protect her. A low evidential threshold for victims' initial identification effectively serves to establish relevant circumstances and

---

[166] *Rantsev v Cyprus and Russia* (n 1) [286]; *Chowdury and Others v Greece* (n 12) [88]. See also *J and Others v Austria* (n 18) [109]; *SM v Croatia* (n 2) [306]; *VCL and AN v United Kingdom* (n 19) [152]; *Zoletic and Others v Azerbaijan* (n 12) [132].

[167] *Rantsev v Cyprus and Russia* (n 1) [286]; *Chowdury and Others v Greece* (n 12) [88]; *VCL and AN v United Kingdom* (n 19) [152].

[168] *Chowdury and Others v Greece* [110] (n 12).

[169] *J and Others v Austria* (n 18) [109] (emphasis added).

[170] *VCL and AN v United Kingdom* (n 19) [160].

[171] ibid [120].

to assess their protection needs, and is separate from establishing the formal elements of the trafficking offence. The Strasbourg Court expressly confirmed this in *J and Others v Austria* and in *SM v Croatia*, where it clarified that:

> [A]dministrative recognition of the status of a potential victim of human trafficking cannot be taken as recognition that the elements of the offence of human trafficking have been made out. Such special treatment of a potential victim of human trafficking does not necessarily presuppose an official confirmation that the offence has been established, and may be independent of the authorities' duty to investigate. Indeed, (potential) victims need support even before the offence of human trafficking is formally established; otherwise, this would run counter to the whole purpose of victim protection in trafficking cases. The question whether the elements of the crime are present has to be answered in subsequent criminal proceedings.[172]

It is therefore clear that the low evidential threshold for triggering the obligation to protect does not run the risk of infringing the rights of the suspects or accused of engaging in 'modern slavery'.

Third part of the test: measures required to protect an individual at risk of or subject to 'modern slavery'

Having found that objective circumstances raise a credible suspicion as to the individual's victim status and, that a state was or ought to have been aware of these, the final task for the Court would be to assess whether the state complied with its duties to protect such an individual. The Court held in *Rantsev* that if the answers to the above questions are affirmative, 'there will be a violation of Article 4 of the Convention where the authorities fail to take *appropriate* measures within the scope or their powers *to remove the individual from that situation or risk*'.[173] While the *Osman* test calls for measures which, judged reasonably, might have been expected 'to avoid' that risk, the *Rantsev* test requires an action 'to remove' the individual from the situation or risk. Thus, while the former invites the assessment of the extent of the risk and the probable capacity of any measure to avoid it, trafficking situations consider victims who have potentially already suffered some harm. This may in turn place stricter duties on states. In fact, the stronger the indicia or evidence of one's trafficking status,[174] the less excuse the state will have for failing to protect the individual.

---

[172] *SM v Croatia* (n 2) [322]. See also *J and Others v Austria* (n 18) [115].
[173] *Rantsev v Cyprus and Russia* (n 1) [286] (emphasis added).
[174] UNODC, 'Human Trafficking Indicators' http://www.unodc.org/pdf/HT_indicators_E_LOW RES.pdf (accessed 4 April 2015).

As discussed in Chapter 5, 'absolute' rights do not confer upon individuals an entitlement to absolute protection. The IACtHR explained in *Hacienda Brasil Verde* that:

> [I]t is evident that a State cannot be responsible for every human rights violation committed among private individuals subject to its jurisdiction. Indeed, the State's treaty-based obligations of guarantee do not entail the unlimited responsibility of the State for every fact or act involving private individuals.[175]

Therefore, the appropriate measures required from the national authorities must be within the scope of their powers and must not be interpreted to impose an impossible or disproportionate burden on them. With respect to the proportionality requirement, while the Court in *Osman* only referred to considerations that act as constraints to the required action, *Rantsev* also presented considerations that fall on the other side of the balancing scale. Hence, the Court noted that the proportionality of any positive obligation will be assessed in the light of the states' obligations under the Palermo Protocol to endeavour to provide for the victims' physical safety, to establish comprehensive policies and programs to prevent and combat trafficking and to provide relevant training for state officials.[176] While this statement clearly signals the preparedness of the Court to take into consideration a more substantive set of duties enshrined in the trafficking-specific instruments when assessing states' compliance with their Article 4 obligations, the question of the nature and scope of protective measures within Article 4 remains the most difficult to answer. In other words, are 'appropriate measures within the scope or [state] powers to remove the individual from that situation or risk' limited to merely rescuing victims from actual or imminent danger, or do they include a range of substantial measures, enshrined in the Anti-Trafficking Convention?

The specific circumstances of the *Rantsev* case must be borne in mind when taking a critical stance towards the Court's failure to state more explicitly the scope of the states' protective duties. The alleged victim died under suspicious circumstances and, irrespective of several worrying signals, the authorities did virtually nothing to establish whether she was actually trafficked or had been exploited. This made the finding of a violation quite straightforward, and the Court may not have felt obliged to address this issue in more detail. In *VCL and AN*, the Court had an opportunity to elaborate further the scope of the operational duty to protect:

> As for the type of operational measures which might be required by Article 4 of the Convention, the Court has considered it relevant that the Anti-Trafficking Convention calls on the member States to adopt a range of measures to prevent

---

[175] *Workers of the Hacienda Brasil Verde v Brazil* (n 2) [323].
[176] *Rantsev v Cyprus and Russia* (n 1) [287].

trafficking and to protect the rights of victims. The preventive measures include measures to strengthen coordination at national level between the various anti-trafficking bodies and to discourage the demand for all forms of exploitation of persons. Protection measures include facilitating the identification of victims by qualified persons and assisting victims in their physical, psychological and social recovery.[177]

This is a clear signal of the Court's preparedness to engage with the substantive content of the Anti-Trafficking Convention to develop positive obligations under Article 4 ECHR. Furthermore, in line with its robust approach to reviewing states' compliance with the procedural obligation, the level of scrutiny over the state's conduct concerning the operational duty is considerable. Accordingly, the Court *VCL and AN* took an issue with the fact that both the prosecutor and the Court of Appeal 'disagreed with the conclusions of the Competent Authority and found that the applicants were not in fact victims of trafficking'.[178] In the Court's view:

> Once a trafficking assessment has been made by a qualified person, any subsequent prosecutorial decision would have to take that assessment into account. While the prosecutor might not be bound by the findings made in the course of such a trafficking assessment, the prosecutor would need to have clear reasons which are consistent with the definition of trafficking contained in the Palermo Protocol and the Anti-Trafficking Convention for disagreeing with it.[179]

In the particular case, the Court concluded that:

> [A]t no stage did [the Prosecutor] put forward any clear reasons for reaching a different conclusion from that of the Competent Authority, and in so far as any reasons can be gleaned from the information provided to the Member of Parliament ... and to the Court of Appeal ... as the Competent Authority itself pointed out they related to peripheral issues and did not go to the core of the elements necessary to establish 'trafficking'.[180]

This represents a particularly hands-on approach to reviewing institutional competence and the decision-making process of the domestic authorities in applying the Convention, which the ECtHR, by its own admission, has not competence to interpret.[181]

---

[177] *VCL and AN v United Kingdom* (n 19) [153].
[178] ibid [113].
[179] ibid [162].
[180] ibid [170].
[181] *VCL and AN v United Kingdom* (n 19) [113].

Some guidance as to the scope of protection that the Court considers adequate is discernible from the decision in *J and Others v Austria*, which concerned two Filipino nationals who claimed to have been exploited while working as maids or au pairs in the United Arab Emirates and who were subsequently brought to Vienna by their employers where they eventually managed to escape. The Court considered, but found no violation of the Austrian authorities' positive obligation to identify and support the applicants as (potential) victims of human trafficking. Its reasoning is worth stating in full:

> From the point when the applicants turned to the police, they were immediately treated as (potential) victims of human trafficking. They were interviewed by specially trained police officers ... were granted residence and work permits in order to regularise their stay in Austria ... and a personal data disclosure ban was imposed on the Central Register so their whereabouts were untraceable by the general public ... During the domestic proceedings, the applicants were supported by the NGO LEFÖ, which is funded by the Government especially to provide assistance to victims of human trafficking. According to the uncontested statements of the Government ... the applicants were given legal representation, procedural guidance and assistance to facilitate their integration in Austria. For the purposes of Article 4 of the Convention, it is paramount that the applicants' claims as a whole were taken seriously and the applicable legal framework was applied, in accordance with the State's obligations under the Convention. From that point of view, the Court considers that the legal and administrative framework in place concerning the protection of (potential) victims of human trafficking in Austria appears to have been sufficient, and that the Austrian authorities took all steps which could reasonably have been expected in the given situation. This was not contested by the applicants. The Court is therefore satisfied that the duty to identify, protect and support the applicants as (potential) victims of human trafficking was complied with by the authorities.[182]

The final chapter of the book presents a detailed overview of the range of protective measures contained in the European anti-trafficking instruments, which are commended for establishing the highest standards of victim protection. The analysis in Chapter 7 therefore examines the extent to which extent these substantive victim protection measures could inform state positive obligations arising out of human rights law to effectively amount to victims' justiciable human rights.

---

[182] *J and Others v Austria* (n 18) [110]–[111].

6.4 Remedies for 'Modern Slavery': Individual Justice, Structural Change, and the Tale of the Two Courts

What happens when states violate their human rights obligations arising out of the prohibition of 'modern slavery'? What, in other words, are the consequences of the states' failure 'to ensure the creation of the conditions required to guarantee that violations of this inalienable right do not occur'?[183]

Previous chapter has highlighted the insufficient attention to the question of remedies for the breach of positive obligations in cases of private infringements of rights, both in the human rights scholarship and in jurisprudence of international tribunals.[184] In particular, positive obligations and remedies for failing to comply with such violations are not clearly distinguished. For instance, the Strasbourg Court often finds a breach of the procedural obligation under the substantive article even though state agents are directly involved in actions infringing upon that right[185]—a situation that ought to trigger an obligation to provide a remedy for the *violation* of a human right guaranteed in Article 13 ECHR.[186] There is furthermore a frequent conflation of remedies for the harm inflicted by non-state actors with remedies for states' own violations of positive duties to respond to such harm.[187]

When it comes to 'modern slavery' cases specifically, the question of remedies is completely overlooked in the Strasbourg jurisprudence. The rare instances when remedies are referenced in the Strasbourg case law illustrate the flaws identified above. For instance, the ECtHR considers that 'positive procedural obligations under Article 4 ... form a *lex specialis* in relation to the general obligations under Article 13'.[188] This statement reveals a conflation of positive obligations for private infringements of rights and remedies for states' own wrongdoing: the former can never be a subset of the latter, as the Court wrongly suggests. This conflation of positive duties with human rights remedies is further evident in the Court's assertion that 'for complaints concerning treatment contrary to Article 4, the adequate remedy to be pursued is a criminal complaint'.[189] This statement fails to distinguish between remedy for the original harm inflicted by private actors (which amounts

---

[183] *Workers of the Hacienda Brasil Verde v Brazil* (n 2) [317] (the scope of the primary obligation set by the Court is broad: '[c]ompliance with Article 6, in relation to Article 1(1) of the American Convention, not only supposes that no one may be subjected to slavery, servitude, trafficking or forced labor, but also requires States to adopt all appropriate measures to end such practices and prevent violations of the right not to be subjected to such conditions').

[184] See Chapter 5, section 5.4.

[185] *McCann and Others v United Kingdom* [1995] ECHR 18984/91; *Hugh Jordan v United Kingdom* (n 73); *Poltoratskiy v Ukraine* (2004) 39 EHRR 43; *Assenov and Others v Bulgaria* (1999) 28 EHRR 652.

[186] Notably, in some cases where states' agents were directly involved in rights infringements, the Court correctly framed an obligation to investigate such allegations under art 13 ECHR. See eg *Aksoy v Turkey* (1997) 23 EHRR 553 [98] (emphasis added). See also *Aydin v Turkey* (1998) EHRR 251 [103]–[109]; *İlhan v Turkey* (2002) 34 EHRR 36 [121].

[187] See the discussion in Chapter 5, section 5.4.

[188] *CN and V v France* (n 12) [113].

[189] *Zoletic and Others v Azerbaijan* (n 12) [175].

to the state's positive human rights obligation) and human rights remedies for states' failure to abide by their positive obligations. What is more, 'modern slavery' cases follow the Court's general policy of relying solely on just satisfaction, which focuses on compensating victims for pecuniary and non-pecuniary damage, as a 'go-to remedy'.[190]

Therefore, both 'modern slavery' case law and the ECHR jurisprudence overall, reveal the Court's reluctance to impose 'specific individual or general measures that ought to be adopted to fully enforce the judgment in the domestic legal system'.[191] Individual measures are intended to end or remedy a specific violation of the Convention rights established by the Court; '[t]hey can be quite concrete: the Court may for example order an applicant's release from prison or the reinstatement of a Supreme Court judge'.[192] In contrast, general measures are forward-looking—they are meant to address structural problems and prevent future violations of the Convention. The need for such measures is especially pressing in the case of systemic problems, which produce numerous repetitive cases and contribute to the significant backlog of the Court.[193] To address such situations, the Court might require a change of legislation or administrative practice.[194]

Fikfak explains the Court's general preference for compensation over specific individual or general measures by its concern about 'over-reaching' and the risk of non-compliance with non-monetary remedies.[195] Instead, she notes that the Court 'relies on the persuasive power of its ruling. The expectation is that the judgment identifies the underlying problem so clearly that states are able to undertake the necessary actions to prevent future breaches at home'.[196] In reality, she warns, the opposite is often true:

> Extensive non-compliance may stem from imprecision in how obligations are framed. If the ECtHR does not specify the actions or remedies required, it is difficult for states to comply and internalize its judgments. If its judgments are meant to persuade states and cajole them into certain behaviour, then they are most useful 'if they sharply reduce uncertainty about the content of obligations' ... Precision, therefore, promotes compliance and internalization.[197]

---

[190] Veronika Fikfak, 'Changing State Behaviour: Damages before the European Court of Human Rights' (2019) 29(4) European Journal of International Law 1091, 1095.

[191] ibid 1099–100.

[192] Helen Keller, Corina Heri, and Réka Piskóty, 'Something Ventured, Nothing Gained? Remedies before the ECtHR and Their Potential for Climate Change Cases' (2022) 22 Human Rights Law Review 1, 3.

[193] Repetitive cases are said to account for almost half of the total number of pending cases before the ECtHR. See European Court of Human Rights, Annual Report The Council of Europe 2016) 13.

[194] Linos-Alexander Sicilianos, 'The Involvement of the European Court of Human Rights in the Implementation of its Judgments: Recent Developments under Article 46 ECHR' (2014) 32(3) Netherlands Quarterly of Human Rights 235, 241–42.

[195] Fikfak (n 190) 1099.

[196] ibid 1093.

[197] ibid 1101–102.

Notwithstanding the uncertainty about the type of non-monetary measures required to render state practice Convention-compliant, even the Court's approach to damages—its preferred type of remedy—appears arbitrary and highly unpredictable. Damages awarded to victims of 'modern slavery' in respect of pecuniary and non-pecuniary damage do not reveal any predictable pattern, which justifies the often repeated criticism of 'the Court's deferential, inconsistent and unreasoned approach to Article 41, and thus to remedies more broadly'.[198] The Strasbourg case law on 'modern slavery' therefore reveals a glaring omission of the Court to articulate and explain the nature, scope, and function of remedies for violations of—in the Court's own words—one of the most fundamental rights.[199]

In contrast, the jurisprudence of the IACtHR is often praised for offering 'a list of highly specific steps that must be undertaken as remedies to adverse judgments'.[200] While this does not necessarily result in better compliance with its rulings, it is noted that 'the specificity nevertheless helps states with enforcement'.[201]

It is worth noting that the IACtHR too uses the term 'remedies' to discuss a series of positive obligations imposed on Member States under the right to judicial protection guaranteed in Article 25(1) IACHR, which contains 'in broad terms, the obligation of States to provide everyone subject to their jurisdiction with an effective judicial remedy against acts that violate their fundamental rights'.[202] For instance, in its first decision that found a violation of the prohibition of slavery, the Court examined whether domestic criminal, civil, and labour proceedings 'were effective remedies to investigate and punish those responsible for the facts verified in *Hacienda Brasil Verde*, and whether an effective remedy existed to make reparation to the presumed victims'.[203] It is clear, however, that when the Court refers to 'remedies', which 'must be appropriate to counteract the violation',[204] it has in mind judicial remedies for the original harm inflicted by non-state actors, and not remedies for harm that results from the state's failing to comply with its obligations to respond to the former. Accordingly, the Court considered a serious of flaws in domestic proceedings against the manager and the owner of the hacienda and concluded that: '[N]one of the proceedings on which it received information

---

[198] Keller, Heri, and Piskóty (n 192) 4.
[199] The Strasbourg Court refers to the rights contained in arts 2, 3, 4, or 5(1) of the Convention, guaranteeing respectively the right to life, the prohibition of torture, inhuman or degrading treatment or punishment, the prohibition of slavery, and the right to liberty and security of person, as the 'core rights'. See European Court of Human Rights, 'The Court's Priority Policy' (22 May 2017).
[200] Fikfak (n 190) 1102.
[201] ibid.
[202] *Workers of the Hacienda Brasil Verde v Brazil* (n 2) [391]. Article 25(1) IACHR contains the right to judicial protection: 'Everyone has the right to simple and prompt recourse, or any other effective recourse, to a competent court or tribunal for protection against acts that violate his fundamental rights recognized by the constitution or laws of the state concerned or by this Convention, even though such violation may have been committed by persons acting in the course of their official duties.'
[203] *Workers of the Hacienda Brasil Verde v Brazil* (n 2) [383]. See in particular the analysis in [391]–[420].
[204] ibid [392]–[394].

determined any type of responsibility for the conducts denounced, and nor were they a means of obtaining reparation for the harm done to the victims, because none of the proceedings examined the merits of each issue.'[205]

Notwithstanding this examination of 'remedies' for the harm inflicted by individual perpetrators, having found a violation of the right to judicial protection established in Article 25 of the American Convention on Human Rights (ACHR) and a violation of the prohibition of slavery recognised in Article 6 ACHR, both on account of the State's failing to act with expected due diligence to prevent, terminate, or punish acts of private individuals, the Court went on to consider appropriate 'reparations' for such violations. These 'reparations' could be considered human rights remedies *stricto sensu* because they concern actions imposed on states in response to a finding of a violation of the state's own international obligation, whether negative or positive.[206] Accordingly, the Court ruled that:

> Reparation of the harm caused by the violation of an international obligation requires, whenever possible, full restitution (*restitutio in integrum*), which consists in the re-establishment of the previous situation. If this is not feasible, as in most cases of human rights violations, the Court will determine measures to ensure the violated rights and to redress the consequences of the violations.[207]

The IACtHR went on to discuss an elaborate set of requirements that Brazil ought to implement in order to comply with its duty to make reparation for the harm caused to the victims as a result of the breach of the Convention rights.[208] These included, first, investigative measures, which required Brazil to 're-open, with due diligence, the required investigations and/or criminal proceedings for the facts verified in March 2000 in this case in order, within a reasonable time, to identify, prosecute and punish, as appropriate, those responsible'.[209] Specifically, the Court ruled that the state should 'examine the possible investigative and procedural irregularities related to this case and, if appropriate, sanction the conduct of the public servants concerned, without the need for the victims in this case to file the pertinent complaints'.[210]

---

[205] ibid [402].
[206] Such reparations are envisaged in art 63(1) of the American Convention, which establishes that: '[i]f the Court finds that there has been a violation of a right or freedom protected by this Convention, the Court shall rule that the injured party be ensured the enjoyment of his right or freedom that was violated. It shall also rule, if appropriate, that the consequences of the measure or situation that constituted the breach of such right or freedom be remedied and that fair compensation be paid to the injured party.'
[207] *Workers of the Hacienda Brasil Verde v Brazil* (n 2) [436].
[208] ibid [440]–[489].
[209] ibid [445].
[210] ibid [446].

Furthermore, as a measure of satisfaction, the Court imposed a duty on Brazil to publish its judgment and inform the Court when it has complied with this obligation.[211] The Court also ordered the state 'within a reasonable time from notification of this judgment, to adopt the necessary legislative measures to ensure that the statute of limitations is not applied to the reduction of a person to slavery and similar conditions'.[212] This measure was meant to guarantee non-repetition. Notably, as part of the same guarantee of non-repetition, the Court examined in detail a range of public policies designed 'to prevent and punish slave labor' in Brazil.[213] While the Court considered that 'barriers still exist in the fight against forced labor in Brazil', it acknowledged a series of actions implemented by the state to eradicate slave labour, concluding that 'the actions and policies adopted by the State are sufficient and does not find it necessary to order additional measures'.[214] Finally, 'taking into account the suffering and anguish [the workers on the hacienda] endured in their situation of a condition similar to slavery' the Court ordered the state to pay to each worker the sum for non-pecuniary damage, which it 'considered to be reasonable and proportionate to the sum requested'.[215]

Such a uniquely comprehensive and strict scrutiny over the state's wider legal and policy framework, followed by a detailed roadmap for both redressing specific violations and for preventing further breaches of this fundamental right, is in stark contrast with the Strasbourg Court's insisting 'that it is not its task to determine what non-monetary remedies would appropriately satisfy the obligations under the ECHR'.[216] While space precludes a detailed discussion of the differences between the two courts when it comes to remedies in general, there is no doubt that the seriousness of the practices of 'modern slavery', the grave impact on victims, and the 'absolute' nature of their prohibition in human rights law, warrant state responses that exceed mere financial compensation. An adequate remedy requires both restoring the rights of affected individuals and forward-looking measures aimed at preventing further violations. The level of detail that the rulings of human rights tribunals should provide when ordering such remedies and the margin of appreciation that states (ought to) have in selecting appropriate measures raise questions that necessitate a comprehensive analysis, which exceeds the scope of this book.

---

[211] ibid [450]–[451].
[212] ibid [455].
[213] ibid [463]–[470].
[214] ibid [468]–[470].
[215] ibid [488]. The Court declined to grant compensation for pecuniary damage on the basis of its inability to determine '(i) the amount that corresponded to each worker at the time he was rescued, and (ii) the possible difference with the amount received by each worker. These two elements are essential to establish the existence of a pecuniary damage. Consequently, the Court rejects the representatives' request in this regard'. ibid [482].
[216] Fikfak (n 190) 1100.

6.5 'Modern Slavery', 'Absolute Rights', and State Responsibility for Acts of Private Violence: New Horizons for the Human Rights Jurisprudence

The analysis in this chapter has shed some light on the potential of human rights law to provide effective and tangible protection to victims of 'modern slavery', grounded in the case law of international tribunals. The analysis of the positive human rights obligations in 'modern slavery' cases thus adds an important dimension and clarity to the general discussion of the positive obligations in the situations of private infringements of human rights, and 'absolute' rights in particular.

These important jurisprudential developments would have undoubtedly benefited from a more robust reasoning by the international tribunals, in order to clarify the nature and scope of positive obligations as well as standards for assessing state compliance with them. The chapter sought to fill these jurisprudential gaps and offer a coherent interpretation of the positive obligations in 'modern slavery' cases established so far.

It is nonetheless clear that such positive obligations are in the state of flux—how they will continue to develop in future is not straightforward. In recent cases, the Strasbourg Court has explicitly referred to the Council of Europe Anti-Trafficking Convention and its expert body (GRETA) when reviewing states' compliance with the ECHR. For instance, in *Chowdury and Others v Greece*, the Court ruled that:

> [M]ember States' positive obligations under Article 4 of the Convention must be construed in the light of the Council of Europe's Anti-Trafficking Convention ... The Court is guided by that Convention and the manner in which it has been interpreted by GRETA.[217]

While the Court was careful to specify that its jurisdiction was limited to the European Convention on Human Rights and that '[i]t has no competence to interpret the provisions of the Anti-Trafficking Convention or to assess the compliance of the respondent State with the standards contained therein',[218] it is clear from the overview of its caselaw that Article 4 duties are decisively shaped by the requirements in these instruments. For example, the Court modelled 'a duty in cross-border trafficking cases to co-operate effectively with the relevant authorities of other states' on the obligations and objectives expressed in the Palermo Protocol.[219] It also shaped the operational duty to protect victims of 'modern slavery' to include 'facilitating the identification of victims by qualified persons and assisting victims

---

[217] *Chowdury and Others v Greece* (n 12) [104]; *VCL and AN v United Kingdom* (n 19) [150].
[218] *VCL and AN v United Kingdom* (n 19) [113].
[219] *Rantsev v Cyprus and Russia* (n 1) [289]; *Zoletic and Others v Azerbaijan* (n 12) [191].

in their physical, psychological and social recovery' by directly invoking similar obligations in the Council of Europe's Anti-Trafficking Convention.[220] The possibility of drawing on the obligations set out in the anti-trafficking instruments to inform the duties arising out of human rights treaties is therefore at the centre of the discussion in Chapter 7.

---

[220] *Chowdury and Others v Greece* (n 12) [110]; *VCL and AN v United Kingdom* (n 19) [153].

7
The Role of Specialised Anti-trafficking Instruments in Shaping Human Rights Obligations of States to Address 'Modern Slavery'

The previous chapter analysed human rights obligations of states owed to the survivors of 'modern slavery' as articulated in the jurisprudence of international human rights tribunals. The Strasbourg Court rulings featured prominently in that analysis because the Court has so far been the most active in addressing this issue. In fleshing out these duties, the Court drew on its jurisprudence on other 'absolute' rights, as well as on the specialised anti-trafficking instruments that set out obligations of states to tackle 'modern slavery' in more detail. The reliance on other international instruments is part of the Court's traditional view that the provisions of the European Convention on Human Rights (ECHR) do not apply in a vacuum.[1] Accordingly, the Court submitted that the extent of the positive obligations arising under Article 4 ECHR must be considered within a broader context of legal instruments (the Palermo Protocol[2] and the Anti-Trafficking Convention[3]) acceded to by almost all Council of Europe Member States.[4] Such a view is similarly endorsed by the Inter-American Court of Human Rights, which explained that:

> [W]hen analyzing the scope of Article 6 of the American Convention, the Court has found it useful and appropriate to use other international treaties, in addition to the Convention, to interpret its provisions in keeping with the evolution of the inter-American system, taking into consideration the corresponding evolution

---

[1] *Rantsev v Cyprus and Russia* (2010) 51 EHRR 1 [273]; *Loizidou v Turkey* (1997) 23 EHRR 513; *Öcalan v Turkey* (2005) 41 EHRR 45.

[2] Protocol to Prevent, Suppress and Punish Trafficking in Persons Especially Women and Children, supplementing the United Nations Convention against Transnational Organized Crime (adopted 15 November 2000, entered into force 25 December 2003) 2237 UNTS 319 (Palermo Protocol).

[3] Convention on Action against Trafficking in Human Beings (adopted 16 May 2005, entered into force 1 February 2008) CETS 197 (Anti-Trafficking Convention).

[4] *Rantsev v Cyprus and Russia* (n 1) [285]. See also *Chowdury and Others v Greece* [2017] ECHR 300 [104].

in the different branches of international law, particularly international human rights law.[5]

It should nevertheless be noted that the provisions of the specialised anti-trafficking instruments, or any other international treaty, could not be simply transplanted into human rights law. In other words, the process of interpreting human rights treaties by taking into account other international law instruments must not be equated with merely importing provisions of such instruments. The Strasbourg Court has tried to navigate that path in the recent case concerning the imprisonment of victims of human trafficking for their involvement in cannabis cultivation, who claimed to have been subject to practice known as 'criminal exploitation' or 'forced criminality'.[6] The obligation of states to consider not applying domestic criminal law to those victims of human trafficking whose involvement in criminal offences is a result of their trafficking situation is established in many anti-trafficking instruments.[7] The Strasbourg Court expressly noted that its role was not to interpret and assess compliance with obligations that stem from other international instruments. Instead, it considered the extent to which the criminalisation and punishment of the trafficking victims in the case at hands contravened the obligation to protect them arising out of Article 4 ECHR. However, even though the Court stopped short of importing the non-punishment provision in the ECHR, its ruling inevitably bolstered such a duty by instructing the states to consider how the prosecution of victims may clash with their Article 4 ECHR obligation to protect such victims.[8]

It is therefore vital to explore the ways in which the specialised anti-trafficking instruments can inform human rights law while maintaining the normative distinction between these different domains of international law.

The chapter considers the provisions of the UN Palermo Protocol and the Council of Europe Anti-Trafficking Convention as the instruments that have decisively shaped normative approaches to anti-trafficking action worldwide. Its focus is on those provisions that are relevant for the protection of victims, critically examining their strength and the potential to shape human rights obligations, identified and analysed in the previous chapter. Notably, while the recent anti-trafficking instruments contain a more victim-centred focus, victim protection

---

[5] *Workers of the Hacienda Brasil Verde v Brazil* (Preliminary Objections, Merits, Reparations and Costs) IACtHR Series C No 318 (20 October 2016) [247].

[6] Anti-Slavery International, *Trafficking for Forced Criminal Activities and Begging in Europe: Exploratory Study and Good Practice Examples* RACE in Europe project (September 2014); UK National Crime Agency, 'NCA Guidance for Councils on How to Identify and Support Victims of Criminal Exploitation'.

[7] Anti-Trafficking Convention, art 26; EU Trafficking Directive, art 8; ASEAN Convention Against Trafficking in Persons Especially Women and Children, art 14(7). See further the discussion in section 7.3.3.

[8] *VCL and AN v United Kingdom* [2021] ECHR 132 [159].

measures do not automatically translate into their human rights, let alone create enforceable obligations for states under human rights law. In light of this 'key distinction', the goal of this chapter is to consider where to draw a line between victim protection measures and their rights justiciable under the ECHR and other general human rights treaties.

Accordingly, in analysing the provisions of the anti-trafficking instruments, the chapter identifies how the Strasbourg Court (and other human rights tribunals) could strengthen protection offered to the survivors of 'modern slavery' by interpreting the ECHR (and other human rights instruments) to take into account victim protection measures contained in the relevant trafficking conventions. It is argued that the role of human rights tribunals is to lay down general guidance as to the scope of protection available to the victims of 'modern slavery' but that the specific measures required to comply with such obligations are to be discerned from the specialised anti-trafficking instruments and national legislation. This creates internal coherence and synergy between different branches of international law as well as the balance between the competence of international human rights tribunals and domestic authorities.

7.1 The Palermo Protocol and States' Obligations to Tackle Human Trafficking

Replacing the outdated concept of human trafficking reserved for specific gender or race, and restricted to prostitution, the Palermo Protocol introduced a modern universal definition of human trafficking. This initiative renewed an interest in trafficking and created a platform for developing a 'human rights dimension' of the problem.[9]

The Protocol has three core purposes: the prevention of human trafficking, the prosecution of the perpetrators of human trafficking, and the protection of victims of human trafficking: the so-called '3Ps'.[10] To achieve those purposes, the Protocol requires state parties to implement a range of measures.[11] The obligations imposed on states are divided into four categories, with varying level of obligation.

---

[9] Ryszard Piotrowicz, 'The Legal Nature of Trafficking in Human Beings' (2009) 4 Intercultural Human Rights Law Review 175. See Chapter 2 for a historical development of the concept of human trafficking and its incorporation in human rights law.

[10] Palermo Protocol, art 2. The fourth 'P', which amounts to 'partnerships' between different actors involved in anti-trafficking action, has been subsequently added and widely accepted. See The United Nations Global Plan of Action to Combat Trafficking in Persons, G.A. Res. 64/293 (30 July 30 2010) Preamble; Jonathan Todres, 'Taking Prevention Seriously: Developing a Comprehensive Response to Child Trafficking and Sexual Exploitation' (2010) 43 Vanderbilt Journal of Transnational Law 1, 41 (suggesting that 'partnerships' should be mainstreamed in each of the original three prongs).

[11] For a good analysis of the issues addressed in the Protocol see Federico Lenzerini, 'International Legal Instruments on Human Trafficking and a Victim-Oriented Approach: Which Gaps Are to Be Filled?' (2009) 4 Intercultural Human Rights Law Review 205, 270.

First, states are required to criminalise human trafficking, as well as to criminalise participating as an accomplice and organising or directing other persons to commit the offence.[12] The second set of duties, which are infamously couched in a discretionary language, includes measures concerned with providing assistance and protection to victims of human trafficking.[13] The third group of obligations is concerned with the prevention of human trafficking, which includes 'comprehensive policies, programmes and other measures',[14] border measures,[15] as well as the security and control of travel or identity documents.[16] Finally, states are obliged to cooperate with each other, and in certain cases, with entities that are not states parties to the Trafficking in Persons Protocol, such as non-governmental organisations, other relevant organisations, and other elements of civil society. State cooperation is focused on information-sharing[17] and the process of repatriation of victims,[18] as well as on matters concerning border measures and travel documents.[19] The Protocol also promotes collaboration with civil society in relation to the provision of assistance to victims[20] and the establishment of prevention measures.[21]

As mentioned above, not all of the required actions carry the same level of obligation. The Protocol therefore distinguishes between measures that are *mandatory*, measures that states parties must *consider* applying or *endeavour to* apply, and measures that are entirely *optional*.[22] Accordingly, whereas states are *required to* 'establish as criminal offences the conduct set forth in article 3 of this Protocol',[23] they are only asked to protect the privacy and identity of victims of trafficking in persons 'in appropriate cases and to the extent possible under its domestic law',[24] or to '*consider* implementing measures to provide for the physical, psychological and social recovery of victims of trafficking in persons'.[25] Similarly, states shall only '*endeavour* to provide for the physical safety of victims of trafficking in persons while they are within its territory'.[26] This is in stark contrast with the *Osman*-style

---

[12] Palermo Protocol, art 5.
[13] ibid arts 6–8.
[14] ibid art 9.
[15] ibid art 11.
[16] ibid arts 12 and 13.
[17] ibid art 10.
[18] ibid art 8.
[19] ibid arts 11–13.
[20] ibid art 6(3).
[21] ibid art 9(3).
[22] UNODC 'Legislative Guide for the Implementation of the Protocol to Prevent, Suppress and Punish Trafficking In Persons, Especially Women and Children, Supplementing the United Nations Convention Against Transnational Organized Crime' (2004)(Trafficking Legislative Guide) para 8.
[23] Palermo Protocol, art 5.
[24] ibid art 6(1).
[25] ibid art 6(3) (emphasis added).
[26] ibid art 6(5) (emphasis added). This provision should nonetheless be read together with arts 24 and 25 of the Organized Crime Convention, which make provisions for victims and witnesses that apply to all cases covered by the Convention. See UNODC, 'Legislative guides for the implementation of the UN Convention Against Transnational Organized Crime and the Protocols Thereto' (2004) pt II, paras

obligation to implement operational measures to protect victims or potential victims of the treatment contrary to Article 4 ECHR, discussed in the previous chapter. Moreover, the Protocol does not establish a duty to identify victims of human trafficking, which is a precondition for any action aimed at providing assistance and protection. Instead, emphasising a strong criminal justice focus of the Palermo Protocol, the Legislative Guide notes that 'apart from criminal proceedings against offenders, there are no formal judicial or administrative proceedings in which the status of victims of trafficking as such can be determined'.[27] The provisions referring to victim protection therefore amount to mere recommendations rather than obligations.

Notwithstanding these design flaws when it comes to victim protection, practice suggests that the Palermo Protocol has made a significant impact on the criminalisation of human trafficking worldwide. Thus, since it was opened for signature on 12 December 2000, the Palermo Protocol 'has reached almost universal ratification, totalling 178 parties'.[28] It should be noted, however, that bringing legislation into line with international requirements is just the first step in the process of addressing the crime of human trafficking. Unless accompanied by effective policing, investigations, and criminal trials, criminal law provisions alone have little meaning. Therefore, while the UNODC notes that 'the conviction rate for trafficking in persons has increased in parallel to a broader adoption of the offence of trafficking in persons in national legislations',[29] it also reports on 'the weak criminal justice actions taken by national authorities to combat trafficking in persons, demonstrated by the limited number of convictions for trafficking in persons reported by countries'.[30]

Overall, beyond giving human trafficking international exposure, the Palermo Protocol seems to have failed to achieve either of its three professed goals, with victim protection most severely impaired by being entirely left to state discretion.

57–59 and pt I, paras 352–75. Therefore, whereas the obligation of the Protocol is only to 'endeavour to provide' for safety, the obligation of the Organized Crime Convention is to take any measures that are appropriate within the means of the state party concerned to provide effective protection from potential retaliation or intimidation. In particular, art 25(1) requires states to take appropriate measures within their means to provide assistance and protection to victims of offences covered by the Organized Crime Convention, especially in cases of threat of retaliation or intimidation. Importantly, 'to meet the requirements of article 25, legislators must either extend them to victims who are not witnesses, or adopt parallel provisions for victims and witnesses. In either case, the substantive requirements will be the same.'

[27] Trafficking Legislative Guide, para 275.
[28] UNODC, Global Report on Trafficking in Persons 2020 (United Nations publication, Sales No E.20.IV.3) 23. For the critique of the effectiveness of the regime envisioned by the Palermo Protocol see Jean Allain, 'No Effective Trafficking Definition Exists: Domestic Implementation of the Palermo Protocol' (2014) 7 Albany Government Law Review 142.
[29] UNODC, Global Report on Trafficking in Persons 2020 (United Nations publication, Sales No E.20.IV.3) 63.
[30] ibid 61.

7.2 The Victim-centred Approach in Post-Palermo Instruments and the 'Key Distinction' between Victim Protection and Victims' Human Rights

Despite its failure to offer meaningful protection to victims of human trafficking, the Palermo Protocol is praised for bringing human trafficking under the spotlight of the international community, which is said to have led to 'the development of a comprehensive international legal framework comprising regional treaties, abundant interpretive guidance, a range of policy instruments, and a canon of state practice'.[31] Gallagher, therefore, claims that:

> [F]ar from damaging human rights, the issue of trafficking provides unprecedented opportunities for the renewal and growth of a legal system that, until recently, has offered only platitudes and the illusion of legal protection to the millions of individuals whose life and labor is exploited for private profit.[32]

Post-Palermo initiatives to tackle human trafficking have therefore brought about greater concern for the protection of victims, leading to the adoption of new international instruments, most notably the Council of Europe Anti-Trafficking Convention.

The Anti-Trafficking Convention is said to embody the 'revolutionary way of thinking about trafficking and about victims of trafficking'[33] by taking 'a victim-oriented perspective to anti-trafficking action and [providing] for a series of measures to protect and assist victims'.[34] It guarantees, inter alia, minimum standards of assistance and protection to *all* victims of trafficking irrespective of their willingness to cooperate with criminal justice authorities,[35] and provides a mandatory recovery and reflection period during which no victim or presumed victim can be deported.[36]

Whereas these guarantees go significantly beyond the requirements established in the Palermo Protocol, the Parliamentary Assembly of the Council of Europe (PACE) was critical of the negotiating process noting that 'the measures for the protection of victims, which should be at the heart of the Convention, have become

---

[31] Anne Gallagher, 'Human Rights and Human Trafficking: Quagmire or Firm Ground? A Response to James Hathaway' (2009) 49(4) Virginia Journal of International Law 789, 791.
[32] ibid 794.
[33] Anne Gallagher, 'Recent Legal Developments in the Field of Human Trafficking: A Critical Review of the 2005 European Convention and Related Instruments' [2006] European Journal of Migration and Law 163, 187.
[34] Petya Nestorova, Executive Secretary of the Council of Europe Convention on Action against Trafficking in Human Beings, 'Trafficking in Europe' (Conference 'Bringing Human Trafficking Out of the Shadows' Cardiff (21 November 2012).
[35] Anti-Trafficking Convention, art 12(2).
[36] ibid art 13.

weaker in the course of the negotiations'.[37] Many recommendations by the PACE for strengthening victim protection did not find a way into the final version of the Convention. The most striking example is the rejection of a suggestion to include the provision granting victims the right to appeal to an independent and impartial body against the decisions on identification. This is particularly problematic given that the explanatory report to the Convention itself expressly warns that 'a failure to identify a trafficking victim correctly will probably mean that victim's continuing to be denied his or her fundamental rights and the prosecution to be denied the necessary witness in criminal proceedings'.[38] Such concern has proved justified as illustrated by the recent case law on both national and international levels.[39]

Furthermore, the PACE called for a significantly stronger protection of victims' safety including the protection of their family members, as part of the unconditional assistance package, and not only during the criminal proceedings as the Convention currently envisages.[40] In addition, the PACE advocated for providing necessary medical or other assistance, securing access to the labour market, to vocational training, and education to *all* victims regardless of their immigration status. On the contrary, the Anti-Trafficking Convention granted access to these benefits only to victims lawfully resident within the territory of a respective state.[41] Finally, the provisions that most obviously substantiate the PACE's criticism of member states' prioritisation of illegal migration over the protection of victims are those dealing with residence permits contained in Article 14. These provisions are considered 'excessively vague' leaving a wide margin of discretion to the states, which weakens the scope of the commitments entered into by states.[42]

While notable, this criticism of the European anti-trafficking framework is not central for the discussion here. The aim of the chapter is to investigate the extent to which the provisions of the anti-trafficking instruments amount to, or could inform, obligations of states under general human rights law. In that context, a claim in the Explanatory Report to the Anti-Trafficking Convention that '[t]he added value provided by the Council of Europe Convention lies firstly in the affirmation that trafficking in human beings is a violation of human rights'[43] could not be interpreted to imply that the Convention itself is a human rights treaty. Thus, even though the Convention is 'geared towards the protection of victims' rights and

---

[37] Council of Europe Parliamentary Assembly (PACE), Draft Council of Europe Convention on Action Against Trafficking in Human Beings (26 January 2005) Opinion 253 (2005) para 8 (PACE Opinion).
[38] Explanatory Report to the Council of Europe Convention on Action against Trafficking in Human Beings (16 May 2005) CETS 197 (Explanatory Report) para 127.
[39] See eg *VCL and AN v United Kingdom* (n 8); *Minh, R (on the application of) v The Secretary of State for the Home Department* [2015] EWHC 1725 (Admin) (18 June 2015).
[40] PACE Opinion, para 8.
[41] Anti-Trafficking Convention, arts 12(3) and 12(4).
[42] PACE Opinion, paras 9 and 12.
[43] ibid paras 36 and 51.

the respect for human rights',[44] it does not *itself* confer enforceable human rights. There is no doubt that the Convention provides 'more attention to the protection of and assistance to victims through more generous and less discretionary provisions on the treatment of victims'[45] compared to the Palermo Protocol. As such, it represents 'an important step away from the dominance of the criminal prosecution approach',[46] reflecting the requirements of an integrated 'holistic' approach to the fight against trafficking.[47] However, the Anti-Trafficking Convention is not a human rights treaty. Rather, it is a hybrid instrument, which combines measures of victim protection with the law enforcement ones including measures of border controls, security and control of travel and identity documents, and various organisational requirements.

Therefore, the Anti-Trafficking Convention obliges Member States 'to promote a human rights-based approach ... in the development, implementation and assessment of the policies and programmes to prevent human trafficking'.[48] However, an obligation 'to promote a human rights-based approach' does not imply that 'measures to protect and assist victims' amount to victim's human rights. Explaining what the human rights approach to human trafficking entails, six UN agencies argue that:

> It ensures compliance with *existing* State obligations under international and regional human rights treaties; it guarantees that anti-trafficking responses do not undermine or otherwise negatively impact on the human rights of trafficked persons or other groups affected by trafficking or anti-trafficking responses, or discriminate against women, migrants, refugees or other groups in a vulnerable situation.[49]

This human rights-based approach therefore implies 'considering, at each and every stage, the impact that a law, policy, practice or measure may have on the human rights of trafficked persons and other groups who may be affected by trafficking or anti-trafficking policies'.[50] Notably, implementing the provisions of the specialised anti-trafficking instruments in a way that respects *recognised* human rights under international and regional human rights treaties is fundamentally

---

[44] Explanatory Report, para 32.
[45] Heli Ascola, 'Article 5: Prohibition of Slavery and Forced Labour' in Steve Peers and others (eds), *The EU Charter of Fundamental Rights: A Commentary* (1st edn, Hart Publishing 2014) 115.
[46] Petra Follmar-Otto and Heike Rabe, *Human Trafficking in Germany Strengthening Victim's Human Rights* (German Institute for Human Rights 2009) 36.
[47] Tom Obokata, *Trafficking of Human Beings from a Human Rights Perspective: Towards a Holistic Approach* (Martinus Nijhoff 2006) 174; UN High Commissioner for Refugees, 'Prevent, Combat, Protect Human Trafficking: Joint UN Commentary on the EU Directive: A Human Rights Based Approach' (November 2011) (Joint UN Commentary on the EU Directive).
[48] Anti-Trafficking Convention, art 5(3).
[49] Joint UN Commentary on the EU Directive 26 (emphasis added).
[50] ibid 28.

different from claiming that the protective measures contained in these instruments represent human rights obligations of states. Accordingly, such measures of victim protection could inform positive obligations under human rights law, as illustrated in the previous and current chapter, but are not to be regarded per se as human rights obligations as such.

7.3 From Victim Protection Measures to Victims' Human Rights: The Criminal Justice Context

The provisions of the Anti-Trafficking Convention that provide protection to victims of human trafficking in the criminal justice context are threefold. First, they stipulate state obligations to criminalise, investigate, and impose appropriate penalties for human trafficking. These duties primarily concern the relationship between a state and a trafficker, prescribing measures required to prosecute and punish those involved in this serious crime. However, as shown in the previous chapter, criminal justice measures against individuals who traffic and exploit others are deemed essential for securing justice and redress for victims, and have been expressly recognised as positive human rights obligations. Secondly, measures of victim protection in the criminal justice context also concern their protection in the course of criminal investigations, prosecutions, and trials. The relevant provisions require states to adapt their criminal procedure in order to 'to protect victims of trafficking and assist prosecution of the traffickers'.[51] Finally, the protection of victims in the criminal justice context also includes their protection from being subject to criminalisation and punishment for crimes they have been 'compelled' to commit in the course, or as a consequence of being trafficked or exploited.[52]

These three sets of provisions relevant for victim protection have a different level of influence on shaping states obligations in human rights law.

7.3.1 Criminalisation, Investigation, and Adequate Penalties for 'Modern Slavery'

The obligation on states to criminalise human trafficking is the first and foremost duty in all specialist trafficking treaties.[53] The Anti-Trafficking Convention places on states a series of obligations aimed at enabling the effective prosecution of

---

[51] Explanatory Report, para 275.
[52] Anti-Trafficking Convention, art 26; Anti-Trafficking Directive, art 8; ASEAN Convention Against Trafficking in Persons Especially Women and Children, art 14(7).
[53] Palermo Protocol, art 5; Anti-Trafficking Convention, art 18; Anti-Trafficking Directive, art 2.

traffickers and ensuring that they are punished in a proportionate and dissuasive manner.

Therefore, in addition to the obligation to criminalise the offence of human trafficking,[54] states are also required to criminalise attempting or being an accomplice in the commission of trafficking offences.[55] Moreover, states 'must consider making it a criminal offence to knowingly use the services of a victim of trafficking'.[56] This is a contentious obligation, because of the difficulty to prove such knowledge in practice[57] and reservations that some have about using criminal law as a prevention tool rather than as punishment for past acts.[58] Moreover, the Anti-Trafficking Convention mandates states to adopt 'legislative and other measures as may be necessary to ensure that a legal person can be held liable for a criminal offence'.[59] This obligation is vital in the light of the emerging knowledge of the exploitative practices being carried out under the cover of legitimate business activities in industries such as agriculture, construction, garment, or food production.[60] In all those instances, states are required to guarantee sanctions that are 'effective, proportionate and dissuasive'.[61] This involves mandatory deprivation of liberty, when committed by natural persons, and monetary sanctions for legal persons, as well as the requirement to adopt legislation and procedures that allow for confiscation of the proceeds of this crime.[62]

Beyond criminalisation, states must ensure effective investigation and prosecution of human trafficking.[63] To that aim, the Anti-Trafficking Convention obliges states to guarantee that investigations and prosecution of human trafficking offences are not dependent upon the report or accusation made by a victim,[64] and to cooperate with each other regarding investigations and/or criminal proceedings related to these offences.[65] The Convention furthermore expressly mandates states to ensure that authorities responsible for investigating or prosecuting trafficking offences 'have adequate training and financial resources for their tasks'.[66]

Overall, the obligations placed on states by the anti-trafficking instruments in the criminal justice context are aimed at ensuring victims' access to justice through

---

[54] Anti-Trafficking Convention, art 18.
[55] ibid art 21.
[56] ibid art 19.
[57] Explanatory Report, para 234.
[58] See further Siobhán Mullally, 'Article 19: Criminalisation of the Use of Services of a Victim' in Julia Planitzer and Helmut Sax (eds), *A Commentary on the Council of Europe Convention on Action against Trafficking in Human Beings* (Edward Elgar Publishing 2020) 269.
[59] Anti-Trafficking Convention, art 22.
[60] See eg Genevieve LeBaron (ed), *Researching Forced Labour in the Global Economy Methodological Challenges and Advances* (OUP 2018).
[61] Anti-Trafficking Convention, art 23.
[62] ibid.
[63] ibid art 1(1)(b).
[64] ibid art 27.
[65] ibid art 32.
[66] ibid art 29.

an appropriate legal and institutional framework, which allows for effective investigations, prosecutions, and adequate punishment of traffickers. These obligations do not confer upon victims an entitlement to have a perpetrator punished in each individual case; instead they require states to put in place adequate mechanisms and procedures that are capable of securing such outcomes.[67]

The discussion in Chapter 6 showed that human rights tribunals have recognised many of these requirements as part of positive obligations within the prohibition of 'modern slavery', extending their application to exploitative practices that do not involve human trafficking. However, courts are rightly exercising caution and restraint when it comes to asking states to deploy criminal law to protect human rights. This is because of the potential for a 'coercive overreach' of such obligations, which could erode the traditional human rights of suspects and defendants and create a spill-over effect that legitimises the expansion of coercive measures.[68]

Accordingly, while courts may not hesitate to require states to implement training for relevant officials 'to ensure that persons or entities are specialised in the fight against trafficking and the protection of victims',[69] it is unlikely and certainly not preferable for human rights tribunals to internalise obligations that require states to criminalise the use of services provided by victims of exploitation,[70] or to criminalise acts relating to travel or identity documents such as forgery.[71] Such measures are only remotely, and at present inconclusively, related to victim protection and are best left to domestic criminal justice policies, which are overseen by GRETA—an expert body established by the Anti-Trafficking Convention to monitor state compliance with this treaty.[72] GRETA issues country reports, which evaluate progress in implementing the Anti-Trafficking Convention by state parties and outline steps that need to be taken to improve compliance.[73] In doing so, GRETA consolidates state practice over time, which in turn provides concrete benchmarks for the Strasbourg Court when evaluating states' compliance with more general and malleable obligations arising from human rights law. In other words, once a number of states have adopted a certain measure required by the

---

[67] *A, B and C v Latvia* (2018) 67 EHRR 31 [149] (The Strasbourg Court ruled that '[t]here is no absolute right to obtain the prosecution or conviction of any particular person where there were no culpable failures in seeking to hold perpetrators of criminal offences accountable'). See also *SM v Croatia*, App no 60561/14 (ECtHR GC, 25 June 2020) [315]–[316].

[68] See further Liora Lazarus, 'Positive Obligations and Criminal Justice: Duties to Protect or Coerce?' in Lucia Zedner and Julian Roberts (eds), *Principles and Values in Criminal Law and Criminal Justice* (OUP 2012); Natasha Mavronicola and Laurens Lavrysen (eds), *Coercive Human Rights: Positive Duties to Mobilise the Criminal Law under the ECHR* (Hart Publishing 2020).

[69] Anti-Trafficking Convention, art 29(1).
[70] ibid art 19.
[71] ibid art 20.
[72] ibid ch VII.

[73] See Fourth GRETA Report, paras 31–33. See also Julia Planitzer, 'GRETA's First Years of Work: Review of the Monitoring of Implementation of the Council of Europe Convention on Action against Trafficking in Human Beings' (2012) 1 Anti-Trafficking Review 1.

Anti-Trafficking Convention, revealing therefore a prevailing consensus among the Council of Europe Member States, the case for reading such a requirement into the ECHR becomes stronger, provided that there is a connection between the measure in question and the protective goals of the ECHR rights. GRETA reports also provide important context which helps the Court understand whether certain deficiencies are part of the broader pattern and flaws in a state's implementation of the applicable international obligation.

7.3.2 Protection of Victims in the Course of Criminal Proceedings against the Perpetrators of 'Modern Slavery'

While every victim is entitled to protection through criminal law, they are not obliged to participate in criminal trials against traffickers and exploiters. Should they decide to take part, they are entitled to protection during and after criminal investigation and trial. The anti-trafficking instruments therefore ask states to guarantee 'effective and appropriate protection from potential retaliation or intimidation in particular during and after investigation and prosecution of perpetrators'.[74] The protection measures are offered to victims, witnesses, collaborators with the judicial authorities, and to members of their families, as well as members of groups, foundations, associations, or non-governmental organisations, which provide assistance and protection to victims. Such measures include, inter alia, physical protection, relocation, identity change, or assistance in obtaining jobs.[75] These are said to be just examples and not a definite list of protections available to the eligible individuals. Therefore, the Explanatory Report to the Anti-Trafficking Convention emphasises that the expression 'effective and appropriate protection' requires states to adapt the level of protection to the threats to the persons entitled to the protection.[76] It also advises that the period in which protection measures have to be provided depends on the threats upon the persons.[77]

Furthermore, Article 30 of the Anti-Trafficking Convention includes procedural measures to be introduced in domestic legislation and institutional practice to safeguard victims' private life, identity, and safety in the course of judicial proceedings. These measures differ from the above mentioned measures of physical protection, which concern situations outside relevant criminal proceedings. The Explanatory Report states that this provision is only compulsory as to the objectives but leaves it to the parties to decide how to attain the objectives.[78] Nevertheless,

---

[74] Anti-Trafficking Convention, art 28. See also Anti-Trafficking Directive, arts 12 and 15; ASEAN Convention against Trafficking in Persons Especially Women and Children, art 16(7).
[75] Anti-Trafficking Convention, art 28.
[76] Explanatory Report, para 286.
[77] ibid para 288.
[78] ibid paras 306–26.

it lists some of the means that may achieve such objectives, which includes, for example, non-public hearings, using audio-visual technology for taking evidence and conducting hearings, recordings of testimony, and anonymous testimony.[79]

These requirements of victim protection during and after criminal proceedings raise two inter-related questions. The first question is whether and how can they be absorbed by the human rights prohibition against 'modern slavery'. And, secondly, if these requirements are to be grounded in the human rights prohibition against 'modern slavery' or any other ECHR right, how do they affect the defence rights?

The potential clash between the defence rights on one hand, and the protection of victims' and witnesses' privacy and safety on the other, is expressly acknowledged in the Explanatory Report to the Anti-Trafficking Convention, which is why it expressly calls for any measures of protection to be 'in accordance with the [ECHR], in particular Article 6'.[80] In the *Osman* case, which concerned the positive obligations to protect individuals from the threats to the right to life by private actors, the Strasbourg Court emphasised:

> [T]he need to ensure that the police exercise their powers to control and prevent crime in a manner which fully respects the due process and other guarantees which legitimately place restraints on the scope of their action to investigate crime and bring offenders to justice, including the guarantees contained in Articles 5 [right to liberty] and 8 [right to private life] of the Convention.[81]

Accordingly, the need secure defence rights constitutes an inherent limitation on any attempt to expand the scope of Article 4 ECHR to guarantee protection of victims and witnesses in the criminal justice process. The process of reconciling State's duties in respect of victim-witnesses and the fair trial rights of defendants is said to be 'multifaceted, relating to the context of the investigation and trial as a whole, the particular vulnerability of the witness-victim and the countervailing measures adopted by the judicial authorities in protecting the defendant's fair trial rights'.[82]

In the context of human trafficking, the Strasbourg Court has engaged with this challenge in *Breukhoven v Czech Republic*.[83] The applicant was convicted of human trafficking of three women from Romania. The Czech Regional Court found that these three victims had been brought to the Czech Republic under the pretext of working as bartenders and that the applicant subsequently forced them to engage in prostitution by using the threats of violence against their families. The applicant

---

[79] ibid.
[80] Anti-Trafficking Convention, art 30.
[81] *Osman v UK* (2000) 29 EHRR 245 [116].
[82] Liora Lazarus, 'Advice for the Stern Review: The Human Rights Framework Relating to the Handling, Investigation and Prosecution of Rape Complaints' in UK Government Equality Office, 'A Report by Baroness Vivien Stern CBE of an Independent Review into how Rape Complaints are Handled by Public Authorities in England and Wales: The Stern Review' (Annexe A) 133.
[83] *Breukhoven v Czech Republic* [2011] ECHR 1177.

contended that his right to a fair trial had been breached because he had been convicted solely on the basis of a testimony of the witnesses whom he had had no opportunity to question at any stage of the proceedings. The three victims gave their testimonies at the initial stage. Their interviews were conducted in the presence of a judge in accordance with domestic Code of Criminal Procedure as an urgent measure because the women said that they wished to return to Romania and never come back to the Czech Republic. Neither the applicant nor his lawyer was present at these interviews because they had taken place before the applicant was formally charged.[84] The Strasbourg Court considered whether domestic courts relied on any other evidence except these witness statements in order to establish the applicant's guilt for this crime. If this was found to be the case, the Court was called upon to determine whether such practice violated Article 6 ECHR.

Both the Government and the Czech Constitutional Court sought to justify the conduct of domestic courts by the serious nature of the applicant's crimes, invoking the positive obligation of States to combat trafficking in human beings, established in *Rantsev*. The European Court of Human Rights (ECtHR) reminded, however, that the *Rantsev* judgment 'did not indicate that the positive obligation of States to prosecute traffickers go as far as infringing the defence rights of persons charged with trafficking'.[85] The Court concluded that the applicant's conviction for trafficking in human beings was based solely on the testimony of the witnesses who did not appear at trial and whom he had no opportunity to question at any time during the proceedings, and that this procedural failure could not be justified by the particular context of the present case, which is a serious crime of sexual exploitation.[86] While the Court showed some concern for the vulnerability of the victims and their plight, the fact that domestic courts made no effort to secure their presence at the trial or to interview them in their home country and that 'no measures were taken by the domestic authorities to counterbalance the handicaps under which the defence laboured'[87] played a decisive role in finding a violation of the right to a fair trial guaranteed by Article 6 ECHR.

It is clear that the Court is unwilling to corrode the fair trial guarantees too easily, even when it comes to the most serious crimes (or especially then) and even when other fundamental rights might be at stake. Therefore, when seeking to reconcile the competing interests of victim-witnesses and the defendant, the Court has suggested that 'only such measures restricting the rights of the defence which are *strictly necessary* are permissible under Article 6'.[88]

It is important to note that the Strasbourg Court considered the interference with the defendants' fair trial rights in the interest of protecting victims and witnesses,

---

[84] ibid [7].
[85] ibid [55].
[86] ibid [57].
[87] ibid.
[88] *PS v Germany* (2003) 36 EHRR 61 [23] (emphasis added).

and ruled on the impact of these limitations on the overall fairness of the criminal proceedings.[89] Therefore, the ECtHR has *not* been called upon to pronounce whether and under which circumstances such limitations *ought* to be imposed in order to protect rights of victims and witnesses. In other words, the Court was not asked to determine whether states have an obligation to protect victims and witnesses in criminal proceedings under the ECHR. On that question, the Court has previously established that as a general rule 'Article 6 does not explicitly require the interests of witnesses in general, and those of victims called upon to testify in particular, to be taken into consideration'.[90] However, it specified that:

> [T]heir life, liberty or security of person may be at stake, as may interests coming generally within the ambit of Article 8 of the Convention. Such interests of witnesses and victims are in principle protected by other, substantive provisions of the Convention, which imply that Contracting states should organise their criminal proceedings in such a way that those interests are not unjustifiably imperilled.[91]

Therefore, while the protection of victims and witnesses may well require certain limitations of the defence rights, Article 6 ECHR does not itself establish any obligation in that regard.

Moreover, given that the protection during criminal investigation and trial is usually sought to secure 'life, liberty or security' of a person or 'interests coming generally within the ambit of Article 8 [ECHR]',[92] it is debatable whether Article 4 ECHR or some other human right(s) are better suited to ground the earlier outlined requirements from the Anti-Trafficking Convention. The prohibition of 'modern slavery' protects against the most serious forms of exploitation and the previous chapter has shown that its application is triggered by the risk of being (continuing to be) subject to such conditions.[93] However, the Strasbourg Court recently clarified that 'the duty to take operational measures under Article 4 of the Convention has two principal aims: to protect the victim of trafficking from further harm; and to facilitate his or her recovery'.[94] This statement potentially opens the possibility of using Article 4 ECHR as a vehicle to secure the protection of victims'

---

[89] *Axen v the FRG* (1983) Series A No 72; *Schenk v Switzerland* (1988) Series A No 140; *Doorson v Netherlands* (1996) 22 EHRR 330; *SN v Sweden* (2004) 39 EHRR 13; *Bricmont v Belgium* (1989) Series A No 158; *Saïdi v France* (1993) Series A No 261-C; *Kostovski v Netherlands* (1989) Series A No 166; *Ludi v Switzerland* (1992) Series A No 238; *Van Mechelen and Others v Netherlands* (1997) 25 EHRR 647; *Kok v Netherlands* [2000] ECHR 706.

[90] *Doorson v Netherlands* (n 89) [70]. See also Ben Emmerson, Andrew Ashworth, and Alison Macdonald, *Human Rights and Criminal Justice* (3rd edn, Sweet & Maxwell 2012) 823–32.

[91] *Doorson v Netherlands* (n 89) [70].

[92] ibid.

[93] Section 6.3.2.

[94] *VCL and AN v United Kingdom* (n 8) [159].

safety and privacy in the context of criminal proceedings against traffickers and exploiters, required by the above discussed provisions of anti-trafficking instruments. This is because the risk of retaliation or intimidation that these provisions are meant to protect against certainly amounts to 'further harm' which hinders victims' recovery.

7.3.3 Non-punishment of the Victims of 'Modern Slavery'

The protection of victims of human trafficking in the criminal justice context also includes an obligation to consider not subjecting them to criminal prosecution or punishment when they 'have been compelled to be involved in unlawful activities' in the course, or as a consequence of being trafficked.[95] Whereas previously described requirements placed on states are concerned with the *deployment* of criminal law to protect victims, the non-punishment principle requires directly the opposite—it effectively *restrains* the operation of the national criminal justice system. The number and complexity of legal issues raised by this provision and the scarcity of interpretative guidance on its implementation, calls for a separate and detailed analysis, which has been explored elsewhere by the book's author.[96]

For the purposes of the present discussion, which concerns the significance of the provisions introduced by the specialised Anti-Trafficking Convention for states' human rights obligations, it is worth recalling the position of the Strasbourg Court expressed in *VCL and AN v United Kingdom*. The case concerned two Vietnamese minors who were prosecuted and convicted for drug-related offences after being discovered by police working on cannabis farms in England. Both applicants had been prosecuted notwithstanding that, as minors working on a cannabis farm, there was a credible suspicion that they were victims of trafficking. After their conviction, both were conclusively recognised as trafficking victims by the Competent Authority through the UK's National Referral Mechanism.[97] Nevertheless, UK courts refused to quash their convictions on this basis, effectively disagreeing with the findings of the Competent Authority, but

---

[95] Anti-Trafficking Convention, art 26; Anti-Trafficking Directive, art 8.
[96] See Marija Jovanovic, 'The Principle of Non-Punishment of Victims of Trafficking in Human Beings: A Quest for Rationale and Practical Guidance' (2017) 1 Journal of Trafficking and Human Exploitation 1; Ryszard Piotrowicz and Liliana Sorrentino, 'Human Trafficking and the Emergence of the Non-Punishment Principle' (2016) 16 Human Rights Law Review 669.
[97] The National Referral Mechanism is the means through which the state identifies and supports potential victims of trafficking in the UK. See National referral mechanism guidance: adult (England and Wales) (updated 16 November 2020) and National referral mechanism guidance: adult (Northern Ireland and Scotland) (updated 16 November 2020). The Home Office has recently announced 'an ambitious NRM Transformation Programme'. See 2020 UK Annual Report on Modern Slavery, 5.

failing to provide any reasons for doing so. The European Court of Human Rights held that the UK violated Article 4 ECHR by failing to comply with its duties to protect the applicants when prosecuting them as minors and potential victims of trafficking.[98]

The ECtHR made it clear that it was not its task to examine how the States choose to operationalise the provisions imposed by other international instruments.[99] Instead, it was solely concerned with the impact of the criminalisation and punishment of the victims of 'modern slavery' on the states' duty to protect them.[100] The Court recognised that even though states are not, in principle, prevented from applying criminal law on victims of 'modern slavery',[101] such application is to be subject to a particularly close scrutiny because it could 'be at odds with the State's duty to take operational measures to protect them'.[102] The Strasbourg Court therefore warned that:

> It is axiomatic that the prosecution of victims of trafficking would be injurious to their physical, psychological and social recovery and could potentially leave them vulnerable to being re-trafficked in future. Not only would they have to go through the ordeal of a criminal prosecution, but a criminal conviction could create an obstacle to their subsequent integration into society. In addition, incarceration may impede their access to the support and services that were envisaged by the Anti-Trafficking Convention.[103]

In the case at hand, the Court had an easy task—the issue was not with the domestic authorities' weighing of the reasons for and against the prosecution of victims of human trafficking. The prosecutor and courts simply decided that the defendants had not been victims of 'modern slavery' in the first place. They provided no official reasons for such a conclusion, which is particularly striking because the designated competent authority repeatedly concluded that they had been. It therefore remains to be seen how the Court approaches situations where domestic authorities did accept one victim's status, but concluded that prevailing reasons justified prosecution.

---

[98] *VCL and AN v United Kingdom* (n 8) [112]. The Court also found that the UK violated 6 of the ECHR because the authorities' failure to conduct a timely assessment of whether the applicants had in fact been trafficked, which amounted to a breach of their positive obligations under art 4 ECHR, prevented them from securing evidence which may have constituted a fundamental aspect of their defence. It therefore concluded that the proceedings against both applicants could not be considered 'fair'. ibid [184]–[210].
[99] ibid (n 8) [113].
[100] ibid [114].
[101] ibid [158].
[102] ibid [159].
[103] ibid [159].

7.4 From Victim Protection Measures to Victims' Human Rights: Beyond the Criminal Justice Context

Measures of victim protection outside the criminal proceedings against traffickers are concerned with three main aspects: victims' safety, material assistance, and their legal status. The relevant provisions include both emergency protection measures as well as measures of longer-term assistance and support. Victims usually need protection long before their official identification can be completed. For that reason, some protection measures are owed as soon as there are reasonable grounds to believe that a person might be a victim, whereas other more extensive measures of protection are due only after the official identification process.

Victim identification is paramount to their access to necessary assistance and protection and accordingly is an expressly prescribed obligation for states. States are therefore required to 'adopt such legislative or other measures as may be necessary to identify victims', with an emphasis on having qualified and trained officials and ensuring that different authorities collaborate with each other, as well as with relevant support organisations throughout this process.[104] This duty has also been recognised as a positive human rights obligation. The Strasbourg Court therefore explained that victim protection measures 'include facilitating the identification of victims by qualified persons and assisting victims in their physical, psychological and social recovery'.[105] It expressly embedded 'the positive obligation to identify and support the applicants as (potential) victims of human trafficking' within the architecture of Article 4 ECHR.[106] These statements confirm that both victim identification and assistance and support represent states' human rights obligations, yet the Court failed to specify the content and scope of obligations.

The following two sections therefore outline obligations to provide assistance and support to victims established by the Anti-Trafficking Convention before considering in the final section the extent to which these provisions could shape human rights obligations.

7.4.1 Pre-identification Measures of Protection: The 'Emergency Package'

Measures that belong to this group apply to victims before they are formally identified as victims of human trafficking. They arise as soon as authorities have reasonable grounds to believe that the person concerned is a victim and are concerned

---

[104] Anti-Trafficking Convention, art 12(2).
[105] *VCL and AN v United Kingdom* (n 8) [153]. See also *Chowdury and Others v Greece* (n 4) [110].
[106] *J and Others v Austria* [2017] ECHR 37 [109]–[111].

with three main aspects of victim protection: material assistance,[107] safety,[108] and immigration status.[109]

The Anti-Trafficking Convention grants presumed victims a reflection and recovery period 'of at least 30 days'[110] during which they cannot be removed from the member state concerned and are provided with emergency assistance. The goal of this 'emergency package' is to allow a presumed victim 'to recover and escape the influence of traffickers and/or to take an informed decision on cooperating with the competent authorities'.[111] As such, this emergency assistance and protection is available to *any* presumed victim of trafficking, and not only to those with irregular immigration status.[112] However, the reflection and recovery period is vital for victims without lawful residence, because it prevents their deportation before they can be formally recognised as victims by the relevant authorities.[113]

Furthermore, the provision of emergency assistance during the reflection and recovery period is not dependent on victims' cooperation with the police or the prosecution.[114] Nevertheless, this guarantee has a substantial limitation since it cannot exclude the obligation to testify when that is required by a judge, given that in the law of many countries it is compulsory to give evidence if requested to do so.[115]

The emergency protection includes a range of substantive benefits.[116] For instance, it requires states to provide appropriate and secure accommodation, psychological and material assistance, and access to emergency medical treatment. It also obliges states to ensure that victims are well aware of their rights and are able to exercise them accordingly. This includes counselling and information concerning their legal rights and available services in a language that they can understand,[117]

---

[107] Anti-Trafficking Convention, art 12(1); Anti-Trafficking Directive, art 11(5).
[108] Anti-Trafficking Convention, art 12(2). It is notable that the Anti-Trafficking Directive, art 11 contains the provision of assistance and support, whereas protection measures envisaged in this instrument are only provided in the framework of criminal investigations and proceedings (art 12).
[109] Anti-Trafficking Convention, art 13. The Anti-Trafficking Directive does not legislate on this point.
[110] Anti-Trafficking Convention, art 13(1). Whereas the reflection and recovery period is primarily established to prevent the expulsion of victims who are 'illegally present' in the territory of a Member State, its overall goal is to enable a presumed victim 'to recover and escape the influence of traffickers and/or to take an informed decision on cooperating with the competent authorities'.
[111] Explanatory Report, para 175.
[112] ibid para 147.
[113] GRETA expressed its concerns about an expedited deportation of presumed victims with an 'illegal' presence in several Member States. See eg Council of Europe, Group of Experts on Action against Trafficking in Human Beings (GRETA) '2nd General Report on GRETA's Activities' (4 October 2012) GRETA (2012)13, para 52; GRETA 2nd report on Norway, GRETA(2017)18, para 143; Council of Europe, Group of Experts on Action against Trafficking in Human Beings (GRETA) '9th General Report on GRETA's Activities' (March 2020) para 155.
[114] Explanatory Report, para 175; Anti-Trafficking Directive, art 11(3).
[115] Explanatory Report, para 176.
[116] Anti-Trafficking Convention, arts 12(1) and (2).
[117] ibid art 12(1)(d).

as well as assistance to enable their rights and interests to be presented and considered at appropriate stages of criminal proceedings against offenders.[118]

Given that many victims do not speak the language of the country they have been brought to for exploitation, the Anti-Trafficking Convention requires states to provide for language assistance, which is 'an essential measure for guaranteeing access to rights, which is a prerequisite for access to justice'.[119] Importantly, this requirement is not limited to the right to an interpreter in judicial proceedings. The Explanatory Report offers a detailed description of information that ought to be conveyed to persons presumed to be victims of human trafficking, which should enable them to evaluate their situation and make an informed choice from the various possibilities open to them.[120] Being appropriately advised on, and assisted in exercising their legal rights, is a fundamental component of the protection and the mandatory language of the provisions containing these requirements is commendable.

In addition to measures that aim to assist victims in their physical, psychological and social recovery, the 'emergency package' of measures in the Anti-Trafficking Convention also includes taking due account of victims' safety and protection needs.[121] This includes a range of measures that depend on victims' personal circumstances, such as age or gender, the type of exploitation, the country of origin, the types and degree of violence suffered, isolation from his or her family and culture, knowledge of the local language, and his or her material and financial resources.[122] For instance, the address of victim's accommodation needs to be kept secret and such accommodation must be protected from any attempts by traffickers to recapture them. These obligations are closely related to the obligation to protect victims' private life and identity,[123] which is said to be 'essential both for victims' physical safety, given the danger from their traffickers, but also ... to preserve their chances of social reintegration in the country of origin or the receiving country'.[124] The specific measures required from states by Article 11 of the Anti-Trafficking Convention, which concern processing and storing of personal data or measures necessary to ensure that the identity of a child victim of trafficking are not made publicly known, through the media or by any other means, are separate from those prescribed by Article 30, which is concerned with protection of victims' private life and identity in the specific context of judicial proceedings.

The Anti-Trafficking Convention and Explanatory Report use mandatory language when referring to assistance and support available to victims during the

---

[118] ibid art 12(1)(e).
[119] Explanatory Report, para 158.
[120] ibid para 160.
[121] Anti-Trafficking Convention, art 12(2).
[122] Explanatory Report, para 164.
[123] Anti-Trafficking Convention, art 11.
[124] Explanatory Report, para 138.

reflection and recovery period. For example, the Explanatory Report refers to the assistance measures which states 'must provide' for trafficking victims and to which victims are 'entitled',[125] emphasising that the required assistance measures are minimum ones.[126] As already noted, neither of these measures depends on the victims' willingness to cooperate with authorities nor on their immigration status.

7.4.2 Post-identification Measures of Protection: The Protective Cloak of Lawful Residence

The Anti-Trafficking Convention also contains a more extensive set of measures that apply to those individuals who have been formally identified as victims of human trafficking by competent authorities. The access to these post-identification measures is, nevertheless, largely dependent on the victims' immigration status and their ability or willingness to assist in criminal investigations against the perpetrators.

Notably, although the Anti-Trafficking Convention explicitly requires states to ensure that this assistance is not made conditional on a victim's willingness to act as a witness,[127] in reality such a requirement is skewed by a wide discretion given to states when it comes to granting them residence permits. Article 14 of the Anti-Trafficking Convention instructs states to issue a renewable residence permit to victims with an irregular migration status 'in one or other of the two following situations or in both': first, when the competent authority considers that their stay is necessary 'owing to their personal situation'; and, secondly, when the competent authority considers that their stay is necessary 'for the purpose of their co-operation with the competent authorities in investigation or criminal proceedings'.[128] However, awarding residence permits on the basis of personal situation is notoriously rare,[129] which makes the stay and further protection of those victims with irregular immigration status entirely dependent on their willingness and ability to contribute to prosecution.[130]

On one hand, the Anti-Trafficking Convention rightly instructs states to take into consideration a range of circumstances including victim's safety, state of

---

[125] ibid paras 146–147 and 149.
[126] ibid para 151.
[127] Anti-Trafficking Convention, art 12(6).
[128] ibid art 14.
[129] The author was able to see statistics provided by Member States in confidential replies to GRETA questionnaires in the first evaluation round during her research visit to GRETA. Some of these statistics are included in the GRETA evaluation reports that are public. See also Fourth GRETA Report, 48–50.
[130] In its recent thematic report on the provision of assistance to victims, GRETA was 'concerned by indications that the provision of assistance to victims of trafficking hinges on their co-operation with law enforcement authorities, even though the link does not exist formally'. See GRETA, 'Assistance to Victims of Human Trafficking: Thematic Chapter of the 8th General Report on GRETA's Activities' Council of Europe (October 2019) 5–6.

health, or family situation when deciding on issuing residence permits based on the personal situation.[131] On the other hand, it allows states to completely sidestep these requirements by giving them freedom to choose whether to include this legal basis in their legislation or not. The broad discretion left to states when deciding whom to grant residence permits has therefore undermined the comprehensive set of protection measures prescribed in other provisions.[132]

Victims of trafficking who are lawfully resident in a State Party are entitled to further assistance in their psychological, physical, and social recovery beyond the 'emergency package' discussed in the previous section. This includes providing access to necessary medical or other assistance to victims who do not have adequate resources and need such help and access to the labour market, to vocational training, and education.[133] Notably, neither the Anti-Trafficking Convention nor its Explanatory Report specifies the duration of the assistance owed to victims beyond the reflection and recovery period.

In contrast with an extended protection guaranteed to victims with lawful residence in their territory, states are entitled to repatriate victims without such residence, although their return 'shall be with due regard for the rights, safety and dignity of that person' and 'shall preferably be voluntary.[134] In that respect, the Explanatory Report to the Anti-Trafficking Convention expressly refers to Article 3 jurisprudence of the ECtHR concerning the prohibition of torture and inhuman or degrading treatment in extradition and deportation cases, which must be considered when organising victims' return.[135] In addition, GRETA expanded this requirement noting that the phrase 'due regard for the rights, safety and dignity' of victims also implies protection from retrafficking, and not just from the risk of being subjected to torture or to inhuman or degrading treatment or punishment.[136] The Strasbourg Court has not had a chance to consider whether Article 4 ECHR could be relied upon to prevent deportation on the basis of the risk of retrafficking. However, some examples from domestic jurisprudence demonstrate how the two instruments could be combined to protect victims from enforced deportation.

---

[131] Explanatory Report, paras 183–84.
[132] Rosa Raffaelli, 'The European Approach to the Protection of Trafficking Victims: The Council of Europe Convention, the EU Directive and the Italian Experience' (2009) 10(3) German Law Journal 205, 211. See also Council of Europe, Group of Experts on Action against Trafficking in Human Beings (GRETA) '4th General Report on GRETA's Activities' (March 2015) 44, 48.
[133] Anti-Trafficking Convention, art 12(3) and (4).
[134] ibid art 16(2).
[135] Explanatory Report, para 203.
[136] GRETA, 'Report Concerning the Implementation of the Council of Europe Convention on Action against Trafficking in Human Beings by UK' First Evaluation Round (12 September 2012) GRETA(2012) 6, para 312; GRETA, 'Report concerning the implementation of the Council of Europe Convention on Action against Trafficking in Human Beings by France' First Evaluation Round (28 January 2013) GRETA(2012)16, para 198; GRETA, 'Report concerning the implementation of the Council of Europe Convention on Action against Trafficking in Human Beings by Italy' First Evaluation Round (4 July 2014) GRETA(2014)18, para 175.

For example, in the case of a trafficked domestic worker from Tanzania, the UK's immigration tribunal found it difficult to accept that 'the removal of the appellant would constitute a further breach of the protective obligations inherent in Article 4 [ECHR]' due to the alleged risk of being re-trafficked.[137] However, since the tribunal previously determined a breach of the appellant's rights under Article 4 ECHR,[138] 'which breach we are satisfied has exposed the victim to harm in this country',[139] it ruled that this finding impacted on the question of whether the appellant should be removed. Accordingly, because the appellant's medical condition was connected to the previously established breach of her rights under Article 4 ECHR, the tribunal concluded that the state should recognise a degree of responsibility for it.[140] The tribunal effectively concluded that the duty to grant a residence permit on personal grounds arising out of Article 14 of the Anti-Trafficking Convention was stronger because the state previously violated its obligations under Article 4 ECHR. This case shows an important interplay between the protective guarantees in the ECHR and the Anti-Trafficking Convention.

Finally, the Anti-Trafficking Convention also requires states to provide in its domestic law the right of victims to compensation from the perpetrators.[141] In order to secure the effective exercise of this entitlement, the Anti-Trafficking Convention requires states to ensure that victims have access, as from their first contact with the competent authorities, to information on relevant judicial and administrative proceedings in a language which they can understand.[142] In addition to the information and counselling that is part of the 'emergency package' described above, these provisions establish the right to legal assistance and to free legal aid in compensation proceedings 'under the conditions provided by its internal law'.[143] Although this provision does not give the victim an automatic right to free legal aid, the Explanatory Report refers to the Strasbourg jurisprudence, which recognises, in certain circumstances, the right to free legal assistance in a civil matter on the basis of Article 6(1) ECHR that must be taken into consideration by domestic courts.[144]

Furthermore, although the traffickers are primarily responsible for compensating victims, recognising that 'in practice there is rarely full compensation whether because the trafficker has not been found, has disappeared or has declared himself bankrupt',[145] the Anti-Trafficking Convention requires states to take steps

---

[137] *EK (Article 4 ECHR: Anti-Trafficking Convention) Tanzania v Secretary of State for the Home Department* [2013] UKUT 313 (IAC) [45].
[138] ibid [29]–[42].
[139] ibid [63].
[140] ibid [64].
[141] Anti-Trafficking Convention, art 15(3). For a more detailed overview of the issues of compensation, see Organization for Security and Cooperation in Europe (OSCE), Office for Democratic Institutions and Human Rights (ODIHR), 'Compensation for Trafficked and Exploited Persons in the OSCE Region' (2008).
[142] Anti-Trafficking Convention, art 15.
[143] ibid art 15(2).
[144] Explanatory Report, para 196.
[145] ibid para 198.

to guarantee such compensation. This means that even though states are left with the choice of means to comply with that duty, they must establish the legal basis, administrative framework, and other operational arrangements for compensation schemes.

Nevertheless, while states may be rightly called to provide compensation when a trafficker has no means, through the established compensation schemes, the other two situations listed in the explanatory report remain highly dubious. Thus, with due respect to the drafters' intentions, if the trafficker 'has not been found, [or] has disappeared', it is virtually impossible for the victim to be provided with compensation, since establishing the basis for calculating such compensation[146] remains inseparable from the circumstances of the trafficking offence.

Furthermore, while the Anti-Trafficking Convention does not explicitly address that question, the immigration status must not preclude victims' right to compensation established in Article 15. This could also be inferred from the Explanatory Report, which notes that 'it would be very difficult for them to obtain compensation if they were unable to remain in the country where the proceedings take place' but does not rule out such a possibility.[147] Also, in the 2013 General report on GRETA's activities, the President of GRETA noted that 'it is not acceptable that compensation is denied to some victims despite what is stipulated in the Convention because they have left the country where judicial proceedings were instituted'.[148] These flaws in framing the obligation to provide compensation to trafficking victims and the disparity between the numbers of convictions for and recognised victims of this offence result in a situation where 'even when there are possibilities in law for granting compensation to victims, in practice this right remains theoretical and few victims benefit from compensation schemes'.[149]

This overview of the provisions of the Anti-Trafficking Convention reveals that even though the Convention insists on detaching victim protection from criminal proceedings against traffickers, any protection and support beyond the 'emergency package' are entirely dependent on their immigration status, which, in turn, mainly rests on their participation in criminal trials. Consequently, protection and assistance available to victims with irregular immigration status is only unconditional during the reflection and recovery period, regardless of their individual needs. As a result, critics have argued that regardless of being proclaimed as one of the main goals of the anti-trafficking instruments, victim protection remains subject to the states' immigration and criminal justice interests, thus 'reflecting the member states' desire to protect themselves from illegal migration rather than of

---

[146] According to the Explanatory Report, para 197, the compensation is pecuniary and covers both material injury (such as the cost of medical treatment) and non-material damage (the suffering experienced).
[147] ibid para 192.
[148] Third GRETA Report, Introduction by the President of GRETA.
[149] Second GRETA Report, para 60.

accepting that trafficking in human beings is a crime and that its victims must be protected'.[150]

The question relevant for the discussion here is which, if any, of these specific measures of victim protection also amount to states' human rights obligations, which could strengthen their normative power and limit the extent to which criminal justice and immigration interests could set them aside. The following section therefore considers the potential of the described requirements to shape obligations established under human rights law discussed in the previous chapter thus creating an important synergy between these two bodies of law.

7.4.3 Victim Protection Measures and Victims' Rights United

According to the former President of GRETA, the requirements enshrined in the Anti-Trafficking Convention concerning 'identification, assistance, recovery and reflection period, compensation, protection against reprisals and non-punishment for illegal acts which victims are compelled to commit by traffickers' represent the set of the victims' 'fundamental rights'.[151]

Similarly, the Group of Experts on Trafficking in Human Beings of the European Commission expressed the opinion that obligations concerning victim protection articulated by the Strasbourg Court in *Rantsev* include: the securing of the immediate physical safety of the trafficked person, or person at risk of being trafficked; their physical, psychological and social recovery, with the immediate provision of information about their rights and options in a language that they understand; referral to assistance and support with the aim of long-term social inclusion.[152] What is more, it is suggested that such measures 'might include, but are not restricted to': ensuring that the person has legal assistance and access to justice; evaluating the need for short or longer-term international protection, whether through refugee status or subsidiary/complementary protection; safe and dignified repatriation involving cooperation with the source state and relevant NGOs and following an individual risk assessment.[153]

It is not, however, apparent that such an extensive set of measures flows from the *Rantsev* ruling. The *Rantsev* decision implies that the appropriate measures of victim protection are only those required *to remove a person from the situation or*

---

[150] PACE Opinion para 8.
[151] Third GRETA Report, Introduction by the President of GRETA (emphasis added). The President adds to this list the right to compensation and non-punishment for illegal acts which victims are compelled to commit by traffickers.
[152] Group of Experts on Trafficking in Human Beings of the European Commission, Opinion on the Decision of the European Court of Human Rights in the Case of Rantsev v. Cyprus and Russia (22 June 2010) Opinion No 6/2010, para 9.
[153] ibid para 10.

risk of being, trafficked or exploited.[154] This clearly requires that an individual is facing an actual or imminent threat. Therefore, providing *immediate* and *basic* protection and assistance outlined in Article 12 (1) and (2) may well be in the function of one's removal from the situation or risk. On this view, a more extensive set of measures aimed at providing for a victim's full recovery, although required by the Anti-Trafficking Convention, could not be read into Article 4 ECHR without distorting the Court's ruling.

In the subsequent cases, the Strasbourg Court expressly instructed states 'to adopt a range of measures to prevent trafficking and to protect the rights of victims' clarifying that '[p]rotection measures include facilitating the identification of victims by qualified persons and assisting victims in their physical, psychological and social recovery'.[155] In *J and Others*, the Court assessed actions of the relevant authorities and found that 'the legal and administrative framework in place concerning the protection of (potential) victims of human trafficking in Austria appears to have been sufficient, and that the Austrian authorities took all steps which could reasonably have been expected in the given situation'.[156] This ruling is instructive in that it illuminates the expectations that the Court may have from any Member state when it comes to victim protection. The Court therefore pointed out that:

> From the point when the applicants turned to the police, they were immediately treated as (potential) victims of human trafficking. They were interviewed by specially trained police officers ... were granted residence and work permits in order to regularise their stay in Austria ... and a personal data disclosure ban was imposed on the Central Register so their whereabouts were untraceable by the general public ... During the domestic proceedings, the applicants were supported by the NGO LEFÖ, which is funded by the Government especially to provide assistance to victims of human trafficking. According to the uncontested statements of the Government ... the applicants were given legal representation.[157]

Furthermore, the decision in *VCL and AN v United Kingdom* has reflected on the type of operational measures which might be required by Article 4 ECHR. The Court 'has considered it relevant that the Anti-Trafficking Convention calls on the Member States to adopt a range of measures to prevent trafficking and to protect the rights of victims' limiting the obligation to take operational measures only by the requirements that such measures 'must be interpreted in a way which does not impose an impossible or disproportionate burden on the authorities'.[158]

---

[154] *Rantsev v Cyprus and Russia* (n 1) [286] (emphasis added). See also *Chowdury and Others v Greece* (n 4) [88].
[155] *Chowdury and Others v Greece* (n 4) [110].
[156] *J and Others v Austria* (n 106) [110]–[111].
[157] ibid [110].
[158] *VCL and AN v United Kingdom* (n 8) [153]–[154].

Could these statements imply that Article 4 ECHR may serve as a vehicle for the enforcement of the full range of victim protection measures prescribed by the Anti-Trafficking Convention?

One reason for caution is the fact that the Anti-Trafficking Convention has established its own mechanism for monitoring states' compliance, and such a mechanism does not envisage individual complaints. Therefore, even though states could have opted for creating an individual complaints mechanism, they clearly chose a different route. Accordingly, it may not be appropriate for the Strasbourg Court to seek to take over the enforcement of obligations prescribed by other international instruments.

Nevertheless, it must be noted that all Member States of the Council of Europe,[159] which are also parties to the ECHR, have signed the Anti-Trafficking Convention, thus expressing their willingness to abide by its provisions. Furthermore, as a consequence of these duties being undertaken, states have indeed adopted laws that provide measures of protection and support to victims. GRETA notes that '[m]ost countries evaluated by GRETA have a statutory basis for the provision of assistance to victims of human trafficking'.[160] The Strasbourg Court in *Rantsev* noted that the Cypriot authorities did not even attempt to comply with its national legislation on human trafficking that contain provisions for victims' protection such as accommodation, medical care, and psychiatric support.[161] Clearly, even though the Court may not be entitled to impose such protective measures itself, let alone rule on their scope, when the state already has such laws in place, it may well be required to comply with them. Significantly, the ECtHR stated in a case dealing with the protection of domestic violence victims that: '[I]n interpreting the provisions of the Convention and *the scope of the state's obligations* in specific cases the Court will also look for any consensus and common values emerging from the practices of European states and *specialised international instruments*.'[162]

In light of this view and the Court's explicit acknowledgment that the extent of positive obligations arising under Article 4 ECHR must be considered within the context of the provisions of the Palermo Protocol and the Anti-Trafficking Convention, it could be argued that obligations contained in the latter serve as a benchmark when assessing compliance with Article 4 ECHR obligations to provide practical and effective protection to the victims of 'modern slavery'. GRETA's supervisory work on the implementation of the Anti-Trafficking Convention has contributed to consolidating and rising the standards of victim protection

---

[159] Except the Russian Federation. However, on 16 March 2022, the Council of Europe's Committee of Ministers expelled Russia from the organisation due to the war in Ukraine. See Council of Europe, Resolution CM/Res(2022) 2 on the cessation of the membership of the Russian Federation to the Council of Europe, under Article 8 of the Statute, CM/Del/Dec(2022) 1428ter/2.3 (16 March 2022).
[160] GRETA, 'Assistance to Victims of Human Trafficking: Thematic Chapter of the 8th General Report on GRETA's Activities' Council of Europe (October 2019) 10.
[161] *Rantsev v Cyprus and Russia* (n 1) [298].
[162] *Opuz v Turkey* (2010) 50 EHRR 28 [164] (emphasis added).

across state parties,[163] which the Strasbourg and other human rights tribunals can draw on when evaluating state compliance with obligations imposed by human rights law.

Were such obligations to be established under Article 4 ECHR, they could be framed in a similar way to obligations concerning the fundamental right to education.[164] The ECtHR clarifies that this right does not oblige states to make education available; it guarantees 'a right of access to educational institutions *existing at a given time*'.[165] Moreover, this right 'by its very nature calls for regulation by the State', thus imposing a positive duty on the state. Such regulation 'may vary in time and place according to the needs and resources of the community and of individuals'.[166] Furthermore, educational institutions have to be accessible to everyone without discrimination.[167] Accordingly, given that most states have established certain mechanisms for providing assistance and support to victims of trafficking (however imperfect),[168] it could be argued that they are required to ensure that victims have equal access to these.[169]

Accordingly, victim protection outside of the criminal justice context could be framed within Article 4 ECHR in the following way. First, these obligations may be covered by the *general* obligation to establish an 'adequate' legal framework that contains 'the spectrum of safeguards ... to ensure the practical and effective protection of the rights of victims or potential victims of trafficking'.[170] What is adequate in each case will be judged by the standards required by the Anti-Trafficking Convention as well as GRETA assessments in individual country reports. The Strasbourg Court was explicit that the adequate legal framework refers to regulatory measures as well as immigration rules, and not just criminal law provisions.[171] Moreover, a *specific* obligation to protect victims or potential victims of 'modern slavery' could be further developed to require, as suggested by the Group of Experts

---

[163] GRETA, 'Practical Impact of GRETA's Monitoring Work' Council of Europe (June 2019).
[164] ECHR Protocol No 1, art 2.
[165] *Case 'relating to certain aspects of the laws on the use of languages in education in Belgium' v Belgium (Belgian Linguistic Case)* (1968) 1EHRR 252 [4] (emphasis added).
[166] ibid [5]. However, this is not an absolute right; limitations must be foreseeable for those concerned and must pursue a legitimate aim. See *Ali v United Kingdom* (2011) 53 EHRR 12.
[167] *DH v Czech Republic* (GC) [2008] ECHR 646; *Oršuš and Others v Croatia* (2011) 52 EHRR 7; *Horvath and Kiss v Hungary* (2013) 57 EHRR 31.
[168] In 28 country evaluation reports, GRETA has urged the authorities to improve different aspects of the provision of assistance to victims of trafficking. See Fourth GRETA Report 42–45.
[169] On the fundamental principle of equality of opportunity in education see also OHCHR, Committee on Economic, Social and Cultural Rights, 'General Comment 13 on the right to education (article 13 of the Covenant)' (2 December 1999) E/C.12/1999/10; UN OHCHR, Special Rapporteur on the right to education, Kishore Singh, 'Report to the Human Rights Council on the promotion of equality of opportunity in education' (18 April 2011) A/HRC/17/29; UNESCO, 'Results of the Seventh Consultation of Member States on the measures taken for implementation of UNESCO's Convention and Recommendation against Discrimination in Education (1960)' (17 August 2007) Doc 177 EX/36.
[170] *Rantsev v Cyprus and Russia* (n 1) [285].
[171] ibid [284].

on Trafficking in Human Beings of the European Commission,[172] a range of substantive assistance and protection measures laid down in the Anti-Trafficking Convention. However, this obligation would only guarantee access to the *existing* assistance and protection schemes and the standard for assessing state compliance could be modelled on the one established in the right to education cases.

Overall, this section has provided a comprehensive assessment of the victim protection measures established by the anti-trafficking instruments and clarified the ways in which these have been, or could be framed within Article 4 ECHR. The Strasbourg Court acknowledged in the *Ranstev* case:

> [T]he paucity of case law on the interpretation of art.4 in the context of trafficking cases, *in particular* in relation to the extent to which art.4 requires Member States to take positive steps to protect potential victims of trafficking *outside of the framework of criminal investigations and prosecutions*.[173]

In the subsequent cases it expanded and elaborated on such obligations, suggesting that the provisions of the Anti-Trafficking Convention play a vital role in shaping the scope of protective duties under Article 4 ECHR. The discussion here is hoped to provide further guidance on how these obligations could be formulated in future.

7.5 The Future of 'Modern Slavery' Jurisprudence

The Council of Europe Anti-Trafficking Convention offers the most comprehensive set of obligations aimed at the protection of trafficking victims. Nevertheless, its enforcement is not in the hands of individual victims unless, depending on the constitutional system of a state, the Convention is either directly applicable or is implemented through the adoption of a statutory instrument. In addition, the Convention is said to leave 'too much discretion to State parties' when it comes to its implementation,[174] which is not a bad thing per se, but it does pose a challenge when it comes to ensuring the equal level of protection and support available to victims in different state parties.

Accordingly, while undoubtedly raising the standards of victim protection, the provisions of specialised anti-trafficking instruments, and the Council of Europe Anti-Trafficking Convention in particular, do not amount to justiciable human rights. Nevertheless, these provisions are vital for shaping human rights

---

[172] Group of Experts on Trafficking in Human Beings of the European Commission, Opinion on the Decision of the European Court of Human Rights in the Case of *Rantsev v Cyprus and Russia* (22 June 2010) Opinion No 6/2010.
[173] *Rantsev v Cyprus and Russia* (n 1) [200] (emphasis added).
[174] Raffaelli (n 132) 213.

obligations. Namely, obligations enshrined in anti-trafficking instruments are binding on their respective state parties as a matter of international law, and even though victims might not enforce them against states, the latter cannot simply ignore them.[175] GRETA—an expert body in charge of overseeing compliance with the Anti-Trafficking Convention—plays a key role in consolidating state practice and raising the standards of victim protection across the state parties. The Strasbourg Court can then draw on such consensus and measures that states envisaged in their domestic legal systems to give effect to Anti-Trafficking Convention when interpreting obligations of states under the ECHR. This way, the Strasbourg Court calcifies and reinforces standards imposed by the Anti-Trafficking Convention in an incremental but steadfast way. The Strasbourg jurisprudence analysed in the previous chapter provides ample evidence of this process, showing that many obligations contained in the anti-trafficking instruments have already been recognised as human rights obligations under the ECHR. Recent jurisprudence therefore shows an increasing willingness of international human rights tribunals to draw on the anti-trafficking instruments in shaping states' human rights obligations, as well as an increasing level of scrutiny over the implementation of the relevant duties by states.

This chapter has explored the potential for continuing to develop the protection guaranteed to victims of 'modern slavery' by the human rights treaties and jurisprudence by incorporating the safeguards and standards established in the specialised anti-trafficking instruments. Whether human rights tribunals, and the Strasbourg Court in particular, will be prepared to follow such a lead depends not only on the perception of their own place among the myriad of institutions and instruments with a role to play in anti-slavery action, but also on the questions raised by the cases that reach these judicial bodies. Therefore, it is of utmost importance to submit well-argued cases which challenge human rights tribunals to engage with these complex questions.

---

[175] For example, the Court of Appeal of England and Wales has expressly stated in *R v LM and Others* [2010] EWCA Crim 2327 [2] that the United Kingdom 'is fully bound by [the 2005 Council of Europe Treaty]'.

8
Conclusion: Human Rights Law, Slavery, and State in the Twenty-First Century

The global initiative to eradicate 'modern slavery' sweeping across the world since the start of the twenty-first century has mobilised a range of legal domains. On the international plane, the impetus emerged from transnational criminal law, and the widely ratified Palermo Protocol, which required states to harmonise their respective legislation to allow for a coordinated criminal justice response to this global phenomenon. International criminal law and international humanitarian law have engaged with the issue through the crimes of enslavement and sexual slavery, as elaborated in the jurisprudence of several international tribunals.[1] Whereas these branches of international law seek to ensure that grave infringements of personal liberty and physical integrity do not go unpunished, human rights law is thought to hold the greatest promise for the victim-centred response to 'modern slavery'. This is because human rights law seeks to divorce victim protection from criminal proceedings against traffickers and exploiters, who might be at large or unknown, while victims of such crimes require assistance and support. On a domestic level, obligations that flow from these different fields of international law have been given effect through criminal law, immigration law, labour law, and, more recently, the regulation of business supply chains.

Two conclusions can be drawn from this. First, no legal domain alone can provide an adequate response to the complex phenomenon such as 'modern slavery' and human rights law is but one tool in the legal toolbox relevant for this cause. Secondly, these various legal domains must be brought into conversation to provide a comprehensive and coherent response to 'modern slavery'. It is often the case that measures developed within one legal domain directly contradict requirements imposed by the other. For example, the preventive measures prescribed by the anti-trafficking instruments include border controls to detect human trafficking[2]

---

[1] See Nicole Siller, 'The Prosecution of Human Traffickers? A Comparative Analysis of Enslavement Judgments Among International Courts and Tribunals' (2015) 2 European Journal of Comparative Law and Governance 236; Patricia Viseur Sellers and Jocelyn Getgen Kestenbaum, 'Sexualized Slavery' and Customary International Law' in Sharon Weill, Kim Thuy Seelinger, and Kerstin Carlson (eds), *Prosecuting the President: the Trial of Hissène Habré* (OUP 2020).

[2] The ECtHR also incorporated these measures as part of positive obligations under art 4 ECHR in *Chowdury and Others v Greece* App no 21884/15 (ECtHR, 30 March 2017) [110].

and these can directly conflict with the duty to offer protection and assistance to victims.[3]

That human rights law could not provide the ultimate answer to this complex problem is particularly important an observation in the context of human rights instruments with judicial or quasi-judicial bodies created to review individual petitions. Beyond providing a remedy to individuals subject to severe forms of exploitation, these human rights mechanisms are ill-equipped to articulate and impose on states a comprehensive anti-slavery strategy. Human rights jurisprudence can nonetheless prompt a structural change. For instance, the judgments of the European Court of Human Rights (ECtHR), bolstered by the continuing and thorough evaluation of states' actions by GRETA—the Council of Europe's expert body on human trafficking—have brought about a slow but steady improvement in the overall framework for addressing 'modern slavery' in some countries. The rulings in the *Rantsev* and *Chowdary* cases, for example, considered broader structural flaws in domestic legal and policy frameworks and their implementation, which allowed traffickers and exploiters to take advantage of victims. These individual rulings have effected a systemic change by inducing legal reform and the change of administrative practices. The Council of Europe has therefore emphasised that, following the *Rantsev* judgment, 'the Cypriot authorities ratified the Council of Europe's Convention on Action against Trafficking in Human Beings', noting that '[c]hanges were also made to Cypriot visa rules'.[4] Similarly, following the judgment in the *Chowdary* case concerning hundreds of Bangladeshi workers subject to human trafficking and forced labour on a farm, the Council of Europe observed that:

> Greece later ratified the Council of Europe convention on human trafficking, passed EU anti-trafficking legislation and created a National Rapporteur to address the issue. The Rapporteur prepared a national action plan for the years 2018-2023, including measures to prevent forced labour, protect victims, investigate allegations and punish wrongdoers.[5]

The analysis in the second part of the book has therefore shown that the ongoing incremental but steady development of positive human rights obligations through the jurisprudence of international tribunals has led to a significant shift in the scope of state responsibility to address 'modern slavery': it evolved from the

---

[3] This was the case eg in *Rantsev v Cyprus and Russia* (2010) 51 EHRR 1 [293], where the ECtHR recognised that 'the regime of artiste visas in Cyprus did not afford to Ms Rantseva practical and effective protection against trafficking and exploitation'.

[4] The Council of Europe, 'Examples of the Impact of the European Convention on Human Rights by Theme: Freedom From Slavery and Human Trafficking' https://www.coe.int/en/web/impact-convention-human-rights/freedom-from-slavery-and-human-trafficking (accessed 25 March 2022).

[5] ibid.

negative prohibition of slavery to the comprehensive set of requirements to address a range of exploitative practices labelled 'modern slavery'.

The book has therefore pursued a particular agenda: it set out to explore the normative content of the human rights prohibition of 'modern slavery' by examining, first, practices that fall within its ambit, the relationship between them, and the underlying wrong or harm embodied in the concept of exploitation that gels these diverse practices into the distinct and often contested category. The second aspect of this enquiry involved examining positive obligations of states to address the infringements of the human rights prohibition of 'modern slavery', most frequently carried out by non-state actors. Accordingly, the book charted out the responsibility of states for 'modern slavery' in human rights law by considering their obligations to respond to the conduct of private actors engaging in such practices and to protect individuals subject to such grave forms of exploitation.

There is nonetheless another dimension of state responsibility for 'modern slavery' that is broader, more elusive, and harder to establish in the strictly legal sense, and which remained outside the scope of this enquiry. It concerns wider legal structures that create conditions in which practices of 'modern slavery' are allowed to flourish, despite a number of instruments and initiatives designed to address it. These legal structures may appear removed from, and thus irrelevant for, the action against 'modern slavery'. They concern, for example, the regulation of labour markets, immigration policy, or the rules pertaining to prison labour. Virginia Mantouvalou uses the term 'state-mediated structures of injustice', suggesting that legal frameworks created to address legitimate issues often create conditions where exploitation is allowed to flourish.[6] One might see these consequences as incidental—a result of ignorance and insufficient attention of states. Yet the convergence of outcomes, which stem from different and seemingly unconnected legal domains[7] and amount to the exploitation of the most vulnerable members of society (usually migrants and those of a lower socio-economic status), may well be interpreted as a deliberate *transformation* of slavery. Thus, instead of seeing 'traditional' slavery—a practice grounded in law—and 'modern' slavery—a practice that continues to persist despite being formally outlawed—as two different and unconnected institutions, we should consider the similarities in their characteristics and role in the modern economy. What if, instead of being abolished, slavery has been redesigned to allow for the continuation of exploitation of the most vulnerable and marginalised groups in a way that is more subtle and palatable to the modern society? What if 'state-mediated structures of injustice', erected and supported by legal rules addressing ostensibly legitimate causes, have been deliberately engineered to mitigate the impact of the formal abolition of slavery?

---

[6] Virginia Mantouvalou, *Structures of Injustice, Workers' Rights and Human Rights* (OUP 2022).
[7] I have examined these in my paper in progress Marija Jovanovic, 'Blurred Lines: Slavery, Law, and Modern State' (forthcoming).

This proposition might strike many as preposterous. The key difference between 'traditional' and 'modern' slavery is the legality of the former and the illegality of the latter. Whereas law once shaped and governed the institution of slavery allowing for the legal ownership of another human being, it was equally instrumental in its abolition in the nineteenth century.[8] Law is thus widely considered as part of the solution to 'modern slavery', not the problem itself.

Yet, it is increasingly obvious that law has played a central role in facilitating both 'versions' of slavery. My recent work, which examines free trade agreements, legal responses to exploitation in global value chains, deregulation of low wage labour, immigration rules, and prison labour demonstrates that severe exploitation, in many respects indistinguishable from historical examples of slavery, still persists and underpins the global economic order.[9] Packaged carefully in the intricate web of laws and policies, and reinforced by the veneer of illegality, the essence and function of slavery in the modern economy remain intact.

Orlando Paterson noted in the preface to his influential work on *Slavery and Social Death* that 'one of the most remarkable features of Western civilization is the critical role of slavery at almost all the high points of its development, from ancient Greece to the rise of industrial capitalism'.[10] Could it be that the modern age is so unique in that it did away with slavery once and for all? Could it be that the relationship between the state, law, and slavery in the twenty-first century is fundamentally different than at any other point in human history? Or might it be that we have found a way to reverse-engineer slavery, making it simultaneously illegal and allowing it to flourish supported indirectly by laws designed to address other legitimate causes? These questions go beyond the scope of this book, which has primarily sought to explain the role of law, and human rights law specifically, as part of the solution to slavery. The full account of the relationship between the state, law, and slavery in the twenty-first century, nonetheless, must also consider the other side of the coin.

---

[8] In 1833, Britain passed the Slavery Abolition Act granting freedom to enslaved people in most of the British Empire. Slavery was formally abolished in the United States with the ratification of the Thirteenth Amendment to the Constitution in 1865.

[9] Jovanovic (n 7).

[10] Orlando Patterson, *Slavery and Social Death: A Comparative Study* (2nd edn, Harvard UP 2018) preface.

Bibliography

BOOKS

Alexy R, *A Theory of Constitutional Rights* (OUP 2002)
Allain J (ed), *The Legal Understanding of Slavery: From the Historical to the Contemporary* (OUP 2012)
Allain J, *Slavery in International Law: Of Human Exploitation and Trafficking* (Brill 2013)
Ashworth A and Redmayne M, *The Criminal Process* (4th edn, OUP 2010)
Bjorge E, *The Evolutionary Interpretation of Treaties* (OUP 2014)
Borg Jansson D, *Modern Slavery: A Comparative Study of the Definition of Trafficking in Persons* (Brill 2014)
Chandran P (ed), *Human Trafficking Handbook: Recognising Trafficking and Modern-day Slavery in the UK* (LexisNexis 2011)
Christoffersen J and Madsen MR (eds), *The European Court of Human Rights Between Law and Politics* (OUP 2011)
Clapham A, *Human Rights in the Private Sphere* (Clarendon Press 1993)
Clapham A, *Human Rights Obligations of Non-state Actors* (OUP 2006)
Clayton R and Tomlinson H (eds), *The Law of Human Rights* (OUP 2009)
Crawford J, *The International Law Commission's Articles on State Responsibility: Introduction, Text and Commentaries* (CUP 2002)
Dubber M, *Victims in the War on Crime* (New York UP 2002)
Emmerson B, Ashworth A, and Macdonald A (eds), *Human Rights and Criminal Justice* (3rd edn, Sweet & Maxwell 2012)
Feinberg J, *The Moral Limits of the Criminal Law Volume 4: Harmless Wrongdoing* (OUP 1990)
Feldman D, *Civil Liberties and Human Rights in England and Wales* (2nd edn, OUP 2002)
Fredman S, *Human Rights Transformed: Human Rights Transformed: Positive Rights and Positive Duties* (OUP 2008)
Gallagher AT, *The International Law of Human Trafficking* (CUP 2010)
Harris DH, O'Boyle M, and Warbrick E, *Law of the European Convention on Human Rights* (2nd edn, OUP 2009)
Hart HLA, *The Concept of Law* (2nd edn, OUP 1994)
Kneebone S and Debeljak J, *Transnational Crime and Human Rights: Responses to Human Trafficking in the Greater Mekong Subregion* (Routledge 2012)
Kotiswaran P (ed), *Revisiting the Law and Governance of Human Trafficking, Forced Labour and Modern Slavery* (CUP 2017)
Kramer M, *Where Law and Morality Meet* (OUP 2008)
Kripke S, *Naming and Necessity* (Harvard UP 1980)
LeBaron G (ed), *Researching Forced Labour in the Global Economy Methodological Challenges and Advances* (OUP 2018)
Lee M, *Trafficking and Global Crime Control* (Sage Publications 2011)

Lavrysen L and Mavronicola N (eds), *Coercive Human Rights: Positive Duties to Mobilise the Criminal Law under the ECHR* (Hart Publishing 2020)

Mantouvalou V, *Structures of Injustice, Workers' Rights and Human Rights* (OUP 2022)

Mavronicola N and Lavrysen L (eds), *Coercive Human Rights: Positive Duties to Mobilise the Criminal Law under the ECHR* (Hart Publishing 2020)

Merrills JG, *The Development of International Law by the European Court of Human Rights* (Manchester UP 1993)

Miers S, *Slavery in the Twentieth Century: The Evolution of a Global Problem* (AltaMira Press 2003)

Mowbray A, *The Development of Positive Obligations Under the European Convention on Human Rights by the European Court of Human Rights* (Hart Publishing 2004)

Munzer S, *A Theory of Property* (CUP 1990)

Nozick R, *Anarchy, State, and Utopia* (Blackwell Publishers 1974)

Obokata T, *Trafficking in Human Beings from a Human Rights Perspective: Towards a Holistic Approach* (Martinus Nijhoff Publishers 2006)

Pasqualucci Jo, *The Practice and Procedure of the Inter-American Court of Human Rights* (CUP 2013)

Pearsall J and Trumble B (eds), *Oxford English Reference Dictionary* (2nd edn, OUP 1996)

Rainey B, McCormick P, and Ovey C (eds), *Jacobs, White & Ovey: The European Convention on Human Rights* (6th edn, OUP 2014)

Rainey B, McCormick P, and Ovey C (eds), *Jacobs, Ovey & White: The European Convention on Human Rights* (7th edn, OUP 2017)

Roach K, *Remedies for Human Rights Violations: A Two-Track Approach to Supra-national and National Law* (CUP 2021)

Shelley L, *Human Trafficking: A Global Perspective* (CUP 2010)

Shelton D, *Remedies in International Human Rights Law* (OUP 2015)

Shue H, *Basic Rights: Subsistence, Affluence, and U.S. Foreign Policy* (2nd edn, Princeton UP 1996)

Starmer K, *European Human Rights Law* (Legal Action Group 1999)

Stoyanova V, *Human Trafficking and Slavery Reconsidered: Conceptual Limits and States' Positive Obligations in European Law* (CUP 2017)

Sumption J, *Trials of the State: Law and the Decline of Politics* (Profile Books 2019)

Wertheimer A, *Exploitation* (Princeton UP 1995)

Xenos D, *The Positive Obligations of the State Under the European Convention of Human Rights* (Routledge 2011)

CONTRIBUTIONS TO EDITED BOOKS

Allain J, 'Conceptualizing the Exploitation of Human Trafficking' in J Bryson Clark and S Poucki (eds), *The SAGE Handbook on Human Trafficking and Modern Day Slavery* (Sage Publications 2018)

Arneson R, 'Exploitation' in L Becker and C Becker (eds) *Encyclopedia of Ethics* (Routledge 1992)

Ascola H, 'Article 5: Prohibition of Slavery and Forced Labour' in S Peers and others (eds), *The EU Charter of Fundamental Rights: A Commentary* (1st edn, Hart Publishing 2014)

Brennan A, 'Necessary and Sufficient Conditions' in Edward N Zalta (ed) *The Stanford Encyclopedia of Philosophy* (Summer 2017 Edition)

Chandran P, 'A Commentary on Interpreting Human Trafficking' in P Chandran (ed), *Human Trafficking Handbook: Recognising Trafficking and Modern-day Slavery in the UK* (LexisNexis 2011)

Chandran P, 'The Identification of Victims of Trafficking' in P Chandran (ed), *Human Trafficking Handbook: Recognising Trafficking and Modern-Day Slavery in the UK* (LexisNexis 2011)

Collins H, 'Exploitation at Work: Beyond a "Criminalization" or "Regulatory Alternatives" Dichotomy' in A Bogg and others (eds), *Criminality at Work* (OUP 2020)

Costello C, 'Migrants and Forced Labour: A Labour Law Response' in A Bogg and others (eds), *The Autonomy of Labour Law* (Hart Publishing 2015)

Crawford J and Keene A, 'The Structure of State Responsibility under the European Convention on Human Rights' in A van Aaken and I Motoc (eds), *The European Convention on Human Rights and General International Law* (OUP 2018)

Dottridge M, 'Trafficked and Exploited: The Urgent Need for Coherence in International Law' in P Kotiswaran, *Revisiting the Law and Governance of Trafficking, Forced Labour and Modern Slavery* (CUP 2017)

Durieux J, 'The Vanishing Refugee' in H Lambert, J McAdam, and M Fullerton (eds), *The Global Reach of European Refugee Law* (CUP 2013)

Engle Merry S, 'Counting the Uncountable: Constructing Trafficking through Measurement' in P Kotiswaran (ed), *Revisiting the Law and Governance of Trafficking, Forced Labor and Modern Slavery* (CUP 2017)

Freedland M and Costello C, 'Migrants at Work and the Division of Labour Law' in C Costello and M Freedland (eds), *Migrants at Work: Immigration and Vulnerability in Labour Law* (OUP 2014)

Goodin R, 'Exploiting a Situation and Exploiting a Person' in A Reeve, *Modern Theories of Exploitation* (Sage Publications 1987)

Heemskerk M and Rijken C, 'Combating Trafficking in Human Beings for Labour Exploitation in the Netherlands' in C Rijken (ed), *Combating Trafficking in Human Beings for Labour Exploitation* (Wolf Legal Publishers 2011)

Himma KE, 'Reconsidering a Dogma: Conceptual Analysis, the Naturalistic Turn, and Legal Philosophy' in M Freeman and R Harrison (eds), *Law and Philosophy* (OUP 2007)

Holmes L, 'Corruption and Trafficking: Triple Victimisation?' in C Friesendorf (ed), *Strategies Against Human Trafficking: The Role of the Security Sector* (National Defence Academy and Austrian Ministry of Defence and Sport 2009)

Kant I, 'Groundwork of the Metaphysics of Morals' in *The Moral Law* (H Paton tr, Hutchinson University Library 1948)

Kotiswaran P, 'From Sex Panic to Extreme Exploitation: Revisiting the Law and Governance of Human Trafficking' in P Kotiswaran (ed), *Revisiting the Law and Governance of Trafficking, Forced Labor and Modern Slavery* (CUP 2017)

Lazarus L, 'Positive Obligations and Criminal Justice: Duties to Protect or Coerce?' in J Roberts and L Zedner (eds), *Principled Approaches to Criminal Law and Criminal Justice: Essays in Honour of Professor Andrew Ashworth* (OUP 2012)

Letsas G, 'The ECHR as a Living Instrument: Its Meaning and Legitimacy' in G Ulfstein, A Follesdal, and B Schlütter (eds), *The European Court of Human Rights in a National, European and Global Context* (CUP 2012)

Mantouvalou V, 'Legal Construction of Structures of Exploitation' in H Collins, G Lester, and V Mantouvalou (eds), *Philosophical Foundations of Labour Law* (OUP 2018)

Marks S, 'Exploitation as an International Legal Concept' in S Marks (ed), *International Law on the Left: Re-examining Marxist Legacies* (CUP 2008)

Mullally S, 'Article 19: Criminalisation of the Use of Services of a Victim' in J Planitzer and H Sax (eds), *A Commentary on the Council of Europe Convention on Action against Trafficking in Human Beings* (Edward Elgar Publishing 2020)

Nickel J, 'Human Rights' in EN Zalta (ed), *The Stanford Encyclopedia of Philosophy* (Winter 2014 Edition)

Patterson O, 'Preface' in *Slavery and Social Death: A Comparative Study* (rev edn, Harvard UP 2018) vii

Pearson E, 'Historical Development of Trafficking: the Legal Framework for Anti-Trafficking Interventions' in *Challenging Trafficking in Persons: Theoretical Debate and Practical Approaches* (Nomos 2005)

Serghides S, 'The Principle of Effectiveness as Used in Interpreting, Applying and Implementing the European Convention on Human Rights (Its Nature, Mechanism and Significance)' in I Motoc, PP de Albuquerque, and K Wojtyczek (eds), *New Developments in Constitutional Law: Essays in Honour of András Sajó* (Eleven International 2018)

Stone Sweet A and Ryan C, 'Introduction and Overview' in A Stone Sweet and C Ryan (eds), *A Cosmopolitan Legal Order: Kant, Constitutional Justice, and the European Convention on Human Rights* (OUP 2018)

Van Krimpen L 'The Interpretation and Implementation of Labour Exploitation in Dutch case law' in C Rijken (ed), *Combating Trafficking in Human Beings for Labour Exploitation* (WLP 2011)

Viseur Sellers P and Getgen Kestenbaum J, 'Sexualized Slavery' and Customary International Law' in S Weill, K Thuy Seelinger, and K Carlson (eds), *Prosecuting the President: the Trial of Hissène Habré* (OUP 2020)

Webber G, 'Proportionality and Absolute Rights' in V Jackson and M Tushnet (eds), *Proportionality: New Frontiers, New Challenges* (CUP 2016)

Wertheimer A and Zwolinski M, 'Exploitation' in EN Zalta (ed), *The Stanford Encyclopedia of Philosophy* (Summer 2015 Edition)

Wolff J, 'Structures of Exploitation' in H Collins, G Lester, and V Mantouvalou (eds), *Philosophical Foundations of Labour Law* (OUP 2018)

Wood AW, 'What Is Kantian Ethics?' in AW Wood (ed), *Rethinking the Western Tradition* (Yale UP 2002)

Wood A, 'Exploitation' in T Honderich (ed), *The Oxford Companion to Philosophy* (2nd edn OUP 2005)

JOURNAL ARTICLES

Allain J, 'Definition of Slavery in International Law' (2009) 52 Howard Law Journal 239

Allain J, 'On the Curious Disappearance of Human Servitude from General International Law' (2009) 11(2) Journal of the History of International Law 303

Allain J, 'R v Tang: Clarifying the Definition of 'Slavery' in International Law' (2009) 10 Melbourne Journal of International Law 246

Allain J, 'Rantsev v Cyprus and Russia: The European Court of Human Rights and Trafficking as Slavery' (2010) 10(3) Human Rights Law Review 546

Allain J, 'No Effective Trafficking Definition Exists: Domestic Implementation of the Palermo Protocol' (2014) 7 Albany Government Law Review 111

Amar AR and Widawsky D, 'Child Abuse as Slavery: A Thirteenth Amendment Response to Deshaney' (1992) 105(6) Harvard Law Review 1359

Buchanan A, 'Exploitation, Alienation, and Injustice' (1979) 9(1) Canadian Journal of Philosophy 121

Bustamante J, 'Immigrants' Vulnerability as Subjects of Human Rights' (2002) 36(2) International Migration Review 333

Campana P and Varese F, 'Exploitation in Human Trafficking and Smuggling' (2016) 22 European Journal on Criminal Policy and Research 89

Chacoón J, 'Tensions and Trade-offs: Protecting Trafficking Victims in the Era of Immigration Enforcement' (2010) 158 University of Pennsylvania Law Review 1609

Chaudary S, 'Trafficking in Europe: An Analysis of the Effectiveness of European Law' (2011) 33 Michigan Journal of International Law 77

Cherneva I, 'Human Trafficking for Begging' (2011) 17 Buffalo Human Rights Law Review 25

Choi-Fitzpatrick A, 'From Rescue to Representation: A Human Rights Approach to the Contemporary Anti-Slavery Movement' (2015) 14(4) Journal of Human Rights 486

Chuang JA, 'Redirecting the Debate over Trafficking in Women: Definitions, Paradigms, and Contexts' (1998) 11 Harvard Human Rights Journal 65

Chuang JA, 'Rescuing Trafficking from Ideological Capture: Prostitution Reform and Anti-trafficking Law and Policy' (2010) 158 University of Pennsylvania Law Review 1655

Chuang JA, 'Exploitation Creep and the Unmaking of Human Trafficking Law' (2014) 108(4) The American Journal of International Law 609

Chuang JA, 'The Challenges and Perils of Reframing Trafficking as "Modern-Day Slavery"' (2015) 5 Anti-Trafficking Review 146

Costa JP, 'The European Court of Human Rights: Consistency of Its Case-Law and Positive Obligations' (2008) 33(5) NJCM Bulletin 719

Collins J, 'Exploitation of Persons and the Limits of the Criminal Law' (2017) 3 Criminal Law Review 169

Cullen H, 'Siliadin v France: Positive Obligations under Article 4 of the European Convention on Human Rights' (2006) 6 Human Rights Law Review 585

Datta MN and Bales K, 'Slavery in Europe: Part 1, Estimating the Dark Figure' (2013) 35 Human Rights Quarterly 817

Dembour MB, 'What Are Human Rights? Four Schools of Thought' (2010) 32 Human Rights Quarterly 1

Duffy H, 'Litigating Modern Slavery in Regional Courts: A Nascent Contribution' (2016) 14 Journal of International Criminal Justice 375

Edwards A, 'Traffic in Human Beings: At the Intersection of Criminal Justice, Human rights, Asylum/Migration and Labour' (2007) 36(1) Denver Journal of International Law and Policy 9

Farrior S, 'The International Law on Trafficking in Women and Children for Prostitution: Making it Live Up to its Potential' (1997) 10 Harvard Human Rights Law Journal 213

Fikfak V, 'Changing State Behaviour: Damages before the European Court of Human Rights' (2019) 29(4) European Journal of International Law 1091–1125

Finnis J, 'Absolute Rights: Some Problems Illustrated' (2016) 61 American Journal of Jurisprudence 195

Fredette K, 'Revisiting the UN Protocol on Human Trafficking: Striking Balances for More Effective Legislation' (2009) 17 Cardozo Journal of International and Comparative Law 101

Gallagher AT, 'Human Rights and the New UN Protocols on Trafficking and Migrant Smuggling: A Preliminary Analysis' (2001) 23 Human Rights Quarterly 975

Gallagher AT, 'Recent Legal Developments in the Field of Human Trafficking: A Critical Review of the 2005 European Convention and Related Instruments' (2006) 8 European Journal of Migration and Law 163

Gallagher AT, 'Human Rights and Human Trafficking: Quagmire or Firm Ground? A Response to James Hathaway' (2009) 49(4) Virginia Journal of International Law 78

Garciandia R, 'State Responsibility and Positive Obligations in the European Court of Human Rights: The Contribution of the ICJ in Advancing Towards More Judicial Integration' (2020) 33(1) Leiden Journal of International Law 177

Gewirth A, 'Are There Any Absolute Rights' (1981) 31(122) The Philosophical Quarterly 1

Gewirth A, 'There Are Absolute Rights' (1982) 32 Philosophical Quarterly 348

Greer S, 'Is the Prohibition against Torture, Cruel, Inhuman and Degrading Treatment Really 'Absolute' in International Human Rights Law?' (2015) 15(1) Human Rights Law Review 101

Hathaway JC, 'The Human Rights Quagmire of "Human Trafficking"' (2008) 49(1) Virginia Journal of International Law 1

Helfer LR, 'Redesigning the European Court of Human Rights: Embeddedness as a Deep Structural Principle of the European Human Rights Regime' (2008) 19(1) European Journal of International Law 125

Hill JL, 'Exploitation' (1994) 79(3) Cornell Law Review 631

Holmstrom N, 'Exploitation' (1977) 7(2) Canadian Journal of Philosophy 353

Jägers N and Rijken C, 'Prevention of Human Trafficking for Labor Exploitation: The Role of Corporations' (2014) 12(1) Northwestern Journal of International Human Rights 47

Jovanovic M, 'The Principle of Non-Punishment of Victims of Trafficking in Human Beings: A Quest for Rationale and Practical Guidance' (2017) 1 Journal of Trafficking and Human Exploitation 1

Jovanovic M, 'The Essence of Slavery: Exploitation in Human Rights Law' (2020) 20(4) Human Rights Law Review 674

Jovanovic M, 'International Law and Regional Norm Smuggling: How the EU and ASEAN Redefined the Global Regime on Human Trafficking' (2020) 68(4) American Journal of Comparative Law 801

Jovanovic M, 'Blurred Lines: Slavery, Law, and Modern State' (forthcoming)

Keller H, Heri C and Piskóty R, 'Something Ventured, Nothing Gained?—Remedies before the ECtHR and Their Potential for Climate Change Cases' (2022) 22 Human Rights Law Review 1

Lenzerini L, 'International Legal Instruments on Human Trafficking and a Victim-Oriented Approach: Which Gaps Are to Be Filled?' (2009) 4 Intercultural Human Rights Law Review 205

Lixinski L, 'Treaty Interpretation by the Inter-American Court of Human Rights: Expansionism at the Service of the Unity of International Law' (2010) 21(3) The European Journal of International Law 585

Mahoney P, 'Judicial Activism and Judicial Self-Restraint in the European Court of Human Rights: Two Sides of the Same Coin' (1990) 57 Human Rights Law Review 66

Mattar MY, 'Incorporating the Five Basic Elements of a Model Anti-Trafficking in Persons Legislation in Domestic Laws: from the United Nations Protocol to the European Convention' (2005) 14(2) Tulane Journal of International and Comparative Law 29

Mayer R, 'What's Wrong with Exploitation?' (2007) 24(2) Journal of Applied Philosophy 137

Mavronicola N, 'What is an "Absolute Right"? Deciphering Absoluteness in the Context of Article 3 of the European Convention on Human Rights' (2012) 12(4) Human Rights Law Review 723

Mavronicola N, 'Is the Prohibition Against Torture and Cruel, Inhuman and Degrading Treatment Absolute in International Human Rights Law? A Reply to Steven Greer' (2017) 17 Human Rights Law Review 483

McBride J, 'Protecting Life: A Positive Obligation to Help' (1999) 24 European Law Review 43

Melish JT and Aliverti A, 'Positive Obligations in the Inter-American Human Rights System' (2006) 15(3) Interights Bulletin: Positive Obligations 120

Milanovic M, 'Special Rules of Attribution of Conduct in International Law' (2020) 96 International Law Studies 295

Mowbray A, 'Creativity of the European Court of Human Rights' (2005) 5(1) Human Rights Law Review 57

Nicholson A, 'Reflections on *Siliadin v France*: Slavery and Legal Definition' (2010) 14(5) The International Journal of Human Rights 705

Norbert WP and others, 'Human Rights Violations in Organ Procurement Practice in China' (2017) 18(11) BMC Medical Ethics 1

Panichas G, 'Vampires, Werewolves, and Economic Exploitation' (1981) 7(2) Social Theory and Practice 125

Piotrowicz R, 'The UNCHR's Guidelines on Human Trafficking' (2008) 20(2) International Journal of Refugee Law 242

Piotrowicz R, 'The Legal Nature of Trafficking in Human Beings' (2009) 4 Intercultural Human Rights Law Review 175

Piotrowicz R, 'International Focus: Trafficking and Slavery as Human rights Violations' (2010) 84 Australian Law Journal 812

Piotrowicz R, 'States' Obligations under Human Rights Law towards Victims of Trafficking in Human Beings: Positive Developments in Positive Obligations' (2012) 24(2) International Journal of Refugee Law 181

Piotrowicz R and L Sorrentino, 'Human Trafficking and the Emergence of the Non-Punishment Principle' (2016) 16 Human Rights Law Review 669

Planitzer J, 'GRETA's First Years of Work: Review of the Monitoring of Implementation of the Council of Europe Convention on Action against Trafficking in Human Beings' (2012) 1 Anti-Trafficking Review 31

Raffaelli R, 'The European Approach to the Protection of Trafficking Victims: The Council of Europe Convention, the EU Directive, and the Italian Experience' (2009) 10(3) German Law Journal 205

Rassam A Y 'Contemporary Forms of Slavery and the Evolution of the Prohibition of Slavery and the Slave Trade under Customary International Law' (1999) 39 Virginia Journal of International Law 303

Reiman J, 'Exploitation, Force, and the Moral Assessment of Capitalism: Thoughts on Roemer and Cohen' (1987) 16(1) Philosophy & Public Affairs 3

Sadurski W, 'Quasi-constitutional Court of Human Rights for Europe? Comments on Geir Ulfstein' (2021) 10(1) Global Constitutionalism 175

Schwartz J, 'What's Wrong with Exploitation?' (1995) 29(2) Noûs 158

Shamir H, 'A Labour Paradigm for Human Trafficking' (2012) 60 UCLA Law Review 76

Sicilianos LA, 'The Involvement of the European Court of Human Rights in the Implementation of its Judgments: Recent Developments under Article 46 ECHR' (2014) 32(3) Netherlands Quarterly of Human Rights 235

Siller N, 'The Prosecution of Human Traffickers? A Comparative Analysis of Enslavement Judgments Among International Courts and Tribunals' (2015) 2 European Journal of Comparative Law and Governance 236

Siller N, 'Human Trafficking in International Law Before Palermo' (2017) 64 Netherlands International Law Review 407

Stoyanova V, 'Dancing on the Borders of Article 4: Human Trafficking and the European Court of Human Rights in the Rantsev Case' (2012) 30(2) Netherlands Quarterly of Human Rights 163

Stoyanova V, 'L.E. v. Greece: Human Trafficking and the Scope of States' Positive Obligations under the ECHR' (2016) 3 European Human Rights Law Review 290

Stoyanova V, 'Sweet Taste with Bitter Roots: Forced Labour and Chowdury and Others v Greece' (2018) 1 European Human Rights Law Review 67

Sullivan B, 'Trafficking in Women: Feminism and New International Law' (2003) 5(1) International Feminist Journal of Politics 67

Todres J, 'Taking Prevention Seriously: Developing a Comprehensive Response to Child Trafficking and Sexual Exploitation' (2010) 43 Vanderbilt Journal of Transnational Law 1

Todres J, 'Widening Our Lens: Incorporating Essential Perspectives in the Fight Against Human Trafficking' (2011) 33 Michigan Journal of International Law 53

Todres J, 'Human Rights, Labor, and the Prevention of Human Trafficking: A Response to a Labor Paradigm for Human Trafficking' (2013) 60 UCLA Law Review Discourse 142

Uhl BH, 'Lost in Implementation? Human Rights Rhetoric and Violations: a Critical Review of Current European Anti-trafficking Policies' (2010) 2 Security and Human Rights 119

Valdman M, 'A Theory of Wrongful Exploitation' (2009) 9(6) Philosophers' Imprint 1

Vijeyarasa R and Villarino JMBY, 'Modern-Day Slavery? A Judicial Catchall for Trafficking, Slavery and Labour Exploitation: A Critique of Tang and Rantsev' (2012) 8 Journal of International Law and International Relations 36

Waldron J, 'The Coxford Lecture Inhuman and Degrading Treatment: The Words Themselves' (2010) 23 Canadian Journal of Law & Jurisprudence 269

Webb P and Garciandia R, 'State Responsibility for Modern Slavery: Uncovering and Bridging the Gap' (2019) 68(3) International and Comparative Law Quarterly 539

Weiss EB, 'Invoking State Responsibility in the Twenty-First Century' (2002) 96(4) The American Journal of International Law 798

Wertheimer A, 'Two Questions about Surrogacy and Exploitation' (1992) 21(3) Philosophy & Public Affairs 211

Wolff J, 'Marx and Exploitation' (1999) 3(2) The Journal of Ethics 105

Wood AW, 'The Marxian Critique of Justice' (1972) 1(3) Philosophy and Public Affairs 244

Wood AW, 'Exploitation' (1995) 12(2) Social Philosophy and Policy 136

NON-BINDING INTERNATIONAL INSTRUMENTS AND GUIDELINES

Council of Europe, Committee of Ministers, Recommendation No R(84)5 of the Committee of Ministers to Member States Relating to Public Liability (18 September 1984)

Council of Europe Parliamentary Assembly (PACE), Draft Council of Europe Convention on Action Against Trafficking in Human Beings (26 January 2005) Opinion 253 (2005)

Council of Europe, Committee of Ministers, 'Guidelines of the Committee of Ministers of the Council of Europe on Eradicating Impunity for Serious Human Rights Violations' 1110th Meeting (30 March 2011)

Council of Europe, Committee of Ministers, Reply to PA Recommendation 2011, Doc 13287 (16 July 2013)

Council of Europe, European Court of Human Rights, 'Guide on Article 4 of the Convention: Prohibition of Slavery And Forced Labour' (2014)

Council of Europe, Resolution CM/Res(2022)2 on the cessation of the membership of the Russian Federation to the Council of Europe, under Article 8 of the Statute, CM/Del/Dec(2022)1428ter/2.3 (16 March 2022)

Explanatory Report to the Council of Europe Convention for the Protection of Human Rights and Fundamental Freedoms (4 November 1950) ETS 5

ILO Recommendation R104: Indigenous and Tribal Populations Recommendation (40th Conference Session Geneva 26 June 1957)

ILO Recommendation R168: Vocational Rehabilitation and Employment (Disabled Persons) Recommendation (69th Conference Session Geneva 20 June 1983)

ILO Recommendation R169: Employment Policy (Supplementary Provisions) Recommendation (70th Conference Session Geneva (26 June 1984)

International Law Commission, Draft Articles on Responsibility of States for Internationally Wrongful Acts, Doc A/56/10 (2001)

UN Conference of the Parties to the United Nations Convention against Transnational Organized Crime, 'Report of the Conference of the Parties to the United Nations Convention against Transnational Organized Crime on its fourth session, held in Vienna from 8 to 17 October 2008' CTOC/COP/2008/19, decision 4/4 (1 December 2008)

UN Conference of the Parties to the United Nations Convention against Transnational Organized Crime, Working Group on Trafficking in Persons, 'Key Concepts of the Trafficking in Persons Protocol, with a Focus on the United Nations Office on Drugs and Crime Issue Papers on Abuse of a Position of Vulnerability, Consent and Exploitation', CTOC/COP/WG.4/2015/4 (25 August 2015)

United Nations Global Plan of Action to Combat Trafficking in Persons, Doc A/RES/64/293 (12 August 2010)

UN High Commissioner for Refugees, 'Guidelines on International Protection-The application of Article 1A (2) of the 1951 Convention and/or 1967 Protocol relating to the Status of Refugees to victims of trafficking and persons at risk of being trafficked' HCR/GIP/06/07 (7 April 2006)

UN High Commissioner for Refugees, 'Prevent, Combat, Protect Human Trafficking: Joint UN Commentary on the EU Directive: A Human Rights Based Approach' (November 2011)

UN Human Right Committee, 'General Comment No 31: The Nature of the General Legal Obligation Imposed on States Parties to the Covenant' CCPR/C/21/Rev.1/Add.13 (26 May 2004)

UN Office of the High Commissioner for Human Rights, 'Informal Note by the High Commissioner for Human Rights', Fourth session of the Ad Hoc Committee on the Elaboration of a Convention against Transnational Organized Crime Doc A/AC.254/16 (28 June-9 July 1999) (1 June 1999)

UN Office of the High Commissioner for Human Rights, Committee on Economic, Social and Cultural Rights, 'General Comment 13 on the Right to Education (Article 13 of the Covenant)' E/C.12/1999/10 (2 December 1999)

UN Office of the High Commissioner for Human Rights, 'Recommended Principles and Guidelines on Human Rights and Human Trafficking' E/2002/68/Add.1 (2002)

UN Office of the High Commissioner for Human Rights, 'Recommended Principles and Guidelines on Human Rights and Human Trafficking: Commentary' (2010)

United Nations Secretariat, 'Special Measures for Protection from Sexual Exploitation and Abuse' ST/SGB/2003/13 (9 October 2003)

UNODC, '*Travaux Préparatoires* of the Negotiations for the Elaboration of the United Nations Convention against Organized Crime and the Protocols Thereto' (2006)

UNODC, 'Legislative guides for the implementation of the UN Convention against Transnational Organized Crime and the Protocols Thereto' (2004)

UNODC, 'Legislative Guide for the Implementation of the Protocol against Smuggling of Migrants by Land, Sea and Air Supplementing the United Nations Convention against Transnational Organized Crime' (2004)

UNODC 'Legislative Guide for the Implementation of the Protocol to Prevent, Suppress and Punish Trafficking In Persons, Especially Women and Children, Supplementing the United Nations Convention Against Transnational Organized Crime' (2004)

UNODC, '*Travaux préparatoires* of the negotiations for the elaboration of the United Nations Convention against Transnational Organized Crime and the Protocols thereto' (2006)

UNODC, 'Model Law against Trafficking in Persons' (5 August 2009)

UNODC 'Guidance Note on "Abuse of a Position of Vulnerability" as a Means of Trafficking in Persons in Article 3 of the Trafficking in Person Protocol' (2012)

UNODC, 'The Concept of "Exploitation" in the Trafficking in Persons Protocol' (2015)

UNODC, 'Assessment Toolkit: Trafficking in Persons for the Purpose of Organ Removal' (2015)

UNODC, 'Interlinkages between Trafficking in Persons and Marriage' (2020)

UK Home Office, 'Modern Slavery Act 2015: Statutory Guidance for England and Wales' (24 March 2020)

UK National Crime Agency, 'NCA Guidance for Councils on How to Identify and Support Victims of Criminal Exploitation' (15 November 2008)

UK, 'National referral mechanism guidance: adult (England and Wales)' (updated 16 November 2020)

UK, National referral mechanism guidance: adult (Northern Ireland and Scotland) (updated 16 November 2020)

REPORTS AND RESEARCH PAPERS

2020 UK Annual Report on Modern Slavery (October 2020)

Anti-Slavery International, 'Trafficking for Forced Criminal Activities and Begging in Europe: Exploratory Study and Good Practice Examples' Race in Europe Project (September 2014)

Caplan and others, 'Trafficking in Organs, Tissues and Cells and Trafficking in Human Beings for the Purpose of the Removal of Organs' Joint Council of Europe/United Nations Study (2009)

Council of Europe, Directorate General of Human Rights and Legal Affairs, 'Practical Impact of the Council of Europe Monitoring Mechanisms in Improving Respect for Human Rights and the Rule of Law in Member States' (2010)

Council of Europe, Group of Experts on Action against Trafficking in Human Beings (GRETA), 'Report concerning the implementation of the Council of Europe Convention on Action against Trafficking in Human Beings by UK' First Evaluation Round GRETA(2012) 6 (12 September 2012)

Council of Europe, GRETA, '2nd General Report on GRETA's Activities' GRETA(2012) 13 (4 October 2012)

Council of Europe, GRETA, 'Report concerning the implementation of the Council of Europe Convention on Action against Trafficking in Human Beings by France' First Evaluation Round (28 January 2013) GRETA(2012) 16

Council of Europe, GRETA, '3rd General Report on GRETA's Activities' Introduction by the President of GRETA (17 October 2013)
Council of Europe, GRETA, 'Report concerning the implementation of the Council of Europe Convention on Action against Trafficking in Human Beings by Italy' First Evaluation Round, GRETA(2014) 18 (4 July 2014)
Council of Europe, GRETA, '4th General Report on GRETA's Activities' (March 2015)
Council of Europe, GRETA, 'Report concerning the implementation of the Council of Europe Convention on Action against Trafficking in Human Beings by Norway' Second Evaluation Round GRETA(2017) 18 (21 June 2017)
Council of Europe, GRETA, 'Assistance to Victims of Human Trafficking: Thematic Chapter of the 8th General Report on GRETA's Activities' (October 2019)
Council of Europe, GRETA, '9th General Report on GRETA's Activities' (March 2020)
Eide A, 'The Right to Adequate Food as a Human Right' (UN Sub-Commission for the Promotion and Protection of Human Rights, UN Doc E/CN4/Sub2/1987/23, Final Report (7 July 1987)
European Commission, 'Report of the Experts Group on Trafficking in Human Beings' (22 December 2004)
European Commission, 'The EU Strategy towards the Eradication of Trafficking in Human Beings 2012-2016' (19 June 2012) COM(2012) 286
European Commission, 'EU Anti-Trafficking Action 2012-2016 at a Glance' (2017)
European Court of Human Rights, 'Annual Report' (2016)
European Court of Human Rights, 'The Court's Priority Policy' (22 May 2017)
European Parliament, Policy Department, Director General for External Policies, 'Trafficking in Human Organs' (2015)
Finnis J and Murray S, 'Immigration, Strasbourg, and Judicial Overreach' Policy Exchange (2021)
Follmar-Otto P and Rabe H, 'Human Trafficking in Germany Strengthening Victim's Human Rights' German Institute for Human Rights (2009)
Group of Experts on Trafficking in Human Beings of the European Commission, Opinion on the Decision of the European Court of Human Rights in the Case of Rantsev v. Cyprus and Russia (Opinion No 6/2010)
International Labour Organisation (ILO), 'Operational Indicators of Trafficking in Human Beings' Results from a Delphi Survey implemented by the ILO and the European Commission (September 2009)
ILO, 'Forced Labour and Human Trafficking: Casebook of Court Decisions' (2009)
ILO, 'Report for Discussion at the Tripartite Meeting of Experts Concerning the Possible Adoption of an ILO Instrument to Supplement the Forced Labour Convention 1930 (No 29)' (11–15 February 2013)
Independent Anti-Slavery Commissioner, 'Combating Modern Slavery Experienced by Vietnamese Nationals en Route to, and Within, the UK' (2017)
Koettl J, 'Human Trafficking, Modern Day Slavery, and Economic Exploitation' World Bank Discussion Paper No 0911 (May 2009)
Lazarus L, 'Advice for the Stern Review: The Human Rights Framework Relating to the Handling, Investigation and Prosecution of Rape Complaints' in UK Government Equality Office, 'A Report by Baroness Vivien Stern CBE of an Independent Review into how Rape Complaints are Handled by Public Authorities in England and Wales: The Stern Review' (Annexe A) 133
Malpani R, 'Legal Aspects of Trafficking for Forced Labour Purposes in Europe' ILO Working Paper (4 January 2006)

Marty A, 'Inhuman Treatment of People and Illicit Trafficking in Human Organs in Kosovo', Council of Europe Parliamentary Assembly, Committee on Legal Affairs and Human Rights (Draft Report), AS/Jur (2010) 46 (12 December 2010)

Nestorova P, Executive Secretary of the Council of Europe Convention on Action against Trafficking in Human Beings, 'Trafficking in Europe' (Conference 'Bringing Human Trafficking Out of the Shadows' Cardiff (21 November 2012)

Organization for Security and Cooperation in Europe (OSCE), Office for Democratic Institutions and Human Rights (ODIHR), 'Compensation for Trafficked and Exploited Persons in the OSCE Region' (2008)

OSCE, 'Trafficking in Human Beings for Purposes of Organ Removal in the OSCE Region: Analysis and Findings' (2013)

Pearson E, 'Human Rights and Trafficking in Persons: A Handbook' Global Alliance Against Traffic in Women (2000)

Plant R, 'Modern Slavery: The Concepts and Their Practical Implications' ILO Working Paper (5 February 2015)

RACE in Europe, 'Victim or Criminal? Trafficking for Forced Criminal Exploitation in Europe: UK Chapter' (2013)

Report of the Ad Hoc Committee on the Elaboration of a Convention Against Transnational Organized Crime on the work of its first to eleventh sessions: Interpretive Notes for the official records (*Travaux Préparatoires*) of the negotiation of the UN Convention Against Transnational Organized Crime and the Protocols thereto, Doc A/55/383/Add.1 (3 November 2000)

Skrivankova K, 'Between Decent Work and Forced Labour: Examining the Continuum of Exploitation' JRF Programme Paper: Forced Labour (November 2010)

The Anti-Trafficking Monitoring Group (ATMG), 'Wrong Kind of Victim? One Year on: An Analysis of UK Measures to Protect Trafficked Persons' (June 2010)

The United States Department of State, 'Trafficking in Persons Report' (2008)

The US Department of State 'Trafficking in Persons Report' (2012)

Thorbjørn J, the EU Ministerial Conference 'Towards Global EU Action against Trafficking in Human Beings' Brussels (19–20 October 2009)

Tomlinson H, 'Positive Obligations Under the European Convention on Human Rights' Matrix Chambers (21 July 2012)

UN Office of the High Commissioner for Human Rights (UN OHCHR), Report of the Special Rapporteur on Violence Against Women, it's Causes and Consequences, Ms Coomaraswamy, on Trafficking in Women, Women's Migration and Violence Against Women, Submitted in Accordance with Commission on Human Rights Resolution 1997/44 UN Doc E/CN.4/2000/68 (29 February 2000)

UN OHCHR, Report of the Special Rapporteur on Trafficking in Persons, Especially Women and Children, 'Integration of Human Rights of Women and the Gender Perspective', UN Doc E/CN.4/ 2005/71 (22 December 2004)

UN OHCHR, Interim Report of the Special Rapporteur on Trafficking in Persons, especially Women and Children, Joy Ngozi Ezeilo, Doc A/65/288 (9 August 2010)

UN OHCHR, Report of the Special Rapporteur on trafficking in persons, especially women and children, Joy Ngozi Ezeilo, The right to an effective remedy for trafficked persons, A/66/283 (9 August 2011)

UN OHCHR, 'Human Rights and Human Trafficking' (Factsheet No 36, 2014)

UN OHCHR, Report of the Special Rapporteur on Trafficking in Persons, Especially Women and Children, Joy Ngozi Ezeilo (1 April 2014) Doc A/HRC/26/37

UN OHCHR, Report of the Special Rapporteur on trafficking in persons, especially women and children, Maria Grazia Giammarinaro, Report of the United Nations High Commissioner for Human Rights, Summary of the consultations held on the draft basic principles on the right to effective remedy for victims of trafficking in persons, Doc A/HRC/26/18 (May 2014)

UN OHCHR, Report of the Special Rapporteur on Trafficking in Persons, Especially Women and Children, Joy Ngozi Ezeilo (28 July 2014) Doc A/69/33797

UN OHCHR, Special Rapporteur on the Right to Education, Kishore Singh, 'Report to the Human Rights Council on the Promotion of Equality of Opportunity in Education' Doc A/HRC/17/29 (18 April 2011)

UNESCO, 'Results of the Seventh Consultation of Member States on the Measures Taken for Implementation of UNESCO's Convention and Recommendation against Discrimination in Education (1960)' Doc 177 EX/36 (17 August 2007)

UNHCR, 'Prevent, Combat, Protect Human Trafficking: Joint UN Commentary on the EU Directive: A Human Rights Based Approach' (November 2011)

United Nations Office on Drugs and Crime (UNODC), 'An Introduction to Human Trafficking: Vulnerability, Impact and Action' Background Paper (2008)

UNODC 'Global Report on Trafficking in Persons' (November 2014)

UNODC, 'Global Report on Trafficking in Persons' (2020)

Weissbrodt D and Anti-Slavery International, 'Abolishing Slavery and its Contemporary Forms' Office of the United Nations High Commissioner for Human Rights, Doc HR/PUB/02/4 (2002)

ONLINE SOURCES

Anti-Slavery International, 'What is Modern Slavery?' https://www.antislavery.org/slavery-today/modern-slavery/

Council of Europe, 'Examples of the Impact of the European Convention on Human Rights by Theme: Freedom From Slavery and Human Trafficking' (2018) https://www.coe.int/en/web/impact-convention-human-rights/freedom-from-slavery-and-human-trafficking

Dottridge M, 'Eight Reasons Why We Shouldn't Use the Term "Modern Slavery"' *Open Democracy* (17 October 2017) https://www.opendemocracy.net/en/beyond-trafficking-and-slavery/eight-reasons-why-we-shouldn-t-use-term-modern-slavery/

Kelly A and McNamara M, '3,000 children enslaved in Britain after being trafficked into Britain' *The Guardian Online* (2015) http://www.theguardian.com/global-development/2015/may/23/vietnam-children-trafficking-nail-bar-cannabis

Oxford English Dictionary (2021) https://www.oed.com/

UNODC, 'Human Trafficking Indicators' http://www.unodc.org/pdf/HT_indicators_E_LOWRES.pdf

UNODC, 'Human Trafficking Case Law Database' https://sherloc.unodc.org/cld/en/v3/sherloc/cldb/index.html?lng=en

UNDOC, Evidential Issues in Trafficking in Persons Cases: Case Digest (2017) file:///C:/Users/majov/Downloads/Case_Digest_Evidential_Issues_in_Trafficking.pdf

Index

For the benefit of digital users, indexed terms that span two pages (e.g., 52–53) may, on occasion, appear on only one of those pages.

absolute rights
  criminal law protection of, 105–7
  positive obligations and, 8, 102–7
  right not to be trafficked, 47–49
abuse of vulnerability, 82–85
access to justice, 173–74
African Charter on Human and People's Rights, 100
African Commission on Human and Peoples' Rights
  exploitation and disproportionate gain, 86
  positive obligations and state responsibility, 100
Anti-Trafficking Convention *see* Council of Europe Convention on Action against Trafficking in Human Beings 2005
Arab Charter on Human Rights 2004, 25–26, 32, 65
Articles on State Responsibility for Internationally Wrongful Acts, 95, 96–97
Association of Southeast Asian Nations (ASEAN)
  Anti-Trafficking Convention, 24–25
  Human Rights Declaration 2012, 65
asylum seekers, 83
Australia
  protection from trafficking for exploitation, 57
  slavery, definition of, 51–52

begging *see* forced begging

Charter of Fundamental Rights of the European Union 2000, 48, 65
children
  child abuse and exploitation, 88
  International Convention for the Suppression of Traffic in Women and Children 1921, 20–21
  recognition of vulnerability, 83
compensation for victims of trafficking, 186–87
consent and vulnerability, 83–84

Convention for the Suppression of the Traffic in Persons and of the Exploitation of the Prostitution of Others 1949, 21–22
Council of Europe Convention against Trafficking in Human Organs, 61
Council of Europe Convention on Action against Trafficking in Human Beings 2005
  access to justice, 173–74
  adequate penalties, 173–74
  compensation for victims, 186–87
  criminalisation of human trafficking, 172–73
  effective investigation, 173
  Group of Experts on Action against Trafficking in Human Beings (GRETA), and, 174–75, 185, 187, 190–92
  non-punishment of victims, 179–80
  Parliamentary Assembly of the Council of Europe, 169–70
  post-identification measures of protection, 184–88
  pre-identification measures of protection, 181–84
  protection from re-trafficking, 185–86
  protection of victims' rights, 188–92
  victim-centred approach, 169–72
  victim protection during criminal proceedings, 175–79
  victims' human rights beyond criminal justice context, 181–92
  victims' human rights in criminal justice context, 172–75
crimes against humanity, 33, 50–51, 104n.63
criminal responsibility
  human trafficking and, 33–36, 172–73
  state responsibility versus, 5–9
criminalisation of human trafficking, 172–73

disproportionate gains, 86–88
domestic servitude, 45
domestic violence
  human rights obligations of states, 131–32
  vulnerability, recognition of, 83

INDEX

duty to establish effective legal framework
   Strasbourg jurisprudence, 124–27
duty to investigate, 127–43
   circumstances engaging the duty, 129–35
   credible suspicion or arguable claim, 129–35
   Inter-American Court of Human Rights jurisprudence, 127–28, 130, 134–35, 142
   principles underpinning, 135–37
   scope of duty, 135–43
   Strasbourg jurisprudence, 128–34, 136–43
duty to protect
   Inter-American Court of Human Rights jurisprudence, 144
   measures required to protect an individual, 153–56
   objective circumstances, 147–49
   official awareness, 149–53
   Osman test, 144–46, 148–49, 153
   Rantsev v Cyprus and Russia, 146–56
   Strasbourg jurisprudence, 143–44
   test for assessing compliance, 143–56

effective investigation, 173
emergency protection, 181–84
EU Anti-Trafficking Directive
   forced begging, 57–58
   victim protection, 24
EU Charter of Fundamental Rights *see* Charter of Fundamental Rights of the European Union
European Court of Human Rights
   anti-trafficking instruments, and, 164, 165, 166
   duty to establish effective legal framework, 124–27
   duty to investigate, 128–34, 136–43
   exploitation, 71–72, 86–87
   forced labour, 54–57
   human trafficking, nature of, 35
   human trafficking as a stand-alone prohibition, 46–47
   living instrument doctrine, 37
   remedies for modern slavery, 157–59
   right not to be trafficked, 40, 41–44
   right to remedy, 111–16
   servitude, definition of, 53–54
   slavery, definition of, 53
exploitation
   abuse of vulnerability, 82–85
   disproportionate gain, 86–88
   Dutch law, 89
   human rights lawC4P56–C4P82
   human trafficking instruments and, 68–71
   international law, and, 66–72
   moral force of exploitation, 80–81
   moral philosophy, in, 72–81
   moralised and non-moralised exploitation, 72–74

   necessary and sufficient conditions, 65–66n.11, 75–80
   Palermo Protocol, 65
   prohibition of modern slavery and, 71–72
   right not to be trafficked, 57–62
   sustained action, 88–90

forced begging, 57–58, 62
forced criminality, 57–58, 62
forced labour
   definition of, 54–55
   ECtHR case law, 54–57
   Forced Labour Convention, 49, 54–55
   sexual exploitation, 57, 59
   see also prohibition of slavery, servitude, and forced labour

GRETA *see* Group of Experts on Action against Trafficking in Human Beings
Group of Experts on Action against Trafficking in Human Beings, 131–32, 133–34, 162, 174–75, 182n.113, 185, 187, 188, 190–93, 195

human rights and exploitation, 81–90
human rights and human trafficking, 24–39
human rights and positive obligations
   duty to establish effective legal framework, 124–27
   duty to investigate, 127–43
   duty to protect victims, 143–56
   remedies, 157–61
human rights law in twenty-first century, 194–97
human trafficking
   as complex phenomenon, 15–18
   as crime and human rights violation, 33–36
   forced begging, trafficking for, 57–58
   forced criminality, trafficking for, 57–58
   history of, in international law, 19–26
   human rights dimension, 24–26
   human rights law, relationship with, 26–30, 38–39
   as hybrid legal concept, 30–36
   organ removal, trafficking for, 57, 59–62
   Palermo Protocol, 22–23
   post-Palermo developments, 24–26
   right not to be trafficked *see* right not to be trafficked
   sexual exploitation, trafficking for, 57, 59
   slavery or servitude without trafficking, 45–46
   state obligations to tackle human trafficking, 166–68
   universal definition of, 30–33
   universalisation of anti-trafficking action, 22–23

INDEX

value of human rights approach, 36–38
victim protection, 169–92
see also exploitation; positive obligations

IACtHR *see* Inter-American Court of Human Rights (IACtHR)
imminent threat, 47–49
Inter-American Court of Human Rights (IACtHR)
   duty to investigate, 127–28, 130, 134–35, 142
   positive obligations, 102–3, 120–21
   remedies for modern slavery, 159–61
   servitude and slavery, 53
   slavery, definition of, 51
International Agreement for the Suppression of the White Slave Traffic 1904, 20
International Convention for the Suppression of the Traffic in Women of Full Age 1933, 20–21
International Convention for the Suppression of the White Slave Traffic 1910, 20
International Convention for the Suppression of Traffic in Women and Children 1921, 20–21
International Criminal Tribunal for the Former Yugoslavia (ICTY)
   evolution of concept of slavery, 42–43
   slavery, definition of, 52
International Labour Organisation (ILO)
   abuse of vulnerability, 83–84
   exploitation, and, 67
   Forced Labour Convention, 49, 54–55, 59
   human trafficking as forced labour, 31
international law
   crimes against humanity, 52
   exploitation, 64–65, 66–72, 79
   human trafficking in, 10–11, 19–26, 33–34, 38
   practices similar to slavery, 53n.77
   right not to be trafficked, 42, 49, 52
   servitude, 53n.77
   see also Palermo Protocol
International Law Commission
   Articles on State Responsibility for Internationally Wrongful Acts, 95, 96–97
investigations *see* duty to investigate

lawful residence, 184–88
living instrument doctrine, 10, 36–37, 42, 100–1

moral philosophy, exploitation in, 72–81
   moral force of exploitation, 80–81
   moralised and non-moralised exploitation, 72–74
   necessary and sufficient elements of concept, 75–80

negative state obligations, 103–5

non-punishment of victims, 179–80
non-state actors
   positive obligations and, 8–9, 98–100
   remedies 107–16
Nuremberg Military Tribunals, 88

organ removal, 57, 59–62
Osman test, 144–46
   measures required to protect an individual, 145–46, 153, 154
   objective circumstances, 144, 148–49
   official awareness, 144
   Rantsev v Cyprus and Russia and, 148–49, 153

Palermo Protocol
   adoption of, 19
   aims and effect of, 22–23
   anti-trafficking instruments, 166–68
   core purposes, 166–67
   exploitation, and, 65, 68
   failure to achieve goals, 168
   human trafficking, definition of, 30–31, 32–33, 49–50
   impact of, 168
   mandatory measures, 167–68
   optional measures, 167–68
   organ removal, trafficking for, 59–60
   post-Palermo developments, 24–26
   pre-Palermo anti-trafficking Instruments, 19–22
   prevention of human trafficking, 166–67
   prosecution of perpetrators of human trafficking, 166–67
   protection of victims of human trafficking, 166–67
Parliamentary Assembly of the Council of Europe, 169–70
penalties, 173–74
positive obligations
   absolute rights and, 8, 102–7
   categorisation of, 119
   duty to aid (provide), 116, 117–18
   duty to conduct effective investigations, 117–18
   duty to protect, 116–17, 121
   duty to provide effective remedy, 120
   duty to respect, 116
   general and specific duties, 122
   legal basis of, 101–2
   negative obligations and, 103–5
   non-state actors, 8–9, 98–100, 107–16
   rationale for, 100–1
   recognition of, 98–100
   remedies where rights infringed by non-state actors, 107–16
   scope of, 102

post-identification measures of protection, 184–88
pre-identification measures of protection, 181–84
principle of effectiveness, 100–1
prohibition of slavery, servitude, and forced labour
　absolute rights, 4, 47, 48–49
　abuse of vulnerability, 82
　anti-trafficking instruments, 164, 165, 167–68, 176, 178–79, 181, 185–86, 188–92
　Australia, 51–52
　credible suspicion, 148
　duty to investigate, 127–28, 129, 130, 132–35, 137–38, 140–42
　effective legal framework, 124–27
　exploitation and, 4–5, 49–62, 64–65, 66, 67, 71–72, 74, 75–76, 78–79, 81–82, 86
　human rights obligations, 123, 124–27, 134, 144, 153, 154–56, 159–60
　human trafficking, nature of, 28, 30, 37
　Osman test, 146
　positive obligations and, 7–8, 99, 105, 109, 118, 157–58, 162–63
　pre-emptive protection, 47–48, 62–63, 105
　prosecution of victims, 152
　protection of victims and witnesses in criminal justice process, 176–79
　right not to be trafficked, 3, 40, 41–44, 45–46
　violation of, 53, 134, 159–60
　see also forced labour; servitude; slavery
prohibition of torture
　African Charter on Human and People's Rights, 100
　anti-trafficking instruments, 185
　domestic violence and, 142
　human rights obligations, 123–25, 128, 138–39, 144, 145, 149
　organ harvesting, 40
　positive obligations and, 103–4, 105, 108–9, 112, 113, 114, 117–18, 144
　pre-emptive protection, 47, 62–63, 105
　right to effective remedy, 112, 113–14
prostitution, 15–16, 20–22, 30–31, 45, 49–50, 57, 59–60, 71–72, 129, 140–41, 148
protection from re-trafficking, 185–86
protection of victims' rights, 188–92
protective rights, 104–5

Rantsev v Cyprus and Russia
　absolute rights and, 154
　duty to investigate, 129–30, 135, 136–37, 142
　duty to protect, 146–56
　human trafficking, nature of, 28, 30, 34–35, 37

objective circumstances, 147–49
official awareness, 149–53
right not to be trafficked, 41–44
remedies
　European Court of Human Rights jurisprudence, 157–59
　infringement of rights by non-state actors, 107–16
　Inter-American Court of Human Rights jurisprudence, 159–61
　modern slavery, 157–61
　right to remedy, 109–10
re-trafficking, 185–86
right not to be trafficked
　absolute rights, 47–49
　case for, 1–5
　express prohibitions under ECHR Art 4, 50–57
　imminent threat, 47–49
　notion of 'modern slavery' in human rights law, 62–63
　Rantsev v Cyprus and Russia, 41–44
　scope of prohibition against modern slavery, 49–62
　trafficking as process versus condition, 44–47
right to fair trial, 35–36, 141–42, 176–78, 186
right to liberty and security, 15, 25, 40, 105, 117, 144, 176
right to life
　anti-trafficking instruments, 176
　human rights obligations, 123–25, 128, 143–44, 149
　positive obligations and, 104–5, 109, 112–13, 114, 117–18
　pre-emptive protection, 47, 62–63, 104–5
right to private and family life, 40, 149, 176, 178–79
right to remedy, 109–10, 115
Roma minority, 83

servitude, definition of, 53–54
　see also prohibition of slavery, servitude, and forced labour
sexual exploitation, protection against, 57, 59
slavery
　definition of, 50–53
　practices similar to, 57, 58–59
　see also prohibition of slavery, servitude, and forced labour
Slavery Convention 1926, 49, 50–51
state responsibility for modern slavery
　anti-trafficking instruments, 164–93
　Articles on State Responsibility for Internationally Wrongful Acts, 95, 96–97
　human rights obligations, 123–63

positive obligations, 95–122
traditional approach to, 95
Osman test, 148
positive obligations, categories of, 118–19, 120
state responsibility versus criminal responsibility, 5–9
Strasbourg court *see* European Court of Human Rights
sustained action, 88–90

torture *see* prohibition of torture

United Nations Convention against Transnational Organized Crime, 22–23
    Conference of the Parties to the Convention, 33, 37
    see also Palermo Protocol
United Nations Human Rights Committee
    positive obligations of states, 101–2
United Nations Human Rights Office of the High Commissioner
    human trafficking as a human rights violation, 26–27
United Nations Office on Drugs and Crime (UNODC)
    exploitation, 69–71, 80–81, 82, 85
    nature of human trafficking, 16–17
    organ removal, trafficking for, 59–60
    process of trafficking, 44–45

United Nations Protocol to the Transnational Organized Crime Convention *see* Palermo Protocol
United Nations Special Rapporteur on Trafficking in Persons
    right not to be trafficked, 40
    right to remedy, 110–11
United Nations Special Rapporteur on Violence against Women, 21–22

victim-centred approach, 169–72
victim compensation, 186–87
victim protection
    criminal proceedings, 175–79
    post-identification measures, 184–88
    pre-identification measures, 181–84
    scope of protection, 188–92
    victim-centred approach, 169–72
    victims' rights and, 9, 26–30, 38–39
victims' rights, 93
    beyond criminal justice context, 181–92
    criminal justice context, 172–75
    criminal proceedings, 175–79
    protection of, 188–92
    victim protection and, 9, 26–30, 38–39
vulnerability
    abuse of, 82–85
    consent and, 83–84
    recognition of, 83

'White Slave Traffic', 20